STRUGGLING FOR EFFECTIVENESS

Struggling for Effectiveness

CIDA and Canadian Foreign Aid

Edited by
STEPHEN BROWN

McGill-Queen's University Press
Montreal & Kingston · London · Ithaca

© McGill-Queen's University Press 2012

ISBN 978-0-7735-4056-9 (cloth)
ISBN 978-0-7735-4057-6 (paper)

Legal deposit third quarter 2012
Bibliothèque nationale du Québec

Printed in Canada on acid-free paper that is 100% ancient forest free
(100% post-consumer recycled), processed chlorine free

This book has been published with the help of a grant from the Canadian
Federation for the Humanities and Social Sciences, through the Awards to
Scholarly Publications Program, using funds provided by the Social Sciences
and Humanities Research Council of Canada. Funding has also been received
from the University of Ottawa.

McGill-Queen's University Press acknowledges the support of the Canada
Council for the Arts for our publishing program. We also acknowledge the
financial support of the Government of Canada through the Canada Book
Fund for our publishing activities.

Library and Archives Canada Cataloguing in Publication

Struggling for effectiveness: CIDA and Canadian foreign aid /
edited by Stephen Brown.

Includes bibliographical references and index.
ISBN 978-0-7735-4056-9 (bound). – ISBN 978-0-7735-4057-6 (pbk.)

1. Economic assistance, Canadian – History – 21st century. 2. Canadian
International Development Agency. 3. Canada – Economic policy.
I. Brown, Stephen, 1967–

HC60.S82 2012   338.91'71   C2012-902511-9

This book was typeset by Interscript in 10.5/13 Sabon.

Contents

Acknowledgments

I owe many thanks to all those who made contributions large and small to this volume. First and foremost are the authors of the various chapters, whose hard work, insights, and congeniality I greatly appreciated. Next on the list is Rosalind Raddatz, who provided invaluable assistance at all stages of the project. You may not see them, but her fingerprints are all over the book. The anonymous peer reviewers and the students in my fall 2011 University of Ottawa graduate seminar on foreign aid also provided shrewd comments and helpful suggestions. I am grateful to all of them for their careful readings of the manuscript. Dana Hayward very efficiently and good-humouredly helped ensure that the manuscript conformed to McGill-Queen's University Press style requirements, a tedious but nonetheless necessary endeavour. At the Press, acquisitions editor Mark Abley was very supportive and ably guided me and the manuscript through all the steps of the publication process. It has been a true pleasure to work with him. Curtis Fahey provided outstanding copy editing, and Megan Sproule-Jones skillfully compiled the index. A grant from the Social Sciences and Humanities Research Council of Canada (SSHRC) greatly facilitated my work on foreign aid over the past few years. This book received additional financial assistance from the Canadian Federation for the Humanities and Social Sciences' Awards to Scholarly Publications Program and the University of Ottawa. Finally, Oxford University Press kindly permitted me to reprint in this volume the chapter "Aid Effectiveness and the Framing of New Canadian Aid Initiatives," which originally appeared in Duane Bratt and Christopher

J. Kukucha, eds., *Readings in Canadian Foreign Policy: Classic Debates and New Ideas*, 2nd ed. (Toronto: Oxford University Press 2011), 469–86.

Avec mes remerciements les plus sincères,

Stephen Brown
University of Ottawa
March 2012

Abbreviations

AAP	Africa Action Plan
AIDS	Acquired Immunodeficiency Syndrome
ANC	African National Congress (South Africa)
AU	African Union
BBC	British Broadcasting Corporation
CACL	Canadian Association for Community Living
CAD	Canadian Dollars
CBC	Canadian Broadcasting Corporation
CCIC	Canadian Council for International Co-operation
CDAI	Conference of Defence Associations Institute (Canada)
CDPF	Country Development Program Framework (CIDA, Canada)
CEO	Chief Executive Officer
C-FAR	Canadians for Foreign Aid Reform
CGD	Center for Global Development (United States)
CGIAR	Consultative Group on International Agricultural Research
CIDA	Canadian International Development Agency
CIGI	Centre for International Governance Innovation (Canada)
CPA	Comprehensive Peace Agreement (Sudan)
CPP	Canada Pension Plan
CRA	Canada Revenue Agency
CSO	Civil Society Organization
CSP	Country Strategy Paper (Ireland)
CSR	Corporate Social Responsibility
CUSO	Canadian University Service Overseas

DAC	Development Assistance Committee (OECD)
DFAIT	Department of Foreign Affairs and International Trade (Canada)
DFID	Department for International Development (United Kingdom)
DND	Department of National Defence (Canada)
DRC	Democratic Republic of the Congo
ECOSOC	Economic and Social Council (United Nations)
EDC	Export Development Canada
EU	European Union
FAO	Food and Agriculture Organization (United Nations)
FCO	Foreign and Commonwealth Office (United Kingdom)
FDI	Foreign Direct Investment
FY	Fiscal Year
GAD	Gender and Development
GBS	General Budget Support
GDP	Gross Domestic Product
GE	Gender Equality
GNI	Gross National Income
GNP	Gross National Product
GOSS	Government of South Sudan
GPG	Global Public Good
GPSF	Global Peace and Security Fund (DFAIT, Canada)
HIPC	Highly Indebted Poor Country
HIV	Human Immunodeficiency Virus
IAE	International Assistance Envelope (Canada)
ICG	International Crisis Group
IDA	International Development Association (World Bank)
IDB	Inter-American Development Bank
IFIS	International Financial Institutions
ILO	International Labour Organization
IMF	International Monetary Fund
IPS	International Policy Statement (Canada)
ISAF	International Security Assistance Force (Afghanistan)
LDC	Least Developed Country
MAC	Mining Association of Canada
MCH	Maternal and Child Health
MDGS	Millennium Development Goals
MINUSTAH	United Nations Stabilization Mission in Haiti
MP	Member of Parliament

NATO	North Atlantic Treaty Organization
NDP	New Democratic Party (Canada)
NEPAD	New Partnership for Africa's Development
NGO	Non-Governmental Organization
NIC	Newly Industrialized Country
NORAD	North American Aerospace Defence Command
NRC	Natural Resources Canada
NSI	North-South Institute (Canada)
OCAE	Office of the Chief Audit Executive (CIDA, Canada)
ODA	Official Development Assistance
ODAAA	Official Development Assistance Accountability Act (Canada)
OECD	Organisation for Economic Co-operation and Development
OEEC	Organisation for European Economic Co-operation
OGDS	Other Government Departments
OICC	Office of the Information Commissioner of Canada
OPEC	Organization of the Petroleum Exporting Countries
PBA	Program-Based Approach
PC	Progressive Conservative Party of Canada
PDAC	Prospectors and Developers Association of Canada
PRBS	Poverty Reduction Budget Support Credit Program (World Bank)
PRT	Provincial Reconstruction Team
PSA	Public Service Agreement (United Kingdom)
QIPS	Quick Impact Projects
QWIDS	Query Wizard for International Development Statistics (OECD/DAC)
RCMP	Royal Canadian Mounted Police
SCEAIT	Standing Committee on External Affairs and International Trade (Canada)
SCFAID	Standing Committee on Foreign Affairs and International Trade (Canada)
SSCFAIT	Senate Standing Committee on Foreign Affairs and International Trade (Canada)
SSR	Security Sector Reform
START	Stabilization and Reconstruction Task Force (DFAIT, Canada)
TBS	Treasury Board Secretariat (Canada)
TSX	Toronto Stock Exchange

UK	United Kingdom
UN	United Nations
UNAMID	United Nations-African Union Assistance Mission in Darfur
UNCTAD	United Nations Conference on Trade and Development
UNDP	United Nations Development Programme
UNFPA	United Nations Population Fund
UNHCR	Office of the United Nations High Commissioner on Refugees
UNICEF	United Nations Children's Fund
UNMIS	United Nations Mission in Sudan
UNRWA	United Nations Relief and Works Agency for Palestine Refugees
UNU	United Nations University
US	United States
USAID	United States Agency for International Development
USD	United States Dollars
USGS	United States Geological Survey
WAD	Women and Development
WEF	World Economic Forum
WHI	World Hope International (Canada)
WID	Women in Development
WOG	Whole of Government
WTO	World Trade Organization

STRUGGLING FOR EFFECTIVENESS

INTRODUCTION

Canadian Aid Enters
the Twenty-First Century

STEPHEN BROWN

Since 2000, development assistance has been undergoing fundamental changes in Canada and other donor countries – a mini-revolution in foreign aid. After a decade of decline, aid volumes have increased dramatically and donors have begun to harmonize new policy initiatives to an unprecedented extent. After decades as aid recipients, countries such as China, Brazil, and India are (re-)emerging as important sources of international development cooperation and frequently employing new forms of assistance. Amid this renewal of interest in foreign aid and innovation in how donors provide it, scholarship has sometimes struggled to keep up, notably in Canada. Since about 2005, however, the study of Canadian aid has experienced a veritable renaissance. A growing number of academic studies and policy reports have put the Canadian International Development Agency (CIDA) and Canadian aid more generally under the microscope, providing intelligent insights and generating lively debates.

Still, many important questions have yet to be answered in full. For instance, how should we understand new foreign aid trends? How appropriate are Canada's recent policy initiatives and what motivates them? How does Canadian aid compare to that of other donors? To what extent is CIDA setting its own policy agenda? What role do other government departments and non-governmental organizations (NGOs) play in the provision of foreign aid? What could be done to improve CIDA's work and what are the impediments to change? The present book seeks to address these questions and many more.

This introductory chapter begins by presenting the broader domestic and international context in which Canadian aid policy is made and aid programs operate, highlighting the changes that have influenced Canada's foreign aid since around 2000. It then explores the contested meanings of two key terms in contemporary aid policy debates that contributors raise repeatedly throughout the book: aid effectiveness and policy coherence. Following a brief review of the literature on Canadian development assistance, it describes this volume's original contributions and the overall approach it adopts, as well as providing an outline of individual chapters.

THE CHANGING DOMESTIC AND GLOBAL CONTEXT

Changes to Canadian aid policy since 2000 can be understood only in the context of broader shifts at both the national and international levels. At home, after almost a decade of cutting foreign aid, Liberal Prime Minister Jean Chrétien's drawn-out retirement permitted him to focus on legacy projects, one of which was an increase in spending on aid, with special attention to Africa, the continent in greatest need of assistance. Amid a wider international policy review, Paul Martin's Liberal government further increased the resources available for development assistance, also emphasizing Africa, and took important steps to integrate foreign aid with Canada's own diplomatic, military, and commercial interests, particularly in Afghanistan. Those changes were in line with shifts in numerous other Western donor countries as well (Woods 2005). Initially, Stephen Harper's Conservative government continued in the same vein, with growth in official development assistance (ODA), additional emphasis on Afghanistan, and a "whole-of-government" approach to international policy coherence. However, after a couple of years in power, it took several initiatives that reversed previous Canadian policy and broke with the broader donor consensus, notably placing greater emphasis on the Americas, where Canada has important commercial interests, followed by an aid budget freeze. Additionally, it made a mantra of transparency and accountability in government spending, including at CIDA.

During this time, changes at the international level also had profound influences on Canada's foreign aid, sometimes in contradictory ways. For instance, donors agreed on the urgent need to address poverty in the short to medium term, epitomized in the Millennium Development Goals (MDGs) adopted in 2000. Depending on one's perspective, these goals complemented, corrected, or contradicted the "Washington Consensus," the donors' dominant neo-liberal approach to development since the 1980s and subsequent additions.[1] Still, various forms of donor assistance, including debt relief, remained predicated on the "Augmented Washington Consensus" and, specifically, recipients' prior adoption of a World Bank-endorsed Poverty Reduction Strategy. The latter maintained basic neo-liberal assumptions, although the MDGs implicitly recognized that such policies had failed to achieve sufficient poverty reduction. Even so, donors, including Canada, retained both as important development paradigms.

At a 2002 conference on finance for development held in Monterrey, Mexico, donors committed to important increases in their aid budgets, reversing a decade of decline – though tempered in some cases by the financial crisis that occurred at the end of the decade. A consensus also emerged, with important contributions from Chrétien and Martin, on the need to recognize that Africa had the greatest and most urgent needs. This was made most explicit by the Commission for Africa, appointed in 2004 by British Prime Minister Tony Blair, who upstaged the Canadian government's role in advocacy for African development. Donors reached a series of new agreements on how they themselves would reform their practices to deliver more effective aid, best illustrated by the 2005 Paris Declaration on Aid Effectiveness, which calls for greater harmonization among donors and their alignment with recipient countries' own development strategies. At subsequent meetings in Accra, Ghana (2008), and Busan, South Korea (2011), donor and recipient governments along with international institutions further refined and expanded on this consensus.

At the same time, countervailing forces reoriented foreign aid flows both geographically and thematically. Since 11 September 2001, donors have dramatically increased their emphasis on security in development policy and practices, including paying far greater attention to so-called failed and fragile states and the potential threat that they might pose to Western interests, especially by hosting terrorist networks. They embarked on massive "state building" exercises after invading Iraq and Afghanistan, with rather limited success. By the end of the first decade of the 2000s, after the global economy went into recession, enthusiasm for development assistance began to wane in several donor countries and aid itself was controversially described as "dead" (Moyo 2009). The economic crisis reversed many development gains of the previous decade and jeopardized the attainment of the MDGs by the 2015 deadline, with many goals seeming increasingly out of reach. Together, the changes at the national and international levels provide the context for understanding the recent shifts in Canadian aid policy.

KEY THEMES IN DEVELOPMENT ASSISTANCE

During this period, two concepts emerged as central to discussions of aid policy, namely aid effectiveness and policy coherence. Neither of these terms was new, but the great emphasis placed on them certainly was. Almost every chapter in this book addresses these themes in relation to Canada. They thus warrant a closer examination here, particularly because of the ambiguities that surround their use.

Aid Effectiveness

Aid effectiveness is a common-sense goal. As I explain in chapter 3, no one would advocate aid being ineffective. The rub, however, lies in how to define and measure effectiveness. There are in fact many different approaches. At its most basic, effectiveness implies good value for money – but how does one assess that value? Does it refer to the value of aid results, aid outcomes, or aid's share of development outcomes?

Aid results refer to the direct consequences of assistance, for instance, the construction of a certain number of schools or the vaccination of a certain number of children. These are assumed to translate into positive outcomes in the longer term, but this is not always the case. Aid-funded school buildings can fail to be maintained or even be destroyed in civil conflicts or they might remain closed for lack of staffing or supplies. Children may be vaccinated, but perhaps not immunized from disease (some immunizations require several doses of a vaccine at given intervals). Even complete achievement of desired aid outputs could thus have little or no impact at all, because of either design flaws or unforeseen changes in conditions. And, even if successful, aid outcomes do not guarantee a concomitant positive impact on broader development outcomes. For instance, educated individuals might never be afforded the opportunity to apply their skills in a productive way owing to a lack of suitable jobs. Further, even when aid does translate into national development, progress is almost impossible to apportion to different contributing actors, since various donors provide different forms and amounts of ODA and, moreover, foreign aid is but one of national development's ingredients. Finally, many types of results are difficult to measure empirically, such as improved governance or women's empowerment. In such a context, aid effectiveness is even harder to assess.

In fact, donors rarely use the term aid effectiveness to refer to results on the ground, applying it instead to their own aid modalities and practices. The central concern of the Paris Declaration and other international agreements on aid effectiveness is more aptly described as efficiency, rather than effectiveness. The international aid effectiveness agenda seeks above all to provide assistance in a way that does not, for example, duplicate or contradict other actors' efforts, including the recipient government's own, or place an unreasonable burden on recipient governments. In other words, donors laudably want to be efficient and avoid wasting precious resources. However, theirs is a preoccupation with form, rather than content. None of the prescribed aid effectiveness measures implies that the aid will actually support an effective strategy. The recipient government and donors might follow all the right processes and agree on a very efficient scheme that nonetheless utterly fails to produce the desired outputs, let alone positive outcomes. The last six decades are unfortunately littered with examples of aid gone wrong. This vision of aid effectiveness is thus insufficient. For that reason, many development actors, led mainly by civil society organizations (CSOs), are beginning to move conceptually beyond aid effectiveness and explore instead the notion of development effectiveness, including for the first time at the most recent international forum on aid effectiveness, held in Busan, South Korea, in November 2011.[2] (The Canadian government, however, generally limits its use of the concept of effectiveness to an even more narrow interpretation, as explained in chapter 3.)

Many failures of development assistance can be attributed to the fact that foreign aid lacks any magic bullets and a certain amount of experimentation is required to determine what works and under what conditions. Although accurate, such explanations belie the fundamental point that donors' actual objectives for providing ODA often relate more to their own commercial, security, economic, or diplomatic interests than to poverty reduction in developing countries or other developmental objectives. The literature on foreign aid is unanimous in this observation, though many authors may differ on the actual degree and nature of self-interest inherent in specific countries' aid programs. In fact, aid agencies themselves, including CIDA, openly acknowledge self-interest as a motivation for aid and a criterion for selecting priority recipient countries.

Given the Canadian government's growing focus on self-interest, rather than recipient countries' priorities – discussed throughout this book – it is not surprising that Canada has been slow to implement the more altruistic elements of the aid effectiveness agenda. In fact, its record is measurably worsening in some areas. For instance, a study by the Organisation for Economic Co-operation and Development (OECD) found that Canada's alignment with national priorities in thirty-two recipient countries surveyed actually declined since it endorsed the Paris Declaration. Compliance with that principle fell from 52 per cent in 2005 to 45 per cent in 2007 and dropped again to 39 per cent in 2010, less than half of the target of 85 per cent for 2010 set by the OECD's Development Assistance Committee (DAC) (OECD 2011, 170).[3]

The lack of altruism has serious implications for the question of aid's actual effectiveness – and not just on the Paris conception of it. For example, if the elimination of security threats to donors themselves, such as insurgent movements linked to international terrorist networks, is the main objective of assistance to a certain country or of a certain aid program, its effectiveness should be measured against those goals, not economic growth, poverty reduction, or other forms of development in recipient countries. It is an inconvenient truth that, when such aid fails to have a significant positive impact on development, the lack of aid effectiveness is not the culprit per se, but rather the fact that development was not the actual objective in the first place. Similarly, when donors provide assistance to governments or other actors that are not credibly committed or able to use it to reduce poverty or undertake other development activities, any lack of aid effectiveness is not the real problem – it is a result of the donors' selection of partners and the motives behind it. Thus, aid that rewards an ally for policies that primarily benefit donors should not be construed principally as development assistance, and thus not be expected to be effective at or efficient in producing development outcomes. Unfortunately, donor countries find it convenient to ignore such matters, in large part in order to avoid embarrassing their peers or incriminating themselves. As a result, these fundamental obstacles are rarely, if ever, raised in discussions of aid effectiveness and how to achieve it.

Policy Coherence

Like aid effectiveness, the term policy coherence is widely used in the development policy context. It also has many distinct uses and interpretations. There are several levels of potential coherence, including: 1) between various aid/development policies of a specific donor; 2) between a donor's aid/development policies and its other policies, both foreign and domestic; 3) between the donor country and the recipient country's policies; and 4) between various donors' aid/development policies (Weston and Pierre-Antoine 2003, 18). International discussions on policy coherence focus almost exclusively on the second level. Aid policy circles refer to the third level as "alignment" and the fourth as "harmonization," rather than policy coherence per se, in the Paris Declaration and other aid effectiveness instruments.

The basic principle of policy coherence is a sound one: that a government's departments should not work at cross-purposes but rather coordinate and cooperate toward common policy goals. The resulting whole-of-government approach can therefore harness resources more effectively to achieve government objectives, however they are defined. At its best, policy coherence *for development* recognizes that more than just aid is required for development, including reforms to the global trading system. As a result, a donor country may consider eliminating tariff and non-tariff barriers to goods from developing countries or dramatically reducing subsidies to domestic industries, both of which would permit developing countries' exports to compete more fairly on an open market and thus facilitate their economic growth. The effects of such endeavours, if widely undertaken by donor countries, could surpass by far the benefits of their current development assistance. Other examples of non-aid policy areas in the global North that can have an important impact in the global South include immigration (for instance, ending the deliberate "poaching" of health professionals in the global South), global public goods (such as ensuring environmental protection and fighting against climate change), and technology transfers (for example, being more flexible about life-saving drug patents). (Chapter 1 compares the degree of policy coherence for development in Canada with two other donor countries.)

Such measures, however, exact a price on the donor country and government, some more so than others. For example, in Canada, ending the protection of the egg, dairy, and poultry sector would turn an influential lobby sector against the ruling party, especially in Quebec. The consequences would be even more severe for an American government that went against its pharmaceutical companies' interests or for a European or Japanese government that ended the protection and subsidization of its farming sector. These political costs can act as extremely powerful incentives against policy coherence for development.

As several authors in this volume argue, the Canadian government's instances of policy coherence tend to undermine development rather than promote it, though chapter 4 provides a couple of contrasting examples. Much depends on what common objective underpins whole-of-government efforts, including what benefits are sought and for whom. For instance, when various Canadian public institutions promote extractive activities in a developing country, is the fundamental purpose to create growth and employment in the recipient country or is it primarily aimed at promoting the profit making of Canadian mining companies? (This is discussed in depth in chapter 8.) To what extent can they achieve both? If the basic goals are growth and employment, was the extractive sector chosen for assistance because it is the most effective way of achieving those goals? More fundamentally even, are economic growth and employment generation the most effective tools of poverty reduction under those circumstances, or are development objectives primarily a smokescreen for ulterior motives? As discussed above, for what is the policy-coherent aid actually meant to be effective? Likewise, to avoid highlighting their own record on such thorny issues, donors generally prefer to sidestep these key concerns in their discussions of policy coherence.

THE STUDY OF CANADIAN AID

Canadian development assistance has long been the object of scholarly analysis and debate, even before CIDA was founded. From the 1960s to the 1990s, much of this literature fell into three broad categories: radical critiques of Canadian self-serving practices (Carty and Smith 1981; Swift and Clarke 1982; Swift and Tomlinson 1991); liberal visions of Canada's potential contributions in this area (Spicer 1966; Miller 1992); or, in a few instances, right-leaning critiques of inefficiency and waste (Fromm and Hull 1981). A number of important studies took less ideological and more nuanced approaches, especially during the 1990s, focusing on a wide range of aspects of Canadian development assistance, including the history of CIDA and Canada's then-declining commitments (Morrison 1998); Canada's motivations in providing development assistance (Nossal 1988; Pratt 2000; Rudner 1989); policy analysis (Pratt 1996; Thérien 1989); and CIDA's relations with other government departments (Pratt 1998). Other studies addressed changes in Canadian aid and development assistance more generally in the context of the first decade of the post–Cold War period (Freedman 2000).

This body of work, however, predates the significant changes in Canada's (and other countries') post-2000 aid policies. One scholar noted in 2007 that ironically, since these important shifts began in 2000, "the volume and level of scholarly debate about Canadian aid policy has declined significantly" (Black 2007, 184). Scholarship had indeed fallen "behind the curve," but it is now catching up. In recent years, a number of researchers from academe and think-tanks have questioned CIDA's policy autonomy (Brown 2008; Campbell and Hatcher 2004) and reacted to government's 2005 *International Policy Statement* chapter on development (Black and Tiessen 2007; Brown 2005, 2007; Cameron 2007; Stairs 2005). Several have gone beyond critiques to explore concrete ways of improving the design and delivery of Canadian foreign aid (Brown and Jackson 2009; Carin and Smith 2010; Goldfarb and Tapp 2006; Gulrajani 2010; Johnston 2010; Swiss with Maxwell 2010). A comprehensive edited volume in French on Canadian development assistance was also recently published (Audet et al. 2008), and a couple of books have highlighted more ominous interpretations of Canadian aid in the context of broader Canadian foreign policy (Engler 2009; Gordon 2010). Though they all provide important analysis, these studies only begin to assess the impact of recent changes.

THIS BOOK

This edited volume seeks to analyze recent trends and evaluate current Canadian aid policy, as well as examine means of improving the work of CIDA and Canadian aid more generally. The contributors come from a range of backgrounds: professors, graduate students, and practitioners with experience in government, Canadian NGOs, and multilateral organizations. Collectively, they provide the most comprehensive analysis of CIDA and Canadian aid policy in more than a decade – since the publication of the volume *Canadian International Development Assistance Policies: An Appraisal*, edited by Cranford Pratt (first edition, 1994; second edition, 1996), and David Morrison's *Aid and Ebb Tide: A History of CIDA and Canadian Development Assistance* (1998).

The book offers insight into a variety of issues concerning CIDA and Canadian foreign aid. It is distinctive in its focus on the post-2000 period, during which time foreign aid has gone through numerous changes, as argued above. It engages scholarship and practice through a variety of approaches. Most contributors draw mainly from qualitative methods (including the analysis of official documents and discourse, as well as interviews with Canadian donor officials) and some make use of quantitative analyses (of aid flows and other statistics). Some chapters assess new policies, others emerging practices. Some focus mainly on the level of government policy, while others consider complex interactions across many levels of the broader aid system. Several chapters compare Canada's performance to other countries' or draw lessons for Canada from other countries' aid programs – notably Ireland, Norway, and the United Kingdom. Others analyze legislation and the political debates concerning Canadian aid. Some are solely empirical while others are also normative. Most focus on the period 2000–11, although a few start with the present and subsequently offer scenarios for improvement. All chapters, however, adopt a critical analytical perspective, based on a thorough understanding of the issues. The goal is to provide solid and grounded analysis – not to dismiss or deconstruct Canadian aid by solely pointing out its flaws, nor to convey uncritically the Canadian government's or NGOs' perspectives. The book seeks to provide robust analysis of the state and recent record of Canadian development assistance, via diverse approaches and voices, with both positive and negative components, and identify possible ways to improve the delivery of Canadian aid and promote development more generally.

A difficulty in discussing Canadian foreign aid is identifying the actors and structures that are responsible for policies, practices, and decisions, as well as potential agents of change within and without CIDA. Part of the problem is the opacity of the decision-making process. A clear example of this was the mystery surrounding the identity of the person who inserted in a memorandum the word "NOT" that reversed the CIDA minister's approval of an NGO's funding application in 2009 (a case discussed in chapters 3, 7, 10, and 11). Though she initially denied in Parliament knowing who had done so, the CIDA minister eventually admitted that she had instructed her staff to alter the document. Whose decision it actually was to override the minister's initial approval remains unknown, though someone in the Prime Minister's Office is a plausible possibility.

When contributors to this volume discuss "CIDA," we refer not only to the institution but also to high-level officials whose decisions determine CIDA's policies and practices. Depending on the issue, such senior officials could be part of CIDA's upper management (president and vice-presidents), work in the minister's office, or in fact be located elsewhere in the government (such as the Prime Minister's Office or Privy Council Office) – it is often unclear, even to lower-level CIDA employees, where specific policy decisions originate. We do not mean to suggest that CIDA's rank-and-file staff members are as a whole involved in the process or at the origin of any decision. Many are acutely aware of serious problems in Canadian foreign aid and unable to participate in solving them, or even openly express their concerns. In order to continue important development work, many CIDA managers struggle to frame their units' programs in terms that fit the policies *du jour*, ironically adopted in the name of aid effectiveness. Anecdotal evidence certainly provides a clear sense of frustration within the agency, particularly about the recent changes that have been effected. Reflecting this, according to a 2008 survey of the federal public service, CIDA employees were far more likely than their colleagues in other government departments to believe strongly that their work suffers as a result of institutional and policy-related problems.[4]

In a context where government officials and development professionals risk significant professional sanctions for speaking freely, a comprehensive assessment of Canadian aid – such as this one – is all the more important. The volume should be of interest to researchers of all kinds, university lecturers, graduate and undergraduate students, and policy makers and practitioners in the area of foreign aid, in government and NGOs as well as in the private sector. We hope it will become a valued source for years to come for anyone conducting research on Canadian foreign aid, seeking to reform it from without or within – or for those just interested in learning more about Canada's development assistance than what can be found in the media and on government websites.

THE CONTRIBUTIONS

In recent years, researchers have published several rankings of aid donors, each differing in criteria. They facilitate comparisons between Canada and other donor countries, essentially on a quantitative basis (indicators). Other studies undertake a more qualitative comparison. In chapter 1, Hunter McGill draws on the Washington-based Center for Global Development's Commitment to Development Index, as well as in-depth "peer reviews" of Western donor countries produced by the OECD/DAC, a process he himself was involved in for several years. McGill systematically compares the performance of Canada, the United Kingdom, and Ireland in four areas: aid strategy, aid volume and distribution, policy coherence for development, and gender equality. The results are sobering, since he fails to find evidence of good Canadian performance, despite government claims to the contrary. McGill concludes that only greater political will and sustained efforts can make Canada a better donor.

Increasingly, Canadians turn to other countries' aid agencies when seeking ideas for reforming CIDA. A key issue for many is the institutional structure for the provision of aid. Should CIDA be folded into the Department of Foreign Affairs and International Trade, as some have suggested? Or should it be granted greater autonomy and a more prominent place at the cabinet table? Nilima Gulrajani, in chapter 2, reviews the experiences of two such examples: Norway's Ministry of Foreign Affairs, which has assumed responsibility for the country's aid program, and the UK's Department for International Development, which is an oft-cited example of the benefits of a higher degree of institutional independence. Both countries, she finds, perform better in delivering foreign aid than Canada does. If governance models based both on autonomy and on the lack thereof can be superior to CIDA's current set-up, the agency's governance structure is unlikely be the root of its deficiencies. What is required to improve performance, she argues, is not tinkering with the institutional model, but rather – similarly to McGill's conclusion – better political vision and greater commitment at the top levels of government to development goals, underpinned by equally strong popular support.

As mentioned earlier, an important new trend is the international aid effectiveness agenda, an evolving set of principles first articulated in the 2005 Paris Declaration on Aid Effectiveness that recognize that the way that donors provide aid has an important impact on the quality of the aid – whereas in the past the responsibility for disappointing development results were almost exclusively attributed to recipient countries. Notions of aid effectiveness have profound implications for which types of countries receive assistance and the very nature of the North-South power differential (Brown and Morton 2008; Hydén 2008). To what extent does Canada translate concerns for effectiveness into practice? In chapter 3, I explore the multiple meanings of aid effectiveness and trace how the Canadian government uses the term to frame its new aid initiatives. I find that, other than the untying of aid from the purchase of Canadian goods, none of CIDA's new policies can be reasonably expected to improve the quality of Canadian aid. Some will, in fact, make Canadian aid less effective. The Canadian government has recast the concept of effectiveness to refer primarily to achieving value for money in ways that can be easily demonstrated to Canadian taxpayers. It uses the term to legitimize its own political preferences by hiding behind the fig leaf of alleged effectiveness. The chapter considers what this tells us about Canada's shifting motivations for foreign aid.

A prominent feature of twenty-first-century aid, mainly in response to the events of 9/11, is the focus on a new category of countries labelled "failed and fragile states," which lack control over their own territories and are unable (or unwilling) to meet the needs of their citizens. Such countries, goes the argument, can become hosts to terrorist groups, crime syndicates, and other vectors of international insecurity. To respond to these "new threats," donors should not only "securitize" their foreign aid but also achieve greater effectiveness through the use of whole-of-government approaches to stabilization and reconstruction. Most analyses of Canada's policies regarding fragile states focus on Afghanistan and chronicle how the military component has overwhelmingly dominated the development and diplomatic components. This raises serious concerns about the use of foreign aid, in particular its instrumentalization by donors and its subservience to counter-insurgency strategies. Stephen Baranyi and Anca Paducel take this analysis two steps further in chapter 4. They not only look at Canada's role in Afghanistan but also compare it with the situation in two other important fragile states, considering a number of local and international actors and factors. Their findings are counterweights to the outright rejections of Canadian whole-of-government endeavours. They argue that, especially in the case of Haiti but also in South Sudan, non-aid actors actually can become important partners for development, albeit only in the absence of security interests. As in Afghanistan, however, such efforts have not yielded many sustainable development results.

Liam Swiss, in chapter 5, also examines the reasons for which Canada provides foreign aid. The debates on the main rationales, self-interested versus selfless, have long dominated the analysis of Canadian foreign aid. Clearly, both have important effects on expenditures, but their relative weight is prone to variation over time. For instance, at different points, researchers have noted how self-interest was increasingly underpinning Canada's aid (Pratt 2000; Rudner 1989). Since the events of 9/11, as mentioned above, national security and donor self-interest have only gained in strength. In his chapter, Swiss documents the securitization of Canadian aid by tracing the rise in aid expenditure on conflict, peace, and security. He asks whether this process is associated with a concomitant reduction in more altruistic programs, using gender equality as a proxy. Though he cannot prove a direct link between the two, he finds that the increase in security-related expenditure is accompanied by a decrease in CIDA programming that seeks gender equality, an area for which Canada used to be a world leader. Moreover, when the government does invoke gender issues, Swiss argues that it is usually to promote Canadian interests, rather than the interest of women in developing countries. The two trends are therefore linked by a common thread: the government's instrumentalization of aid for its own national interests, rather than in the interest of recipient countries and their citizens.

The most recent global food crisis that emerged in 2007, characterized by a rapid spike in prices of dietary staples across the world, required new responses from donors. CIDA, for instance, adopted increased food security as one of its three priority themes in 2009. Still, though everyone can agree on the need to ensure an adequate access to nutritious food for all, there is no consensus on the means to achieve it. Should smallholder food self-sufficiency be promoted or should aid support large-scale, mechanized plantations to bolster crop exports, thereby maximizing revenues for the subsequent purchase of food? In chapter 6, Denis Côté and Dominique Caouette examine the history of CIDA's land and food policies, criticizing its promotion of neo-liberal market mechanisms for being insufficient and, moreover, failing to respect fundamental human rights, in particular the right to food. CIDA's twenty-first-century policies and strategies on food and land, they find, might provide assistance to the hungry but do not address the basic cause of food insecurity: poor people's lack of access to land.

Critics of CIDA regularly complain about Byzantine bureaucratic requirements. One might think that this results from having too many policies, each with its own requirements. Molly den Heyer studied CIDA's partnership with Tanzania and, as she explains in chapter 7, found that there are actually few formal policies that CIDA officials can use to guide their activities. Instead, CIDA representatives take a number of small decisions, based on a wide variety of de facto policies and less formal understandings that together constitute what one might call a "shadow policy," which can have inconsistencies and internal contradictions. Having to negotiate through this diffuse web (or "ecosystem") often causes serious delays, since risk-averse officials want to avoid accepting responsibility for ill-received decisions made without sufficient guidance. As a result, the timeliness and the effectiveness of Canadian aid can suffer greatly. This is most acutely felt by CIDA staff in field offices, and their circumstances will only worsen if CIDA continues to decentralize its operations and move its personnel to recipient countries without providing them with clearer guidance and greater approval authority.

Aid agencies often emphasize the private sector as the engine that drives growth in recipient countries. Many donors have special programs for encouraging private investment in developing countries, for instance, through special credits and guarantees. Much of the economic growth in developing countries since 2000 has relied heavily on the extraction of natural resources, such as oil, gold, or diamonds, especially in Africa. Yet, though the extraction of these commodities gives a rapid boost to gross national product, it does not necessarily contribute to poverty reduction, other than providing modest salaries for a small number of manual labourers for as long as resources are still available to be extracted. It also can create serious new problems, such as extensive environmental damage and violations of human rights, as well as exacerbating conflict and repression. Many therefore speak of the "natural resource curse." This is an important issue for Canada, since it is the home to a majority of the world's mining companies, whose overseas activities are only minimally regulated under Canadian law. Elizabeth Blackwood and Veronika Stewart, in chapter 8, explore the link between government agencies, including CIDA, and private mining interests. Canada, they argue, has adopted a whole-of-government approach to supporting the activities of mining companies, which has included the use of CIDA funds to pave the way for the greater involvement of Canadian companies in resource extraction. This use of foreign aid, they find, appears to be illegal under the provisions of Canada's 2008 Official Development Assistance Accountability Act.

The Harper government initially paid little attention to Canadian foreign aid, content to continue along the path set by the Liberals. Since 2008, however, the government has instituted a number of changes in Canada's development assistance. The first notable portent of a break with the past – and with the international consensus – was Harper's surprise announcement in 2007 that Canada would henceforth focus more on Latin America and the Caribbean and, by implication, less on Africa. This was entrenched two years later when CIDA dropped eight African countries that had been designated as priorities only in 2005. Later, at the 2010 G8 summit in Huntsville, Ontario, Harper used his host's position to push for a new initiative: maternal and child health. This suggested that *more* aid would be directed to Africa, where maternal and child health require the most assistance. In chapter 9, David Black tries to make sense of the confusing tug-of-war over Africa's place in Canadian aid, as well as the Conservative Party's engagement (or lack thereof) with foreign aid more generally. Without romanticizing the record of the previous Liberal governments, his sobering analysis traces a decline in engagement from which it may be difficult to recover.

The importance of civil society organizations (CSOs), also known as non-governmental organizations, in development has been widely recognized, even enshrined (for instance, in the 2008 Accra Agenda for Action). Both Northern and Southern NGOs, as development actors in their own right, receive funding from bilateral donors. CIDA is a vital source of funding for numerous Canadian NGOs. Some became overly dependent and a few prominent organizations suffered greatly from CIDA decisions not to renew funding in recent years, without providing a coherent explanation. Through these funding decisions, the Conservative government strongly reinforced a concern that many NGOs already shared: How far can Canadian NGOs criticize CIDA or the government without jeopardizing their funding? Ian Smillie argues in chapter 10 that the government deliberately seeks to silence NGOs' plural voices and that the NGOs are too often reduced to contracted service providers. NGOs can be complicit in this process, when they bite their tongues in exchange for important contracts or grants. Advocacy – including public debate and education on development issues – is a crucial activity if actors want to effect actual change, and not just alleviate problems.

Chapter 11, by the editor, analyzes a different aspect of Canadian NGOS' relationship with the government. I focus on changes to CIDA's funding mechanisms for NGOS, announced in 2010. Though CIDA presents them as "modernizing" the partnership and increasing aid effectiveness, many aspects of these new modalities reflect a step backwards. In the past, CIDA was a global leader in policies on channelling assistance through NGOS, including core funding, as well as recognizing their original contributions and their complementarity with government-to-government forms of assistance. Now, CIDA is seeking to influence much more strongly the countries and sectors that NGOS work in, so that they align more closely with the Canadian government's own priorities and interests – rather than those of developing country NGOS and citizens – and further muzzling their critical voices. This, I argue, fits well with two broader trends in Canadian development assistance: the government's desire to centralize control over foreign aid and its growing instrumentalization of aid and CIDA to achieve self-serving objectives.

Many of this book's chapters have raised the need to alter fundamentally the ways that CIDA and the rest of the Canadian government deliver foreign aid. In chapter 12, Adam Chapnick considers the politics involved in effecting such change, and helps to explain why reform is so difficult to achieve. In doing so, he discusses what few authors have mentioned: how electoral politics and the interaction of political parties in the House of Commons reflect the little weight that MPS – or their constituents – place on the issue of foreign aid. In the Machiavellian environment of Parliament Hill (including the Langevin Block, which houses the Prime Minister's Office), there are few incentives for and little interest in improving aid performance. Nonetheless, the chapter provides some practical advice that may bolster the aid reform agenda.

The concluding chapter, co-authored by the editor and Rosalind Raddatz, reviews the common themes that permeate the book, considering the points of convergence as well as some relatively minor points of divergence. In it, we sum up the basic contributions of the book and identify remaining gaps in efforts to understand better – and potentially favourably influence – CIDA and Canada's aid policy.

NOTES

1 The donors' "Washington Consensus" advocated minimal government regulation, privatization, emphasis on trade, and global market integration. Other requirements were later added, such as good governance, seeking to enable the policies to bear fruit. See Rodrik (2001, 14–16) for further explanations and an in-depth analysis.
2 There is, however, no shared conception of development effectiveness. See Kindorney (2011) for an analysis of four different ones.
3 Canada is not the only donor failing to meet its Paris Declaration commitments. The same report's main finding is that DAC members have collectively attained only one of the thirteen aid effectiveness targets that they set for themselves for 2010 (OECD 2011, 19).
4 The most significant discrepancy between CIDA employees' responses and those from the public service as a whole relates to the question, "I feel that the quality of my work suffers because of ..." A far greater proportion of CIDA employees, compared to their colleagues elsewhere, identified the following reasons as "always/almost always" or "often": constantly changing priorities (66 per cent vs. 41 per cent), lack of stability (61 per cent vs. 34 per cent), and too many approval stages (71 per cent vs. 41 per cent) (Treasury Board 2009). By the time this book is published, results from the 2011 Public Service Employee Survey should be available on the Treasury Board website.

REFERENCES

Audet, François, Marie-Eve Desrosiers, and Stéphane Roussel, eds. 2008. *L'aide canadienne au développement: bilan, défis et perspectives.* Montreal: Presses de l'Université de Montréal.
Black, David R. 2007. "Editorial Introduction: Problems and Prospects of Canadian Aid Policy." *Canadian Journal of Development Studies* 28, no. 2 (June): 183–5.
Black, David R., and Rebecca Tiessen. 2007. "The Canadian International Development Agency: New Policies, Old Problems." *Canadian Journal of Development Studies* 28, no. 2 (June): 191–212.
Brown, Chris, and Edward T. Jackson. 2009. "Could the Senate be Right? Should CIDA be Abolished?" In Allan M. Maslove, ed., *How Ottawa Spends, 2009–2010: Economic Upheaval and Political Dysfunction.* Montreal and Kingston, ON: McGill-Queen's University Press. 151–74.

Brown, Stephen. 2005. "Achieving the Development Objectives of Canada's
International Policy Statement." *McGill International Review* 6, no. 1
(fall): 52–5.
– 2007. "'Creating the World's Best Development Agency'? Confusion and
Contradictions in CIDA's New Policy Blueprint." *Canadian Journal of
Development Studies* 28, no. 2 (June): 213–28.
– 2008. "CIDA under the Gun." In Jean Daudelin and Daniel Schwanen,
eds., *Canada among Nations 2007: What Room for Manoeuvre?*
Montreal and Kingston, ON: McGill-Queen's University Press. 91–107.
Brown, Stephen, and Bill Morton. 2008. "Reforming Aid and
Development Cooperation: Accra, Doha and Beyond." Policy Note.
Ottawa: North-South Institute.
Cameron, John. 2007. "CIDA in the Americas: New Directions and Warning
Signs for Canadian Development Policy." *Canadian Journal of Develop-
ment Studies* 28, no. 2: 229–49.
Campbell, Bonnie, and Pascale Hatcher. 2004. "Existe-t-il encore une place
pour la coopération bilatérale? Réflexions à partir de l'expérience cana-
dienne." *Revue Tiers Monde* 45, no. 179 (July): 665–87.
Carin, Barry, and Gordon Smith. 2010. *Reinventing CIDA.* Calgary, AB:
Canadian Defence and Foreign Affairs Institute.
Carty, Robert, and Virginia Smith. 1981. *Perpetuating Poverty: The Political
Economy of Canadian Foreign Aid.* Toronto: Between the Lines Press.
Engler, Yves. 2009. *The Black Book of Canadian Foreign Policy.* Winnipeg
and Black Point, NS: Fernwood Publishing.
Freedman, Jim, ed. 2000. *Transforming Development: Foreign Aid for a
Changing World.* Toronto: University of Toronto Press.
Fromm, Paul, and James P. Hull. 1981. *Down the Drain? A Critical Re-
Examination of Canadian Foreign Aid.* Toronto: Griffin House.
Goldfarb, Danielle, and Stephen Tapp. 2006. *How Canada Can Improve
Its Development Aid: Lessons from Other Aid Agencies.* Commentary
No. 232. Toronto: C.D. Howe Institute.
Gordon, Todd. 2010. *Imperialist Canada.* Winnipeg: Arbeiter Ring.
Gulrajani, Nilima. 2010. *Re-Imagining Canadian Development
Co-operation: A Comparative Examination of Norway and the UK.*
Toronto: Walter and Duncan Gordon Foundation.
Hydén, Goran. 2008. "After the Paris Declaration: Taking on the Issue of
Power." *Development Policy Review* 26, no. 3 (May): 259–74.
Johnston, Patrick. 2010. *Modernizing Canadian Foreign Aid and Development:
Challenges Old and New.* Toronto: Walter and Duncan Gordon Foundation.

Kindornay, Shannon. 2011. "A New Agenda for Development Assistance? From Aid to Development Effectiveness." Policy Brief. Ottawa: North-South Institute.

Miller, Robert. 1992. *Aid as Peacemaker: Canadian Development Assistance and Third World Conflict*. Ottawa: Carleton University Press.

Morrison, David R. 1998. *Aid and Ebb Tide: A History of CIDA and Canadian Development Assistance*. Waterloo, ON: Wilfrid Laurier University Press.

Moyo, Dambiso. 2009. *Dead Aid: Why Aid Is Not Working and How There Is a Better Way for Africa*. New York: Farrar, Strauss and Giroux.

Nossal, Kim R. 1988. "Mixed Motives Revisited: Canada's Interest in Development Assistance." *Canadian Journal of Political Science* 21, no. 1: 35–56.

Organisation for Economic Co-operation and Development. 2011. *Aid Effectiveness 2005–10: Progress in Implementing the Paris Declaration*. Paris: Organisation for Economic Co-operation and Development.

Pratt, Cranford, ed. 1994 (1st ed.) and 1996 (2nd ed.). *Canadian International Development Assistance Policies: An Appraisal*. Montreal and Kingston, ON: McGill-Queen's University Press.

– 1998. "DFAIT's Takeover Bid of CIDA: The Institutional Future of the Canadian International Development Agency." *Canadian Foreign Policy* 5, no. 2 (winter): 1–14.

– 2000. "Alleviating Global Poverty or Enhancing Security: Competing Rationales for Canadian Development Assistance." In Jim Freedman, ed., *Transforming Development: Foreign Aid for a Changing World*. Toronto: University of Toronto Press. 37–59.

Rodrik, Dani. 2001. *The Global Governance of Trade – As If Development Really Mattered*. Background Paper. New York: United Nations Development Programme.

Rudner, Martin. 1989. "New Dimensions in Canadian Development Assistance Policy." In Brian Tomlin and Maureen Appel Molot, eds., *Canada among Nations 1988: The Tory Record*. Toronto: James Lorimer.

Spicer, Keith. 1966. *A Samaritan State? External Aid in Canada's Foreign Policy*. Toronto: University of Toronto Press.

Stairs, Denis. 2005. "Confusing the Innocent with Numbers and Categories: The International Policy Statement and the Concentration of Development Assistance." Calgary, AB: Canadian Defence and Foreign Affairs Institute.

Swift, Jamie, and Brian Tomlinson. 1991. *Conflicts of Interest: Canada and the Third World*. Toronto: Between the Lines Press.

Swift, Richard, and Robert Clarke, eds. 1982. *Ties That Bind: Canada and the Third World*. Toronto: Between the Lines Press.

Swiss, Liam, with Simon Maxwell. 2010. *A New National Project for Canadian Development Cooperation*. Toronto: Walter and Duncan Gordon Foundation.

Thérien, Jean-Philippe. 1989. "Le Canada et le régime international de l'aide." *Études internationales* 20, no. 2: 311–40.

Treasury Board of Canada Secretariat. 2009. *Organizational Report: Canadian International Development Agency*. http://www.tbs-sct.gc.ca/ pses-saff/2008/results-resultats/res-eng.aspx?o1=22&cd=#i4. Accessed 29 June 2011.

Weston, Ann, and Daniel Pierre-Antoine. 2003. "Poverty and Policy Coherence: A Case Study of Canada's Relations with Developing Countries." Ottawa: North-South Institute.

Woods, Ngaire. 1995. "The Shifting Politics of Foreign Aid." *International Affairs* 81, no. 2 (March): 393–409.

1

Canada among Donors:
How Does Canadian Aid Compare?

HUNTER McGILL

Analysis and criticism of Canada's performance as an aid donor is, for the most part, based on assessments of how the country rates against targets it has set for itself or in relation to international undertakings, commitments, and goals. This chapter takes a different approach. It uses two credible international assessment processes, one mainly qualitative and the other quantitative, to provide perspectives on how Canada is performing relative to other donors, with respect to both aid and non-aid policies and programs.

Using evidence drawn primarily from those sources, I argue that while operating under conditions similar to those of the United Kingdom and Ireland, Canada has underperformed in terms of the quality of its aid policies and programming. The three countries' records are compared in four areas recognized globally as key to successful development cooperation: aid strategy; aid volume and distribution; policy coherence for development; and gender equality. Owing in part to the government's general lack of interest and engagement in foreign policy from a strategic perspective, the effectiveness of Canadian aid has been eroded. Instead, the government has favoured an episodic, transactional approach tied to high-profile international events such as G8 and G20 summits. As a result, Canada's visibility and influence in foreign policy and aid spheres have ebbed considerably.

METHODS FOR INTERNATIONAL COMPARISONS

The performance of aid donors is difficult to compare, since there is little in the way of international agreement on an assessment framework within which to judge how well individual donor countries are doing, especially with respect to their bilateral aid policies and programs. Two benchmarking exercises, however, offer some basis for assessing country performance: the Peer Review process of the Organisation for Economic Co-operation and Development's Development Assistance Committee (OECD/DAC), and the Commitment to Development Index annual rankings of the Center for Global Development (CGD).[1] Both processes have been undertaken for some time – the DAC Peer Reviews for almost fifty years and the CGD Index since 2002 – and thus provide useful material on trends in donor-country performance.

The DAC Peer Reviews are based on the systematic assessment of the performance of a state by other donor states, with the objective of helping the reviewed state improve its policy making, adopt best practices, and comply with established standards and principles (OECD 2003, 9). Countries are reviewed every four or five years and consenting to peer review is a condition of membership in the DAC.[2] The framework for the Peer Reviews – the agreed-on set of principles, standards, and criteria against which country performance is to be viewed – is derived from the DAC's collection of recommendations for effective aid, as well as from the principles and best practice for bilateral aid in areas such as governance, gender equality, environmental sustainability, and poverty reduction, in addition to the 2001 agreement on the untying of aid to the poorest countries and the commitments embedded in the 2005 Paris Declaration on Aid Effectiveness. These parameters are all of a qualitative character and are reached by consensus within the DAC. The sole quantitative measure of performance, which is really a gauge of level of effort, is the United Nations target for donors of 0.7 per cent of gross national product (GNP) (now gross national income – GNI), first proposed by the 1969 Commission on International Development (the Pearson Commission) and subsequently adopted by the UN General Assembly. Only five countries have met or exceeded this target (Denmark, Luxembourg, Netherlands, Norway, and Sweden).

As a complement to the DAC Peer Reviews, and to illustrate the good practice which the reviews can highlight, it is helpful to look at the synthesis study published in 2008 as "Effective Aid Management: Twelve Lessons from DAC Peer Reviews" (OECD 2008). This study draws on the Peer Reviews' insights into the management of bilateral aid programs across a wide spectrum of

government systems as represented by the member countries of
the DAC.[3]

Another valuable tool is the integrated approach used by the
Washington, DC-based CGD. The CGD's Commitment to Development
Index was developed as part of an effort to rate how the public policies of twenty-two wealthy nations, all currently members of the
DAC, affect the prospects and progress of developing countries. The
spectrum of policies covered by the Index includes aid, trade, investment, environment and climate change, migration, security, and
technology. Since 2002, the Index has been published annually as
part of the CGD's mission to demonstrate that "helping takes more
than aid" (CGD 2009, 19). This view reflects the reality that rich and
poor countries are linked by more than just the transfers of aid monies and that policies in non-aid areas can affect, positively and negatively, the growth and stability possibilities for developing countries
to a significantly greater extent than aid. The CGD publishes the
Index as part of its work in raising public awareness of the work
required to facilitate the development of poor countries.

In addition to the Index, the CGD published in October 2010 a
new analytical study, the "Quality of Official Development Assistance
Assessment" or QUODA, which attempts to rank countries in terms
of aid agency effectiveness, in other words, to judge the quality of
the aid a particular country provides. The four main dimensions of
the assessment are: maximizing efficiency (aid linked to poverty-
reducing growth); fostering institutions; reducing the burden on
recipients; and transparency and learning (Birdsall and Kharas 2010,
9). The relevance and validity of the methodology and conclusions
are debatable; for instance, the report represents a single snapshot in
time, as opposed to the series of reports from the DAC Peer Reviews
and the decade of material supporting the CGD's Commitment to
Development assessments. This new comparison, however, offers a
useful and complementary perspective on strengths and weaknesses
that reinforces the work of the other two approaches to judging
donor performance.

Together, these tools provide a helpful and valuable view, though
admittedly incomplete, of how Canada performs as a donor relative
to its peers in the G8 and, more broadly, in the twenty-four-member
DAC group of "traditional" donor countries. While the DAC does not
rank its members, it is possible to extrapolate from Peer Review
findings and recommendations where the committee believes Canada

stands in relation to aid effectiveness. In the case of the Commitment to Development Index, the CGD has listed the countries assessed using a quantitative methodology from the start, which complements the mainly qualitative OECD approach in a number of ways. Both provide evidence-based input that helps the reader/observer appreciate how Canada is doing in terms of results, as opposed to the attention-seeking, input-oriented nature of official statements and reports generated by the Canadian government and the Canadian International Development Agency (CIDA).

USEFUL POINTS OF COMPARISON

The approaches to rating aid donor countries' efforts described above provide valuable material for comparing Canada's development-cooperation program with those of other established donors.[4] This chapter examines several themes, namely aid strategy, aid volume and distribution/allocation, policy coherence for development, and gender to determine how Canada is doing in the realm of official development assistance (ODA) relative to two well-performing members of the DAC, the United Kingdom and Ireland. These themes reflect both the DAC and the CGD areas of emphasis, the global consensus around the 0.7 per cent ODA/GNI ratio, and the importance of gender as a crosscutting issue in aid policy and programming. The countries selected for comparison are seen generally as well-performing donors by both the DAC and the CGD, and they deliver most if not all of their aid through a single agency. Additionally, they bracket Canada in terms of the volume of aid provided, with the United Kingdom among the largest bilateral donors and Ireland in the ranks of the low-to-medium volume donors. Other points in common among the three countries are a similar legislative arrangement and having an elected member of the government with the title of minister for international development/international cooperation, that is, one person accountable for aid policy and expenditure. The balance of this chapter compares the three countries on the basis of their performance in the four areas identified above.

AID STRATEGY

In its publication "Effective Aid Management: Twelve Lessons from DAC Peer Reviews," the DAC lists as first the importance of having

a clear, top-level statement of the purpose of development cooperation, whether in legislation or in another form, that has wide ownership and can remain relevant for a sufficient period (OECD 2008, 4).
This is essential to show that development cooperation is a major
foreign policy interest, as well as to provide a framework within
which competing short-term pressures can be dealt with so as to not
put at risk the long-term interest in sustainable, effective international development. A clear, national strategy for aid is also necessary for mobilizing and maintaining a high level of public support.

Canada

For several years (2003–05), Canada attempted mightily to produce
a foreign policy statement which situated diplomacy, development,
defence, and trade in a medium- to long-term time frame. The resulting International Policy Statement, issued in 2005, involved extensive inter-ministerial discussions, consultations with civil society and
international partners, and consideration of the views of development practitioners. The document was close to being formally
endorsed by Parliament when the government changed in 2006.
Since that time there has been no overarching statement of Canadian
foreign and development policy. Instead, there have been ministerial
speeches and press announcements communicating elements of a
strategy without any sense of an overall picture and how individual
components of the government's approach relate to one another (see
den Heyer, this volume). For key strategic decisions, such as the concentration of Canadian bilateral aid in fewer – and often different –
countries, there were no public consultations or discussions with
Canadian or partner developing countries prior to the announcement of a new orientation in a press release from Minister of
International Cooperation Beverley Oda on 23 February 2009 (CIDA
2009). Interestingly, the decision was labelled a further step in
Canada's aid effectiveness agenda, though concentration in fewer
countries is not an explicit component of the Paris Declaration on
Aid Effectiveness which is the global reference point on this issue
(see Brown, chapter 3, this volume).

The last DAC Peer Review of Canada called for "a development
cooperation policy that puts poverty reduction at the heart of its
international development assistance. Whilst the government has
produced several sector policies, strategies and reports which cite

Canada's goal of reducing poverty, these documents generate a diffuse set of orientations. There is no clear single point of reference for
Canada's development cooperation" (OECD 2007, 11). Since this
2007 assessment by Canada's donor peers, there has not been any
action on the part of the Canadian government to correct this significant gap in the country's development-cooperation framework.

The CGD rankings in its 2009 Commitment to Development Index
are based on the assumption that the donor countries examined
have adopted a strategy that situates the seven policy categories in a
coherent overall framework. In this light, it is easy to understand
why Canada, while scoring well in certain areas considered beneficial to developing countries – investment and trade, for example –
receives a lower overall ranking owing to the weight of environmental
policies viewed as unfavourable to the interests of developing countries, especially regarding climate change, as well as the absence of a
global aid strategy.

An important element of Canada's development-cooperation
strategic framework was announced by International Cooperation
Minister Oda in a speech on 20 May 2009. Again billed as a new
and effective approach to Canadian aid, the speech merely reiterated
previous announcements on untying food aid and bilateral assistance and repeated the February 2009 message on geographic focus.
The minister then announced a thematic focus on food security, sustainable economic growth, and children and youth. Not stopping
there, however, she committed the use of ODA to promote democracy and ensure security and stability. Finally, she noted the importance of governance, the environment, and equality between men
and women, all of which were to be integrated into CIDA's activities
(Oda 2009). In fact, however, it is difficult to discern any focus at all
in this array of themes, topics, and issues. The minister did not mention a global Canadian aid strategy, the Millennium Development
Goals (MDGs), or the efforts of partner developing countries.

While the government outlined aspects of aid policy through
ministerial speeches and positions taken at international meetings,
Parliament adopted the Official Development Assistance Accountability Act, a private member's bill, in 2008. This act is direct and
straightforward in its language, requiring the government to apply
three tests for the use of ODA funds: that the expenditure contributes
to poverty reduction; that the activity funded takes account of the
perspectives of the poor; and that the aid provided is consistent with

international human-rights standards. An important aspect of the act is the requirement for a report to Parliament annually on implementation and conformity with the provisions of the legislation. The first of these reports was produced in early 2010, covering the period 2008–09. Labelled "Summary of the Government of Canada's Official Development Assistance," it lists the activities of twelve departments and agencies (Canada 2009). For each departmental/agency chapter of the report there is an identical attestation, in the form of a brief footnote, that the assistance reported meets the requirements of the ODA Accountability Act and is consistent with the DAC's definitions of ODA. Apart from these footnotes, there is little if any evidence to show how the expenditures meet the three tests listed above. There was no parliamentary debate on this report when it was presented. In late 2010 the government released its second annual report to Parliament, with much the same approach to reporting described above, this time covering 2009–10 (Canada 2010). The publication of the second report was not announced on CIDA's website and hard copies were not made available to the public.

In summary, the absence of an integrated overall policy framework for aid means that Canada has no statement of the purpose and objectives of its development-cooperation programs that brings together the various elements, situating aid within its foreign policy and linking aid to the recently enacted (2008) legislation. Poverty reduction has not been acknowledged by the government as the principal purpose of Canadian aid, and partners, whether developing countries or international organizations, do not have a comprehensive policy framework to which they can relate their programs.

United Kingdom

Unlike Canada, the United Kingdom has invested significantly in a strong policy framework to support the poverty-reduction focus of its aid program, as might be expected from a country considered one of the best performers in the DAC. Beginning with a White Paper in 1997 produced by the newly elected Labour government, followed by an International Development Act in 2002 and further White Papers in 2006 and 2009, the British authorities have regularly spelled out their policy framework for aid. The most recent White Paper (2009) set out four overarching priorities: achieving sustainable growth in the poorest countries; combating climate

change; supporting conflict prevention and fragile states; and rein-
forcing the international system's efficiency and effectiveness.
Gender equality is a priority crosscutting theme for all United
Kingdom ODA (see below).

A very important step in enabling the UK to play its current leading role in development cooperation was the creation of the Department for International Development (DFID) in 1997. DFID, led by
a senior cabinet minister, was given a wide-ranging mandate, with
responsibilities including international trade and development and
multilateral financial institutions (World Bank, African Development Bank, and other regional development banks), as well as
the full portfolio of bilateral and multilateral/UN aid operations.[5]
The clear policy and legislative framework mentioned above ensures
the centrality of poverty reduction as the purpose of British ODA and
reinforces DFID's reputation as a well-performing aid agency.

Under the UK government's budgeting and planning system,
departments are required to enter into three-year Public Service
Agreements (PSAS), which for DFID are based on the MDGS. DFID
submits an annual report on its performance against the PSA, a
report that is notable for its frankness in identifying where the UK
has not been able to make progress in supporting the achievement of
the MDGS and meeting its own targets. The report, published in a
reader-friendly format, covers the entire range of activities related
to development cooperation, including, for example, increasing the
share of the United Kingdom's ODA going to low-income countries,
improving the effectiveness of the multilateral system, and working
to improve trade opportunities for developing countries through the
reduction of trade barriers.

Ireland

Despite recent economic setbacks, Ireland has managed to build an
admirable and focused development-cooperation program. The key
document for Irish development cooperation is the 2006 White
Paper on Irish Aid, a comprehensive statement of the principles and
values that underpin Ireland's foreign aid. This White Paper, the
result of extensive analysis and consultation with the Irish public
and Ireland's development partners, situates development cooperation at the centre of Ireland's foreign policy and emphasizes that
the purpose of aid is reducing poverty and vulnerability. Two key

elements of the White Paper, support for increased aid effectiveness and partners' ownership of their own development, help shape the supporting strategies and policies that guide implementation. A strong feature of Ireland's aid program is the White Paper requirement that gender, governance, environment, and HIV/AIDS be mainstreamed across all Irish aid interventions. In 2009 the DAC noted, "The forward-looking orientations outlined in the White Paper are a good foundation for Ireland's overall objective of poverty reduction" (OECD 2009b, 11). Ireland has maintained the strategic orientations set out in its 2006 White Paper, while refining the guidelines, strategies, and policies that govern program delivery. The Irish government publishes a comprehensive annual report on progress made against the development objectives it has set for itself, as well as the contributions Ireland is making to the achievement of global goals (Irish Aid 2009a).

Summary

Compared with the United Kingdom and Ireland, Canada appears significantly under-equipped to deliver a comprehensive aid program, given the absence of an integrated, overarching strategy which would enable Canadians and international partners to understand why and how Canada is implementing an aid program and the goals and objectives the country has set itself. In the absence of such a strategy for its aid program, there is considerable ambiguity as to how important poverty reduction is for Canada. Unlike the United Kingdom, when the Canadian government has reported to Parliament on its ODA programs, there has been no critical self-assessment of its performance, even against the targets it has set for itself.

AID VOLUME AND DISTRIBUTION/ALLOCATION

While aid volumes are not the critical determinant of commitment to development cooperation, they are a useful indicator of level of effort and one of the very few quantitative tools to help compare national performance. The extent to which a donor's aid program is distributed across a wide range of partner countries and allocated to a large number of international and civil society organizations (CSOs) is also valuable in assessing impact and effectiveness. Finally, the extent of commitment to aid untying serves as clear measure of a donor's engagement with value-for-money principles and effectiveness.

Canada

For decades the Canadian government has subscribed to the UN ODA/GNP target of 0.7 per cent, without ever committing to a specific schedule to achieve this goal. Consequently, Canada's aid volume performance, as measured by the OECD, has fluctuated dramatically, at times surpassing 0.5 per cent and then dropping as low as 0.22 per cent. In its last Peer Review of Canada, in October 2007, the DAC "encouraged Canada to draw up a timetable for achieving the UN 0.7 per cent ODA/GNI target. It should continue to scale up its development aid to help achieve the MDGs in line with its ambition to become a major donor" (OECD 2007, 15). Rather than setting a date for achieving 0.7 per cent and a specific path to achieve that target, however, the government placed a cap on Canadian ODA in 2009 and has since made no mention of the UN target in any government announcements about aid, suggesting that it has abandoned this goal. In 2010 Canada's ODA/GNI performance was 0.33 per cent, ranking fourteenth out of twenty-four DAC members (OECD 2011b, Table 4).

Canada's approach to untying aid is another interesting indicator of how the country subscribes in principle to the international consensus but lags in taking actions to implement a commitment. In 2001 the DAC member countries agreed to the Recommendation on Aid Untying to the Least Developed Countries (LDCs). This recommendation was amended in 2006 and 2008 to include non-LDC highly indebted poor countries (HIPCs). Extensive studies (Bhagwati 1985; Clay et al. 2009; Jepma 1991) have demonstrated that untied aid is more consistent with the value-for-money principle, more cost effective, and more in line with the ownership and partnership elements of the Paris Declaration on Aid Effectiveness.

As a member of the DAC, Canada joined the consensus on the 2001 Recommendation. At that time around 50 per cent of Canadian bilateral aid was tied and 6 per cent partially untied, a category not recognized by the DAC but reported by Canada anyway (Clay et al. 2009, 22). By 2007, the untied element of bilateral aid had risen to 69 per cent, the bulk of the remaining tied aid being technical cooperation and emergency or disaster relief. The debate in Canada with respect to untying food aid, long a significant component of Canadian ODA, was then reaching its conclusion, propelled by pressures from World Trade Organization (WTO) agricultural negotiations and further OECD evidence on resource-transfer efficiency. In 2008 Canadian food aid was fully untied, with immediate effect. Also in 2008, Canada agreed to untie all its bilateral aid by 2013.

Since the 2001 consensus on aid untying, the majority of DAC members have fully untied their bilateral aid. To a certain degree, this has been a consequence of the decision of European Union (EU) member states to do so. Other countries – Australia and Norway as examples – have accepted the evidence that untied aid is much more efficient and effective and have also untied their programs. Several DAC members, however, notably the United States and Japan, for reasons specific to their political and legislative situations, have remained within the strict boundaries of the 2001 Recommendation to untie aid only to countries classified as LDCs and HIPCs. Given Canada's professed wish to increase the effectiveness of its ODA and the evidence that untying indeed supports that objective, it is difficult to understand why it is taking more than a decade (2001 to 2013) to untie fully Canadian bilateral aid. In its 2010 QUODA assessment of tied aid, the Center for Global Development analyzed the country-programmable aid share of donors' assistance, as well as the straightforward proportion of tied aid.[6] In the composite ranking on "maximizing efficiency" which includes both factors, Canada ranked twenty-third of the thirty-one countries and agencies covered (CGD 2010, 25).

The broad distribution of Canadian bilateral aid has attracted the attention of a number of external observers. In 2007 the DAC noted that "the Canadian programme has for a long time been dispersed over a large number of countries" (OECD 2001, 14). Similarly, the CGD in 2009 observed that "Canada's positive impact is reduced by its aid to less poor and relatively less democratic governments" (CGD, Commitment to Development Index, Canada's country report 2009, 1). By the DAC's reckoning, using 2006 data, 142 countries then received Canadian ODA, up from 136 countries in 1999–2000. By CIDA's own calculation, Canada had eighty-nine bilateral partners in 2000 and seventy-seven bilateral partners in 2006 (Canada 2007).[7] By way of comparison, DFID (UK) delivered 90 per cent of its programs to twenty-three countries in 2008 with a budget of US$11 billion (OECD 2010, 16). CIDA's budget that same year was US$4.75 billion.

In February 2009 the Canadian government announced that it would focus 80 per cent of its bilateral assistance on twenty countries. The criteria for the selection of these countries – chosen

without any consultation with Canadian stakeholders or international partners – were "their real needs, their capacity to benefit
from aid, and their alignment with Canadian foreign policy priorities" (CIDA 2011). The announcement made no reference to poverty
reduction, to the MDGs, or to existing long-term commitments to
support bilateral partner countries' ongoing programs. Key points
in the government's statement were efficiency, focus, and accountability. There were no references to partnership or to development
results. In the list of twenty countries of focus, there was a shift away
from sub-Saharan LDCs to Latin American middle-income countries
including Colombia, Peru, and Honduras, as well as Vietnam and
Ukraine, countries not known for high levels of structural poverty.[8]
Also on the list of twenty focus countries is Indonesia, a member of
the Organization of the Petroleum Exporting Countries (OPEC).

Moreover, despite Minister Oda's aforementioned February
2009 announcement of a geographic focus in bilateral aid, in April
2010 she announced "up to" $178 million of commitments for
nine African countries, three of which were not on Canada's list of
countries on which it was supposedly concentrating its aid (CIDA
2010a). It would appear that geographic concentration of Canada's
aid program, while a stated target, is not about to be implemented
any time soon.

United Kingdom

By comparison, it is worth noting the DAC's findings with respect to
the United Kingdom, in its Peer Review carried out in June 2010. On
the basis of 2008 data, showing total ODA of US$11.5 billion, the UK
had reached 0.43 per cent of GNI, against a commitment to arrive at
0.7 per cent by 2013. Complementing this performance was the government's introduction, in early 2010, of draft legislation to enshrine
the 0.7 per cent target in law. The new (2010) UK government,
despite the fiscal difficulties it inherited, has not backed away from
a strong commitment to ODA volume growth. For this and other
reasons, the DAC has labelled the UK "an international leader in
times of global crisis" (OECD 2010, 13).

With respect to aid untying, the UK was an early proponent of
fully untied aid to least developed countries, supporting the 2001
Recommendation, and it has since taken this approach further, in
keeping with EU decisions, by untying all its bilateral assistance.

Following several high-profile scandals in the 1990s involving tied-aid projects, most notably the Pergau Dam project in Malaysia, one key objective of the UK's aid legislation since 1998 has been to ensure that British ODA is used for poverty reduction and to benefit the poorest populations, without being influenced by the commercial interests of British enterprises.

Since 2006 DFID has concentrated its aid geographically, closing programs in thirty-six countries, with the result that 90 per cent of its bilateral assistance went to twenty-three partner countries in 2009. While this shift was underway, the UK maintained its focus on low-income countries and on assisting these partners to achieve the MDGs. On the other hand, non-DFID aid expenditures are still dispersed across a wide range of recipients. The British government took into account the particular needs of fragile states when it streamlined its list of bilateral recipients, in recognition of the high levels of poverty characteristic of this group of states. A notable feature of UK assistance is the significant level of country-programmable aid going directly to partners' development activities, a level above the DAC member-country average, another consequence of a fully untied bilateral-aid program (OECD 2009c).

Ireland

Ireland's budget situation is less positive, given the very serious fiscal difficulties the country experienced after 2008. After reaching 0.59 per cent of GNI in 2008, Irish ODA slipped to 0.54 per cent in 2009 as all government expenditure was cut. Still, Ireland has not renounced its intention to reach 0.7 per cent by 2015, in keeping with the EU Council decision of 2006. During the Irish fiscal crisis, foreign aid was not targeted for special treatment as part of the government's program to reduce the deficit. It is worth noting that 99 per cent of Irish development assistance is delivered by Irish Aid, a directorate of the Ministry of Foreign Affairs, thus substantially reducing the likelihood of contributing to overload of recipient-country systems and authorities through the involvement of multiple Irish government agencies (Birdsall and Kharas 2010, Table 7).

Ireland's development assistance has been completely untied since it signed on to the DAC Recommendation on Aid Untying to the Least Developed Countries in 2001, and it complies with the EU consensus on aid untying. Irish discussions regarding untying do not dispute that it contributes to enhancing aid effectiveness. An interesting feature of Ireland's shift to a fully untied cooperation program has been the cancellation of government support for volunteer-sending programs and other forms of donor-driven technical cooperation, although the Catholic Church's missionary activities in developing countries still receive financial assistance, though at lower levels than in the past.

The DAC has referred to Ireland's concentration of its assistance in a limited number of sub-Saharan African countries as one of its main strengths and has noted the intensive, long-term nature of these relationships (OECD 2009b, 37). Irish bilateral aid is also highly concentrated on LDCs and this has been a constant factor over a number of years, consistent with the 2006 White Paper on Irish Aid. While giving considerable attention to country-to-country assistance, Ireland has not overlooked multilateral aid. It has been a strong supporter of the delivery of global public goods (GPGs) through contributions to the Global Fund to Fight AIDS, Tuberculosis and Malaria and the Global Alliance for Vaccines and Immunization, and it has also demonstrated a strong preference for core, as opposed to project-specific, funding though UN agencies (United Nations Development Programme, United Nations Children's Fund, and United Nations High Commissioner for Refugees).[9]

Summary

Evidence from the last decade, as taken from DAC Peer Reviews and annual statistical reports, shows that Canada has consistently underperformed in terms of ODA volume, though it has met the modest goals it has set for itself with respect to increasing aid. Despite strong economic growth, successive Canadian governments have never committed to an explicit ODA growth path linked to the international 0.7 per cent ODA/GNI target. In addition, unlike comparable donors such as Ireland and the UK, Canada has been very slow to untie fully all its bilateral aid, despite conclusive evidence that untying aid increases its effectiveness. Finally, Canada has made important shifts in concentrating its bilateral aid, moving away from providing substantial levels of predictable assistance to low-income sub-Saharan African countries in favour of middle-income Latin American nations (see Brown, chapter 3, this volume; and Black, also this volume).

POLICY COHERENCE FOR DEVELOPMENT

The current global environment requires attention to more than donors' development-cooperation policies if partner countries are to grow sustainably and benefit from integration with the global economic and trade system. In 2002 OECD member countries agreed that, when formulating policies across the spectrum of public-policy issues and themes, they should consider the potential impact on developing countries (OECD 2002). Assessing countries' performance in this area is challenging, but the DAC in its Peer Reviews and the CGD in its Commitment to Development Index have done so, each from different angles, providing complementary perspectives. The CGD methodology, as mentioned above, considers countries' policies with regard to trade, investment, migration, environment, security, and technology, as well as aid quality and volume. The DAC considers specific policy measures regarding non-aid sectors and themes and also looks at the mechanisms and structures its members have adopted to support greater coherence. This latter aspect of the assessment of OECD countries' performance recognizes that policy coherence for development is built on sound analytical work and effective inter-ministerial coordination and consultation.

The generally accepted best performer when it comes to policy coherence for development is Sweden. In 2003 the Swedish parliament adopted a "Policy for Global Development" which incorporated guidelines for the full range of government policies – domestic as well as international – to support the achievement of an integrated policy which acknowledges that national policy has to address trans-boundary issues and that national decisions have international consequences and impact. An important aspect of the Swedish approach is the requirement for an annual report to parliament on progress in implementing global development policy. This annual reporting provides an occasion for parliamentarians to examine Sweden's and other industrialized countries' policy choices and chart their progress toward fulfilling their commitments to developing countries.

An additional dimension to policy coherence, which the CGD's QUODA has addressed, is how countries contribute to the promotion of global public goods. The data are limited and – as mentioned previously – the methodology is subject to debate, but the perspective offered is useful nonetheless. Considered through this lens, Canada, according to the CGD, emerges with a higher than average rating given Canadian contributions to such GPG vehicles as the advanced market commitments for pharmaceuticals,[10] the Consultative Group on International Agricultural Research, and the International Finance Facility for Immunizations. According to the initial report by the CGD, Ireland is among the lower-ranking donor-country supporters of GPGs, while UK data suggest a high ranking for the same reasons that Canada scores well (Birdsall and Kharas 2010, 81–2).

Canada

The CGD assessment of Canadian policy coherence, in its 2009 report, was mixed. On the positive side, it praised Canada for technological innovation and dissemination, as well as for lowering barriers to developing-country exports and policies that appear to promote investment in poor (developing) countries. On the other hand, Canada's lower-than-potential aid volume and the channelling of a significant portion of that aid to less-poor countries, along with its modest contributions to international peacekeeping efforts and most notably its poor environmental record as viewed from the standpoint of developing countries, reduced its overall ranking. In the latter case, Canada's disproportionately high use of non-renewable natural resources and high greenhouse gas emissions placed it twenty-first out of twenty-two countries in the Index. Canada lost a chance to improve its record when, in 2006, the newly elected Conservative government cancelled a commitment of $1.5 million to assist developing countries via the Clean Development Mechanism to gain access to improved technologies for emissions reduction (*Globe and Mail*, 9 October 2006).

The DAC, in its 2007 Peer Review, ascribed Canada's poorer-than-expected performance partly to a lack of policy continuity and consistency and partly to the government's emphasis on how development cooperation could benefit Canadian foreign policy rather than the reverse. As well, the committee noted that greater attention was given to making policy internally more coherent than to supporting aid effectiveness. The DAC observed, "Canada does not have a clear statement promoting policy coherence for development, which hinders CIDA's leadership on development issues in government discussions and negotiations" (OECD 2007, 13). Whereas in Sweden and in the UK the development-cooperation agencies have the capacity to review the policy proposals of other government departments to determine the impact of these proposals on development and developing countries, this is not the case at CIDA. The DAC also cited migration and the issue of brain drain/brain gain as an example of an issue that could benefit from better analysis and clearer policy statements. The CGD placed Canada more or less in the middle of the pack with respect to migration, with points gained for the large numbers of migrants and students from developing countries, and points lost for the small number of low-skilled migrants admitted and the much higher post-secondary tuition charged to students from developing countries.

In fact, no Canadian government has articulated a clear national commitment to pursue policy coherence for development and there is no government machinery to support inter-ministerial consultations and dialogue to identify and help resolve policy incoherence. The absence of an overarching strategy for development cooperation is a further gap in Canada's framework to support policy coherence.

United Kingdom

Clare Short, Britain's first minister for the Department for International Development, has said, "Development is more than aid. If we really mean to establish a more equitable and sustainable world order, then all areas of policy must be re-examined. It is a mistake to confine thinking on development to how aid budgets are managed" (Short 2009). In 2010 the DAC stated, "By clearly specifying DFID's objectives, the International Development Act of 2002 has helped to ensure that the potentially competing objectives of other foreign policy, trade, climate change and national security priorities do not overwhelm development objectives" (OECD 2010, 15). Both statements illustrate a certain level of recognition that non-aid policies can have a positive or negative effect on development.

The UK's International Development Act of 2002 unambiguously designated DFID as the lead government agency/ministry with the legal mandate to implement British development-cooperation programs. This has allowed DFID to influence cross-government work on all aspects of development policy and has resulted in the department being given the lead with respect to all issues associated with trade with developing countries and the formulation of the UK position for the United Nations Conference on Trade and Development (UNCTAD) and the Doha Round of trade negotiations.

In the 2009 Commitment to Development Index, the CGD assessed the United Kingdom as twelfth in this area, out of twenty-two countries reviewed (Canada was eleventh). The UK's strengths were in the areas of investment, environment, and aid, while it was ranked low on technology (access and transfer), security, and migration. An interesting aspect of the ranking was the UK's negative weighting as a result of arms sales to undemocratic governments and restrictive policies regarding immigrants from developing countries, which help explain why this very well-regarded donor country was surprisingly not ranked higher.

Ireland

Ireland's 2006 White Paper acknowledges the links between policies on development, trade, agriculture, investment, and migration. In 2009 the DAC found that "there is broad consensus among officials, parliamentarians, academia and civil society that the fight against poverty is not merely a matter of providing ODA" (OECD 2009b, 31). Ireland has maintained its 2006 policy framework consistently over time and complemented its statement of principles with successor initiatives such as the Hunger Task Force in 2008, calling for a coherent, multifaceted approach on food and hunger issues, including special attention to least developed countries and gender inequality (Irish Aid 2010).

Ireland placed sixth in the CGD's Commitment to Development Index of 2009, due to its "high quality" aid program, generally open migration policies, and middle-of-the-road environmental position. On the investment and trade side, however, Ireland was seen as lacking policies to facilitate outflows of portfolio investment in developing countries and maintaining high tariffs on agricultural exports and high agricultural subsidies. Following the publication of the White Paper, in 2007 the Irish government set up the Inter-Departmental Committee on Development with a mandate to consult and advise on issues requiring policy coherence. According to the DAC, while the committee serves a useful function as a consultative forum and has facilitated Ireland's policy development with respect to issues such as the Doha Development Agenda on trade and international discussions on climate change, it could play a stronger role in addressing policy inconsistencies and conflicts (OECD 2009b, 32).

Summary

Performance comparisons on the issue of policy coherence for development are difficult to make since the concept can be interpreted in various ways. Nonetheless, with regard to key indicators of engagement with policy coherence, Canada is performing poorly, notably with regard to aid volume, global environmental issues, and contributions to international peacekeeping. These three issues have particular weight when it comes to poverty reduction in the least developed countries and fragile states. As well, there is no internal government system in place to identify and resolve cases of policy incoherence, unlike in the United Kingdom and Ireland. The example of the UK is useful because it demonstrates how political engagement can drive a significant reorientation of departmental and agency mandates to facilitate engagement with policy coherence. This has resulted in DFID being considered a model for donor countries, even if some of the UK's non-aid policies are less worthy of emulation.

GENDER EQUALITY

An important element of the consensus that resulted from the 2008 Accra High Level Forum on Aid Effectiveness was the declaration that "gender equality, respect for human rights and environmental sustainability are cornerstones for achieving enduring impacts on the lives and potential of poor women, men, and children. It is vital that all our policies address these issues in a more systematic and coherent way" (Accra Agenda for Action, para. 3). According to the DAC Network on Gender, donor actions required to support the achievement of gender equality and women's empowerment include: ensuring that the aid agency has the required institutional practices to address gender inequalities through development cooperation, including leadership and high-level support for the issue (in the agency's strategic framework, for example); clear policies and strategies on gender equality and resources to implement the strategies;

and disseminating information about gender equality and women's empowerment so as to influence policies and budgets across the board. These actions have been identified through synthesis of Peer Review findings and DAC member evaluations of what constitutes good practice in supporting gender equality (OECD 2009d).

Canada

For over three decades, Canada, through CIDA and civil society organizations, has been working for the full and equal involvement of all people, regardless of gender, in the sustainable development of communities and societies. During the 1980s, CIDA's policies on gender equality were at the leading edge of international practice, and its 1999 policy framework linked these policies directly to the agency's poverty-reduction strategy.[11] The 1999 Policy on Gender Equality was highly innovative when issued given its explicit linking of poverty and gender equality. The policy stated, "For poverty reduction to be achieved, the constraints that women and girls face must be eliminated" (cited in Informal Civil Society Working Group on Women's Rights 2009, 2). In the view of many, the policy remains a very relevant and important tool directly linked to poverty reduction and social and economic justice (Informal Civil Society Working Group on Women's Rights 2009).

Since 2004–05, however, Canada has made little effort to be a gender-equality trendsetter or to keep up with efforts by other donors (see Swiss, this volume). The absence of policy progress and application of lessons learned has led to public embarrassments, such as when the government announced, as its "signature" aid project during G8 and G20 summits it chaired in 2010, the $1.1-billion Muskoka Initiative to support maternal and child health, which initially did not include family planning or ensuring access to safe abortions. Even after considerable public commentary in the media on the need to enhance the initiative to ensure its effectiveness, the true content and impact of the program remained undisclosed. It was also never clear where funding for the initiative would come from and whether the program needs would be met with additional financing to supplement existing budgets.

Indeed, since 2006, it has become much more difficult to assess CIDA's performance with respect to gender equality. This is due to a shift away from programs supporting women's empowerment and women's rights toward activities focused on service delivery to women. At the same time, in keeping with the Canadian government's approach to aid effectiveness (emphasis on accountancy and tracking expenditures, rather than impact and outcomes – see Brown, chapter 3, this volume), there is much more talk of results in quantitative terms. For crosscutting policies such as gender equality, where progress and outcomes are difficult to measure, a purely quantitative approach would seem to be inconsistent with the lessons learned by DAC member countries over the last few decades. This is particularly true for the four lead dimensions of equality: access, decision making, women's rights, and capacity building, all of which involve long-term commitment and sustained engagement of resources and donor attention.

In February 2009 CIDA published an assessment of its gender-equality policy, entitled "Evaluation of CIDA's Implementation of Its Policy on Gender Equality." The evaluation was a multifaceted exercise, involving surveys with staff, donor benchmarking, field visits, and a thorough review of program, policy, and other documentation. In all, the evaluation tracked 10 per cent (or $1.64 billion) of Canada's ODA expenditures between 1998–99 and 2005–06 in terms of its gender-equality specific programming and gender-equality integrated programming.

The evaluation provided valuable insight into the growing disconnect between CIDA's programming and the international policy consensus on gender equality and the role and importance of women as drivers of social change and key actors in achieving the reduction of poverty as set out in the Millennium Development Goals. It also provided evidence of a gap between Canadian development-cooperation programming and the requirements of Canada's ODA Accountability Act, with its emphasis on consistency with international human-rights standards (see Blackwood and Stewart, this volume). It is hardly surprising, then, that the Canadian government's Reports to Parliament on Official Development Assistance, in response to the ODA Accountability Act, do not mention gender equality or relations/ equality between men and women.

In mid-2010 CIDA issued a Gender Equality Action Plan (2010–13). While the stated aim of the plan is to "better equip ... CIDA to plan, implement, and report on gender equality ... results in its programming and gender equity dialogue with its partners" (CIDA 2010b, 1), it does not set targets or specific outcomes for what are process objectives. Simultaneously with the release of the Action Plan, CIDA reissued its Policy on Gender Equality, in effect the 1999 statement without the references to now-outdated sectoral and thematic priorities.

The Center for Global Development does not address gender equality explicitly in the Commitment to Development Index. As a result, the rest of this section does not mention its assessments.

United Kingdom

The DAC has characterized DFID's performance on gender equality as having "strong leadership and an innovative approach" (OECD 2010, 31). The UK's work in this area is guided by the 2007 DFID Gender Equality Action Plan, driven by a director general who champions gender for the department, and involves a program to mainstream gender equality across policies, programming, internal systems, and resources. DFID's strategic-objectives reporting now incorporates a gender-equality indicator. The result is that gender equality has a higher profile, though, to maintain momentum and extend its impact, the DAC felt that attention should be given to the system of incentives for strong management leadership and a specific reporting mechanism. With leadership comes responsibility, and the DAC evidently envisages the UK extending its work on gender equality into such areas as trade and humanitarian aid. For example, the 2009 White Paper on development cooperation set out several specific gender-equality objectives in the multilateral context, one of which, the creation of a single United Nations women's agency, has already been realized with significant support from the UK.

Ireland

Gender equality is an important crosscutting theme for Irish Aid and a separately funded program, as specified in the 2006 White Paper on Irish Aid. The 2004 Irish Aid Gender Equality Policy situates gender as a human-rights issue. It emphasizes initiatives to mainstream gender equality across Ireland's aid program, as well as prevent and respond to gender-based violence, particularly in emergency and conflict situations. There is a dedicated gender-equality budget to support testing new approaches, strategies, and partnerships. While respecting the authority of embassies in partner countries to develop their own strategies for Irish development cooperation, in keeping with the decentralization principles for the design and delivery of programs, Irish Aid headquarters expects all country strategy papers (CSPs) to address mainstreaming of gender, and guidelines for CSPs are clear in this regard (Irish Aid 2009b). Mid-term monitoring and evaluation of the implementation of the CSPs must address gender as well.

Ireland does not limit its efforts to advance gender equality to the orientation of its bilateral programs but works with partners multilaterally as well. The 2009 DAC Peer Review noted, "Ireland's intellectual leadership at the high level meeting on cross-sectoral issues and aid effectiveness, held in Dublin in 2007, led to substantial gender equality outcomes which were fed into the High Level Forum on Aid Effectiveness held in Accra" (OECD 2009b, 40). The outcomes of the Accra Forum were reflected also in Irish Aid's Operational Plan, 2008–12, illustrating how Ireland continues to hone its approach to gender equality in light of lessons learned through its own and others' experience.

Summary

Canada, once a leader among aid donors with regard to gender equality in both policy and programming, has slipped since 2001. In contrast to the steps taken by the United Kingdom and Ireland to ensure that their gender-policy frameworks are current and reflect good practice and evaluation-based evidence and experience, Canada has not updated the substantive content of CIDA's 1999 Policy on Gender Equality. Here, as in other contexts, the absence of a Canadian development-cooperation strategy means there is no overall framework within which to situate a horizontal issue such as gender equality and thereby show how various components of Canada's aid program are gender-sensitive.

CONCLUSION

Despite CIDA Minister Oda's claims in 2009 that "Canada is going to lead the world in ending ... ineffective aid" and that "Canada lives up to its commitments" (Oda 2009), external analysts take a different view. The absence of an overarching development-cooperation strategy leaves Canadians, partner developing countries, and international partners at a loss to know what Canada's vision is for development cooperation. There is no way to show how Canada is designing and delivering its aid programs to support partner developing countries in achieving the MDGs and, similarly, no global framework within which bilateral strategies for the countries of focus can be situated. The Harper government has repeatedly claimed that its primary concern is what it calls "aid effectiveness" (CIDA 2008), but, to many observers, it looks rather like accountancy and a preoccupation with inputs rather than development results and outcomes (Smillie 2010; also see Brown, chapter 3, this volume).

As noted, other donor countries such as the United Kingdom and Ireland have revamped and reformed their aid programs to incorporate good practice as identified by the DAC and as called for by other international observers, such as the CGD. The four issues/themes selected for this comparison serve as useful proxies for assessing the degree of commitment by governments to improving the impact and effectiveness of development-cooperation programs. In all four cases, Canada is nowhere near delivering a peak performance to alleviate poverty, defend human rights, or support sustainable development in recipient countries.

While most other member countries of the DAC have committed to increase their ODA flows – in the case of the core member countries of the European Union, to 0.7 per cent of GNI by 2015 – Canada has not pledged to increase development aid since the 2002 United Nations Conference on Financing for Development in Monterrey, Mexico. This despite having, by the Canadian government's own attestation, the strongest economy in the G8, least affected by the 2008–09 global economic downturn. Meanwhile, Canada seeks credence as a major player in international forums such as the G20, but it lacks the will to undertake necessary and expected commitments in terms of financial-resource transfers to developing countries, which undermines its efforts.

In the absence of an overarching development-cooperation strategy, it comes as no surprise that Canada's performance is mixed with respect to constructing an international policy framework that incorporates policy coherence for development. Other than opening Canadian markets to the exports of least developed countries, except for dairy products, Canada's approach is unclear with respect to policy issues of great importance to all developing countries, such as climate change and migration. The government has not created any mechanism, backed by sufficient analytical capacity, to identify and address questions of policy incoherence so that the costs of trade-offs and of minimizing the negative impact of national policy decisions can be weighed. If Canada wants to have a mutually beneficial dialogue with the emerging economic superpowers and help shape global discussions on development, it will need to engage on the full spectrum of policy issues this requires.

At one time, Canada was a leader and innovator in gender equality, but lack of leadership or interest has resulted in an erosion of its position in this area and a decrease in the proportion of ODA resources dedicated to the cause (CCIC 2009; also see Swiss, this volume). Mainstreaming gender equality across CIDA's range of programs remains difficult and presents challenges that are related to the absence of an integrated Canadian development-cooperation strategy which otherwise would provide links between sectoral and thematic goals and gender. Such a strategy could provide a platform for emphasizing the importance of gender equality in achieving sustainable poverty reduction and improved equity. This would also enable improved monitoring and reporting, as required by the ODA Accountability Act.

In summary, Canada lags behind two well-performing DAC member countries, the United Kingdom and Ireland, when it comes to development-cooperation performance, and appears to be slipping in several important areas, such as aid volume and gender equality. Moreover, Canada shows little interest in pursuing development issues that are crucial to developing countries' long-term prospects, including through policy coherence for development. There is no shortage of evidence on how these issues can be addressed, as is illustrated by DAC Peer Reviews' documentation of other donors' performance and identification of good practices. As well, through the CGD's Commitment to Development Index, useful perspectives demonstrate how non-aid policies can be shaped to be more supportive of the development prospects of partner countries. What Canada requires is the political will to invest in the necessary strategic and programming instruments that will guide the actions of CIDA and other national agencies responsible for aid programs, as well as enable Canada to intervene in international policy discussions. Together, this would constitute a properly funded and oriented development-cooperation effort, in keeping with Canadians' expectations and Canada's international undertakings.

NOTES

1 The OECD is a forum where the governments of thirty-four countries work together to "promote policies that will improve the economic and social well-being of people around the world" (OECD 2011a, n.p.). One of the OECD's specialized committees is the Development Assistance Committee, "whose members have agreed to secure an expansion of aggregate volume of resources made available to developing countries and to improve their effectiveness" (OECD 2007, 3).

  The CGD describes itself as a "nimble, independent, nonpartisan, and nonprofit think tank" that "works to reduce global poverty and inequality through rigorous research and active engagement with the policy community." Its Commitment to Development Index "quantifies the full range of rich country policies that have an impact on poor people in developing countries" (CGD 2011, n.p.).

2 In December 2010 the members of the DAC were: Australia, Austria, Belgium, Canada, Denmark, Finland, France, Germany, Greece, Ireland, Italy, Japan, Korea, Luxembourg, the Netherlands, New Zealand, Norway, Portugal, Spain, Sweden, Switzerland, the United Kingdom, the United States, and the Commission of the European Communities.

3 The lessons identified in the synthesis as contributing to or supporting effective aid management include: (1) appropriate legal and political foundation; (2) management of competing national interests; (3) policy coherence for development; (4) investment in delivering, measuring, and transmitting results of aid-financed activity; (5) a leadership structure that works; (6) resolving institutional dispersion; (7) managing contributions to multilateral institutions; and (8) decentralized management.

4 It is necessary to distinguish between the traditional donors of the DAC and newer donors such as China, Brazil, and India and private foundations and vertical funds, that is, international funds focused on specific diseases or medical themes, such as the Global Alliance for Vaccines and Immunization or the Global Fund to Fight AIDS, Tuberculosis and Malaria. None of these latter donors has been assessed on the same basis as the traditional bilateral donors.

5 In the case of Canada, the Department of Finance manages contributions to the World Bank (and contributions to the International Monetary Fund that qualify as ODA).

6 Country-programmable aid is the amount of aid that can be programmed by the donor at the partner-country level, that is, excluding administration costs, debt forgiveness, food aid, etc. See OECD 2009a.

7 The variance between the distribution of Canada's aid and CIDA's reporting on its budget is largely due to the growing share of Canadian ODA managed by the Department of Foreign Affairs (Canada 2009).
8 The twenty priority countries/areas are: Afghanistan, Bangladesh, Bolivia, the Caribbean region, Colombia, Ethiopia, Ghana, Haiti, Honduras, Indonesia, Mali, Mozambique, Pakistan, Peru, Senegal, Sudan, Tanzania, Ukraine, Vietnam, and West Bank/Gaza (CIDA 2011).
9 Global public goods are goods whose characteristics of "publicness" (non-rivalry in consumption and non-excludability of benefits) extend to more than one set of countries or more than one geographic region. Examples of GPGs are environmental sustainability, peace and security, and financial stability (Kaul et al. 1999, 4).
10 An advance market commitment is a binding commitment, offered by a government or an international financial institution, guaranteeing a viable market if a successful vaccine or other medical treatment is developed.
11 The framework's programming objectives are: to advance women's equal participation with men as decision makers; to support women and girls in the realization of their full human rights; and to reduce gender inequalities in access to and control over the resources and benefits of development.

REFERENCES

Bhagwati, Jagdish N. 1985. "The Tying of Aid." In *Dependence and Interdependence: Essays in Development Economics, Vol. 2*. Oxford: Blackwell. 204–51.
Birdsall, Nancy, and Homi Kharas. 2010. "Quality of Official Development Assistance Assessment 2010." Washington, DC: Center for Global Development.
Canada. 2007. *Memorandum of Canada to the Development Assistance Committee*. Gatineau, QC: Canadian International Development Agency.
– 2009. *Report to Parliament on the Government of Canada's Official Development Assistance 2008–2009*. Gatineau, QC: Canadian International Development Agency.
– 2010. *Report to Parliament on the Government of Canada's Official Development Assistance, 2009–2010*. Gatineau, QC: Canadian International Development Agency.
Canadian Council for International Co-operation. 2009. "A Civil Society Response to the Evaluation of CIDA's Policy on Gender Equality," Annex 2. Ottawa: Canadian Council for International Co-operation.

Canadian International Development Agency. 2008. "Canada Is Committed to Building a New Aid Relationship: A Canadian Statement for the Third High-Level Forum on Aid Effectiveness." http://www.acdi-cida.gc.ca/acdi-cida/ACDI-CIDA.nsf/eng/NAT-95153928-R38. Accessed 30 June 2011.

– 2009. "Canada Moves on Another Element of Its Aid Effectiveness Agenda." 23 February 2009. http://www.acdi-cida.gc.ca/acdi-cida/ACDI-CIDA.nsf/eng/NAT-223132931-PPH. Accessed 30 June 2011.

– 2010a. "CIDA Announces New Initiatives for Africa." 29 April 2010. http://www.acdi-cida.gc.ca/acdi-cida/ACDI-CIDA.nsf/eng/FRA-429183116-UEM. Accessed 30 June 2011.

– 2010b. "Gender Equality 2010–2013." Gatineau, QC: Canadian International Development Agency.

– 2011. "Regions and Countries." 13 June. http://www.acdi-cida.gc.ca/acdi-cida/acdi-cida.nsf/eng/NIC-5482847-GN3. Accessed 30 June 2011.

Center for Global Development. 2009. "Commitment to Development Index." Washington, DC: Center for Global Development.

– 2011. "About CGD." http://www.cgdev.org/section/about. Accessed 3 December 2011.

Clay, Edward J., Matthew Geddes, and Luisa Natali. 2009. "Untying Aid: Is It Working? An Evaluation of the Implementation of the Paris Declaration and of the 2001 DAC Recommendation of Untying ODA to the LDCs." Copenhagen: Danish Institute for International Studies.

Informal Civil Society Working Group on Women's Rights. 2009. "Strengthening Canada's International Leadership in the Promotion of Gender Equality: A Civil Society Response to the Evaluation of CIDA's 1999 Policy on Gender Equality." September.

Irish Aid. 2009a. "Annual Report 2009." Limerick: Irish Aid.

– 2009b. "Guidelines for the Preparation of Country Strategy Papers." Limerick: Irish Aid.

– 2010. "Report on the Millennium Development Goals." Limerick: Irish Aid.

Jepma, Catrinus J. 1991. The Tying of Aid. Paris: Organisation for Economic Co-operation and Development.

Kaul, Inge, Isabelle Grunberg, and Marc A. Stern. 1999. Global Public Goods: International Cooperation in the 21st Century. New York: Oxford University Press.

Oda, Beverly J. 2009. "Speaking Notes for Beverley J. Oda, Minister of International Cooperation, at the Munk Centre for International Studies, University of Toronto." 20 May.

Organisation for Economic Co-operation and Development. 2002. "OECD
    Action for a Shared Development Agenda." Final Communiqué,
    Organisation for Economic Co-operation and Development Council at
    Ministerial Level. 16 May.
– 2003. "Peer Review: An OECD Tool for Cooperation and Change."
    Paris: Organisation for Economic Co-operation and Development.
– 2007. "DAC Peer Review of Canada." Paris: Organisation for Economic
    Co-operation and Development.
– 2008. "Effective Aid Management: Twelve Lessons from DAC Peer
    Reviews." Paris: Organisation for Economic Co-operation and
    Development, Development Assistance Committee.
– 2009a. "2009 DAC Report on Aid Predictability: Survey on Donors'
    Forward Spending Plans 2009–2011." Paris: Organisation for Economic
    Co-operation and Development.
– 2009b. "DAC Peer Review of Ireland." Paris: Organisation for Economic
    Co-operation and Development.
– 2009c. "Development Cooperation Report 2009." Paris: Organisation
    for Economic Co-operation and Development.
– 2009d. "Managing for Gender Equality Results in Donor Agencies."
    Paris: Organisation for Economic Co-operation and Development.
– 2010. "DAC Peer Review of the United Kingdom." Paris: Organisation
    for Economic Co-operation and Development.
– 2011a. "About the Organisation for Economic Co-operation and
    Development (OECD)." http://www.oecd.org/pages/0,3417,en_3673_
    4052_36734103_1_1_1_1_1,00.html. Accessed 25 November 2011.
– 2011b. "Development Cooperation Report 2011." Paris: Organisation
    for Economic Co-operation and Development.
Short, Clare. 2009. "Notes for an Address by Clare Short." Conference on
    the Future of Canadian Overseas Development Assistance, Gatineau,
    QC. September 29.
Smillie, Ian. 2010. "CIDA under Oda." *Globe and Mail*, 8 January.

2

Improving Canada's Performance as a Bilateral Donor: Assessing the Past and Building for the Future[1]

NILIMA GULRAJANI

Observers of Canada's aid program are discernibly uneasy. There is a palpable sense that the Canadian International Development Agency (CIDA) is increasingly ineffectual in its mission to "help people living in poverty" (CIDA 2011). Since 2006, a string of reports have suggested that CIDA is a poorly performing aid agency (Auditor General of Canada 2009; Canada 2007; Canadian International Council 2010; Carin and Smith 2010; Goldfarb and Tapp 2006). Limited concentration in its sectoral and geographic programs, high administrative costs, unmotivated staff, inadequate accountability, lack of results, poor policy coherence – all leave the impression that CIDA is a relatively inefficient and unimpressive bilateral donor. A primary purpose of this chapter is to investigate the empirical basis for this pessimism by examining Canada's performance against quantitative metrics associated with both aid effectiveness and donor effectiveness.[2] While there is reason to lament the fact that Canada's performance lags behind its ambition to be a leading player in the donor community, it is also important to recognize that Canada ranks above the Organisation for Economic Co-operation and Development/Development Assistance Committee (OECD/DAC) average on many of the common proxies for donor performance.

This chapter also explores the merit of the argument that donor-governance structures are conduits for improving Canada's performance as a donor. *Donor governance structures* are formal

institutional arrangements that unite actors who either manage aid
resources or are involved in development policy. The term is used
synonymously with the term "aid architecture," although the latter
perhaps connotes a more direct reference to international rather
than national aid structures (International Development Association
2007, 1). Donor governance structures, by contrast, underline the
domestic government structures that oversee a donor nation's development policy and its implementation. While the rationale of effectiveness has come to frame a host of aid policy initiatives (see Brown,
chapter 3, this volume), donor governance structures have recently
been identified as key to improving CIDA's performance (Canada
2007; Canadian International Council 2010; Carin and Smith 2010).

Three donor governance structures are typically discussed as
options for Canada: 1) a strengthened CIDA with unquestioned and
primary responsibility for development policy formulation and its
implementation across government; 2) the assimilation of CIDA's
development functions into, and subordination to, the Department
for Foreign Affairs and International Trade (DFAIT); and 3) an independent agency structured like a private corporation existing outside direct government departmental accountability but nonetheless
owned by government (what is known in Canada as a crown corporation). The last of these options has become a favoured governance
structure for solving the ills plaguing CIDA (Brown and Jackson
2009; Canadian International Council 2010; Carin and Smith 2010).
However, not one of the twenty-two donors belonging to the DAC
has exclusively adopted such an autonomous governance structure
(OECD 2008b; 2009a). While certain bilateral donors possess separate "executing" agencies, these remain directly accountable to a
government department and operate within the realm of the public
sector to ensure adequate policy coherence and deep political engagement. There is neither precedent for a crown corporation-like structure among bilateral donors to date nor any evidence to suggest that
autonomous governance is a driver of donor performance.[3] The
third option is therefore not a governance model that can be easily
assessed in terms of its effectiveness.

Consequently, this chapter will explore the value of the first two
governance options and their contributions to donor performance.
To do so, I will compare Canada's achievement on quantitative metrics of effectiveness against that of Norway and the United Kingdom.
These two countries are chosen as comparative cases to make sense

of Canadian governance dilemmas because Norway merged its development program with the Ministry of Foreign Affairs in 2004, while the UK created a development ministry independent of the Foreign and Commonwealth Office (FCO) in 1997. Many researchers laud the UK as a strong model for Canadian donor governance (Brown 2007; Goldfarb and Tapp 2006; Gulrajani 2009). The ability of its Department for International Development (DFID) to set and innovate development policies of substance, the commitments and quality of its political and bureaucratic leadership, and DFID's strong financial and political dedication to development issues are all cited as reasons to look to the United Kingdom for a model governance structure. By comparison, Norway is less understood as a model of donor performance, although its Scandinavian-style generosity and reputation for progressive internationalism are often cited positively. Canada is a hybrid of these two models; while it possesses a physically separate development agency like the UK's, this separation lies more in convention than in the letter of the law, since CIDA's status, like that of its Norwegian counterpart, is considerably subordinated to foreign affairs concerns.[4] While the 2010 election of a Conservative/Liberal Democrat coalition government in the UK suggests that there is risk of a similar subordination there, at the time of writing the UK's strong developmentalist credentials, including its commitment to the 0.7 per cent official development assistance/gross national income (ODA/GNI) target, remain intact.

The chapter begins by presenting key analytical dimensions of donor performance, including aid effectiveness and donor effectiveness. The next section examines Canada's standing relative to Norway and the UK on quantitative measures of aid and donor effectiveness, culminating in an assessment of overall donor performance. The comparative analysis of these three countries underlines the generally high level of donor performance of the UK and Norway, and provides some early evidence that governance structure alone cannot explain high donor performance. Based on a more detailed qualitative understanding of each donor agency, the final section offers some thoughts on what might be driving development success in Norway and the UK, and offers recommendations on how Canada might consider replicating their examples. Evidence suggests it would be hasty and short-sighted for Canada to conclude that a simple reform to governance structures will remedy the woes that currently afflict CIDA and Canadian development cooperation more generally.

Rather, a multiplicity of factors is likely to explain high donor performance. There is more value in first considering how support for a robust development policy can be fostered in order to maintain Canada's commitment to global humanitarianism, equality, and human rights. Both Norway and the UK demonstrate the importance of strong leadership, cross-party political support, and a coherent vision for progressive international development policy in achieving higher donor performance.

ASSESSING DONOR PERFORMANCE

Aid effectiveness is defined and framed by the 2005 Paris Declaration on Aid Effectiveness, which represents a certain ideal of how aid could be better managed (Hayman 2009, 581–2). The declaration defines aid effectiveness in terms of five core principles: aid recipients exercising leadership over development policies and strategies and coordination (ownership); donors basing their support on recipients' systems and priorities (alignment); reducing the transaction costs of donor interventions (harmonization); and introducing mechanisms for assessing measuring results and improving accountability (results and mutual accountability). Aid effectiveness emphasizes one input to development, namely foreign aid, and underlines certain qualities of this flow and of the immediate processes involved in its delivery. Nevertheless, the causal link between the improvements to aid and tangible progress in reducing poverty is both unspecified and contestable. For example, Lauchlan T. Munro (2005) claims that aid's supposed increased effectiveness when it is "focused" within geographic areas is actually based on "impressionistic and anecdotal" evidence. Aid effectiveness is presumed rather than proven to be a vehicle for *development effectiveness*, the latter defined in terms of the positive effects to be had on the lives of the poor (Stern et al. 2008).

The ongoing debate in Canada over which governance structures are most appropriate for coaxing higher donor performance suggests that the organization and management of donors themselves may be an important variable in improving aid outcomes. Nevertheless, the dominant aid effectiveness discourse remains silent on the relationship between donor organization and development results. The Paris Declaration ultimately has minimal implications for the ways donors manage themselves in processes of aid giving, other than encouraging joint missions and collaborative analytical work, program-based delivery mechanisms, and the elimination of parallel project units. In other words, one can distinguish between strategies for enhancing aid effectiveness in terms of the inputs of development effectiveness, namely aid, and those strategies that seek to improve *donor effectiveness*. The latter refers to the donor-related organizational processes and dynamics that have an impact on aid effectiveness and thus presumably on development effectiveness as well. For example, decentralization and de-concentration of staff to field offices is widely assumed to increase the likelihood that aid will be delivered in ways that are more sensitive to local conditions, and thus more likely to deliver development outcomes that improve the lives of the poor. Decentralization is an example of a donor organizational process that has indirect implications for aid effectiveness and positive externalities for development effectiveness. Current interest in donor governance systems as a vehicle for improving Canadian aid effectiveness illustrates this growing concern with donor effectiveness.

Assessments of donor performance must therefore focus on both the quality of aid inputs (aid effectiveness) and the organizational processes that indirectly contribute to aid effectiveness (donor effectiveness). International benchmarking of donor countries via the use of metrics typically combines indicators representing both aid and donor effectiveness, even if the distinction between the two components is rarely made (Easterly and Pfutze 2008; Knack et al. 2010; Roodman 2006; Williamson 2010). Moreover, there is little consideration of the relative importance of donor and aid effectiveness in their contribution to overall donor performance in improving development outcomes. Although most would agree that assessing individual donors' performance via their contribution to development effectiveness would be the ideal way to proceed, this is methodologically challenging, especially given that development is a complex public good produced by multiple actors. Development often lacks a shared definition and, even when common purpose exists, is frequently beyond explicit measurement. Estimating donor contributions to development effectiveness ultimately suffers from the same limitations as affect assessments of other areas of public-sector performance.[5] There is ultimately no robust way to causally attribute development effectiveness to individual donors except in small project-related activities where randomized controlled evaluations are used,[6] with the result that macro-level donor performance is conventionally measured by variables that combine aid effectiveness and donor effectiveness. Assessing donor performance in a holistic sense, especially when relying exclusively on quantitative indicators, clearly has its weaknesses. It would be preferable that quantitative analysis be accompanied by qualitative analysis of donor dynamics and aid processes, since the latter is better able to investigate the causal mechanisms that bring about higher levels of performance. Nevertheless, quantitative assessments of aid and donor effectiveness do provide some initial indicative evidence of Canada's comparative performance against Norway and the UK that can be further investigated through more qualitative means.[7]

ASSESSING CANADA'S PERFORMANCE IN NUMBERS

Assessing Canada's performance as a donor against measures of both aid effectiveness and donor effectiveness is one way to establish the severity of the challenges it now faces. Too often, laments about Canada's performance are not contextualized with international comparisons of the wider donor community (Canadian International Council 2010; Carin and Smith 2010; Government of Canada 2007). Explicitly comparing Canada's position against the UK's and Norway's can provide additional indications of what kind of governance structure – a strengthened independent development ministry or a ministry of foreign affairs that assimilates responsibilities for international development – is associated with higher levels of donor performance. The variables we examine under each dimension of effectiveness are not exhaustive of each category; rather, they represent the most commonly examined variables of donor performance in both the academic and policy literature to date.

Aid Effectiveness

FINANCIAL INPUTS
The UK is among the largest bilateral donors in the DAC in terms of disbursement of funds, while both Canada and Norway are mid-sized donors. The latter two are quite similar in terms of absolute resources devoted to development assistance, notwithstanding the fact that Norway's gross national income (GNI) is approximately one-third Canada's (Table 1).

Table 1
Donor Aid Inputs, ODA Net Disbursement, 2008

ODA (million USD)		Per cent of global ODA	ODA per cent of GNI	Donor rank*
Canada	4,795	3.52	0.35	10
Norway	3,963	2.91	0.88	12
UK	11,500	8.44	0.44	4
DAC AVERAGE**	5,924			

* Donor rank by per cent share of total ODA.
** Based on twenty-three bilateral donors.

Sources: Data taken from Williamson (2010, 29) and OECD, International Development Statistics online.

Figure 1 tracks ODA as a percentage of GNI from 1980 to 2008 for all three countries. Whereas Norway has exceeded the United Nations target of 0.7 per cent of GNI for several decades, both Canada and the UK have hovered between 0.2 per cent and 0.5 per cent over the same period, with the UK distancing itself from Canada in the last decade. During this time, Canada's aid ratio has roughly mirrored the DAC average.

CHANNELS FOR AID SPENDING

Donor countries possess dual channels for aid spending: bilateral and multilateral. Multilateral channels are thought to be superior, since they tend to be less biased toward national prerogatives and are a way to coordinate donor flows (Riddell 2007). Table 2 illustrates how Canada directs roughly the same amount as Norway through bilateral channels, though there are important reasons to suspect this figure. The category "bilateral" in the table includes monies given to multilateral agencies that are earmarked to initiatives specified by the donor. While Norwegian statistics define such spending in a third category called multi-bilateral finance (mainly because implementation is multinational though driven by bilateral imperatives and conditionalities), the UK and Canada include these flows in the bilateral category. Over the 2008–09 period, multi-bilateral finance represented 35 per cent of Norway's bilateral assistance and 20 per cent of the UK's (Department for International Development 2009c, 13; Norwegian Agency for Development Cooperation [NORAD],

Figure 1
ODA as a Percentage of Gross National Income (1980–2008)

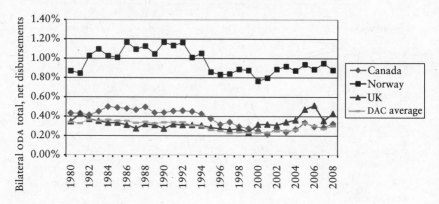

Source: OECD (2010).

in-house publication). However, if one were to count *multi-bilateral* finance as "multilateral," Norway would be providing 41.3 per cent of its funding in bilateral channels and 58.7 per cent in multilateral channels, with the UK closely following with 39.8 per cent bilateral and 60.2 per cent multilateral. This would mean that the UK and Norway allocate similar proportions of their budget to bilateral and "multi" channels. Unfortunately, it is not possible to calculate a similar statistic for Canada because figures breaking down Canada's multi-bilateral assistance are not publicly available.

Claudia Williamson (2010) ranks donors according to their overhead costs and suggests that Norway has a lower cost structure than both the UK and Canada. Nevertheless, she cautions against inferring too much from these rankings because overhead calculations are not standardized across agencies. In 2009 Norway reported 5 per cent of its total ODA as administrative cost, while the UK reported 4.1 per cent in 2008–09. Canada reported administrative costs only for CIDA, rather than the entire aid program, representing 7 per cent of all CIDA's International Assistance Envelope (IAE)-related expenditures in 2008–09.[8] Given intractable measurement problems, all comparative administrative-cost data need to be interpreted with care.

AID SELECTIVITY
While there is an academic debate about the merit of aid selectivity and the conditions necessary for making aid effective at the country level, both the Paris Declaration on Aid Effectiveness and the

Table 2
Channels for Aid Spending*

Country	per cent bilateral** ODA to total ODA	per cent multilateral ODA to total ODA
Canada	72.0	27.0
Norway	76.3	23.7
UK	59.8	40.2

*These figures do not include administrative costs.
**Earmarked trust funds to multilateral organizations, or multi-bilateral aid, are treated as bilateral aid for the purposes of this table.

Sources: Canadian data are for 2008–09 and are taken from CIDA (2010, 11). In the absence of ODA figures, we assume that the IAE figures for CIDA are a reasonably proxy for ODA. United Kingdom data are for 2008–09 and are taken from DFID (2009b, 13), whereas Norwegian data are for 2009 and are taken from NORAD (2010, in-house).

Table 3
Aid Selectivity, 2008

	Rank	Per cent of ODA to non-corrupt	Per cent of ODA to politically free	Per cent of ODA to low-income country
Canada	11	33.49	18.74	59.01
Norway	15	40.23	10.04	43.32
UK	4	42.36	21.59	47.92
DAC average**		39.13	18.30	38.43

*Based on twenty-three bilateral donors.

Sources: Data taken from Williamson (2010, 35).

subsequent Accra High Level Forum emphasize that aid should go to poor countries that are democratic and where corruption is low (Williamson 2010, 14). Williamson (2010) measures donors' portfolios in terms of aid going to countries whose levels of corruption are minimal, whose political systems are free and/or democratic, and whose populations have low incomes. As Table 3 shows, aid from Canada in 2008 was better targeted to low-income countries in comparison with other donors, including the UK and Norway. It is, of course, conceivable that Canada's recent shift in priority away from Africa and toward the Americas may jeopardize this relative concentration. In comparison to Norway and the UK, Canada has less of its ODA concentrated in non-corrupt countries.

TIED AID

Tied aid is aid given with the condition that it may only be spent procuring goods and services from the country that provides the aid or from a defined group of sources. In 2008 five bilateral donors had less than 1 per cent of their aid tied. Several donors, however, still maintain large shares of tied aid, notably southern European donors and the United States. Canada's share of tied aid was 9.23 per cent in 2008, down from 43 per cent in 2004 (Table 4). In 2008 the Canadian minister for international cooperation announced that all Canadian aid would be untied by 2013. Norway began untying its aid in the 1980s and by 2002 there were only a few residual areas of tying. The UK fully untied its aid in 2000 (Clay et al. 2009).

FRAGMENTATION

Donors are regularly advised to focus their bilateral aid on fewer countries, sectors, and projects in order to minimize duplication, reduce transaction costs, and specialize in areas of comparative advantage (OECD 2008b). Canada is almost obsessive in its search for such focus and the data below suggest that its approach may be bearing fruit. While Canada has almost consistently had less aid concentration than Norway and UK, recent figures suggest that some amount of concentration is emerging in its geographic allocations (Figure 2). Yet Canada still has a higher number of aid recipients (173) compared to the UK (150) and Norway (132) (OECD 2010).

A further proxy for aid fragmentation is the number of donor projects. While Canada disburses less than half of the UK's aid budget, it is largely comparable to the UK in terms of the number of aid projects it finances (Table 5). Canadian project aid is, however, currently less fragmented than both Norway's and the DAC average.

Williamson (2010) grades donors according to their overall specialization in certain countries, sectors, and projects. Interestingly, Canada, Norway, and the UK all achieve rankings at the lower end of the table. Each country achieves similar levels of sectoral fragmentation in their program, and their geographic and project allocation are all relatively fragmented.[9] She concludes that Canadian aid on the whole is more fragmented than UK aid and less fragmented than Norwegian aid, although all fare poorly on her metrics (Table 6). Aid from some smaller donors, notably Austria, Portugal, and Italy, is considerably less fragmented.

Table 4
Share of Tied Aid, 2008

Canada	9.23
Norway	0.01
UK	0.00
DAC average*	13.52

*Based on twenty-two bilateral donors.

Source: Data taken from Williamson (2010, 37).

Figure 2
Partner Country Fragmentation (1980–2008)

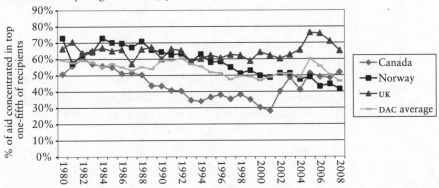

Source: OECD (2010).

Table 5
Project Fragmentation, 2008

	Number of projects	ODA per project (million USD, net disbursed)
Canada	2,049	2.34
Norway	4,208	0.94
UK	2,460	4.67
DAC AVERAGE*	3,591	1.65

* Based on twenty-three bilateral donors.

Sources: Data taken from Williamson (2010, 29) and OECD International Development Statistics online.

Table 6
Aid Fragmentation, 2008*

Country, sector, and project fragmentation (rank)	
Canada	14
Norway	16
UK	12

*Adjusted ranking among twenty-three bilateral donors.

Source: Data taken from Williamson (2010, 33).

In summary, Canadian aid is generally of inferior quality and quantity to that of either Norway or the UK. This is validated by a recent benchmarking exercise to assess twenty-eight bilateral donors' "aid quality" in terms of selectivity, alignment, harmonization, and specialization that ranked the UK fourth, Norway eighth, and Canada twenty-first (Knack et al. 2010). It also corroborates the recent Quality of ODA (QUODA) study which ranks donors systematically on four alternative dimensions of aid quality: maximizing efficiency, fostering institutions, reducing burden, and transparency and learning. In this study, Canada ranked below the UK and Norway on all but one dimension (Canada ranked higher than Norway in the efficiency category by one place) (Birdsall and Kharas 2010: 42). In the analysis presented here, the only area where Canada achieves higher scores than either Norway or the UK is in its aid selectivity to low-income countries. Canada does better than Norway on aid fragmentation but still performs worse than the UK. Norway distinguishes itself from UK in terms of its higher ODA/GNI ratio, higher aid fragmentation, and lower ranking in aid selectivity. Otherwise, both roughly channel equivalent amounts of their aid through "multi" channels and both have untied virtually all their aid. Overall, the differences between the UK and Norway in terms of aid effectiveness appear to be quite marginal.

Donor Effectiveness

DECENTRALIZATION AND DE-CONCENTRATION
The decentralization of staff and the de-concentration of authorities to field level are increasingly associated with a donor's ability to build local relationships, quickly respond to programming needs, and facilitate improved donor collaboration (see den Heyer, this

Table 7
Decentralization in Donor Employment, 2008–09

	Total no. of employees	Per cent at headquarters	Per cent in the field	ODA per employee (million USD)
Canada	2,838	62.3	37.7	1.69
Norway	1,176	49.7	50.3	3.37
UK	2,671	52.2	47.8	5.06
DAC average*	1,996	48.6	51.4	

*Based on nineteen bilateral donors.

Sources: Data on employment are taken from OECD (2009b, 7); ODA data are taken from OECD, International Development Statistics online.

volume). A common proxy for an aid donor's decentralization is the allocation of employees across headquarters and field offices. Table 7 suggests that CIDA is both a large organization (its ratio of ODA committed per employee is lower than both Norway's and the UK's) and a highly centralized one. High centralization is not always negative; for example, one can imagine that an efficient administrative system might require less staff in the field (OECD 2009b). Nevertheless, Canada has yet to be described in these terms.

Another measure of donor performance is the financial authority that is delegated to field offices. According to an OECD donor survey conducted in 2008–09, Canada's field offices do not have the authority to commit new ODA monies and their authority to disburse existing funds has a ceiling of US$500,000 (OECD 2009b). By contrast, Norway's field offices can commit and disburse unlimited amounts of ODA as long as there is some basis for this outlay within an approved strategic plan. The UK can also disburse an unlimited amount at the field level, but with an upper limit of US$15 million for new commitments (OECD 2009b, 5–6).

MINISTERIAL TURNOVER
Stable leadership structures are believed to be important organizational features that enhance the effectiveness of aid (OECD 2008b). The frequent turnover of Canada's political leadership has been often blamed for negatively affecting Canadian development cooperation, providing an unstable and uncertain context for planning

(Auditor General of Canada 2009; Brown and Jackson 2009; Lalonde 2009, 140). From mid-1997 to mid-2007, Canada had six different ministers for international cooperation.[10] This compares to four different ministers for international development in Norway and three in the UK over the same period.

EMPLOYEE SATISFACTION

Employee satisfaction is thought to contribute to donor performance because it reflects motivation to accomplish organizational goals. While Canada and UK have recently published public-service employment surveys by department, no comparable study for Norway was found. In the UK, an in-house employee-engagement score that assesses loyalty, retention, and commitment is calculated for each department and the civil service at large. DFID's employee-engagement index was one of the highest among all ministries, almost 20 per cent higher than the average civil-service score (Cabinet Office 2010). The 2008 Canadian Public Service Employee Survey (Treasury Board Secretariat 2008) suggests that CIDA staff are approximately 10 per cent below the public-service average (68 per cent) in terms of satisfaction with their department. While a meaningful direct comparison of this data is difficult, it provides some anecdotal evidence for differing levels of employee satisfaction across these donors.

PUBLIC SUPPORT FOR AID

Public awareness of, and support for, development cooperation is the best guarantee for ensuring continued political and legislative support for development assistance (OECD 2008b, 8). This support can be an important determinant of aid effectiveness since it provides aid agencies with the credibility to engage in challenging environments and can buffer aid budgets. A 2007 poll by the Canadian Defence and Foreign Affairs Institute indicated that 70 per cent of respondents surveyed felt Canada had a moral obligation to help poor countries (Canadian Defence and Foreign Affairs Institute 2007). While this support may appear substantial, aid often polls at the top of the list when in comes to areas targeted for cutbacks, leading many to believe that Canadian public support for aid is "a mile wide and an inch deep" (Smillie 1998, 23). This finding is similar to a recent survey on British public attitudes to development, which highlights that aid may enjoy considerable public support when viewed in isolation but is given low priority when presented against domestic priorities (Department for International Development 2009b). Further, while public support for foreign aid in the UK has been over 70 per cent since 1999 (OECD 2006, 25), a recent poll showed that a large share of respondents thought that people in poor countries were not as deserving of UK tax money as people in the UK (International Development Select Committee 2009, 43). The situation is similar in Norway, where public support for foreign aid reached an all-time high of 90 per cent in 2007, though there is a strong sentiment expressed that aid is often wasted (OECD 2008a, 24–5). These numbers reflect the general principle that the noble aims of aid are often far too intangible for the public, particularly when contrasted to the practical benefits of domestic expenditures. Although this may make aid nearly always politically expendable in times of fiscal austerity (White as quoted in Morrison 1998, 443), the decision of the current UK coalition government to exempt the aid budget from cuts to programmatic spending of 25 per cent over four years suggests otherwise. It should be noted, however, that questions are emerging in the UK about the strength of the exemption (BBC 2010).

CIVIL SOCIETY PARTNERS

An active strategy for engaging with civil society is one way to ensure that aid reaches those who both need assistance and can make best use of it, as well as enhancing overall awareness of development issues. A range of organizations with development interests populates civil society, including non-governmental organizations (NGOs), church groups, and unions. Civil society actors can either be domestically registered or registered in other jurisdictions, the latter category including indigenous and regionally and internationally based groups. In Canada, funding for civil society organizations (CSOs) went through two major channels at CIDA until recently: Canadian Partnership Branch and Geographic Programs.[11] The former provided financial support (including operational funding) to CSOs, while the latter funded civil society actors executing specific CIDA projects.[12]

Canada is certainly channelling the lion's share of its civil society funding to domestic-based organizations, much more than Norway and the UK (Table 8). The difference may be explained by the fact

Table 8
Funding to Civil Society as a Percentage of Total Civil Society Spending

	Domestic civil society	Non-domestic civil society*
Canada**	84.5	15.5
Norway	65.9	34.1
UK	72.8	27.2

* Non-domestic includes funding for local (i.e., indigenous), regional,
  and international NGOs.
** Includes all CIDA spending on civil society via all existing channels.

Sources: Canadian data are for 2008–09 and are taken from CIDA (2010, 20);
Norwegian data are for 2009 and are taken from NORAD (in-house statistics);
United Kingdom data are taken from DFID (2009c, 13, 28).

Table 9
Concentration of Support for Civil Society

	No. of organizations	Funding (million USD)	Average grant/organization (million USD)
Canada (2006–07)	294*	216	0.73
Norway (2010)	103	244	2.37
UK (2008–09)	96	510	5.31

* This figure only includes NGOs receiving core funding from Partnership Branch.

Sources: CIDA (2009), DFID (2009b, 28 and Table 19), NORAD (in-house statistics).

that both the UK and Norway provide direct financing to local civil society actors, whereas Canada rarely does – although data currently inaccessible to the public would be required to ascertain whether this is in fact the case. The reason may be Canadian concerns over the financial accountability of foreign-based partners.

For fiscal year 2006–07, the most recent year for which data are available, CIDA supported 294 CSOs with operational funds (i.e., via Canadian Partnership Branch) of US$216 million. If NGOs receiving funds for program execution are also included (via Geographic Programs), the number of organizations rises to 581. Civil society recipients are fewer and better funded in the UK and Norway than in Canada (Table 9).

Overall, Canada's effectiveness as a donor agency is of lower standard than both Norway and the UK on all the metrics examined here. Canadian aid is more centralized and reliant on staff for each dollar of ODA, with higher ministerial turnover, greater dispersion in support for civil society actors, and far less support for local actors embedded in communities in the developing world. Norway and the UK appear to have achieved relatively similar levels of donor effectiveness, notwithstanding their divergent governance structures. Approximately half of their total staff are located in field offices and they have had comparable low levels of ministerial turnover. Norwegian and British support for non-domestic civil society is of equivalent proportion to their support for domestic actors, and they both offer relatively concentrated support. Overall, it would appear that Norway and the UK achieve similar levels of donor effectiveness, while Canada lags behind both.

Donor Performance

Based on a holistic reading of the above data, Canada's performance as a donor is lower than both Norway's and the UK's. On both aid effectiveness and donor effectiveness indicators, the latter two countries unequivocally outperform Canada. This finding is supported by all existing efforts to benchmark donor performance. For example, in 2008, William Easterly and Tobias Pfutze ranked Canada fifteenth out of twenty-three bilateral donors, while the UK placed first and Norway second (Easterly and Pfutze 2008). In 2010 Williamson ranked Canada thirteenth out of twenty-two donors, with the UK ranked third and Norway twelfth.[13] As noted, while there is definite reason to lament Canada's low achievement on these metrics, it is also important to recognize that Canada ranks above the DAC average on many of them. Nevertheless, this may be cold comfort for those with greater ambitions for Canadian development assistance.

There is also little evidence to suggest that a separate development ministry exhibits any significant comparative advantage in its performance over an aid program amalgamated into a ministry of foreign affairs. Norway and the UK achieve relatively similar levels of donor effectiveness, with marginally higher achievement by the UK on aid effectiveness variables. Nevertheless, there is nothing in this comparative quantitative assessment of Norway and the UK to suggest that one mode of donor governance is consistently achieving higher levels of effectiveness than another. This points to other potential drivers of donor performance beyond governance structures in Norway and the UK.

EXPLAINING HIGH DONOR PERFORMANCE:
IMPLICATIONS FOR CANADA

What else might be driving Norway's and the UK's success? Deeper qualitative analysis of organizational dynamics within each country's development program reveals a number of potential clues, which together suggest that it is the subtle process-based features of reform, rather than the actual shifts in governance themselves, that are the likely drivers of donor performance.

In both the UK and Norway, reforms to donor governance emerged only after senior political figures who had a stake in improving donor performance actively championed the international development portfolio. In the UK, Robin Cook, Labour opposition critic on foreign affairs until 1997, committed the party to stop serving national commercial and geopolitical interests with the aid budget and create a separate ministry with independence over development policy. The first secretary for international development, Clare Short, became a powerful and visible advocate for the new ministry that would ultimately become her political legacy to New Labour. As one DFID staff member acknowledged: "The political ambition comes first; there was no point in having all the capability pulled together in DFID if the purpose was to run an old fashioned aid program" (confidential interview with DFID employee, London, March 2010). In Norway circa 2004, a political vision of a program centred on country-led development led the incumbent minister of international development, Hilde Franfjord Johnson, to demand greater oversight and control over NORAD, the implementing agency of Norwegian aid that was not under her ministerial control. In the cases of both Norway and the UK, then, a radical overhaul of governance required both a bold vision for the development program and the political leadership to achieve it, particularly at the early stages of reform.

Other common features across the Norwegian and UK cases include the presentation of a political vision in a clear and coherent written statement on development policy, supported by the minister of development, the finance ministry, and senior civil servants. These documents provided a compelling discussion of matters of substantive policy and served as aspirational statements for their development programs. Since 1997, the UK has produced four White Papers with an exclusive focus on international development (Department for International Development 1997; 2000; 2006; 2009a), while

Norway has produced two (Norwegian Ministry of Foreign Affairs 2004; 2009). In Canada, technically only one White Paper has exclusively treated the theme of international development (CIDA 2002). Most White Papers in Canada have presented development policy within the context of broader foreign policy reviews, as in the case of the 2005 International Policy Statement. Combining development topics within a foreign policy White Paper risks relegating development to a second-tier concern with only grudging support from the aid ministry and minister, ostensibly chief executors of the policy. Moreover, incorporating development in a foreign policy review is no guarantee of policy coherence in practice. In both Norway and the UK, a strong White Paper focused on development, in combination with some key statements from the head of government and/or minister of development, provided a robust platform for policy and empowered their aid agencies to aim higher in their work.

Also shared across the Norwegian and UK cases was an effort to foster cross-party support for development, based on shared values. In the UK, development policy has gradually been turned into an area where political consensus is achievable; for example, the Conservative/Liberal Democrat coalition government, elected in 2010, committed itself to maintaining the independence of DFID as well as the 0.7 per cent ODA/GNI target, both of which were flagship Labour Party policies. In Norway, all parties sought a progressive international policy that could cultivate their country's identity as a generous peacemaker throughout the world.

Adopting a meaningful internationalist vision of development can transcend political divisions in productive ways, secure global external legitimacy, and militate against vested interests that threaten to ambush the humanitarian and human-rights impulses of development (Morrison 1998, 447). In Canada, it might have the added value of linking the goal of national unity with the goal of international solidarity. There is a precedent for such unity in Canada, often displayed in times of international crisis. The Indian Ocean tsunami in 2004 and the Haitian earthquake in 2010 come to mind as instances where Canadians moved beyond parochial interests and affiliations and generously united in common cause. Nevertheless, as David Morrison (1998) tells us in detail that is sometimes painful to read, Canadian development cooperation has been a long tale of exploiting aid to service ethnic, corporate, geopolitical, regional, and linguistic interests – in other words, as a tool to divide Canadians.

In the current political environment, it is the institutionalized association between a progressive development policy and the Liberal Party that is particularly debilitating, since it seems to discredit many Canadian NGOs, academics, and policy avenues in the eyes of the Conservative government. This association is partly the product of the credit granted to former Liberal prime ministers, especially Lester B. Pearson and Pierre Trudeau, for their leadership during the halcyon days of Canadian aid policy. Yet it is not self-evident that the Liberals remain the vanguard of a humane aid policy (Ibbitson 2010; see also Black, this volume, and Brown, chapter 3, this volume). Ways need to be found to make the cause of international solidarity attractive to all political parties. This is not necessarily a fool's errand if one considers that, in a recent poll, 61 per cent of self-declared Conservatives solidly supported development assistance (OECD 2007, 27). The search for cross-party agreement on Canadian development policy is not beyond the realm of the possible (Paris 2010).

As Canada weighs different governance options, it makes sense to consider whether there is sufficient clarity over the aims of Canada's development program and adequate political championship of reforms across the political spectrum to buffer the journey to higher donor performance. No governance structure can improve donor performance in the absence of strong champions. And, should a dearth of political vision and leadership exist, what will be needed are efforts by Canadians themselves to articulate compelling visions for development policy around which political, media, and public support can be harnessed. Both traditional and newer forms of social networking, lobbying, and public campaigning will be critical both for generating a convincing vision for Canada's foreign aid programming and for fostering support in diverse quarters. Addressing the lack of political will and leadership on development policy in Canada ultimately requires the support of a grassroots political movement.

Assessing donor performance is not an exact science, and drawing lessons from the performance of others is harder still. Nevertheless, this chapter has attempted to tackle the broad question of what fosters donor performance in the UK and Norway, with a view to informing current debates on the renewal of Canadian development cooperation. The comparative analysis of Canada, the UK, and Norway presented here underlines the superior performance of the

UK and Norway when compared to Canada on key measures of aid effectiveness and donor effectiveness. This evidence provides some basis to reject the tenet that changes to donor governance structures are the key to unlocking excellence in aid agencies, given that Norway and the UK display similar levels of donor performance notwithstanding widely divergent governance structures. Norway's and the UK's success as donors derives from the clear articulation of a political vision for development, supported by strong political champions and relatively broad cross-party encouragement. Enthusiasts of radical donor governance reform in Canada who do not have a strategy to tackle endemic domestic political challenges thus ultimately risk having their ambitious dreams of a highly performing development program left unfulfilled.

NOTES

1 I would like to thank Patrick Johnston for extending me an invitation to participate in a project on Canadian aid effectiveness in comparative perspective supported by the Walter and Duncan Gordon Foundation. Linnea Jonsson's invaluable research assistance for this chapter is gratefully acknowledged. Comments from participants at a workshop held in May 2010 at the Munk Centre at the University of Toronto, as well as from David Black, Alasdair Roberts, and Donny Surtani, greatly improved earlier drafts. A British Academy grant has also generously supported this research. The usual caveats regarding author responsibility for content apply.

2 While the 2005 Paris Declaration on Aid Effectiveness and the subsequent Accra Agenda for Action frame and define the current aid effectiveness debate, *donor effectiveness* refers to the donor-related organizational features that can have a credible positive impact on development outcomes (Gulrajani 2011). More details on this distinction in the next section.

3 Canada's International Development Research Centre is a crown corporation but not a bilateral donor with representation on the DAC.

4 CIDA is still legally subordinate to DFAIT via an order-in-council dating from 1968 (see Morrison 1998, 63).

5 For a discussion of the challenges of measuring and managing public-sector performance, see de Bruijn (2007), Harford and Klein (2004), March and Sutton (1997), Moynihan (2008), Radin (2006), and Townley (1997).

6 Even in the case of randomized controlled evaluations, the nature of the causal mechanism remains elusive (see Deaton 2010).

7 A lengthier qualitative analysis of Canada's performance as compared to Norway and the UK can be found in Gulrajani (2010; 2011).
8 The International Assistance Envelope is the overarching framework within which ODA is programmed in Canada.
9 The average ODA project data in Table 5 is but one of the factors contributing to the rank allocated in Table 6. For more details, see Williamson (2010).
10 CIDA also had four presidents over those ten years.
11 In chapter 11 of this volume, Stephen Brown discusses recent changes to the CIDA/NGO relationship.
12 At the time of writing, financing for civil society via both branches was undergoing a dramatic reorganization and this division may no longer be applicable.
13 It is impossible to judge whether this is a case of improvement by Canada since the Easterly and Pfutze (2008) study or suggestive of methodological non-equivalence between the two studies.

REFERENCES

Auditor General of Canada. 2009. "Report of the Auditor General of Canada to the House of Commons: Chapter 8: Strengthening Aid Effectiveness – Canadian International Development Agency." Ottawa: Office of the Auditor General of Canada.

Birdsall, Nancy, and Homi Kharas. 2010. "Quality of Official Development Assistance Assessment." Washington, DC: Center for Global Development.

British Broadcasting Corporation. 2010. "Forecast Suggests 600,000 Public Sector Jobs to Go." *British Broadcasting Corporation.* 30 June.

Brown, Chris, and Edward Jackson. 2009. "Could the Senate Be Right? Should CIDA Be Abolished?" In A.M. Maslove, ed., *How Ottawa Spends, 2009–2010: Economic Upheaval and Political Dysfunction.* Montreal and Kingston, ON: McGill-Queen's University Press.

Brown, Stephen. 2007. "'Creating the World's Best Development Agency'? Confusion and Contradictions in CIDA's New Policy Blueprint." *Canadian Journal of Development Studies* 28, no. 2: 213–28.

Canada. 2007. "Overcoming 40 Years of Failure: A New Road Map for Sub-Saharan Africa." Ottawa: Senate Standing Committee on Foreign Affairs and International Trade.

Canadian Defence and Foreign Affairs Institute. 2007. "Survey Conducted by Innovative Research Group." Calgary, AB: Canadian Defence and Foreign Affairs Institute.

Canadian International Council. 2010. "Open Canada: A Global Positioning Strategy for a Networked Age." Toronto: Canadian International
Council.

Carin, Barry, and Gordon Smith. 2010. "Reinventing CIDA." Ottawa:
Canadian Defence and Foreign Affairs Institute.

Canadian International Development Agency. 2002. "Canada Making a
Difference in the World: A Policy Statement on Strengthening Aid
Effectiveness." Ottawa: Canadian International Development Agency.

– 2009. "Statistical Report on International Assistance Fiscal Year 2006–
2007." Gatineau, QC: Canadian International Development Agency.

– 2010. "Statistical Report on International Assistance Fiscal Year
2008/2009." Gatineau, QC: Canadian International Development Agency.

– 2011. "CIDA's Mission and Mandate." http://www.acdi-cida.gc.ca/acdi-
cida/acdi-cida.nsf/eng/NIC-5493749-HZK. Accessed 14 December 2011.

Clay, Edward J., Matthew Geddes, and Luisa Natali. 2009. "Untying Aid:
Is It Working? An Evaluation of the Implementation of the Paris
Declaration and of the 2001 DAC Recommendation of Untying ODA to
the LDCs." Copenhagen: Danish Institute for International Studies.

Deaton, Angus. 2010. "Instruments, Randomization, and Learning about
Development." *Journal of Economic Literature* 48: 424–55.

De Bruijn, Hans. 2007. *Managing Performance in the Public Sector.*
London: Routledge.

Department for International Development. 1997. "Eliminating World
Poverty: A Challenge for the 21st Century." White Paper on
International Development. http://www.dfid.gov.uk/Pubs/file/whitepa-
per1997.pdf. Accessed 14 December 2011.

– 2000. "Eliminating World Poverty: Making Globalisation Work for the
Poor." White Paper on International Development. http://www.dfid.gov.
uk/Pubs/file/whitepaper 1997.pdf. Accessed 14 December 2011.

– 2006. "Eliminating World Poverty: Making Governance Work for the
Poor." White Paper on International Development. http://www.dfid.gov.
uk/Pubs/file/whitepaper 1997.pdf. Accessed 14 December 2011.

– 2009a. "Eliminating World Poverty: Building our Common Future."
White Paper on International Development. http://www.dfid.gov.uk/
Pubs/file/whitepaper1997.pdf. Accessed 14 December 2011.

– 2009b. "Public Attitudes towards Development TNS Report Prepared
for coi on behalf of DFID." London: Department for International
Development.

– 2009c. "Statistics on International Development." London: Department
for International Development.

Easterly, William, and Tobias Pfutze. 2008. "Where Does All the Money Go? Best and Worst Practices in Foreign Aid." *Journal of Economic Perspectives* 22, no. 2: 29–52.

Goldfarb, Danielle, and Stephen Tapp. 2006. "How Canada Can Improve Its Development Aid." Working Paper No. 232. Vancouver: C.D. Howe Institute.

Gulrajani, Nilima. 2009. "How Politicization Has Been Silently Killing CIDA's Aid Effectiveness." *Globe and Mail*. 5 June.

– 2010. "Re-Imagining Canadian Development Cooperation: A Comparative Examination of Norway and the UK." Toronto: Walter and Duncan Gordon Foundation.

– 2011. "Organising for Donor Effectiveness: An Analytical Framework for Improving Aid Effectiveness Policies." Unpublished manuscript.

Harford, Tim, and Michael Klein. 2004. "Donor Performance: What Do We Know, and What Should We Know?" In *Public Policy for the Private Sector*. Washington, DC: World Bank.

Hayman, Rachel. 2009. "From Rome to Accra via Kigali: 'Aid Effectiveness' in Rwanda." *Development Policy Review* 27, no. 5: 581–99.

Ibbitson, John. 2010. "Robert Fowler Attacks Ottawa's Inaction in Africa." *Globe and Mail*. 29 March.

International Development Association. 2007. "Aid Architecture: An Overview of the Main Trends in Official Development Assistance Flows." Washington, DC: International Development Association.

International Development Select Committee. 2009. "Aid under Pressure: Support for Development Assistance in a Global Economic Downturn." London: House of Commons.

Knack, Stephen, Halsey Rogers, and Nicholas Eubank. 2010. "Aid Quality and Donor Rankings." World Bank Policy Research Working Paper. Washington, DC: World Bank.

Lalonde, Jennifer. 2009. "Harmony and Discord: International Aid Harmonization and Donor State Domestic Influence. The Case of Canada and the Canadian International Development Agency." PhD thesis. Baltimore: Johns Hopkins University.

March, James, and Robert Sutton. 1997. "Organizational Performance as a Dependent Variable." *Organization Science* 8, no. 6: 698–706.

Morrison, David 1998. *Aid and Ebb Tide: A History of CIDA and Canadian Development Assistance*. Waterloo, ON: Wilfrid Laurier Press.

Moynihan, Donald. 2008. *The Dynamics of Performance Management: Constructing Information and Reform*. Washington, DC: Georgetown University Press.

Munro, Lauchlan T. 2005. "Focus-Pocus? Thinking Critically about Whether Aid Organizations Should Do Fewer Things in Fewer Countries." *Development and Change* 36, no. 3: 425–47.

Norwegian Ministry of Foreign Affairs. 2004. "Fighting Poverty Together: A Comprehensive Development Policy." Report No. 35, 2003/2004, to the Storting. Oslo: Norwegian Ministry of Foreign Affairs.

– 2009. "Climate, Conflict and Capital: Norwegian Development Policy Adapting to Change." Report 13, 2008/2009, to the Storting. Oslo: Norwegian Ministry of Foreign Affairs.

Organisation for Economic Co-operation and Development. 2006. "DAC Peer Review of the United Kingdom." Paris: Organisation for Economic Co-operation and Development.

– 2007. "DAC Peer Review of Canada." Paris: Organisation for Economic Co-operation and Development.

– 2008a. "DAC Peer Review of Norway." Paris: Organisation for Economic Co-operation and Development.

– 2008b. "Effective Aid Management: Twelve Lessons from DAC Peer Reviews." Paris: Organisation for Economic Co-operation and Development.

– 2009a. "Managing Aid: Practices of DAC Member Countries." Paris: Organisation for Economic Co-operation and Development.

– 2009b. "Survey of the Levels of Decentralisation to the Field in DAC Members' Development Co-operation Systems." Paris: Organisation for Economic Co-operation and Development.

– 2010. "OECD Stat Extracts: Aggregate Aid Statistics." 13 April. Paris: Organisation for Economic Co-operation and Development, Development Assistance Committee.

Paris, Roland. 2010. "Minority Governments are Hobbling Canadian Foreign Policy." *Globe and Mail.* 30 March.

Radin, Beryl. 2006. *Challenging the Performance Movement.* Washington, DC: Georgetown University Press.

Riddell, Roger. 2007. *Does Foreign Aid Really Work?* Oxford: Oxford University Press.

Roodman, David. 2006. "An Index of Donor Performance." Working Paper. Washington, D.C.: Center for Global Development.

Smillie, Ian. 1998. "Optical and Other Illusions: Trends and Issues in *Public Thinking about Development Co-operation*." In Ian Smillie et al., eds., Public Attitudes and International Development Co-operation. Paris: Organisation for Economic Co-operation and Development, Development Assistance Committee.

Stern, Elliot D., et al. "Thematic Study on the Paris Declaration, Aid Effectiveness and Development Effectiveness." Cophenhagen: Danish Ministry of Foreign Affairs.

Townley, Barbara. 1997. "The Institutional Logic of Performance Appraisal." *Organization Studies* 18, no. 2: 261–85.

Treasury Board Secretariat. 2008. "The Public Service Employee Survey (pses): Organization Report for the Canadian International Development Agency." Ottawa: Treasury Board Secretariat.

United Kingdom. 2010. "Civil Service People Survey (csps): DFID Engagement Index." London: Cabinet Office.

Whaites, Alan. 1998. "The New UK White Paper on International Development: An NGO Perspective." *Journal of International Development* 10: 203–13.

Williamson, Claudia. 2010. "Fixing Failed Foreign Aid: Can Agency Practices Improve?" Paper presented at the AidData Conference. Oxford, UK, 25 March.

Aid Effectiveness and the Framing of New Canadian Aid Initiatives[1]

STEPHEN BROWN

At the end of the twentieth century, foreign aid appeared to be in almost terminal decline, both in Canada and in other Western countries. During the 1990s, Canada's official development assistance (ODA) dropped from $3.0 billion in 1990–91 to $2.6 billion in 2000–01. Relative to the size of the Canadian economy, the decline was even more dramatic. The government cut aid disbursements almost in half during this same period, from 0.45 per cent to 0.25 per cent of gross national income (GNI) (Canada 2009, 10). The optimism that accompanied the end of the Cold War quickly evanesced, while the widely heralded "peace dividend" failed to materialize.[2] Disillusioned with the lack of tangible results and as part of deficit-cutting strategies, Canada and most other donors slashed their aid budgets, turning their backs on long-standing commitments to reaching 0.7 per cent of GNI. After thirty years of growth, it felt like the end of an era. Across the world, a new term gained currency: aid fatigue. Imbued with *fin de siècle* pessimism, analysts used expressions such as an "ebb tide" and an "uncertain future" in the titles for their publications on Canadian development assistance (Morrison 1998; 2000).

The new century ushered in a radical reversal of this trend. The Millennium Development Goals (MDGs), adopted at the United Nations in 2000, epitomized the new thinking. Donors recognized that massive efforts were required to reduce poverty drastically over a fifteen-year period, including through increased spending to improve access to health and education. At the beginning of the twenty-first century, at UN conferences and G8 summits, Western donors renewed and reiterated their commitments to providing

higher levels of aid, to target poverty reduction, and to focus especially on Africa, the continent where needs are the greatest. They
also sought to improve aid effectiveness, so as to provide not only
more but also better aid. Canada participated enthusiastically in
this, at least for the first few years. By 2008, Canadian ODA disbursements had bounced back to 0.32 per cent of GNI (OECD 2009a),
though this remained less than half the international target.

A year after the adoption of the MDGs, another event was to shape
profoundly the context in which foreign aid operated: the al-Qaeda
terrorist attacks of 11 September 2001. The new mindset of the
"Global War on Terror," as well as the US-led invasions of Iraq and
Afghanistan, recast how Canada and other donors framed and oriented their aid programs. Almost overnight, security concerns gained
a central importance, often eclipsing the focus on the MDGs. Within
the context of these contradictory trends at the international level,
Canada began to rethink its place in the world and especially its
relationship with the United States.

Successive Canadian prime ministers each brought a new direction to foreign aid, usually building on his predecessor's achievements. For instance, Jean Chrétien reversed the decline in aid flows
and designated Africa a priority. Paul Martin integrated aid more
closely with other foreign policy "instruments" (known as the
"whole-of-government" approach) and took steps to focus on a
smaller number of countries. Stephen Harper sought to concentrate
and integrate aid even further, notably focusing resources on
Afghanistan but also replacing Africa with the Americas as the priority region for aid.

This chapter analyzes the main trends in Canadian development-
assistance policy since 2000–01, the pivotal "international moment"
that pulled ODA simultaneously in two new directions: a preoccupation with the immediate and medium-term needs of the poor
embodied in the MDGs and the donor countries' own security concerns in the post-9/11 era.[3] It argues that shifts in Canadian aid
policy reflect the government's broader foreign policy concerns,
especially a preoccupation with prestige (the quest for a personal
legacy under Chrétien and for Canada's place among peers and in
the post-9/11 world under Martin and Harper) and most recently
commercial self-interest, with the new geographical focus on the
Latin America and the Caribbean. Though these forms of self-
interest are not new or unique to Canada, the language used usually

frames the changes as improvements in aid effectiveness and thus as being for the benefit of poor countries, rhetorically reflecting the growing international concern with improving the quality of aid. With the notable exception of the gradual untying of aid, however, most of the initiatives' impact on effectiveness would be unclear or even detrimental. Through these changes, couched in aid effectiveness terms, the Canadian government is increasingly seeking to instrumentalize the Canadian International Development Agency (CIDA) and its aid programs, including through the whole-of-government approach, to reflect non-development-related interests.

This chapter is organized as follows. Its first section analyzes the politics of aid effectiveness by examining in turn the main components in the effectiveness discussions that have been part of Canadian aid policy initiatives in recent years: the untying of aid, the questioning of impact and search for results, the issue of aid volume, the "focus on focus" (fewer recipient countries and economic sectors), and the coherence between aid policy and policies in other areas. It then explores the motivations that underpin recent Canadian aid policy initiatives. The conclusion summarizes the main argument and speculates on the effect of global changes on Canadian foreign aid in the years to come.

THE POLITICS OF AID EFFECTIVENESS

Virtually every time the Canadian government announces changes in aid policy, it evokes the need for aid to have greater impact, regardless of who is in power.[4] At first blush, this might appear impossible to be anything but a good thing. After all, it would be hard to oppose effectiveness. Upon further examination, however, the concept's malleability permits its use to justify any new initiative, preventing it from having any fixed connotations. "Effectiveness" becomes a substitute for "good policy," which in turn is really the government's preferred policy, but with an aura of supposed objectivity and benevolence underpinned by cost-effectiveness and international legitimacy.

"Aid effectiveness" is currently one of the most important buzzwords in aid circles. In recent years, the term has acquired two distinct meanings. First, in the late 1990s, the World Bank published an influential report entitled *Assessing Aid: What Works, What Doesn't, and Why* (World Bank 1998). It argued that, based on econometric analysis, aid produces growth only in countries with a "good" policy environment and "sound" fiscal, monetary, and trade policies, without which, it inferred, aid is wasted (further argued in Burnside and Dollar 2000). Though the methodology and reasoning were roundly criticized (Lensink and White 2000), this strand of aid effectiveness came to signify the ability to produce economic growth (not a synonym for development) when combined with the "right" policies in recipient countries.

Simultaneously, a different meaning emerged in a consensus among the twenty-two member countries of the Organisation for Economic Co-operation and Development's Development Assistance Committee (OECD/DAC), where Western donors discuss and try to coordinate aid policy. Concerned not only with policies in recipient countries, as the World Bank had been, they considered how *donors'* aid policies could improve the effectiveness of their contributions. The 1996 report, *Shaping the 21st Century*, began to lay out basic principles, including not just the responsibilities of recipients but also those of donors: a sustained commitment from donors, improved coordination among them, increased support for "locally-owned development strategies," and greater coherence among donors' aid and non-aid policies (OECD 1996, 2). These principles evolved into the 2005 Paris Declaration on Aid Effectiveness, supplemented by the 2008 Accra Agenda for Action, which formalized as basic principles the centrality of the harmonization among donors, alignment with recipient-country ownership, and the predictability of aid flows, among others. In other words, aid's effectiveness depended not on the "correct" neo-liberal policy environment in recipient countries but rather on enhanced commitment and cooperation of donors among themselves and with recipient countries.[5]

As a member of the DAC and part of the DAC-led process in defining the principles of aid effectiveness, the Canadian government often invoked these principles to outline the basic philosophy of Canadian assistance. However, it continued to use the World Bank's approach and present its neo-liberal justifications in its policy documents for directing aid to certain countries (Canada 2002; 2005) – even after donors as a whole had abandoned not only the logic behind that argument but also that particular use of the term "effectiveness."[6] Lacking any robust empirical evidence to support this approach, Canada was embracing what was essentially a political or ideological preference for countries with minimal state intervention in their economy and great openness to international finance and investment (Killick 2004).

More recently, however, the government and especially the minister of international cooperation (who is responsible for CIDA) have been invoking effectiveness to justify any changes the government makes, even if they contradict the basic consensus principles. Canada's version of aid effectiveness is clearly "a distinct, more narrow version" of the internationally endorsed agenda and concentrates on internal organizational issues and accountability to Canadian taxpayers (Lalonde 2009, 169; see also Brown and Jackson 2009). Some Canadian initiatives, such as completely untying aid (that is, not requiring that funds be spent on Canadian products and services), are fully in line with aid effectiveness principles. Others are less so, such as frequently changing priority countries and sectors. This raises the question of effectiveness for what and for whom, to be further addressed below. Some have gone so far as to argue that a measure of aid effectiveness should include a consideration of the extent to which aid helps donors achieve their own non-aid-related goals (Gillmore and Mosazai 2007).

This chapter does not seek to assess Canada's progress in the actual implementation of the international "aid effectiveness agenda."[7] Rather, it examines recent Canadian policy initiatives and the extent to which they can be justified by the aid effectiveness rationale, by which I mean whether they improve the quality of aid from the point of view of the beneficiaries in recipient countries. The rest of this section thus analyzes the recent evolution of the five main components of Canadian aid policy changes and their links to aid effectiveness: tied aid, impact and results, volume, focus, and policy coherence.

Tied Aid: The Long Goodbye

Tied aid is a practice that involves making ODA conditional on the purchase of goods and services from the donor country. Tied aid adds on average an extra 15–30 per cent to costs because it prevents the funds from being used to buy the best value for money on a competitive market (Jepma 1991, 15). This benefits the donor country but provides no benefit to the recipient. Tied aid is thus antithetical to the notion of aid effectiveness.

The most unambiguous advance in Canadian aid policy since 2000 is the progressive, albeit slow, untying of aid. In 2002 the government recognized that tied aid was "at odds with trends towards trade liberalization and the dismantling of investment barriers" and that tying its aid benefited Canada rather than developing countries. At the time, Canada tied more of its ODA than the majority of its peers. At least 50 per cent of aid to African and least-developed countries and two-thirds of aid to other countries had to be spent in Canada. No more than 10 per cent of the cost of emergency food aid could be used to purchase food in countries other than Canada. Under pressure from G8 and DAC partners, Canada initially agreed to untie certain categories of aid to least developed countries only, but not food aid (Canada 2002, 19–23).

After a tsunami devastated the coastal areas of many Asian countries in 2004, the Canadian response highlighted the shortcomings of tied food aid. Rather than buy rice available in nearby Asian countries, the government shipped Canadian surplus wheat, which cost more, took longer to arrive, and was less suited to local diets. The government responded to widespread criticism by reducing the tied component of food aid to 50 per cent.

In 2005 Canada signed the Paris Declaration on Aid Effectiveness, which committed the government to untying aid, though with no specific deadline for eliminating the practice altogether (OECD 2005, 6, 9). In 2007 Canada remained one of the countries with the highest rate of tied aid: 25.4 per cent, compared to the DAC average of 15.2 per cent. By then, several countries, including Ireland, Sweden, and the UK, had completely untied all assistance (OECD 2008, Table 23). In 2008 the government announced its intention to untie fully all aid by 2012–13 (CIDA 2008). This will eliminate the ineffectiveness caused by tying procurement to the donor country and bring Canada in line with the international norm, though only slowly and rather belatedly.

Show Me the Impact! Criticisms of CIDA from within Government

Outside actors raise a litany of criticisms against CIDA and Canadian foreign aid with great regularity. Commonly raised themes include CIDA's excessive bureaucratization and centralization; lack of both geographic and sectoral focus, leadership, and overall vision or clearly articulated purpose; and failure to commit to a firm timetable for achieving the goal of disbursing 0.7 per cent of GNI on ODA (Chapnick 2008; OECD 2002; 2007; Goldfarb and Tapp 2006). On occasion, government bodies, such as parliamentary committees, have published critical examinations of Canadian aid policy as well (for instance, Canada 1987). A distinctive trend in recent years has been the number and at times vociferousness of attacks on CIDA from *within* government, as well as how drastic some of the remedies suggested are. Three government reports stand out in this regard, two from the Senate and one from a government-appointed panel, all of which lament in particular the lack of visible impact of Canadian aid. In addition, recent attacks by the minister responsible for CIDA on the agency can only be interpreted ominously.

In 2007 the Canadian Senate threw CIDA a one-two punch. First, the Standing Senate Committee on National Security and Defence complained about the lack of visibility of CIDA's efforts in Kandahar, the province of Afghanistan where Canada is playing a central role, and recommended that CIDA turn over $20 million per year to the Canadian Forces for them to use for development projects (Canada 2007b, 9, 26). Second, the Standing Senate Committee on Foreign Affairs and International Trade deplored CIDA's "40 years of failure" in Africa and raised the possibility that the agency be abolished and its functions taken over by the Department of Foreign Affairs and International Trade (DFAIT). Among other things, it recommended focusing aid on the private sector and economic growth, at the expense of social spending and fighting poverty directly, which it considered unproductive welfare spending (Canada 2007b). The media seized upon the mooted possibility of abolishing CIDA, which was actually not the Senate committee's first preference.

Despite being very poorly argued and justified (for a detailed analysis, see Brown 2007b), some of these recommendations squared well with pre-existing government beliefs and intentions, including the rationale for increased support to the private sector. The tenor of the report also supported the shift of focus away from Africa, first announced a few months after the report's publication. The government did not act on other recommendations, such as promoting trade with and investment in African countries or increasing support for UN peace operations in Africa.

In 2008 the government-appointed Independent Panel on Canada's Future Role in Afghanistan expressed its concern that more than 85 per cent of Canadian aid was being channelled through the Afghan government or multilateral institutions, with little left for "quick-action" local projects or for initiatives that could be recognized as Canadian contributions. It recommended that CIDA fund at least one "signature" project that would ensure that Canada achieved visibility, status, and gratitude for its development contributions (Canada 2008, 25–6, 36). This resonated with public demands for demonstrable results for the hundreds of millions of dollars being poured into what had quickly become Canada's top foreign aid recipient.

Within a few months, the Canadian government announced three signature projects in Afghanistan: repairing the Dahla Dam and the connected irrigation system in Kandahar province, supporting the education sector, and eliminating polio. Results to date, however, have proved disappointing. More than a year later, as of September 2009, the Canadian company SNC-Lavalin had not yet begun its work on the Dahla Dam because a key access road and bridge had not yet been completed, and only about 200 of the promised 10,000 jobs for Afghans had actually been created. Construction or repair work had been completed on only five of the promised fifty schools, with another twenty-eight underway. During this period, violence forced the closure of 180 or roughly half of the schools in Kandahar, suggesting that security should be a higher priority than new schools. The security situation also hindered immunization and the number of new cases of polio actually increased (A. Woods 2009).

The Senate reports brought high-profile attention to CIDA's shortcomings, real and imagined, and placed the agency in a more vulnerable position. In 2009 an unprecedented event occurred: CIDA's own minister, Bev Oda, after spending her first two years in office talking up CIDA and its achievements, rather suddenly went on the attack and criticized the agency for its lack of technical expertise and focus on inputs rather than results (Berthiaume 2009). The patent unfairness of her criticisms further eroded morale among CIDA employees and raised the spectre that the government was laying the groundwork for future budget cuts (Brown 2009).

These critiques all centred on the apparent lack of impact of Canadian aid. However, a fixation on immediately visible results has a negative effect on effectiveness.

An Unhealthy Obsession with Results

Since around 2007, CIDA has demonstrated an increased preoccupation with demonstrable results. The need to focus on results has long been a concern for the DAC (see OECD 1996) and CIDA itself (reflected in its use of "results-based management" tools since the 1990s). The new fixation, bordering on obsession, is linked to both the Conservative leitmotif of accountability and the need to justify massive expenditures in Afghanistan, which rapidly became by far the largest recipient of Canadian aid. It also reflects the skepticism of the Conservative Party and important parts of its constituency toward the actual desirability of foreign aid, as well as the party's desire to demonstrate to taxpayers that their money is being well spent.

Unfortunately for donor governments seeking to claim credit, development-assistance results are not always tangible or quick. For instance, "qualitative changes in gender relations" are difficult to monitor and measure (Edwards and Hulme 1996, 968). Likewise, aid to the governance sector cannot be immediately assessed by quantifiable indicators – or if it is, they can only capture some components of results. Others can take a generation to bear fruit with any certainty. Even then, causality is difficult to establish. Long-term development successes are not attributable to a single source, especially when donors work closely with each other or a recipient government. As a growing proportion of aid funds are channelled to development programs and even sector-wide approaches, rather than individual projects (in line with current thinking on aid effectiveness), the task of attributing results becomes more difficult (Brown and Morton 2008, 3–4). Moreover, foreign aid is but one contribution to the development process in a given country. Others include domestic policies and planning, national and international investment, international trade policies, and resource endowments.[8]

As a result, CIDA has trouble identifying what it has accomplished. On its website, for instance, under the heading "What Are CIDA's Achievements?," it mentions the global reduction in poverty levels, the increase in primary-school enrolment, and the decline in infant mortality (CIDA 2009b). No evidence, however, indicates that these accomplishments are the direct result of Canadian foreign aid, rather than other donors' assistance or in fact the policies of recipient governments themselves.

The inability to claim direct credit leaves CIDA vulnerable to unfair accusations of failure, epitomized by the Senate report on Africa, which concluded that Canadian aid had failed miserably because committee members could not find signs that CIDA's efforts had made a significant difference on a continental scale. It is not clear what kind of visible impact senators expected from an annual

Canadian contribution that averaged only about thirty-five cents per African (Brown 2007b). The lack of demonstrable results imputable to Canada does not mean, however, that Canadian aid was wasted.

By embracing the fetishization of immediately visible results, Canada biases its assistance towards short-term, stand-alone project assistance in sectors where results can be tangible and quick, exemplified by Canada's signature projects in Afghanistan. This can easily backfire when the high-profile projects fall behind schedule or fail to meet their targets, as is currently the case, further discrediting CIDA. Moreover, this type of assistance is at odds with the principles of the aid effectiveness agenda, which emphasizes the long-term integration of development efforts with recipient government institutions, based on recipient needs and strategies, rather than scoring quick points for individual donors. It also contradicts the state-building objectives that underpin assistance to "fragile states" such as Afghanistan, whose future depends far more on its government gaining legitimacy among Afghans than the Canadian government doing so. In sum, a fixation on short-term visible results emphasizes "accountancy" more than it does actual "accountability," which requires a longer time horizon (Edwards and Hulme 1996, 968).

A more productive approach would also acknowledge the inherent uncertainties in development assistance, especially in conflict zones, and adopt aid modalities that try to mitigate these problems over the medium to long term. Rather than pandering to public pressure and aiming for "quick wins" for Canada, the government could educate the Canadian public about the challenges of development, the importance of strengthening local institutions, and the real principles of effectiveness in the longer term – in Afghanistan and in other recipient countries.

Low Volume, Low Impact

Though the question of the quantity of ODA can be considered independently of its quality, the volume of a country's aid program is strongly related to its impact. A country delivering a very small amount of highly effective aid is making a very limited contribution, no matter how effective it might be. For that reason, the volume of Canadian assistance is important to consider under the rubric of the effectiveness of Canada's aid. Moreover, when a country such as Canada contributes only limited resources, it will have difficulty claiming a leadership role among donors, an attempt that Denis Stairs (2003, 252) derides as the "value-imperialism of the weak."

In 2008, of the twenty-two OECD/DAC members, Canada was only the tenth-largest donor and, in terms of generosity (as measured by the ODA/GNI ratio), it ranked sixteenth (OECD 2009a, 1).[9] Although Canada has become more generous since 2000, its global ranking has not improved. Other countries' aid programs, especially European ones, have grown faster and Canada's position may in fact slip further in coming years if this trend continues. This is consistent with Canada's historical decline in importance as a donor. Whereas in 1975, when Canadian ODA represented 0.54 per cent of GNI, Canada provided approximately 6 per cent of global ODA, in 2008 the figures had dropped to 0.32 per cent and about 4 per cent (OECD 2009b). With the Obama administration's planned massive increase of US aid expenditure, the rise of "philanthrocapitalism" (best illustrated by the Bill and Melinda Gates Foundation), and the increased importance of China and other non-OECD donors (Marten and Witte 2008; N. Woods 2008), Canada will be further marginalized on the global aid scene, even if it increases its aid budget modestly every year.

In 2002 Chrétien announced that Canadian foreign aid would grow by 8 per cent annually and that aid to Africa would double by 2009. Martin subsequently reaffirmed these two commitments and the Conservatives honoured them.[10] However, the Harper government was the first to abandon the commitment to eventually allocating 0.7 per cent of GNI to ODA, in line with the Conservatives' doubts about the value of foreign aid. Even while the Chrétien government was cutting expenditure in the 1990s, it always reiterated its commitment to the goal set in 1970 at the United Nations and in fact proposed by Canadian political icon Lester B. Pearson. The 2006 Conservative election platform, however, stated that it would "increase spending on Overseas Development Assistance beyond the currently projected level and move towards the OECD average level" (Conservative Party of Canada 2006, 46). It is worth noting that "moving towards" is not the same as "reaching" and that it is not clear if the "OECD average level" refers to the average DAC country effort, which was 0.47 per cent in 2008, or the average for the entire DAC, which was 0.30 per cent, a ratio that Canada has already exceeded (OECD 2009a, 1).

Also unclear is what is to happen after 2010. The government has given no concrete indication that ODA levels will continue to increase or even be maintained. Though no official policy announcement has been made on this issue, Minister Oda stated in an interview that there will be "no new major injections of funding until she is satis-fied the agency is working properly" (Berthiaume 2009). Likewise, now that aid to Africa has doubled but Africa is no longer Canada's top-priority region, it could well remain stagnant or be cut, possibly even dramatically.

Given Canada's relatively paltry generosity when compared to its peers and its lack of commitment to increasing aid flows substan-tially, it is logical that the government prefers instead to emphasize improving effectiveness, increasing Canada's prestige, and maximiz-ing the benefits that accrue to Canada, all discussed below. As part of its effectiveness mantra, the government constantly repeats the word "focus."

Focus, Focus, Focus

Increasing focus is the cornerstone of most aid policy announce-ments. Greater focus, both geographical and thematic, is assumed but never demonstrated to improve effectiveness. The constant shift-ing in priority countries, continents, and sectors, however, unam-biguously decreases effectiveness.

Canadian aid has been very widely dispersed since the early 1970s (Morrison 2000, 26). Canada is the only donor country to belong to the Commonwealth, the Francophonie, and the Organization of American States. Membership has its privileges, but also obligations – or at least an interest in providing assistance to developing coun-try members in Asia, francophone and anglophone Africa, Latin America, and the Caribbean. Canada's aid also is spent in a broad range of sectors. The donor consensus, however, underlines the need to focus on a smaller number of both countries and sectors in order to increase effectiveness. Canada's donor peers, like its domestic crit-ics, have often criticized CIDA programming for being excessively scattered (OECD 2002; 2007). Successive Canadian governments have taken steps to concentrate not only on a subset of countries but also on a handful of sectors.

In 2002 the Chrétien government announced its intention to enhance its relationship with "a limited number of the world's poor-est countries," emphasizing how this would improve the impact of Canadian ODA (Canada 2002, 11).[11] Of the nine countries selected for "enhanced partnerships," two-thirds were in Sub-Saharan Africa.[12] Unable to achieve this degree of concentration, the Martin government announced in 2005 that Canada would increase the impact of its aid by dedicating two-thirds of its bilateral aid to twenty-five "development partners" (Canada 2005).[13] To the existing nine countries, it added eight Sub-Saharan African ones, two Latin American ones, five Asian ones, and one European one.[14] In 2009 the Harper government radically redrew the list, retaining the original core of nine, adding the West Bank/Gaza and four new countries in the Americas, while dropping twelve of the sixteen additions from 2005, including all eight African ones.[15] Since only four years had elapsed, it was too soon to see results in the countries added in 2005, since CIDA projects take an average of three and a half years just to be to be approved (Auditor General of Canada 2009, 27).

Successive governments also announced a focus on a limited number of sectors. In 2001 CIDA adopted social-development priorities in health and nutrition, basic education, HIV/AIDS, and children, all of which were meant to include the promotion of gender equality. These aligned well with Canada's commitment to the Millennium Development Goals. In the 2002 development-policy statement, the minister added rural development and agriculture, as well as the private sector (Canada 2002, 14–16). In Martin's 2005 policy statement, the list was redrawn to focus on good governance, health, basic education, private-sector development, and environmental sustainability, again with gender as a crosscutting theme (Canada 2005, 11). In 2009 the government announced three "priority themes": increasing food security, stimulating sustainable economic growth, and securing the future of children and youth. This unexpected announcement created confusion in the Canadian development community since "themes" are not quite the same as sectors and could in fact encompass numerous sectors. For instance, the future of children and youth would certainly include health and education but arguably also a variety of efforts in technical training, job creation, and peacebuilding, to name but a few. The press release that announced the three themes also named a few specific sectors that would be strengthened via the themes, including the environment, gender equality, human rights, and governance (CIDA 2009), further muddying the waters as to what was to be included and, more to the point, excluded.[16]

Though one could endlessly debate the merits of individual country recipients and sectors, two points put into perspective the question of focus. First, despite the consensus among donors on the need to focus on fewer recipients and sectors, the theoretical argument that this approach actually increases aid effectiveness has serious weaknesses, and claims to that effect lack empirical evidence (Munro 2005). If all donors adopt such focus without coordinating their efforts, this also creates new risks, including the possibility of "aid orphans," countries that donors have abandoned. Furthermore, a decision by a donor to focus only on certain sectors or themes contradicts its commitment in previous aid policy statements (Canada 2002; 2005) and under the Paris Declaration to recipients' ownership of their development strategy and donors' alignment with recipients' national priorities. Moreover, when a donor government seeks to pick specific sectors in which it has a comparative advantage, it reintroduces a more subtle form of tied aid through the back door.

Second, even if increased focus were in fact beneficial, radically changing the list of priority countries and sectors every few years – even in the name of effectiveness – increases aid volatility and thus actually reduces aid effectiveness. According to the latest report of the auditor general of Canada (2009, 21), "the lack of clear direction," in large part due to frequently changing priorities and senior staff, including presidents and ministers, "has confused CIDA staff, recipient governments, and other donors, effectively undermining the Agency's long-term predictability." The designation of priority sectors also contradicts other fundamental principles of aid effectiveness, particularly the national ownership of development planning and donors' alignment with recipient countries' priorities, which Canada endorsed when it signed the Paris Declaration in 2005.[17] "Focusing on focus" rather than on more substantive issues of the origins of and solutions to poverty and inequality serve as a convenient justification for a given government's own preferences, while providing a veneer of selflessness and assuaging peer pressure.

Nevertheless, focus is not the only major donor preoccupation that often emphasizes form over content. Another is the question of policy coherence, to which this chapter now turns.

The Quest for Policy Coherence

The question of coherence among different government departments and policies has been on the donor agenda for over a decade

(OECD 1996; Pratt 1999). The Chrétien government mentioned it in its 2002 development policy statement (Canada 2002, 17–18), but it was under Paul Martin that it became an important practice. Initially known as the "3-D approach" (referring to diplomacy, defence, and development), it was later expanded to include commerce and other areas and rebaptized the whole-of-government approach, which featured prominently in the Martin government's International Policy Statement.

Though, in principle, coherence and consistency (much like aid effectiveness) can only be seen as a good thing, their impact on development goals is not necessarily positive. In essence, it depends on what becomes the overriding concern. If other departments, such as Foreign Affairs, International Trade, and Defence, were to line up behind development goals, this could help a donor government achieve aid objectives. Notably, the interests of developing countries themselves could be better reflected in donor policies, at home and at the international level. For example, the lowering or elimination of tariff barriers and other protectionist measures would promote developing-country exports and could raise incomes more than foreign aid does. Likewise, the use of donor troops to stabilize countries emerging from civil war could improve the impact of aid.

In practice, however, evidence from other donor countries suggests that policy integration leads to the subordination of development objectives to donors' foreign policy and defence priorities, not the other way around (Smillie 2004, 15), which reduces rather than increases aid effectiveness. For many donors, the Global War on Terror has profoundly influenced their aid disbursements with the goal of enhancing their own security, in an international trend toward the increased "securitization" of foreign aid (N. Woods 2005). Such is clearly the case for Canada's involvement in Afghanistan, which commands a disproportionate amount of CIDA's attention and resources. Canadian ODA to that country ballooned from a paltry US$7 million in 2000 to US$345 million in 2007, representing about 8.5 per cent of total Canadian ODA (OECD 2009c). The government presented Afghanistan as a "laboratory" for a new way of carrying out foreign policy. In spite of the unprecedentedly high expenditures, it is becoming increasingly but unsurprisingly clear that aid effectiveness is especially difficult in a war zone like Kandahar.[18] In 2007 CIDA President Robert Greenhill actually indicated that in the future Canada would focus less on "failed and fragile states" such as Afghanistan and Haiti and more on countries where "we've actually seen real results" (Berthiaume 2007), suggesting that the "lab experiment" had failed. In spite of the attempts to link Canadian defence, diplomatic, and development initiatives in Afghanistan (Gillmore and Mosazai 2007; Simpson 2007), none of the three DS appears to be producing any clear progress, be it the defeat of the Taliban insurgency in Kandahar province, the strengthening of the Afghan state with a legitimate government, or the improvement of the lives of millions of impoverished Afghans.

Without this form of policy coherence, CIDA would be able to function with greater autonomy (Brown 2008a) and have a greater impact on development by spending its funds in countries where they could be used more effectively, rather than being used – and ineffectually at that – to shore up Canada's and other donors' strategic priorities in Afghanistan and other countries engulfed in the Global War on Terror, as is increasingly the case in Pakistan. It might nonetheless be too early to call for the end of the whole-of-government approach, since it might prove more effective for promoting development in countries in the midst of complex crises unrelated to the Global War on Terror, such as Haiti (Baranyi 2011). Much will depend on the mix of motivations that underpin donors' policy coherence in such cases, addressed in the next section of this chapter.

MORPHING MOTIVATIONS

States are not monolithic unitary actors and it is generally not possible to discern clear overarching motivations. As Ilan Kapoor (2008, 78) points out, one should avoid "presupposing a homogeneous nation-state and fully and rational controlled policy-making." Just as individuals can have mixed motives, so too can states. Moreover, different actors within government (CIDA, DFAIT, Prime Minister's Office) or within a government department or agency (CIDA President's Office, Policy Branch, country desk officers) can differ widely in their approaches to ODA.

Analysts have long recognized that the simultaneous pursuit of political, commercial, and development objectives hampers aid efficiency (Canada 1987, 7; Morrison 2000, 15). The recent aid policy changes discussed above illustrate shifts in the government's thinking about ODA and the motivations that underpin them, even if the initiatives do not necessarily have a large impact on the actual day-to-day implementation of Canadian aid outside Afghanistan, especially not in the short term. Most CIDA employees try to keep their heads down and carry on with their jobs as before, regardless of new policy initiatives. In other words, though self-interested motivations characterize recent Canadian aid policy *changes*, one should not infer that those motives underlie Canadian foreign aid as a whole.

Traditionally, the motivation debate has been set up as a tug-of-war between self-interest ("realism," epitomized by Morgenthau 1962) and selflessness ("humane internationalism," such as Lumsdaine 1993). Though self-interest has become more important (Brown 2007a; Pratt 2000), the desire for prestige (as suggested by Nossal 1988), in particular Canada's international reputation, better explains most recent changes than do more tangible commercial or even national-security interests – including the emphasis placed on Afghanistan.

Throughout the 1990s, under Prime Minister Chrétien, Canada's ODA declined steadily. Assistance to Africa was especially hard hit: it was cut from US$601 million in 1992 to $270 million in 2000, corresponding to a drop from 31 per cent of total Canadian aid to 19 per cent (Brown 2008b, 272). It is thus a particularly noteworthy achievement – and compelling evidence of Canadians' capacity for collective amnesia – that Chrétien managed to reinvent himself in the early 2000s as a vociferous proponent of development assistance in general and aid to Africa in particular. Chrétien's sudden about-face in the final years of his mandate, including the renewal of aid itself and increased attention to Africa, was closely linked to his own concerns for personal legacy, a generous imprint he could make in Canada and on the global stage – though he was more successful at home than internationally (Black 2005; 2006; Brown 2008b).

Chrétien's successor, Paul Martin, focused less on personal credit than on trying to improve Canada's global presence, notably mending its relations with the United States, which had suffered under Chrétien, most recently because of Canada's refusal to take part in the US-led invasion of Iraq. Martin's international policy statement was tellingly titled *A Role of Pride and Influence in the World*, which played to both the domestic and the international audience. The priority the Liberals and later the Conservatives accorded to Afghanistan reflected a concern to prove that Canada could make important contributions to the NATO alliance, including by sending Canadian soldiers to Afghanistan in 2002 in the aftermath of the Taliban's fall, assuming lead responsibility in Kandahar province in

2006, and making Afghanistan a top-priority recipient of Canadian ODA in 2009.

The Conservative government of Stephen Harper, in power since 2006, has not yet released any official documents outlining its approach to foreign aid. Despite the brevity of the section on international assistance, the federal budget is often the most detailed statement of the government's aid policies and priorities in any given year. For that reason, any analysis of aid policy initiatives is only slightly better than reading tea leaves. One must glean information from relatively brief press releases and vague public statements made by politicians, none of which has provided any in-depth rationale or justification for changes. As such, the making of aid policy under Prime Minister Harper has been done "by stealth" and is being drip fed to Parliament, CIDA employees, and the Canadian public.

Still, some statements by top officials strongly suggest that international prestige has been a crucial consideration for the Conservative government as well. For example, in 2007 the government indicated that Canada would concentrate efforts in countries where Canada could be among the top five donors, a clear desire to have a place at the table with the major donors (Canada 2007a, 262) – assuming, of course, that there are actually five seats at the metaphoric and literal table. At the time, International Cooperation Minister Josée Verner noted that in some cases increasing expenditures only slightly would place Canada there, suggesting that the government was more interested in impressing voters and donor peers than it was in actual impact (Brown 2008a).

After Bev Oda replaced Verner as CIDA minister in 2007, prestige abroad became less central – though it still characterized the desire for signature projects in Afghanistan. As Kapoor (2008, 87) notes, "nationalist symbols permit donors to be identified, thanked, or envied; they also enable it to stake its territory, and perhaps to gloat." Signature projects mark Canada's international presence and enhance its national credibility, but they also contradict widely held principles of aid effectiveness. For that reason, they can actually detract from Canada's reputation among other donors and development workers in Canada and abroad. According to Nilima Gulrajani (2009, A13), "in the world of international aid, Canada is reputed as a money-grubbing flag planter rather than effectively and selflessly serving the world's poor." A discredited Canada makes it harder for the Canadian government and individual Canadian officials to influence donor debates within the OECD/DAC and in donor-coordination groups on the ground in recipient countries. If the government ceases to increase or even fails to maintain aid budgets, its international reputation will suffer further.

With the shift in focus from Africa to the Americas, first announced by Harper at the 2007 G8 summit, the government's motivation ostensibly started to move away from rather symbolic prestige concerns and toward more concrete economic, and more specifically commercial, self-interest. The new list of twenty "core countries" released in 2009 operationalized this new regional priority when, as mentioned above, it dropped many poor African countries and added wealthier ones in Latin America and the Caribbean, notably ones of particular trade interest to Canada.[19] Soon after, CIDA President Margaret Biggs listed for the first time Canada's foreign policy considerations as an explicit official criterion for selecting core recipients (Lupick 2009).

A concern for personal or national prestige, however, should not be overemphasized in the analysis of policy shifts.[20] Pressure from the donor community, notably within the OECD/DAC, plays an important but under-recognized part in shaping Canadian aid policy, as was the case with Canada's renewed emphasis on Africa in 2001–02 (Black 2006). Chrétien and Martin generally followed the donor consensus, at times contributing to it. Harper, on the other hand, seemed at times to relish breaking with it and distancing himself from global norms (and Liberal priorities), especially eschewing the focus on Africa in favour of the Americas. Oda recognized this departure when outlining the government's new orientation in 2009, noting that it was "not something that aims to please Irish rock stars," again framing it as beneficial for aid effectiveness (York 2009, F7) when in fact it might be more beneficial for Canada than for the poor.

In this tale, one significant effort sought to push the Canadian government in the opposite direction. The ODA Accountability Act (Bill C-293) was passed by Parliament in 2008 as a private member's bill. It aimed to ensure that all Canadian aid would contribute directly to poverty reduction, take into account the perspectives of the poor, and be consistent with international human-rights standards. However, its provisions lack teeth. According to the government's interpretation, Canadian ODA is already in compliance with the new law, even if one can only at best expect a very indirect, long-term contribution of certain aid activities to poverty reduction. The new law may thus have no discernible effect on aid (Halifax Initiative 2009). Certainly, the government would prefer to ignore the act's attempt to reorient aid, much to the consternation of Canadian development NGOs. Tellingly, none of the government's announcements since the law was passed has made any reference to the act as providing any guidance on aid policy.

CONCLUSION: WHAT WOULD LESTER DO?

Prior to 2001, observers such as Cranford Pratt (2000) noted with concern that the government was increasingly justifying Canadian aid on the basis of global security, rather than the need to fight poverty and inequality. Most lamented the decline of Pearsonian idealism and a global-justice imperative. This trend intensified after the al-Qaeda attacks on the United States in 2001, impelling the government to focus on specifically Canadian security, rather than global security (Brown 2007a; Simpson 2007). As mentioned above, Canada is not exceptional in the "securitization" of its foreign aid and the increased focus on self-interest, rather than poverty eradication (N. Woods 2005).

At the same time, since 2000, a counter-trend has been emerging in the global aid regime. Epitomized by the MDGs' underlining of the urgency of the fight against poverty, emerging donor norms dictated increased aid volumes, especially to Sub-Saharan Africa, and much greater attention to social spending. This new trend also underscored the importance not only of policies in recipient countries but also ways that Canada and other donors themselves could improve their aid delivery, embodied in the Paris Declaration on Aid Effectiveness.

Since Chrétien's final years in office, and increasingly so under Harper, the government has presented its policy initiatives as ways of improving the effectiveness of Canadian aid. Some efforts, particularly the untying of aid, were clear contributions to that goal, even if Canada was one of the last holdouts in this area. Similarly, Canada lags behind most of its peers in terms of the relative generosity of its aid. Other efforts, such as concentrating aid in fewer countries and sectors, have not been demonstrated to have a positive or negative effect on aid effectiveness – and raise some concerns and potential new risks for developing countries. Moreover, the frequency of changes in priority countries and sectors have in themselves undermined CIDA's aid effectiveness, as has the rapid turnover of senior officials. Other policies and practices, especially the emphasis on signature projects in Afghanistan and the redefining of core sectors and countries every few years, are political decisions and preferences, which directly or indirectly contradict stated Canadian policies on local ownership, the predictability of aid flows, the centrality of long-term relationships with recipients, and other internationally accepted principles of aid effectiveness. The continuing heavy concentration of Canadian ODA in Afghanistan, despite the severe security-related impediments to effective aid, epitomizes politically motivated aid priorities. Finally, the adoption of a whole-of-government approach to foreign policy could theoretically enhance aid effectiveness. However, to date, policy coherence has instead been undermining it by generally subjecting development priorities to donor self-interest, rather than the other way around.

Throughout this period, new Canadian policies and priorities usually reflected the desire for prestige: personal prestige in Chrétien's final years as prime minister, but more often Canada's international prestige, especially under Martin and the early Harper years, when the government sought to use aid to bolster Canada's place in the world, including improving its relationship with the United States. The size and nature of Canada's involvement in Afghanistan best illustrates the government's desire for the US and other Western allies to consider it a team player. The relative feebleness of Canada's renewal of aid, however, ensured that Canadians, rather than other donor countries, would be these efforts' main audience. By 2009, notwithstanding continued involvement in Afghanistan, it appeared that the Harper government was less interested in using foreign aid to redefine Canada's place in the world and gain international prestige. It has failed to make any commitment to increasing or even maintaining aid flows after 2010, it ended Africa's privileged position as the continent that most urgently needed aid, and it embraced instead the open use of ODA for Canadian commercial self-interest in Latin America and the Caribbean.

It should be noted, however, that self-interest and the seeking of international prestige need not be incompatible with development efforts, depending on how national interest is constructed. If Canada were to seek prominence through renewed Pearsonian internationalism, to be a leader in generous, innovative, poverty-fighting foreign aid, it could gain respect in the eyes of its donor peers and the developing world. Canada has brought new perspectives to donors' discussions in the past, including the importance of gender issues and NGOs (Morrison 1998; 2000). Spearheading a similar issue in the future, such as human-rights-based approaches to development, could help provide a platform for global leadership and enhance Canada's influence, helping it, for instance, to obtain a non-permanent seat at the UN Security Council. The question of aid policy thus encompasses not only the volume of aid and the underlying objective of Canadian assistance but also the kind of country Canada wants to be, Canada's place in the world, and the kind of world Canada envisions.[21]

The coming years will pose additional challenges to the aid regime in general and to Canadian policies in particular. In the short term, Canada and other donors are likely to cut aid expenditure owing to the global economic crisis, despite the even greater effect of the crisis on poor countries. Over the medium and long term, climate change will increase the developing world's need for international assistance, particularly because of more frequent and severe natural disasters, lower crop yields, food scarcity, and higher food prices (Ayers and Huq 2009). Alongside this process, Canada's place among donors is waning, as its share of global aid flows decreases, accelerated by the rise of non-traditional donors such as China and non-state donors. The G20, where Canada's influence is limited, is supplanting the G8, in which Canada sits among a select few. Canada could respond by further concentrating on narrowly defined self-interest, thereby sealing its fate as a minor player on the world stage, or it could radically rethink how and to whom it provides assistance and try to make niche contributions that would actually contribute to aid effectiveness on the ground.

NOTES

1 For helpful comments and suggestions, I thank Chris Brown, Molly den Heyer, Brigette DePape, Tristen Naylor, Rosalind Raddatz, Arne Rückert, Jennifer Salahub, Liam Swiss, and two CIDA employees who prefer to remain anonymous. All remaining deficiencies are strictly my own. I am also grateful to the Social Sciences and Humanities Research Council of Canada and the University of Ottawa for funding that made this research possible. This book chapter originally appeared in Duane Bratt and Christopher J. Kukucha, eds., *Readings in Canadian Foreign Policy:*

Classic Debates and New Ideas, 2nd ed. (Toronto: Oxford University Press 2011), 469–86. Oxford University Press has kindly permitted it to be reproduced in this volume.

2 Lumsdaine (1993) epitomizes the short-lived initial optimism of the post-Cold War period, celebrating the constant increase in aid budgets, an increased focus on humanitarian and egalitarian goals, greater emphasis on very poor countries and very poor people within those countries, the untying of aid, and the replacement of loans with grants.

3 It is worth underlining that this chapter focuses its analysis on changes at the policy level and does not examine the concrete impact of new initiatives on the ground, which may not yet be discernible and are only beginning to be studied in depth.

4 For instance: "CIDA will reorient its programming in the poorest countries towards new approaches that are based on the principles of effective development" (Canada 2002, 7); "In order to increase the effectiveness of the development cooperation program, we will focus our efforts in a few priority sectors and in a small group of countries and will engage in value-added, selective partnerships with Canadians and with the most effective multilateral institutions" (Canada 2005, 31); "By fully untying Canada's aid, the Government is delivering on its commitment in the 2006 Speech from the Throne to support 'a more effective use of aid dollars' and the 2007 Budget's promise not only to increase the amount of Canada's international assistance envelope, but also 'to make our existing resources work more effectively'" (CIDA 2008, 1); and "With greater efficiency, focus, and accountability, our Government's new approach to Canadian aid will be even more effective" (CIDA 2009a, 1).

5 I don't mean to accept uncritically the principles of the Paris Declaration (see Hyden 2008). Still, it represents the standing consensus on what constitutes aid effectiveness, to which Canada has subscribed and against which Canada's policies and practices can be assessed.

6 A notable exception is the United States, which embraced the concept of the presence of the "right" policy environment as the basis for selecting recipients by its new bilateral development agency, the Millennium Challenge Corporation.

7 This is analyzed in Lalonde (2009), with a focus on the harmonization component.

8 As a result, the concept of *development* effectiveness is emerging as an alternative to *aid* effectiveness. Its meaning, however, has yet to be clearly defined and the term is used in many different ways (Kindornay and Morton 2009).

9 By way of comparison, Canada was the fifth-largest OECD donor in the mid-1980s. Measured as a ratio of GNI, Canada's place slipped even further: it was the sixth most generous country as recently as 1994 (Morrison 2000, 21).

10 Because its Africa expenditures for the baseline year of 2003–04 were lower than expected, the Harper government was able to cut $700 million from its targeted expenditure of $2.8 billion and still claim to have kept its promise.

11 As the policy document's title, *Canada Making a Difference in the World: A Policy Statement on Strengthening Aid Effectiveness*, suggests, it emphasized better aid rather than just more aid. Much of the thinking on effectiveness reflected, belatedly, the principles of the DAC/OECD's 1996 document, *Shaping the 21st Century: The Contribution of Development Assistance* (OECD 1996), which Canada had endorsed six years earlier. It also reflected a concern with orienting Canadian assistance in support of the MDGs.

12 Namely Ghana, Ethiopia, Mali, Mozambique, Senegal, and Tanzania. The others were Honduras, Bolivia, and Bangladesh.

13 As Stairs (2005) pointed out, two-thirds of bilateral aid was already going to twenty-five countries – though not the same twenty-five. This new policy would therefore not necessarily achieve any greater concentration.

14 Benin, Burkina Faso, Cameroon, Kenya, Malawi, Niger Rwanda, and Zambia; Guyana and Nicaragua; Cambodia, Indonesia, Pakistan, Sri Lanka, and Vietnam; and Ukraine.

15 The other additions to the list in the Americas were Colombia, Haiti, Peru, and the Caribbean regional program. The other countries dropped were the two Latin American countries added in 2005 (Guyana and Nicaragua) and two newly added Asian ones (Cambodia and Sri Lanka).

16 The confusion was exacerbated in late 2009, when CIDA Minister Bev Oda unexpectedly rejected a grant application by KAIROS, an NGO affiliated with Canada's main Christian denominations. Though the NGO had developed the proposal in close cooperation with CIDA officials and it focused on human rights, good governance, and environmental sustainability, which were all listed as priority areas on the latest policy press release, Oda's spokesperson stated that the "project does not meet CIDA's current priorities" (Payton 2009). The decision was widely interpreted as retaliation for the NGO's criticism of some Harper government policies.

17 As CIDA itself has recognized, "long-term development requires a predictable and stable source of funding to be effective" and "effective international assistance involves long-term relationships with development partners" (Canada 2005, 10).

18 This commonsensical fact explains why donors are currently providing only humanitarian assistance to Darfur. Before attempting to achieve longer-term development, they are waiting for security to be re-established.

19 Though ODA to Latin America can legitimately fight poverty and inequality (Cameron 2007), the new list notably included comparatively well-off countries (the English-speaking Caribbean) and ones with which Canada was actively pursuing free-trade agreements (Colombia and Peru).

20 Prestige seeking and compliance with norms are not incompatible. As Lumsdaine (1993, 67) argues, "doing something costly and right but doing it out of desire for approbation" is evidence of the strength of peer pressure and norms.

21 For a critique of this national(ist) framework for situating the aid relationship, see Kapoor (2008).

REFERENCES

Auditor General of Canada. 2009. "Chapter 8. Strengthening Aid Effectiveness – Canadian International Development Agency." *Report of the Auditor General of Canada to the House of Commons*. Ottawa: Office of the Auditor General of Canada.

Ayers, Jessica M., and Saleemul Huq. 2009. "Supporting Adaptation to Climate Change: What Role for Official Development Assistance?" *Development Policy Review* 27, no. 6: 675–92.

Baranyi, Stephen. 2011. "Canadian Policy towards Haiti." In Jorge Heine and Andrew S. Thompson, eds., *Fixing Haiti: MINUSTAH and Beyond*. Tokyo and New York: UNU Press. 205–28.

Berthiaume, Lee. 2007. "CIDA Boss Hints at Shift to Stable Nations." *Embassy*, 27 June.

– 2009. "CIDA Consultations on the Way, Minister Reassures." *Embassy*, 27 May.

Black, David R. 2005. "From Kananaskis to Gleneagles: Assessing Canadian 'Leadership' on Africa." *Behind the Headline* 62, no. 3: 1–17.

– 2006. "Canadian Aid to Africa: Assessing 'Reform.'" In Andrew F. Cooper and Dane Rowlands, eds., *Canada among Nations 2006: Minorities and Priorities*. Montreal and Kingston, ON: McGill-Queen's University Press. 319–28.

Brown, Chris, and Edward T. Jackson. 2009. "Could the Senate Be Right? Should CIDA be Abolished?" In Allan M. Maslove, ed., *How Ottawa Spends, 2009–2010: Economic Upheaval and Political Dysfunction*. Montreal and Kingston, ON: McGill-Queen's University Press. 151–74.

Brown, Stephen. 2007a. "'Creating the World's Best Development Agency'? Confusion and Contradictions in CIDA's New Policy Blueprint." *Canadian Journal of Development Studies* 28, no. 2: 213–28.

– 2007b. "Le Rapport du Sénat sur l'aide canadienne à l'Afrique: une analyse à rejeter." *Le Multilatéral* 1, no. 3: 1, 6–7.

– 2008a. "CIDA under the Gun." In Jean Daudelin and Daniel Schwanen, eds., *Canada among Nations 2007: What Room for Manoeuvre?* Montreal and Kingston, ON: McGill-Queen's University Press. 91–107.

– 2008b. "L'aide publique canadienne à l'Afrique: vers un nouvel âge d'or?" In François Audet, Marie-Eve Desrosiers, and Stéphane Roussel, eds., *L'aide canadienne au développement: bilan, défis et perspectives.* Montreal: Presses de l'Université de Montréal. 267–90.

– 2009. "CIDA under Attack (from its own Minister)." *The Mark*, 23 June.

Brown, Stephen, and Bill Morton. 2008. "Reforming Aid and Development Cooperation: Accra, Doha and Beyond." Policy Note. Ottawa: North-South Institute.

Burnside, Craig, and David Dollar. 2000. "Aid, Policies, and Growth." *American Economic Review* 90, no. 4: 847–68.

Cameron, John. 2007. "CIDA in the Americas: New Directions and Warning Signs for Canadian Development Policy." *Canadian Journal of Development Studies* 28, no. 2: 229–47.

Canada. 1987. *For Whose Benefit? Report on Canada's Official Development Assistance Policies and Programs.* Ottawa: House of Commons Standing Committee on External Affairs and International Trade.

– 2002. *Canada Making a Difference in the World: A Policy Statement on Strengthening Aid Effectiveness.* Hull, QC: Canadian International Development Agency.

– 2005. *Canada's International Policy Statement: A Role of Pride and Influence in the World; Development.* Gatineau, QC: Canadian International Development Agency.

– 2007a. *Budget Plan 2007.* Ottawa: Department of Finance.

– 2007b. *Canadian Troops in Afghanistan: Taking a Hard Look at a Hard Mission.* Ottawa: Senate of Canada, Standing Senate Committee on National Security and Defence.

– 2007c. *Overcoming 40 Years of Failure: A New Road Map for Sub-Saharan Africa.* Ottawa: Senate of Canada, Standing Senate Committee on Foreign Affairs and International Trade.

– 2008. *Report of the Independent Panel on Canada's Future Role in Afghanistan.* Ottawa: Manley Commission.

– 2009. *Statistical Report on International Assistance, Fiscal Year 2006–2007.* Gatineau, QC: Canadian International Development Agency.

Canadian International Development Agency. 2008. "Canada Fully Unties its Development Aid." http://www.acdi-cida.gc.ca/acdi-cida/ACDI-CIDA.nsf/eng/NAT-9583229-GQC. Accessed 28 September 2008.

– 2009a. "Canada Introduces a New Effective Approach to its International Assistance." 20 May. http://www.acdi-cida.gc.ca/acdi-cida/ACDI-CIDA.nsf/eng/NAT-5208514-G7B. Accessed 27 September 2009.

– 2009b. "CIDA in Brief." 5 August. http://www.acdi-cida.gc.ca/acdi-cida/ACDI-CIDA.nsf/eng/JUD-829101441-JQC. Accessed 27 September 2009.

Chapnick, Adam. 2008. "Canada's Aid Program: Still Struggling after Sixty Years." *Behind the Headlines* 65, no. 3: 1–28.

Conservative Party of Canada. 2006. *Stand up for Canada, Conservative Party of Canada: Federal Election Platform 2006.*

Edwards, Michael, and David Hulme. 1996. "Too Close for Comfort? The Impact of Official Aid on Nongovernmental Organizations." *World Development* 24, no. 6: 961–73.

Gillmore, Scott, and Janan Mosazai. 2007. "Defence, Development, and Diplomacy: The Case of Afghanistan, 2001–2005." In Jennifer Welsh and Ngaire Woods, eds., *Exporting Good Governance: Temptations and Challenges in Canada's Aid Program.* Waterloo, ON: Wilfrid Laurier University Press. 143–67.

Goldfarb, Danielle, and Stephen Tapp. 2006. *How Canada Can Improve Its Development Aid: Lessons from Other Aid Agencies.* Commentary No. 232. Toronto: C.D. Howe Institute.

Gulrajani, Nilima. 2009. "How Politicization has been Silently Killing CIDA's Effectiveness." *Globe and Mail.* 8 June. A13.

Halifax Initiative. 2009. "Official Interpretations of the 'ODA Accountability Act' One Year Later." Issue Brief. Ottawa: Halifax Initiative.

Hyden, Goran. 2008. "After the Paris Declaration: Taking on the Issue of Power." *Development Policy Review* 26, no. 3: 259–74.

Jepma, Catrinus J. 1991. *The Tying of Aid.* Paris: Organisation for Economic Co-operation and Development.

Kapoor, Ilan. 2008. *The Postcolonial Politics of Development.* London and New York: Routledge.

Killick, Tony. 2004. "Politics, Evidence and the New Aid Agenda." *Development Policy Review* 22, no. 1: 5–29.

Kindornay, Shannon, and Bill Morton. 2009. "Development Effectiveness: Towards New Understandings." Issues Brief. Ottawa: North-South Institute.

Lalonde, Jennifer. 2009. "Harmony and Discord: International Aid Harmonization and Donor State Domestic Influence. The Case of Canada and the Canadian International Development Agency." PhD thesis. Baltimore: Johns Hopkins University.

Lensink, Robert, and Howard White. 2000. "Assessing Aid: A Manifesto for Aid in the 21st Century?" *Oxford Development Studies* 28, no. 1: 5–17.

Lumsdaine, David Halloran. 1993. *Moral Vision in International Politics: The Foreign Aid Regime, 1949–89*. Princeton, NJ: Princeton University Press.

Lupick, Travis. 2009. "CIDA Refocused International Aid with Foreign Policy in Mind." *Georgia Straight*. 21 May.

Marten, Robert, and Jan Martin Witte. 2008. "Transforming Development? The Role of Philanthropic Foundations in International Development Cooperation." GPPi Research Paper Series No. 10, Berlin.

Morgenthau, Hans. 1962. "A Political Theory of Foreign Aid." *American Political Science Review* 56, no. 2: 301–9.

Morrison, David R. 1998. *Aid and Ebb Tide: A History of CIDA and Canadian Development Assistance*. Waterloo, ON: Wilfrid Laurier University Press.

– 2000. "Canadian Aid: A Mixed Record and an Uncertain Future." In Jim Freedman, ed., *Transforming Development: Foreign Aid for a Changing World*. Toronto: University of Toronto Press. 15–36.

Munro, Lauchlan T. 2005. "Focus-Pocus? Thinking Critically about Whether Aid Organizations Should Do Fewer Things in Fewer Countries." *Development and Change* 36, no. 3: 425–47.

Nossal, Kim R. 1988. "Mixed Motives Revisited: Canada's Interest in Development Assistance." *Canadian Journal of Political Science* 21, no. 1: 35–56.

Organisation for Economic Co-operation and Development. 1996. *Shaping the 21st Century: The Contribution of Development Cooperation*. Paris: Development Assistance Committee, Organisation for Economic Co-operation and Development.

– 2002. "Development Co-operation Review: Canada." Paris: Development Assistance Committee, Organisation for Economic Co-operation and Development.

– 2005. "Paris Declaration on Aid Effectiveness." http://www.oecd.org/dataoecd/11/41/34428351.pdf. Accessed 28 September 2009.

– 2008. "Statistical Annex of the 2009 Development Co-operation Report." Tables updated on 5 December 2008. http://www.oecd.org/dac/stats/dac/dcrannex. Accessed 28 September 2009.

– 2009a. "Net Official Development Assistance in 2008." Paris: Organisation for Economic Co-operation and Development. http://www.oecd.org/dataoecd/48/34/42459170.pdf. Accessed 20 September 2009.

– 2009b. "OECD International Development Statistics." http://www.oecd.org/dac/stats/idsonline. Accessed 27 September 2009.

– 2009c. "OECD International Development Statistics." http://www.oecd.org/dac/stats/idsonline. Accessed 28 December 2009.

Payton, Laura. 2009. "KAIROS Funding Cuts Chill Community." *Embassy*, 9 December.

Pratt, Cranford. 1999. "Greater Policy Coherence, a Mixed Blessing: The Case of Canada." In Jacques Forster and Olav Stokke, eds., *Policy Coherence in Development Co-operation*. London and Portland, OR: Frank Cass. 78–103.

– 2000. "Alleviating Global Poverty or Enhancing Security: Competing Rationales for Canadian Development Assistance." In Jim Freedman, ed., *Transforming Development: Foreign Aid for a Changing World*. Toronto: University of Toronto Press. 37–59.

Simpson, Erin. 2007. "From Inter-Dependence to Conflation: Security and Development in the Post-9/11 Era." *Canadian Journal of Development Studies* 28 no. 2: 263–75.

Smillie, Ian. 2004. "ODA: Options and Challenges for Canada." Ottawa: Canadian Council for International Co-operation.

Stairs, Denis. 2003. "Myths, Morals, and Reality in Canadian Foreign Policy." *International Journal* 58, no. 2: 239–56.

– 2005. "Confusing the Innocent with Numbers and Categories: The International Policy Statement and the Concentration of Development Assistance." Calgary: Canadian Defence and Foreign Affairs Institute.

Woods, Allan. 2009. "Polio Defeats Canada's Pet Project." *Toronto Star*, 16 September.

Woods, Ngaire. 2005. "The Shifting Politics of Foreign Aid." *International Affairs* 81, no. 2: 393–409.

– 2008. "Whose Aid? Whose Influence? China, Emerging Donors and the Silent Revolution in Development Assistance." *International Affairs* 84, no. 6: 1205–21.

World Bank. 1998. *Assessing Aid: What Works, What Doesn't, and Why*. New York: Oxford University Press.

York, Geoffrey. 2009. "Banned Aid." *Globe and Mail*. 30 May, F1, F6–7.

4

Whither Development in Canada's Approach toward Fragile States?

STEPHEN BARANYI AND ANCA PADUCEL

Since the end of the Cold War and especially post-9/11, certain Western states and international organizations have become increasingly involved in fragile states and situations. In 2007 ministers and heads of development agencies of the Organisation for Economic Co-operation Development's Development Assistance Committee (OECD/DAC), including the Canadian International Development Agency (CIDA), committed themselves to the Principles for Good International Engagement in Fragile States and Situations, complementing the commitments set out in the Paris Declaration on Aid Effectiveness, adopted by the international community in 2005.[1] According to this emerging policy consensus, fragile states are seen as having weak state authority and legitimacy, a limited capacity to deliver public services, and severe economic and social problems, such as extreme poverty and widespread violence (Carment et al. 2009). This multidimensional nature of state fragility is commonly seen as requiring special attention and integrated responses, that is, whole-of-government (WOG) approaches (Patrick and Brown 2007; World Bank 2011).

In 2005 this concern was translated into Canadian policy through the Liberal government's International Policy Statement (IPS). Under subsequent Conservative governments, Ottawa deepened the mechanisms for WOG engagement in a small group of high-priority fragile states – mainly Afghanistan and Haiti. In those countries, CIDA and other government departments (OGDs) established international assistance programs that dwarfed Canada's cooperation with traditional aid recipients. Even in second-tier fragile 'situations' like Sudan or West Bank/Gaza, Canadian assistance attained or

surpassed programs in long-standing development partner countries. The social dynamics driving those large increases in aid to fragile states are among the issues explored in this chapter.

In 2007 the OECD/DAC peer review of Canada singled out its
"promising approach toward fragile states, such as Haiti and
Afghanistan" as a distinct strength of the Canadian cooperation
program (OECD 2008, 263). The Canadian government has reported
impressive results from its cooperation in fragile states, as we shall
see in this chapter. Yet independent analysts have questioned those
claims. With regard to Afghanistan, Nipa Banerjee (2009; 2010),
Stephen Brown (chapter 3 of this volume), and others have argued
that the WOG approach brought greater coordination but also more
security-driven and less locally sustainable programming. In Haiti,
Yasmine Shamsie (2008) and Nancy Thede (2008) have suggested
that Canadian WOG approaches also yielded more security-oriented
programming, while reinforcing inappropriate neo-liberal economic
policies. In Sudan, the North-South Institute (2009) has suggested
that Canada's WOG approach exhibits biases toward short-term and
foreign-executed projects.

Such independent analyses offer alternatives to government
reports and to the DAC peer review. Yet they also have limitations.
Although some analysts cross-reference each other's work, intellectual dialogue is rare, particularly across cases. Moreover, several
authors generalize from the case of Afghanistan despite the unique
features of that situation. Few explicitly draw on social theory to
enrich their interpretations of Canadian engagement. This chapter
addresses those gaps through a theoretically informed, focused comparison of the development pillar of Canadian WOG engagement in
Afghanistan, Haiti, and Sudan.[2]

These cases were selected for several reasons. In 2010 they were
among the top twelve of the "alert" category in the Failed States
Index because they all suffered from humanitarian crises, extremely
low economic development, severe deficits of state legitimacy, and
large international interventions (Fund for Peace 2011). They were
also among the top twelve recipients of Western development assistance (OECD 2010, 3). In 2009–10 Haiti was the largest recipient of
Canadian international assistance ($334 million through all chan-
nels) and Afghanistan the second at $317 million. Sudan was the
sixth, receiving $157 million (CIDA 2010, 6). Until the escalation of
international intervention in Libya in 2011, these countries also

hosted the largest Canadian military deployments outside NATO's historic area of operations (DND 2010).

This chapter explores the extent to which there has been a securitization of aid,[3] as suggested by critical analyses of Western and particularly of Canadian WOG engagement in fragile states. Are there significant variations in the way development has emerged from WOG processes there? How have dynamics on the ground in host states, along with Canadian and broader international factors, shaped commonalities and differences across these cases?

We show how Canadian engagement in these contexts has been characterized by common tendencies, namely large development programs informed by WOG strategies and market-oriented economic policies, which emphasize humanitarian assistance and other short-term projects as well as the channelling of Canadian assistance through multilateral agencies and non-governmental organizations (NGOs). Yet there are also important variations with respect to the way Canadian aid has been employed in these contexts: from a tight integration into a Western-driven military strategy in Afghanistan, to an approach characterized by greater attention to strengthening the state and fostering long-term development, particularly in Haiti, which is more in line with international aid effectiveness principles. We also explain how those patterns result from the distinct alignment of forces on the ground, in Canada and in the international arena.

Our analysis is oriented by various strands of critical thought. We build on the work of critical security analysts such as Mark Duffield (2001), who view current Western engagement in fragile states as rooted in centuries-old interventions by modern capitalist states in Southern societies and as driven today by the need to ensure order on the chaotic borderlands of an increasingly violent globalized system. Critical security analysts from the Copenhagen School argue that discourses and specific instruments such as aid have been "securitized" to advance Western agendas, especially since 9/11 (Buzan and Hansen 2007). Our approach is akin to these analysts' "critical social constructivism" because we explore the interplay between human agency, discourses, and structures shaping history. Yet we also follow Robert Cox's (2002) critical theory in placing more emphasis on how agency is informed by material factors (e.g., transnational economic structures and relations of power between states and social forces). In particular, we draw on Cox to continue an earlier exploration (Baranyi 2008) of how the agency of certain states and social forces can align to alter historical trends in some contexts – in this instance the practices of Canadian intervention in less geopolitically salient fragile states such as Haiti.

CANADA AND DEVELOPMENT IN AFGHANISTAN

Afghanistan has been engulfed in warfare since the late 1970s. Despite some development gains after the US-led overthrow of the Taliban regime in 2001, violence escalated in 2005. Decades of armed conflict, foreign occupation, and a war economy fuelled by the production and sale of opium have converged to undermine development. Despite extensive international investment, including the deployment of over 140,000 international troops on the ground, ten years after the events of 9/11 Afghanistan remained a fragile state characterized by weak governance, armed violence, an expanding drug economy, and low human development (Barfield 2010).

Canadian engagement in Afghanistan evolved greatly over the decade following the US-led invasion. After Afghan and world leaders signed the Bonn Agreement in December 2001 – an agenda for guiding Afghanistan toward "national reconciliation, a lasting peace, stability, and respect for human rights" (Embassy of Afghanistan 2006) – the UN mandated the International Security Assistance Force (ISAF) to continue the campaign against Taliban and al-Qaeda forces. The objective set by the international community, including Canada, was to "build a new Afghan nation through the promotion of reconstruction, reform, and development" (Banerjee 2008, 25). Increasing the legitimacy of the Afghan government and its capacity to achieve the Millennium Development Goals was seen as integral to achieving stability and development in the country (Goodhand and Sedra 2010).

In support of those objectives, from late 2001 to 2005, Canada committed a growing number of troops and civilian advisers, as well as significant reconstruction assistance, to Afghanistan. Canadian officials moved towards a WOG approach by coordinating diplomacy, defence, and development efforts, even before the IPS was adopted in 2005. As security deteriorated in 2005–06, NATO deployed additional troops and in January 2006 Afghan and world leaders launched the Afghanistan Compact – the successor to the Bonn Agreement.[4] The Compact comprises nine goals that fall under three "critical and interdependent" areas of activity for the five years following its adoption: security, governance, rule of law and human rights, and economic and social development, with the elimination of the narcotics industry being a crosscutting area of work (Afghanistan Compact 2006, 2). Canada adapted its WOG strategy to support the Compact, increased its aid and military contingent, and redeployed most of its forces to Kandahar (Canada 2008b; Stein and Lang 2007).

In 2007–08 the war continued to escalate, placing the government of Canada's policies under increased public scrutiny. Prime Minister Stephen Harper responded by convening an independent panel, led by John Manley, a prominent Liberal politician. In early 2008 Harper instructed officials to implement the Manley Report's central recommendation: that Canada should more closely integrate its WOG resources in Afghanistan, particularly by redirecting at least 50 per cent of Canada's development assistance to Kandahar to support the almost 3,000 Canadian military personnel there (CIDA OCAE 2009). WOG efforts subsequently focused on six priorities: security; strengthening economic growth and social services; humanitarian assistance; enhancing border security and Afghanistan-Pakistan dialogue; promoting democratic governance; and facilitating political reconciliation (Canada 2011l). By 2010, almost half of the CIDA-supported projects were in Kandahar (CIDA OCAE 2009).

In 2010 the US deployed an additional 30,000 troops to Afghanistan in response to deteriorating security conditions. In turn, the Harper government announced that, after the pull-out of combat troops from Kandahar in 2011, Canada's military deployment would shift back to Kabul. Official development assistance (ODA) and broader Canadian assistance would focus on security training, the rule of law, children and youth, humanitarian assistance, and regional diplomacy (Canada 2011k).

There is much debate over how much Canada has spent in Afghanistan. The parliamentary budget officer has suggested that Canada's military mission in Afghanistan cost between $5.9 billion and $7.4 billion from 2001 to 2008 (Robinson 2009). A parliamentary committee estimated that Canadian development and reconstruction assistance amounted to approximately $1.9 billion during the same seven years (SCFAID 2008). The data compiled in Table 1 suggest that Canada spent about $9 billion in Afghanistan from 2005 to 2010, of which about $7.8 billion (87 per cent) went to

Table 1
Canadian Bilateral Assistance to Afghanistan
(in Millions, Fiscal Years 2005–10)[5]

CAD *millions*	2005–06	2006–07	2007–08	2008–09	2009–10
ODA					
CIDA	101	179	280	224	230
OGDS	0.8	38	38	63	68
Total ODA	102	217	318	287	299
Non-ODA					
DFAIT	N/A	N/A	N/A	42	40
DND	1,066	1,919	1,478	1,856	1,478
Total	1,168	2,136	1,796	2,185	1,817

Sources: See n.5.

military operations via the Department of National Defence (DND) and only $1.23 billion (13 per cent) to humanitarian and development aid via CIDA and OGDs.

From CIDA's viewpoint, Canadian ODA to Afghanistan was aligned with Canada's WOG strategy, the Afghanistan Compact, and other national strategies (TBS 2010b). Within those frameworks, CIDA suggested that its funding had generated development results in the areas of education, democratic governance, and economic growth. In 2010 twenty-seven schools were under construction in Kandahar and, for fiscal year 2009–10, 110,000 teachers and principals received basic training and 23,500 people received literacy training, while another 1,240 people graduated from CIDA-funded vocational training programs (of whom 59 per cent were women) (CIDA 2011a). With respect to democratic governance, CIDA helped establish 22,000 Community Development Councils, representing more than half of all communities in Afghanistan (CIDA 2011a). Nevertheless, CIDA acknowledged that the precarious situation on the ground prevented sufficient progress in the area of governance reform (CIDA 2011a). The rehabilitation of the Dahla Dam irrigation system in Kandahar continued: in 2009–10, 80,000 cubic metres of silt were removed, improving water flow and in turn agricultural output (CIDA 2011a).

These results appear impressive given the difficult environment in Afghanistan. Canada invested huge resources there and CIDA's program was tightly coordinated with other government departments, particularly after 2008. However, analysts have questioned the results claimed by Canadian officials, as well as the long-term sustainability of development efforts in that context. Four patterns stand out. First, CIDA reports rarely provide detailed information on results, making it difficult to assess the success of development efforts (Banerjee 2009, 68). Few independent sources corroborate the results claimed by CIDA. Furthermore, few results are based on joint evaluations with Afghan institutions, while others are downright dubious. For example, media reports suggested that, despite ambitious goals set in 2008, the $50-million Dahla Dam "signature project" was seriously delayed because of the war and particularly because of rent-seeking activities by a security firm linked to the Karzai family (Potter 2010; CBC 2011).

Second, many CIDA-supported projects bypassed Afghan state institutions, thus undermining the state's legitimacy and its ability to deliver core public services to its people (Banerjee 2009). This was the case with the Dahla Dam project, managed by Canadian firms, and with hundreds of "quick-impact projects" (QIPs) that the Provincial Reconstruction Team (PRT) implemented in Kandahar (Moens 2008, 579).[6] While Ottawa's supply-driven approach to aid delivery raised Canada's visibility in Kandahar, it did little to foster national ownership or strengthen the central state (Banerjee 2009). According to Jonathan Goodhand and Mark Sedra (2010), the broader insistence of Western donors on fairly orthodox market-oriented economic policies has also undermined national ownership and the emergence of a viable Afghan state.

Third, many Canadian development projects were components of ISAF's counter-insurgency strategy, aiming to win the hearts and minds of ordinary Afghans (Holland 2010, 272). Although the OECD ODA eligibility criteria precluded CIDA from using ODA for certain security-related activities, much of Canadian aid directly or indirectly served the military-led counter-insurgency strategy and PRT-led activities in Kandahar. Securitized aid practices made it difficult to uphold development principles such as consultation and community participation, as well as proper monitoring and evaluation (Banerjee 2009). The overwhelming presence and resources of the DND also limited the influence of CIDA at the WOG table – in Ottawa and in Afghanistan.

Fourth, the gap between results claimed and actual outcomes is also apparent in the realm of democratic governance. The ruling elite around the Karzai family control politics in Afghanistan, despite achievements at the level of new laws, institutions, and women's participation. Many observers agree that this network stole the 2009 and 2010 elections through intimidation and fraud (Banerjee 2010). As such, despite its stated intentions, Canada actually aided the consolidation of an illiberal, neo-patrimonial democracy, rather than contributing to genuine democratic transformation in Afghanistan.

Such tendencies are inconsistent with Canada's commitments in the Paris Declaration and the Fragile State Principles – such as strengthening the state, ensuring mutual accountability for development results, and fostering the local sustainability of development efforts. Together, they beg the deeper question of "how much development work can be carried out in a war zone" (Brown 2008, 97). They also offer strong support for critical analysts who see Western involvement in fragile states as an attempt to impose order and security on the violent peripheries of the global political economy, even at the expense of other values such as liberal democracy.

CANADA AND DEVELOPMENT IN HAITI

Haiti shares common features of state fragility such as weak public institutions, a dependent economy, recurrent governance and environmental crises, and periodic international interventions (Fatton 2007). A major difference between this Caribbean society and the other two cases is that Haiti has not recently been engulfed in a major war. Nonetheless, the governance crisis in February 2004 led to a US-French-Canadian military intervention that removed President Jean-Bertrand Aristide from power. Since mid-2004, over 10,000 foreign military and police personnel have been deployed in the country under the aegis of the UN Stabilization Mission in Haiti (known by its French acronym, MINUSTAH). In January 2010 Haiti suffered the most destructive earthquake in its history, leaving about 220,000 dead and two million persons displaced – out of a population of ten million (ICG 2010).

Canada has been involved in Haiti for generations. However, in the aftermath of the 2004 intervention, Ottawa redoubled its engagement. As Brazil and other South American states took over the military lead through the UN, Canada and other Western states reoriented their roles to provide diplomatic support to MINUSTAH and development assistance to Haiti. In 2004–06 Ottawa developed a WOG approach to support the transitional government and help prepare the election of a more legitimate regime.[7] It included restoring core state functions such as public security and development planning, helping to organize elections, and contributing to economic reactivation and the restoration of social services. Canada disbursed over $200 million in international assistance during the first two years, distributing it fairly evenly among governance, security, humanitarian, and economic and social development efforts (Baranyi 2011).

Shortly after Haiti's 2006 elections, Ottawa made a five-year commitment of $555 million to Haiti, situating the country as the largest recipient of Canadian assistance in the Americas and the second-largest in the world after Afghanistan (Canada 2011i). CIDA developed a country program aligned with the Haiti Interim Poverty Reduction Strategy, focusing on strengthening national governance, access to basic social services, and humanitarian relief.[8] Through its Stabilization and Reconstruction Task Force (START), the Department of Foreign Affairs and International Trade (DFAIT) established its own portfolio in Haiti, mostly in the area of security. The Harper government underscored Canada's intent to remain a major international actor in Haiti.

As indicated in Table 2, from April 2005 to March 2010, CIDA and other government departments disbursed almost $823 million (88 per cent) of the almost $939 million in Canadian assistance to Haiti. In addition, DFAIT spent about $44 million (4.6 per cent) on activities related to public security (police, prisons, and border security), while DND spent about $71 million (7.5 per cent) of Canadian contributions in four military operations during that time frame.

After the earthquake, Canadians citizens and private institutions contributed $220 million to Haiti. CIDA matched that amount and pledged $400 million in new funds over two years to assist the country's reconstruction, based on the government of Haiti's Action Plan (CIDA 2011c). Motivated partly by humanitarian compassion, Canada's large official commitments were also driven by the Harper government's desire to remain a major player in Haiti and specifically to obtain a seat on the Interim Haiti Recovery Commission (Baranyi 2011).

CIDA has pointed to significant results from those investments in Haiti in several priority areas. For children and youth, CIDA's $17.5-million grant via the Pan-American Health Organization helped reactivate the Ministry of Health's Expanded National

Table 2
Canadian Bilateral International Assistance to Haiti
(in Millions, Fiscal Years 2005–10)

CAD millions	2005–06	2006–07	2007–08	2008–09	2009–10
ODA					
CIDA	96	93	103	135	247
OGDs	2	17	21	38	71
Total ODA	98	110	124	173	318
Non-ODA					
DFAIT	N/A	15	N/A	15	14
DND	0.1	1.4	61	7	2
Total	98.1	126.4	185	195	334

Sources: See n.5.

Vaccination Program (CIDA 2008a; 2011a). With respect to economic growth, a $15-million CIDA grant greatly reduced Haiti's debt to the Inter-American Development Bank (IDB), a $14-million grant strengthened the planning capacity of the Ministry of Planning and External Cooperation, and a $75-million grant via the IDB helped initiate the construction of new roads linking Jérémie to Les Cayes in the southwestern region (CIDA 2008a; 2011a). CIDA's support for the distribution of seeds, grains, compost, and manure to Haitian farmers also helped improve food production and reduce food insecurity (CIDA 2011a). As for democratic governance, CIDA support for the preparation and distribution of over 480,000 identification cards during the 2010 elections enabled people to access public services and vote (CIDA 2011a).

Those activities and results seem impressive, but few have been corroborated by systematic, publicly available evaluations. Moreover, Ottawa's claims have fuelled healthy debates about the appropriateness and outcomes of Canadian development assistance. Robert Muggah (2007) notes that, over the previous three decades, Canada's programming in Haiti swung between reinforcing state institutions and supporting civil society. After 2004, Canadian officials remained distrustful of Haitian public institutions and continued to channel funds mainly through NGOs and international organizations. Still, other observers (including Baranyi 2011) have accepted Ottawa's claim that much assistance has gone to strengthening Haitian state institutions, including central agencies like the Ministry of Planning and Cooperation and departments such as the Ministry of Health. That trend also applies to the security sector, where DFAIT and CIDA funds have gone mostly to state institutions, such as the police.

This has led some analysts to argue that Canadian WOG engagement in Haiti has, as in Afghanistan, also privileged security instruments (Zebich-Knos 2008; Shamsie 2008). Security funding did indeed increase after 2005, yet, as the data in Table 2 indicate, security received only 12 per cent of Canadian assistance to Haiti. The lion's share (88 per cent) was directed at relief, reconstruction, access to social services, and economic reactivation, rather than security activities per se. Promoting stability was certainly one aim of those humanitarian, economic, and social investments. Yet, given that they were oriented by development strategies and controlled by civilian agencies, it is inaccurate to speak of a securitization of Canadian (or broader) assistance in Haiti.

Shamsie (2008) suggests that Canada invested mainly in the institutions of liberal democracy without promoting the participation required for transformative development. For her, that approach failed to address the predatory character of elites or the need to support struggles for radical change. Shamsie and others have also argued that Canada supported inappropriate market-oriented approaches to development in Haiti from the late 1980s, especially after 2004 (Shamsie 2008; Thede 2008). In particular, they have suggested that Canada supported a strategy privileging export-processing activities while neglecting agriculture and rural development. An assessment by Rights and Democracy (2010) of Canada's assistance after the earthquake suggests that Canada has also privileged short-term relief, early recovery, and security, disproportionately channelling funds via Canadian and international executing agencies.

Without contesting the essence of that analysis, Stephen Baranyi (2011) argues that CIDA has nurtured the social basis of democracy through modest support to women's organizations and through Rights and Democracy's dedicated support to civil society organizations. He also notes that CIDA and DFAIT have in fact supported the reconstitution of state functions in areas from public security to health and financial planning. Moreover, CIDA's support for agriculture increased significantly after the 2008 food-security crisis (Baranyi 2011).

Nonetheless, the earthquake reminds us that Canadian investments are fragile, even though Haiti is not at war. The earthquake killed numerous officials whose capacities were being developed with Canadian assistance and destroyed infrastructure that was built with Canadian aid. The ruling party Inité's resort to fraud during the 2010–11 elections and the international community's initial embrace of President Michel Martelly – despite his party's use of violence and an extremely low voter turnout in the March 2011 presidential elections – also illustrate how tenuous democracy remains in Haiti.

Those events certainly raise questions about the sustainability of aid. In 2010 Canada and other donors pledged over $10 billion over two years to help Haiti "build back better." Yet the slow pace of reconstruction, the shaky legitimacy of the new government, and the minimal investment in structural change (e.g., in the creation of sustainable livelihoods for poor urban youth) could converge to rekindle protest and donor fatigue. These mixed tendencies suggest that Brown's (2008) question about the viability of development is also germane to fragile situations that are not "war zones."

More critical analysts, such as Thede (2008), have concluded that Canada's approach in Haiti reflected the post-9/11 wave of Western interventions aiming to control chaotic peripheries through strategies combining security and market-oriented reforms. Yet a careful analysis of the record suggests a more nuanced picture. Canada has certainly backed market-oriented economic policies and contributed to security-sector reform there. Yet it has also adhered to international aid effectiveness principles by making a serious effort to respect national ownership, strengthen the state, and link development to security without letting the latter dominate the effort. Likewise, Canada has supported civil society rights-based advocacy. A subtle analysis, informed by critical social constructivism, is required to capture these important distinctions.

CANADA AND DEVELOPMENT IN SUDAN

Sudan is a vast East African country with a population of over forty-two million, whose economy is based on agriculture, commerce, and oil extraction. Its authoritarian state has faced deep legitimacy crises, especially in the South, since it gained independence in 1956. While South Sudan became an independent state in July 2011, based on the 2005 Comprehensive Peace Agreement (CPA) and the January 2011 referendum, war persisted in Darfur after 2003. The UN Mission in Sudan (UNMIS), staffed by about 10,000 security personnel, oversees the CPA's implementation, while the UN-African Union (AU) Mission in Darfur (UNAMID), with about 22,000 security personnel, monitors the more limited accords in Darfur (Collins 2008; ICG 2011).

Although Canada has been engaged in Sudan for decades, the CPA and the crisis in Darfur provided the Canadian government with the opportunity to apply its emerging WOG approach to its policies and programming in an important part of Africa. In 2005 the government established the interdepartmental Sudan Task Force to coordinate Canada's humanitarian assistance, early recovery programming, peacekeeping, peacebuilding, and diplomatic efforts in Sudan (Canada 2010).

In Darfur, Canada financed the provision of large-scale humanitarian assistance to persons displaced by violence and supported the deployment of successive African Union peace missions by providing military assets, senior personnel, and training. In addition, Ottawa furnished direct assistance to African-led peace talks on Darfur, while actively supporting the indictment issued by the International Criminal Court against Sudanese president Oman al-Bashir (Canada 2010). In the rest of Sudan, Canada directed its efforts toward the implementation of the CPA by deploying Canadian Forces personnel and civilian police officers to UNMIS and providing diplomatic and technical support to the historic 2010 elections – the first multiparty elections in more than twenty years – and the 2011 referendum (Canada 2010). DFAIT and CIDA also funded projects to enhance the capacity of the new government of South Sudan (GOSS).

As shown in Table 3, between 2005 and 2010, Canada contributed about $626 million to those activities in Sudan. Of that amount, CIDA and other government departments contributed $452 million (73 per cent), mostly to humanitarian and early recovery activities. DFAIT contributed $115 million (18 per cent) in non-ODA assistance while DND spent $59 million (9 per cent) on military-support operations during that period.

CIDA claims significant results from these investments in its priority areas for Sudan. For children and youth, CIDA support facilitated vocational training and income-generating activities for 20,000 people, training for 2,300 teachers, and the rehabilitation of 250 schools during fiscal year 2009–10 (CIDA 2011a). During that year, CIDA also contributed to a 30 per cent increase in births attended by a skilled health staff and a 33 per cent increase in the number of doctors in

Table 3
Canadian Bilateral International Assistance to Sudan
(in Millions, Fiscal Years 2005–10)

CAD millions	2005–06	2006–07	2007–08	2008–09	2009–10
		ODA			
CIDA	69	64	65	98	101
OGDS	3	6	9	21	16
Total ODA	72	70	74	119	117
		Non-ODA			
DFAIT	N/A	60	N/A	40	15
DND	5	5	7	17	25
Total	77	135	81	176	157

Sources: See n.5.

South Sudan (CIDA 2011a). With respect to food security, CIDA's support – for the distribution of agro-forestry inputs (seeds, tools, etc.), business training, and the dissemination of improved agricultural technologies – benefitted 154 farmer groups (CIDA 2011a). CIDA funding also enabled the training of 500 trainers in civic and voter education, contributing to the free and fair elections in 2010 and to the legitimate referendum process in early 2011 (CIDA 2011a).

Several patterns stand out with regard to those activities. First, much Canadian aid was delivered through multilateral channels, particularly in Darfur and in the North, because of Canada's objections to Khartoum's allegedly genocidal policies. It was easier to align Canadian aid with governmental plans in the South, given Ottawa's broad agreement with the policies of the GOSS. There, CIDA focused its aid on children and youth, food security, and governance, in the framework of CPA implementation (CIDA 2011a). Through the Joint Donor Team, Canada and other like-minded donors strengthened the planning, management, and service-delivery capacities of the GOSS (North-South Institute 2009). Those were important steps toward adhering to the Paris Declaration and the Fragile States Principles, at least in South Sudan.

Second, Ottawa made substantial contributions to AU and UN peace missions in the country. The bulk of the non-ODA assistance noted in Table 3 went to UNMIS and UNAMID, which sought to protect lives and facilitate humanitarian aid. As indicated in Table 3, the rest (73 per cent) of Canadian assistance to Sudan was directed to relief or development. The bulk of Canadian aid was managed by civilian agencies and did not directly serve security strategies. In Sudan as in Haiti, one can therefore also conclude that Canadian aid was not securitized.

Third, although Canada has supported civil society in Sudan for decades, the North-South Institute (2009) suggests that such support has been ad hoc and limited. That observation was echoed by a report of the parliamentary Standing Committee on Foreign Affairs and International Development (SCFAID 2010), which suggested that much more could be done to support civil society organizations, such as the churches and women's organizations. SCFAID also noted that, even in the South, CIDA has not made substantial investments in longer-term development activities, essential for forging a viable South Sudanese state.

A multi-donor evaluation of peacebuilding in South Sudan, in which Canada participated, confirms that donor coordination and capacity-building support for GOSS institutions increased in recent years. Yet the report highlights the "dearth of activities focused specifically on supporting young peoples' livelihoods and/or employment opportunities" (Bennett et al. 2010, xvii). It also notes disconnects between GOSS attempts to decentralize development to the regions, continued donor focus on Juba, and the fragmentation of community-based activities supported by NGOs.

Canadian involvement in Sudan underscores the difficulties of fostering development in fragile situations, especially those affected by war. It lends support to critical interpretations of Western attempts to impose security on the peripheries of the global political economy. Yet, as in the Haitian case, a careful reading of the record suggests a more nuanced picture. In South Sudan, Canada took steps to adhere to international-aid effectiveness principles by respecting national ownership, strengthening the state, and jointly evaluating results. Canada pursued development and security without letting the latter dominate the effort. In South Sudan, there was also limited support for civil society and longer-term development. Such nuances underscore the need for a more textured analysis of Canadian engagement in fragile states.

REVISITING THE BIG PICTURE

A comparison of Canadian involvement in Afghanistan, Haiti, and Sudan confirms the common shape of the development pillar in Canada's WOG approaches. DFAIT and especially CIDA established large assistance programs in those fragile states. Their programs were coordinated with central agencies and OGDs, in Ottawa and in the field. They were aligned with national development plans in each context, though they also reflected Canadian priorities, such as CIDA's focus on children and youth. Despite commitments to the Paris Declaration and the Fragile States Principles, Canadian aid was largely channelled through international agencies. There also was a strong focus on humanitarian assistance and other short-term activities. Thus, while advances have been made in each context, the most striking pattern is the modest nature of development results despite the scale of investments made by Canada. The general weakness of evaluating development programming in these contexts is a corollary of this trend.

Beyond those common patterns, there are important divergences. In Afghanistan, the use of aid for security purposes was a dominant tendency, with DND leading WOG efforts through the PRT in Kandahar. In Haiti and Sudan, that feature was much less salient, with CIDA playing an important role in WOG efforts. Moreover, while defence expenditures were the largest share of WGO efforts in Afghanistan, owing to Canada's commitment of almost 3,000 troops to the US/NATO-led counter-insurgency efforts, in Haiti and Sudan the bulk of WOG spending was directed toward humanitarian aid, governance, and socio-economic development.

While Canada's focus on security in Kandahar influenced the geographic distribution and the delivery mechanisms of Canadian ODA in Afghanistan, in Haiti and Sudan ODA was more national in scope. In Haiti and in South Sudan, CIDA and DFAIT also invested significant funds in strengthening the state – not only its security agencies, but also its financial, judicial, public-health, and other institutions. In South Sudan and in Haiti before the earthquake, Canada made concerted efforts to strengthen state capacity in order to diminish dependence on international agencies. Despite the emphasis on humanitarian aid and short-term projects, Canada also invested in infrastructure, agriculture, democratic governance, and other aspects of longer-term development, especially in Haiti.

What combination of factors explains these commonalities and differences? As Stewart Patrick and Kaysie Brown (2007) have noted, successive Canadian governments' decisions to adopt WOG approaches and make Afghanistan, Haiti, and Sudan priorities set the parameters for Canada's development engagement in those fragile states. The drive to position Canada as a key player in strategic places, present under previous Liberal governments but more explicit under Harper's Conservatives, certainly influenced the scale and tenor of Canada's engagement in those fragile states. The post-9/11 international discourse also pushed Canada and to some extent CIDA toward framing the fragile states as a security threat requiring WOG responses linking development to security (see Brown, chapter 3, this volume).

Similarities on the ground also pulled Canada and other donor countries in common directions. It was partly the weakness of the state and the persistence of neo-patrimonial politics that explain why CIDA and DFAIT tended to channel most ODA through international organizations and NGOs, despite Canada's adherence to the Paris Declaration and the Fragile States Principles. Similarly, persistent violence and human vulnerability made it difficult to move from relief and recovery to sustainable development in those societies.

Yet those countries' distinct situations also shaped the differing outcomes of Canadian action in each context. Different forms and intensities of armed violence were central in this regard. The fact that Afghanistan was engulfed in a mid-intensity insurgency linked to a "Global War on Terror" in which the US and NATO were the leading powers on the ground, and that Canada had many combat forces in Kandahar province, compelled CIDA to contribute directly to counter-insurgency efforts. The political-military situation in Haiti was completely different. Although confrontations between military and irregular forces occurred in Haiti after 2004, the fact that Haiti was not at war and that foreign military forces operated under a UN umbrella (with Brazil and other Latin American states in the lead and no Canadian combat troops on the ground) gave CIDA more room to focus on poverty. Sudan had a mixture of these situations. In the South, the war's end, the presence of UNMIS, and the relative legitimacy of the new government opened space for putting international-aid effectiveness principles into practice. Nonetheless, Khartoum's policies, the conflict in Darfur, and territorial disputes in the South still greatly constrained long-term development cooperation, particularly in Darfur and in the North.

Canada is also connected to each of these fragile states in distinct ways. Shamsie (2008) and Thede (2008) credit the over 100,000 Canadians of Haitian origin living mostly in Quebec for motivating Canadian governments to provide generous aid to Haiti. Yet one cannot underestimate the influence of the thousands of other

Canadians (especially Québécois) who have passed through Haiti over the past twenty years – as diplomats, peacekeepers, visiting members of Parliament, NGO staff, investors, or journalists – and exerted low-profile pressure to keep Canada engaged in the country. The $220 million that ordinary Canadians donated to Haiti immediately after the earthquake is a poignant reminder of that constituency's presence.

Transnational relationships also connect Canada to Afghanistan and Sudan. But it is only in Haiti that a large, informed domestic constituency, the government of Quebec, and a strong Latin American presence on the ground have provided counterweights to influences coming from Washington or from NATO headquarters in Brussels. In Haiti, an informed Canadian constituency and a diverse group of international actors increased space for a balanced, development-oriented Canadian approach. In Afghanistan, transnational forces aligned the other way: there was neither a diverse domestic constituency nor a coherent regional presence to counterbalance the dominance of political and military actors determined to win the war and use ODA as a tool for that goal. Sudan lay between those situations, with transnational pressures privileging Canadian support for humanitarian action in Darfur, as well as peacekeeping and peacebuilding in South Sudan.

This comparison enriches critical analyses of Canadian and broader Western engagement in fragile states. While it confirms common tendencies like the linkage between development and security agendas, it also underscores differences across contexts. It validates critical analysts' views of how Western military engagement in the Afghan war has securitized aid there. Yet it shows how that version of the security-development nexus has not emerged in Haiti and in Sudan, given the distinct security situations on the ground, the different configuration of Canadian and Western actors there, and the roles that international organizations and regional coalitions played in mediating Western influence. The focused comparison also shows how, despite the greater room for development-oriented agency in Haiti and South Sudan, that space remained tenuous in both contexts. Finally, and in keeping with the spirit of critical social constructivism (notably its interest in understanding constraints and possibilities for human agency), these cases also extend the reach of Brown's (2008) question about what kind of development cooperation is possible in fragile states, whether or not they are involved in war.

CONCLUSION

At the time of writing, officials in Ottawa are completing an exercise to tease out lessons learned in Afghanistan and reflect on how they could be applied in other fragile states. This chapter will be published after that process has ended, yet it might inform the broader debate and help ground it in Canada's varied experiences in different fragile states. The election of a majority Conservative government in Canada in 2011 will probably facilitate the consolidation of WOG engagement in priority fragile states where Canadian diplomatic, security, and domestic political interests converge – albeit in different mixes. Afghanistan, Haiti, and Sudan are likely to remain priorities, though the trend toward decreasing aid to Afghanistan, given the West's pullback from that country, will probably continue. Conversely, assistance to South Sudan may increase because of its relatively smooth transition to independence in 2011.

Still, our research suggests that there are limits to higher levels of ODA in these contexts, owing both to their limited absorptive capacity and to the volatile situation on the ground. In Haiti as in Afghanistan, problematic elections, recurrent violence, and the paucity of tangible results will make it difficult to convince Canadians that huge sums of tax dollars are being well spent. Those conditions will persist unless those states and their main donors innovate outside the box of economic orthodoxy that has constrained policy in fragile states – for example, by investing much more in sustainable, labour-intensive activities like smallholder agriculture.

Given its understanding of structural constraints such as Western donors' bias toward market-oriented economic policies, critical social constructivism suggests that such innovation is unlikely and that violence will endure, thus justifying more security-driven approaches originating in Ottawa and in other Western capitals. This may not add up to the grand project of controlling chaotic borderlands suggested by some critical analysts, yet appreciating the enduring weight of historical structures helps us understand why development practices still fall so short of international ideals, in war zones and in other states of fragility.

Further research is required on what has happened with Canadian engagement in fragile states since 9/11. Our preliminary analysis has underscored the need for more studies of development results in each context, preferably rooted in field research on samples of

Canadian-supported projects there. Systematic comparisons of development cooperation by Canada and other donors in those contexts – not only other Western donors but also new donors and investors like Venezuela in Haiti, China in Sudan, and India in Afghanistan – would fill major knowledge gaps. Finally, our analysis has highlighted the need to explore more sophisticated explanations of Canadian assistance, particularly how the host society and international forces converge to shape uneven development outcomes. We hope this chapter will provoke further reflection on how critical social constructivism could help generate more textured understandings of the forms of international engagement in distinct fragile states.

NOTES

1 The Fragile States Principles emphasize the need to "take context as the starting point ... ensure activities do no harm, [prioritize] state-building [and] prevention, recognize the links between political, security and development objectives, align [activities] with local priorities, [and] act fast and for a sustainable period of time" (OECD 2007).

   The Paris Declaration affirms the following principles: aid recipients, in partnership with their parliaments and electorates, must forge their own national development strategies (ownership); donors must support national development strategies (alignment); donors must work to streamline their efforts in-country (harmonization); development policies and programs should aim to achieve clear goals, which require monitoring (results); and donors and recipients must be jointly responsible for achieving those goals (mutual accountability) (OECD DAC 2005).

2 As this study is a focused comparison, it sacrifices depth on particulars to gain a broader perspective. It is based mainly on a review of the secondary literature and of publicly available official documents. We have not delved into parliamentary debates or media coverage, nor have we carried out formal interviews for this preliminary analysis.

3 For the following analysis, securitization is defined as the direct linkage of development assistance to the promotion of the donor's military or security objectives.

4 The Compact emerged out of consultations between the government of Afghanistan, the UN, and the international community "to present the interim Afghanistan National Development Strategy and to ensure the

Government of Afghanistan has adequate resources to meet its domestic ambitions" (Embassy of Afghanistan 2006).

5 Sources: ODA disbursement figures were retrieved from the CIDA 2005–06, 2006–07, 2007–08, 2008–09, and 2009–10 Statistical Reports on Official International Assistance. Defence spending figures were retrieved from the DND 2005–06, 2006–07, 2007–08, 2008–09, and 2009–10 Departmental Performance Reports. DFAIT spending figures were retrieved from the 2006–07, 2008–09, and 2009–10 Departmental Performance Reports and CIDA's 2005–06 and 2007–08 Statistical Reports on Official International Assistance.

6 The PRT in Kandahar was taken over from the US-led Operation Enduring Freedom with the purpose of extending the authority of the Afghan government by promoting security, reconstruction, and improved governance structures. The personnel of the PRT consisted of members from the Canadian Forces, an RCMP civilian police contingent, CIDA representatives, and a DFAIT political director (Canada 2008a).

7 The transitional government was appointed in April 2004, shortly after the US-led intervention toppled President Aristide. It governed Haiti until the national elections in 2006.

8 The Interim Poverty Reduction Strategy (Document de Stratégie Nationale pour la Croissance et la Réduction de la Pauvreté) was officially adopted in November 2007.

REFERENCES

Afghanistan Compact. 2006. *Building on Success: The London Conference on Afghanistan.* London. 1–15.

Banerjee, Nipa. 2008. "Ineffective Aid Hobbles Afghan Transition." *Policy Options* (June). 24–7.

– 2009. "Afghanistan: No Security, No Governance." *Policy Options* (November). 66–71.

– 2010. "Aid Development for a Secure Afghanistan." *Policy Options* (November). 48–52.

Baranyi, Stephen, ed. 2008. *The Paradoxes of Peacebuilding Post-9/11.* Vancouver: University of British Columbia Press.

– 2011. "Canada and the Travail of Partnership in Haiti." In Andrew S. Thompson and Jorge Heine, eds., *Fixing Haiti: MINUSTAH and Beyond.* Tokyo and New York: UNU Press. 205–28.

Barfield, Thomas. 2010. *Afghanistan: A Cultural and Political History.* Princeton, NJ: Princeton University Press.

Bennett, Jon, Sara Pantuliano, Wendy Fenton, et al. 2010. "Aiding the Peace: A Multi-Donor Evaluation of Support to Conflict Prevention and Peacebuilding in Southern Sudan 2005–2010." The Hague: Netherlands Ministry of Foreign Affairs.

Brown, Stephen. 2007. "'Creating the World's Best Development Agency'? Confusion and Contradictions in CIDA's New Policy Blueprint." *Canadian Journal of Development Studies* 28, no. 2: 213–28.

– 2008. "CIDA under the Gun." In Jean Daudelin and Daniel Schwanen, eds., *Canada among Nations 2007: What Room to Manoeuvre?* Montreal and Kingston, ON: McGill-Queen's University Press. 91–107.

Buzan, Barry, and Lene Hansen. 2007. *International Security*. Vol. 4: *Challenging State Security*. London: Sage.

Canada. 2008a. "Afghanistan: Canadian Diplomatic Engagement." *Parliamentary Information and Research Service Publication* (PRB 07–38 E), 2–7.

– 2008b. *Report of the Independent Panel on Canada's Future Role in Afghanistan*. Ottawa: Ministry of Public Works and Government Services.

– 2010. "Canada's Approach." 20 October. http://www. canadainternational.gc.ca/sudan-soudan/approach-approche. aspx?lang=eng. Accessed 20 April 2011.

– 2011a. "Canada – Haiti Relations." 7 January. http://www. canadainternational.gc.ca/haiti/bilateral_relations_bilaterales/canada_ haiti.aspx. Accessed 20 April 2011.

– 2011b. "Canada's Approach in Afghanistan." 6 April. http://www. afghanistan.gc.ca/canada-afghanistan/approach-approche/index. aspx?lang=eng. Accessed 27 April 2011.

– 2011c. "Canada's Engagement in Sudan: Priorities and Objectives." 22 March. http://www.canadainternational.gc.ca/sudan-soudan/ engagement.aspx?lang=eng. Accessed 20 April 2011.

– 2011d. "Canada's Four Themes for Afghanistan: 2011–2014 (November 16, 2010)." 6 April. http://www.afghanistan.gc.ca/canada- afghanistan/news-nouvelles/2010/2010_11_16b.aspx?lang=eng. Accessed 27 April 2011.

– 2011e. "Canada's Priorities." 6 April. http://www.afghanistan.gc.ca/ canada-afghanistan/priorities-priorites/index.aspx?lang=en. Accessed 27 April 2011.

– 2011f. "Canadian Aid to Sudan." 21 March. http://www. canadainternational.gc.ca/sudan-soudan/humanitarian_aid-aide_ humanitaire.aspx?lang=eng. Accessed 20 April 2011.

– 2011g. "Development Projects." 6 April. http://www.afghanistan.gc.ca/
canada-afghanistan/projects-projets/dev.aspx. Accessed 20 April 2011.

– 2011h. "Diplomacy." 19 April. http://www.canadainternational.gc.ca/
sudan-soudan/diplomacy-diplomatie.aspx?lang=eng. Accessed 27 April
2011.

– 2011i. "Documents." 2 February. http://www.canadainternational.gc.ca/
sudan-soudan/brochure-depliant.aspx?lang=eng. Accessed 20 April
2011.

– 2011j. "FAQs: Rebuilding Haiti after the Earthquake." 7 January. http://
www.canadainternational.gc.ca/haiti/highlights-faits/Faq-Foire-
Reconstruction.aspx#. Accessed 26 June 2011.

– 2011k. "Our Priorities: Prosperity, Security, and Democratic Governance."
7 January. http://www.canadainternational.gc.ca/haiti/engagement/
priorities-priorites.aspx. Accessed 20 April 2011.

– 2011l. "Our Whole-of-Government Team." 11 January. http://www.
canadainternational.gc.ca/haiti/engagement/whole_of_government-
pangouvernementale.aspx. Accessed 20 April 2011.

Canadian Broadcasting Corporation. 2011. "Afghanistan: What's Next?"
The National. 12 May. http://www.cbc.ca/thenational/indepthanalysis/
story/2011/03/16/national-afghanistan2011.html. Accessed 7 June 2011.

Canadian International Development Agency. 2006. "Statistical Report on
Official Development Assistance (ODA) Fiscal Year 2005–2006." http://
www.acdi-cida.gc.ca/INET/IMAGES.NSF/vLUImages/Publications/$file/
StatisticalReport-ENG-2008-04-29_SM.pdf. Accessed 14 December
2011.

– 2007. "Statistical Report on ODA Fiscal Year 2006–2007." http://www.
acdi-cida.gc.ca/INET/IMAGES.NSF/vLUImages/ stats/$file/CIDA_
STATS_ REPORT_ON_ODAper cent202006-07-E.pdf. Accessed
14 December 2011.

– 2008a. "Haiti: CIDA Results 2007–2008." Gatineau, QC: Canadian
International Development Agency.

– 2008b. "Statistical Report on ODA Fiscal Year 2007–2008." http://www.
acdi-cida.gc.ca/INET/IMAGES.NSF/vLUImages/ stats/$file/Statistical_
Report_InternationalL_Assistance_2007-2008_EN.pdf. Accessed
14 December 2011.

– 2009a. "Afghanistan – Overview." http://www.acdi-cida.gc.ca/acdi-cida/
ACDI-CIDA.nsf/eng/JUD-125135935-QAA. Accessed 20 April 2011.

– 2009b. "Statistical Report on ODA Fiscal Year 2008–2009." http://www.
acdi-cida.gc.ca/INET/IMAGES.NSF/vLUImages/stats/$file/ STATISTICAL-
REPORT-2008-2009_ENG.pdf." Accessed 14 December 2011.

– 2010. "Statistical Report on ODA Fiscal Year 2009–2010." http://www.
acdi-cida.gc.ca/INET/IMAGES.NSF/vLUImages/stats /$file/Statistical_
Report_2009-2010_eng.pdf. Accessed 14 December 2011.
– 2011a. "Development for Results 2009–2010: At the Heart of Canada's
Efforts for a Better World." Gatineau, QC: Canadian International
Development Agency.
– 2011b. "Sudan." http://www.acdi-cida.gc.ca/acdi-cida/ACDI-CIDA.nsf/
Eng/JUD-217124359-NT2#tphp. Accessed 20 April 2011.
– 2011c. "Summary of Canada's Financial Contributions to Haiti in
Response to the Earthquake." http://www.acdi-cida.gc.ca/acdi-cida/
ACDI-CIDA.nsf/eng/FRA-4810272-JXY. Accessed 20 April 2011.
Canadian International Development Agency, Office of the Chief Audit
Executive (OCAE). 2009. "Audit of the Afghanistan Country Report –
Internal Audit Report." Gatineau, QC: Canadian International
Development Agency.
Carment, David, Stewart Prest, and Samy Yiagadeesen. 2009. *Security,
Development and the Fragile State: Bridging the Gap between Theory
and Policy*. London: Routledge.
Collins, Robert O. 2008. *A History of Modern Sudan*. Cambridge:
Cambridge University Press.
Cox, Robert. 2002. *The Political Economy of a Plural World: Critical
Reflections on Power, Morals and Civilisation*. London and New York:
Routledge.
Department of Foreign Affairs and International Trade. 2007.
"Departmental Performance Report 2006–2007 – Section II: Analysis of
Program Activity by Strategic Outcome." http://www.tbs-sct.gc.ca/dpr-
rmr/2006-2007/inst/ext/ext02-eng.asp. Accessed 7 June 2011.
– 2008. "Departmental Performance Report (DPR) 2007–2008:
Supplementary Information (Tables)." http://www.tbs-sct.gc.ca/dpr-rmr/
2008-2009/inst/ext/st-tspr-eng.asp?format=print. Accessed 7 June 2011.
– 2011. "Departmental Performance Report 2009–2010: Supplementary
Information (Tables)." http://www.tbs-sct.gc.ca/dpr-rmr/2009-2010/inst/
ext/st-tspr-eng.asp?format=print. Accessed 7 June 2011.
Department of National Defence. 2006. "Departmental Performance
Report for the period ending March 31, 2006. Section 7: Canadian
Forces Operations." http://www.collectionscanada.gc.ca/webarchives/
20061216162331/http://www.vcds.forces.gc.ca/dgsp/pubs/rep-pub/ddm/
dpr2006/sec7g_e.asp. Accessed 7 June 2011.
– 2007. "Departmental Performance Report for period Ending March 31,
2007. Section III: Financial and Human Resource Reporting." http://

www.tbs-sct.gc.ca/dpr-rmr/2006-2007/inst/dnd/dnd03-eng.asp. Accessed
   7 June 2011.
– 2008. "Departmental Performance Report 2007–2008. Supplementary
   Information (Tables)." http://www.tbs-sct.gc.ca/dpr-rmr/2007-2008/inst/
   dnd/st-tspr-eng.asp?format=print. Accessed 7 June 2011.
– 2009. "Departmental Performance Report 2008–2009. International
   Operations – Cost Estimates for Canadian Forces." http://www.vcds-
   vcemd.forces.gc.ca/sites/page-eng.asp?page=7445. Accessed 7 June 2011.
– 2010. "Departmental Performance Report 2009–2010. International
   Operations – Cost Estimates for Canadian Forces." http://www.vcds-
   vcemd.forces.gc.ca/sites/page-eng.asp?page=9424. Accessed 7 June 2011.
Duffield, Mark. 2001. *Global Governance and New Wars*. London and
   New York: Zed Books and Palgrave.
Embassy of Afghanistan, Washington. 2006. "Frequently Asked
   Questions." http://www.embassyofafghanistan.org/faqs/faqpolitics.html.
   Accessed 25 June 2011.
Fatton, Robert. 2007. *The Roots of Haitian Despotism*. Boulder, CO:
   Lynne Rienner.
Fund for Peace. 2011. "Failed States Index Scores 2010." http://www.
   fundforpeace.org/web/index2.php?option=com_content&task=view&
   id=452. Accessed 9 January 2011.
Goodhand, Jonathan, and Mark Sedra. 201. "Who Owns the Peace? Aid,
   Reconstruction and Peacebuilding in Afghanistan." *Disasters* (S1),
   S78–S102.
Holland, Kenneth. 2010. "The Canadian Provincial Reconstruction Team:
   The Arm of Development in Kandahar Province." *American Review of
   Canadian Studies* 40, no. 2: 276–91.
International Crisis Group. 2010. "Haiti: The Stakes of the Post-Quake
   Elections." Latin America/Caribbean Report 35. Bogotá and Brussels:
   International Crisis Group.
– 2011. "Politics and Transition in the New South Sudan." Nairobi and
   Brussels: International Crisis Group.
Moens, Alexander. 2008. "Afghanistan and the Revolution in Canadian
   Foreign Policy." *International Journal* 63, no. 3 (summer): 569–86.
Muggah, Robert. 2007. "The Perils of Changing Donor Priorities in Fragile
   States: The Case of Haiti." In Jennifer Walsh and Ngaire Woods, eds.,
   *Exporting Good Governance: Temptations and Challenges in Canada's
   Aid Program*. Waterloo, ON: CIGI and Wilfrid Laurier University Press.
   190–223.

North-South Institute. 2009. "The Future of Canada's Engagement in
Sudan." Ottawa: North-South Institute.

Organisation for Economic Co-operation and Development, Development
Assistance Committee. 2005. "Paris Declaration and Accra Agenda for
Action." http://www.oecd.org/document/18/0,3343 ,en_2649_3236398_
35401554_1_1_1_1,00.html. Accessed 27 June 2011.

– 2007. "Principles of Good International Engagement in Fragile States
and Situations." http://www.oecd.org/document/46/0,3343,en_2649_
33693550_35233262_1_1_1_1,00.html. Accessed 27 June 2011.

– 2008. "DAC Peer Review of Canada." OECD *Journal of Development* 8,
no. 4: 263–387.

– 2010. "Ensuring Fragile States Are Not Left Behind. Summary Report."
Paris: Organisation for Economic Co-operation and Development.

Patrick, Stewart, and Kaysie Brown. 2007. "Canada." In Stewart Patrick
and Kaysie Brown, eds., *Greater Than the Sum of Its Parts? Assessing
Whole of Government Approaches to Fragile States*. New York:
International Peace Academy. 56–74.

Potter, Mitch. 2010. "Security Standoff Stalls Canadian Dam Project in
Kandahar." *Toronto Star*. 9 June.

Rights and Democracy. 2010. "Canada's Assistance and Foreign Policy in
Haiti – Background and Strategic Directions Prior to the 2010
Earthquake." http://www.dd-rd.ca/site/_PDF/haiti/Canada_s_engagement_
in_Haiti_ Analysis_and_Perspectives_on_Canada_s_Post-Earthquake_
Assistance_to_Haiti.pdf. Accessed 25 April 2011.

Robinson, Bill. 2009. "Canadian Military Spending 2009." *Foreign Policy
Series* (March): 1–10.

Shamsie, Yasmine. 2008. "Canada's Approach to Democratization in
Haiti: Some Reflections for the Coming Years." *Canadian Foreign
Policy*, 14, no. 3: 87–101.

Standing Committee on Foreign Affairs and International Development.
2008. "Canada in Afghanistan." *Report of the Standing Committee on
Foreign Affairs and International Development, 39th Parliament, 2nd
Session*. Ottawa: Communications Canada.

– 2010. "The Referendum in Sudan: Where to after 2011?" *Report of
the Standing Committee on Foreign Affairs and International
Development, 40th Parliament, 3rd Session*. Ottawa: Communications
Canada.

Stein, Janice Gross, and Eugene Lang. 2007. *The Unexpected War:
Canada in Kandahar*. Toronto: Viking Canada.

Thede, Nancy. 2008. "Human Security, Democracy, and Development in the Americas: The Washington Consensus Redux?" *Canadian Journal of Latin American and Caribbean Studies*, 33, no. 65: 33–56.

World Bank. 2011. *World Development Report 2011. Conflict, Security and Development*. Washington and Oxford: World Bank and Oxford University Press.

Zebich-Knos, Michele. 2008. "The Honest Broker? Canada's Role in Haitian Development." *Revista Mexicana de Estudios Canadienses* 15: 29–51.

5

Gender, Security, and Instrumentalism: Canada's Foreign Aid in Support of National Interest?

LIAM SWISS

For decades, foreign aid has been portrayed as a tool of foreign policy and national interest (Morgenthau 1962). Nowhere has this been more evident in recent years than in the alignment of aid priorities with security concerns by an array of donors. This chapter examines the "securitization" of Canadian bilateral aid as an example of this instrumentalization of aid and argues that it has been conducted at the expense of other development objectives in Canada's aid program, including its nearly thirty-five-year focus on women's rights and gender equality (GE). By examining quantitative patterns in the allocation of aid, and drawing on qualitative data collected during interviews with Canadian International Development Agency (CIDA) officials, I argue that as Canadian aid becomes increasingly instrumentalized to support Canadian security interests and foreign policy objectives, the room to prioritize altruistic issues like GE – perceived by many as a traditional Canadian strength – is simultaneously diminishing. This is most evident in the creation of new pools of money and funding mechanisms to focus on security at the same time that the priority attached to aid in support of GE is waning, a trend connected to the increasing reliance on weak mainstreaming efforts and to the growing unacceptability of GE discourse at CIDA. Mainstreaming in this context is the process of incorporating a gender analysis into all aid programming or policy to be sure that the intervention is cognizant of its impact on GE and/or makes a positive contribution toward promoting equality. Not only is priority accorded to GE on the decline, recent events suggest that gender appears now to be a priority for Canada only when it serves an instrumental purpose or Canadian interest.

In recent years Canadian official development assistance (ODA) has shifted to include a greater focus on countries in conflict or post-conflict situations. The fact that in 2007–08 three of the top four recipient states of Canadian bilateral ODA fell into this category, and the top recipient (Afghanistan) received more than 6 per cent of Canada's bilateral aid, provides stark evidence of this shift. Only a decade earlier, just one of the top four recipients of Canadian aid fit these criteria (OECD 2009).[1] The shift toward a greater concentration of Canadian aid to states in conflict or prone to conflict is reflective of a corresponding trend in the global distribution and focus of ODA. Indeed, since the early 2000s, the relationship between development, conflict, and security has become a central preoccupation of aid donors globally, resulting in new approaches to aid and security and the expansion of aid delivery in areas previously avoided by the aid sector. Some have labelled this shift the "securitization" of aid to denote the extent to which development funds have been employed as a tool for achieving a variety of security and defence objectives (Woods 2005). Aside from the growing concentration of aid in conflict-prone countries, a new focus for aid has emerged in the area of security-sector reform (SSR), where ODA funds are employed to achieve improvements in the quality of recipient countries' security apparatus, including national institutions such as customs and borders agencies, correctional systems, the police, the judiciary, and in some cases even the military (Brzoska 2003; Ebo 2007; OECD 2005).

Arguments in favour of the securitization of aid usually refer to the concept of enlightened self-interest. By helping key recipient countries improve their security and development, donor countries benefit in a variety of ways – not least with their own national security being better protected from outside attacks and terrorism. Thus, the perceived security of donor countries becomes tied directly to foreign aid's ability to improve security in recipient countries and make them less hospitable to insurgents and terrorist groups that might attack the West. In this context, the link between the securitization of aid and the recent "Global War on Terror" cannot be easily dismissed. Through the securitization of aid, ODA is being used instrumentally to achieve security objectives in the developing world that directly contribute to domestic security in donor states.

The impact of this process on ODA globally, and more specifically on Canadian aid, has been little studied until now. This is due largely to the novelty of the securitization phenomenon. In this chapter, therefore, I examine the trend of securitization of Canadian aid in the broader context of changes to traditional support of GE as one of Canada's aid priorities. By examining the securitization process within the Canadian context, I will demonstrate how in recent years Canadian aid has experienced an increased degree of instrumentalization as a tool of foreign policy. I will argue that the global phenomenon of securitization conveniently subverts Canada's aid program to foreign policy and security objectives, while making poverty reduction and other altruistic aims like GE, child protection, sexual and reproductive health, or human rights more difficult to promote.

The main hypothesis under examination is that this instrumentalization of aid in the name of security occurs simultaneously with a pattern of diminishing resources and priority accorded to GE and other altruistic aid objectives. Accordingly, I will address the following questions: What relationship is there between the securitization of aid and the reduced commitment to GE? In other words, are there links between the two trends or is it a mere coincidence that they occur simultaneously? To what extent are both trends reflective of increasing instrumentalism in Canadian aid policy? The chapter will first undertake an examination of the securitization process in Canadian aid provision, with a particular focus on the motivations for providing aid. Subsequently, I will demonstrate that the securitization of aid reflects a closer alignment of aid objectives with foreign policy objectives.

BACKGROUND

Canadian Aid Motivations

Since its inception, Canadian development assistance has oscillated between the often contradictory motivations of maintaining Canadian national interests and assisting worse-off countries and peoples (Pratt 1994b; Rawkins 1994; Morrison 1998; Otter 2003; Noël et al. 2004). As Canada has no geographic proximity to the developing world, and no foreign colonial history, its direct ties to most countries of the developing world are limited, although these have expanded in recent years with increased immigration and trade.

In the early years of aid, before the formation of CIDA, Canada's aid was more closely linked to commercial objectives, trade relationships, and foreign policy objectives – all issues of national interest. After 1968 and the formation of CIDA, some research indicates a departure from the national-interest position, with an attempt by CIDA to make Canadian aid truly benefit poor countries, supported by lobbying from civil society (Lumsdaine 1993). However, after 1977, the inter-linking of Canadian aid to foreign policy and other national interests became a more prominent characteristic of Canada's aid program (Morrison 1994; Pratt 1994a). After a swing back toward humani-tarianism in the late 1990s, the last decade has seen a resurgence of national interest in aid motivation. Against this background, it would appear that Canada's development assistance is underpinned by altru-istic humanitarian concerns and the promotion of Canadian interests alike. Efforts in recent years to narrow the number of countries to which Canada provides aid have also furthered national-interest motivations, given that many of the countries prioritized attained this status because of some foreign policy (Afghanistan, Iraq), economic (China), or diasporic (Philippines, Ukraine) tie to Canada rather than because they were among the poorest of poor countries. The most recent list of CIDA focus countries sustains this trend in many ways (CIDA 2009). The priority accorded to national interest as an aid motivation has thus peaked in recent years. Quantitative analysis of trends in the destination of Canadian aid confirms the growing impor-tance of self-interest as a motive (Macdonald and Hoddinott 2004).

Canada's motivations for providing aid have been mixed in the past and it is fair to assume that they will remain so in the future. However, reducing motivations for providing aid to a dichotomy of altruism versus interest does a disservice to the complexity of the politics of aid. Indeed, it is more accurate to depict Canada's instru-mental use of aid as a tool to achieve other objectives as selective and in constant flux. This chapter shows how the securitization trend in recent years reflects this fluctuating set of motivations. Indeed, securitization has occurred in parallel with diminishing attention paid to other concerns such as GE which are more closely aligned with international humanitarian altruism.

The Securitization of Aid

For much of the early history of ODA, spending tended to dry up when a country experienced conflict and insecurity. Instead, attention would shift to managing humanitarian crises arising from the conflict. With the apparent increase in intrastate conflict in the developing world following the end of the Cold War, a new perspective on the relationship between conflict and development has emerged (Woods 2005). Serious concerns about the possible impact of aid on the Rwandan genocide (Uvin 1999; Andersen 2000) and the realization that protracted conflict in recipient countries could no longer be ignored by donors have led to widespread acceptance of the idea that the development of a state is directly linked to its security status. Consequently, development assistance has become more closely linked to the arena of national security in both recipient and donor countries. Recipient-country security is discussed as a prerequisite for effective development and simultaneously cast as a concern for the national security of donor countries. This interrelationship is typified in discourse on how donors must prevent states from collapsing so they do not become safe havens for terrorist groups and other movements that threaten national security in the West. Regardless of the veracity of these concerns, donors are responding by adapting their aid programs in two ways: 1) aid donors are more frequently continuing ongoing medium-term development-assistance programming in countries in the midst of conflict or in its immediate aftermath; and 2) new models for ODA have emerged specifically targeting the improvement of security in recipient countries through support to SSR. These two trends comprise what can broadly be labelled the "securitization of aid."

This phenomenon has not been explored to any great extent in the context of Canadian aid. Indeed, from most standpoints, the securitization process within Canada has been a quiet and implicit one. There are two reasons for this: the securitization of aid at CIDA has occurred in the absence of an overall institutional policy for engaging in situations of conflict and insecurity, and, as a result, interventions and increases in aid to states in conflict have been conducted in an ad hoc manner responding to larger Canadian foreign policy interests; and much of the funding for security-sector interventions and other peacebuilding interventions that qualify as Canadian ODA are implemented through the Stabilization and Reconstruction Task Force (START) and the Global Peace and Security Fund (GPSF), both managed by the Department of Foreign Affairs and International Trade (DFAIT), leaving this spending disconnected from the larger part of Canadian bilateral ODA. Securitization in Canada has therefore not been studied rigorously within the research literature on

Canadian aid. Stephen Brown (2008) makes reference to the fact that CIDA is increasingly subject to decisions made by the Prime Minister's Office and other external actors in efforts to shore up security concerns; however, a more specific examination of the impacts of this process remains absent in the literature. Other recent examinations of Canadian aid have emphasized the set-up of the aid architecture or the implementation of aid effectiveness (Black and Tiessen 2007; Brown 2007; Lalonde 2009) rather than addressing the creeping securitization of Canadian ODA.

The fact that the impact of the securitization of Canadian aid on other aid priorities has not been examined is particularly relevant to the research context of this chapter. Though I cannot make direct causal links between the two phenomena, it is important to question how this implicit shift in focus has paralleled diminishing or flat aid spending on other areas of traditional Canadian leadership in the aid field. The case that I examine in this chapter is Canada's aid in support of GE.

Gender Equality and Canadian Aid

Canada has a long history of supporting women's rights and GE through its aid programs. From its first policy on women in development in 1976, Canada has been perceived for more than thirty years as a leader on women's issues in the development process (Rathgeber 1990; Rathgeber 1995; Swiss 2009). CIDA has carried the banner of GE for most of this time. Since 1999, its GE policy has called for the integration of gender as a crosscutting issue in all CIDA programming while outlining approaches to gender-specific programming that explicitly target gender equality and women's rights (CIDA 1999). With this long history of support and strongly institutionalized framework, Canada has been lauded by its donor peers for its leadership and support of GE and women's rights. Indeed, recent Organisation for Economic Co-operation and Development/ Development Assistance Committee (OECD/DAC) peer reviews refer to Canada's management of aid in this regard in glowing terms (OECD 2007b). Given the aid effectiveness agenda's focus on long-term commitments and capitalizing on donor strengths, the seeming desertion of its strong commitment to GE is troubling.

For all this, a disturbing trend has since emerged within CIDA: support for gender equality is flagging, marked by reduced levels of spending and support for GE at the top levels of management and ministerial oversight – a phenomenon noted in other departments such as DFAIT (Plewes and Kerr 2010). The 2010 decision to stop funding MATCH International, a leading Canadian development non-governmental organization (NGO) in the GE field, is but one indication of this decline in support of gender equality at CIDA (Plewes and Kerr 2010). In 2007 CIDA changed its rhetoric; it would no longer refer to "gender equality," preferring instead to discuss "equality between women and men." This shift in discourse is further indication of an institutional distancing from previous principles of supporting GE through reform of socially constructed gender relations in recipient states. Labelling gender inequalities in such a manner disassociates CIDA and Canada from the globally established discourse on gender and development and panders to a conservative domestic constituency within Canada that perceives GE as outside the desired ambit of the present government. As a result, organizations submitting applications for funding to CIDA are reportedly being told to "remove the words 'gender equality' from their proposal if they want a chance at funding" (Plewes and Kerr 2010).

This diminishing support for GE coincides with an increase in aid to states in situations of conflict and fragility. To better understand this, we need to examine the links between GE support and the achievement of broader foreign policy and security objectives.

Instrumentalizing Aid and Gender Equality

The most apparent link between these aid policy trends is seen in the instrumentalization of GE as a tool for generating support for international objectives or for staged or overt demonstrations of international leadership. The former has frequently been the case when nations try to legitimize military intervention against other states or insurgent groups for reasons to do with liberating women from oppression (Cohn and Enloe 2003). This is evidenced by NATO's rhetoric around the invasion of Afghanistan in 2001 to supposedly save Afghan women from oppression under the Taliban regime (Blanchard 2003). In this instance, GE was employed as a tool to legitimize significant military intervention and the achievement of NATO and Canadian security objectives.

Instrumentalization of gender was also apparent in Canada's announced focus on maternal and child health as its significant priority at the June 2010 G8 meetings it hosted. In its attempts to shore up support for international goals around maternal and child health, the government forced CIDA's hand to focus efforts around these two priorities while simultaneously generating significant domestic and international controversy by questioning whether the full range of sexual and reproductive health options – including access to abortion – would fall under the proposed funding. The aim of the government of Canada in spearheading a G8 initiative of this sort seems to reflect a legitimate concern for a significant health challenge in the developing world, as well as a desire to put a Canadian stamp on a worthwhile international initiative so as to generate prestige and positive reporting around the Summit. Here again, we see how GE is being used as a tool to achieve broader foreign policy aims. The obvious contradiction inherent in concentrating on maternal and child care while concurrently gutting CIDA's focus on GE has not been lost on the government's critics (Plewes and Kerr 2010).

The securitization of aid and the recent diminishing priority accorded GE within Canadian aid programs both reflect the explicit instrumentalization of aid as a tool of Canadian foreign policy. In this respect, Canadian aid is again witness to a shift in motivations, with the pendulum swinging toward national interests rather than international humanitarianism. The diminishing support for gender equality is part and parcel of this shift and manifests the shrinking space for more altruistic objectives within the Canadian aid envelope, as well as the wider ideological project of the Conservative Party of Canada. This rejection of GE was evident in the advice of Conservative Senator Nancy Ruth to aid groups ahead of the June 2010 G8 conference that they should "shut the fuck up" regarding sexual and reproductive health and women's rights because "if you push there will be more backlash" (Delacourt 2010). The backlash she mentions is representative of the Conservative abandonment of GE across government. Such comments highlight how aid groups in Canada have been actively silenced by Conservative politicians (see Smillie, this volume) – even in a case where the motive may have been to preserve some positive progress in terms of maternal health. Where GE still is accorded focus, it is in instances where it can be instrumentally deployed as a justification for other diplomatic or defence objectives. Consequently, conventional areas of Canadian aid provision, like women and gender, are being marginalized.

The remainder of this chapter will thus test the hypothesis that securitization reflects a broader trend of instrumentalization of Canadian aid for foreign policy and defence objectives.

ASSESSING THE EVIDENCE[2]

Securitization by the Numbers

Tracking disbursement of Canadian ODA figures as a reflection of the priorities of the Canadian aid program is a difficult endeavour. Two commonly accepted sources for data include the annual statistical reports on ODA prepared by CIDA and other government of Canada departments responsible for delivering parcels of the International Assistance Envelope (IAE), and the data collected by the OECD's Development Assistance Committee. Problems arise, however, when trying to examine these numbers since they do not always correspond one-to-one, making meaningful comparison difficult. Both sources tell us a story of securitization in two ways. First, the increasing amounts of Canadian ODA directed to countries in conflict or post-conflict situations speak to the recent concentration of aid in states where security and development are intrinsically linked; and second, increased aid to states where Canada has specific security objectives that run parallel to or even dominate the developmental objectives of Canadian aid similarly highlight the salience of foreign policy concerns in aid programming. Table 1 illustrates the increased concentration of Canadian aid in conflict and post-conflict societies.

According to Table 1, aid to recipient countries with significant recent or ongoing insecurity in 2007–08 (Afghanistan, Haiti, Iraq, and Sudan) accounted for 13 per cent of total ODA. When we contrast this to the situation in 1997–98, when 1.4 per cent of ODA went to one country experiencing significant insecurity, Haiti, and to 1987–98, when none did, we see a marked departure in the spending decisions Canada has made regarding the destination of its aid. The geographic allocation of Canadian aid to reflect conflict, insecurity, and geopolitical concerns as well as foreign policy objectives is a clear marker of the securitization of its aid.

Other markers to consider are OECD and CIDA reports of ODA disbursements designated to address issues related to securitization. Here, the DAC sector category of greatest relevance is "Conflict, Peace, and Security" (see Figure 1). Canadian ODA coded as fitting within this category has been increasing rapidly since 2002.

Table 1
Top Ten Recipients of Canadian Bilateral ODA, 1987–2008

1987–88		1997–98		2007–08	
Country	%	Country	%	Country	%
Bangladesh	5.0	Bangladesh	3.3	Afghanistan	6.2
Pakistan	2.7	China	2.5	Haiti	3.0
India	2.4	India	1.5	Ethiopia	2.7
Indonesia	2.0	Haiti	1.4	Iraq	2.1
Tanzania	1.8	Pakistan	1.3	Indonesia	1.8
Jamaica	1.6	Côte d'Ivoire	1.3	Mali	1.7
China	1.6	Cameroon	1.3	Sudan	1.7
Kenya	1.4	Indonesia	1.2	Ghana	1.7
Zambia	1.3	Peru	1.2	Bangladesh	1.6
Thailand	1.3	Egypt	0.8	Mozambique	1.5

Source: OECD 2009.

From disbursements on peace, conflict, and security of just over US$8.5 million in 2002, Canadian ODA spending in this area increased nearly nineteen times to US$160.8 million in 2008. The percentage rise has also been significant, jumping from just under 1.5 per cent of Canadian sector-allocable ODA in 2002 to nearly 5 per cent in 2008.[3] This sharp surge in conflict, peace, and security disbursements in just a six-year period is another telling indicator of the increased priority accorded to securitization of aid in recent years.

CIDA data show similar patterns. Drawing on data from the agency's recent reports on ODA and the IAE, Table 2 provides differing, albeit complementary, data to those seen in Figure 1. Data for 2004–05 through to 2008–09 indicate that, along with an overall increase in the levels of bilateral aid, there was a corresponding growth in the amount of aid dedicated to issues of conflict, peace, and security as defined by the DAC categorization. Over those five years, the level of spending fluctuated, both expanding and shrinking as an overall percentage of total bilateral aid. Still, the overall magnitude of total spending in this area increased sharply, more than doubling between 2004–05 and 2008–09.

Particularly striking in Table 2 is the steep spending increase in other government departments aside from CIDA. With more than ten times the spending in 2008–09 than in the initial observation in

Figure 1
Canadian ODA Disbursements Directed to Conflict, Peace, and Security, 2002–08

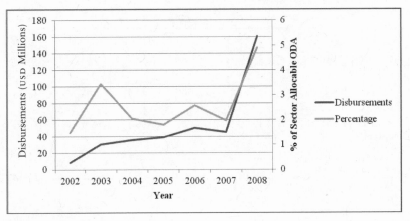

Source: OECD 2010b.

2004–05, this trend indicates that, in order to better understand Canada's aid in support of conflict, peace, and security, we must examine more closely the spending of departments other than CIDA. Indeed, upon closer inspection of the annual statistical reports on Canadian assistance, we see that the largest share of non-CIDA aid in this sector was delivered by the Department of Foreign Affairs and International Trade (CIDA 2009; 2010). In fact, DFAIT's overall contribution to the IAE was 8 per cent of the total in 2008–09, with nearly CAD423 million disbursed, of which $114 million was ODA related to "security and stability programming" (CIDA 2010). This marks a sizable increase from only $141 million of total ODA disbursed by Foreign Affairs in 2004–05, of which only $13 million could be classified as spending on security-related issues (CIDA 2006).

The growth of DFAIT-handled ODA and more specifically the increase in DFAIT's ODA dedicated to security issues is a direct result of the creation of the Stabilization and Reconstruction Task Force in 2005. This unit of DFAIT, along with the Global Peace and Security Fund it manages, are primarily responsible for the delivery of conflict-, peace-, and security-related ODA in the Canadian IAE. It is through this channel of delivery that Canada's aid has most sharply come to focus on security issues. In the 2010–11 fiscal year, the GPSF had a budget of CDN$146 million, which exceeds what the overall

Table 2
Conflict, Peace, and Security as Percentage of Total Bilateral Aid,
2004–09 (Millions Current CAD)

	2004–05	2005–06	2006–07	2007–08	2008–09
CIDA	65.40	58.51	110.12	64.80	44.42
Other government departments	11.29	21.33	127.31	101.95	142.60
Total conflict, peace, and security	76.69	79.84	237.43	166.76	187.02
Total sector allocable bilateral assistance	2454.33	3153.87	3566.17	3449.79	4769.77
Conflict, peace, security as per cent of total	3.12	2.53	6.66	4.83	3.92

Source: CIDA 2006; 2007; 2008; 2009; 2010.

ODA budget for DFAIT was just five years earlier (DFAIT 2010).
Thus, while CIDA spending on conflict and security issues (see
Table 2) has fluctuated but not shown a marked increase, DFAIT has
accounted for much of the overall increase in ODA spending on security in the Canadian IAE.

This close relationship between the securitization of aid in Canada
and the delivery of aid by DFAIT is a telling indication of the extent
to which such aid is used to further Canadian foreign policy and
security objectives. The concentration of aid in a number of countries with important political considerations for Canadian foreign
policy augments this trend. Substantial increases in aid to countries
like Afghanistan and Iraq clearly are linked to foreign policy objectives and aim to support Canadian and NATO defence efforts abroad.
The Canadian aid program in Afghanistan has, consequently,
adopted a whole-of-government approach to development assistance (Brown 2008). ODA funds are used in such as way as to align
closely with the funding of other government departments, with the
goal of ensuring that development results in Afghanistan yield complementary benefits to Canada's security objectives in Kandahar
province and the rest of the country. So apparent is this integrated
approach to aid that development officers have been working in tan-
dem with the military through the use of Provincial Reconstruction
Teams as a means to assemble development and security objectives
under one umbrella (Maloney 2005).

The securitization of aid in Canada and its obvious links to aid and foreign policy objectives suggest that Canadian aid is becoming increasingly motivated by national self-interest and less informed by altruistic international humanitarianism. This pattern of shifting aid motivations is not new. As mentioned above, research shows that Canadian aid cycles frequently between competing motivations of self-interest and altruism (Lumsdaine 1993; Pratt 1994c; Morrison 1998). The impact of this shift in motivation and the dedication of new resources to securitization needs to be better understood. Through the cursory examination cited above, it is manifest that security is an emerging and increasingly important priority for Canadian aid, with resources directed to reflect this priority. What does this mean for other aid priorities, particularly those less directly linked to Canadian foreign policy and security objectives? How do aid priorities like gender equality weather the securitization of Canadian aid?

Does Gender Count? Aid in Support of Gender Equality

Are aid priorities with altruistic or humanitarian motivations receiving continued support in the context of augmented securitization of aid? Canadian aid data show a significant rise in the portion of aid being dedicated to conflict, peace, and security; however, the same cannot be said for aid allotted to the issue of gender equality. Both CIDA and DAC sources on Canadian ODA spending on gender equality provide evidence of mixed and flagging support for GE at CIDA. The scale of resources dedicated to GE in Table 3 appears to underscore ongoing focus on gender equality in the Canadian ODA program. However, if we determine that only aid categorized as having GE as its principal objective can be justified as being "gender" programming, then the overall commitment to GE in Canada has been rather stagnant and, aside from an aberration in 2006,[4] has declined in recent years when examined as a percentage of total sector-allocable aid.[5] Indeed, though the total amount of sector-allocable aid grew intensely during 2004–08, the overall percentage of aid dedicated to GE, either as a principal or significant objective, declined significantly. Notably, total GE-focused aid dropped considerably after 2006, the year in which the Conservative-led minority government first took power, with total aid focused on gender

Table 3
GE-Focused Aid Portion of Sector-allocable Aid, 2004–08
(Millions Current USD)

	2004	2005	2006	2007	2008
GE as principal objective	38	60	146	55	51
GE significant objective	585	622	685	963	744
Total sector-allocable aid	1406	1366	1455	2121	2372
GE principal as per cent of ODA	2.7	4.4	10.0	2.6	2.2
GE significant as per cent of ODA	41.6	45.5	47.1	45.4	31.4
Total GE-focused aid as per cent of ODA	44.3	49.9	57.1	48.0	33.6

Source: OECD 2007a; 2008; 2010a.

equality either as a significant or principal objective declining from slightly more than 57 per cent of total ODA to a mere 33.6 per cent in 2008.[6]

Reports in the media confirm the quantitative evidence, suggesting that CIDA has been actively de-prioritizing gender equality in recent years. The rejection of proposed large-scale gender programming in Pakistan and Kenya is one such indication of this trend (Plewes and Kerr 2010). Indeed, public and media discourse on aid were gripped in 2010 with increasingly divisive arguments about gender equality in Canada's aid program. The refusal to continue funding MATCH International (Plewes and Kerr 2010) is one indicator of this overall trend of flagging support for GE at CIDA. The place for gender in Canadian aid is thus increasingly in doubt, despite the fact that large amounts of Canadian aid are directed to programs considered to be "significant" in their support of GE. These programs are reflective of the overall move toward gender mainstreaming by bilateral donors globally (Swiss 2012), a cause promoted widely in the aftermath of the UN's Fourth World Conference on Women, held in Beijing in 1995 (Moser and Moser 2005; Moser 2005; Swiss 2012). This pattern has seen gender mainstreamed into a wide array of programming whose principal objectives are focused on other developmental outcomes. The new reliance on gender-mainstreaming as the primary avenue through which Canada can support GE makes gender the responsibility of all the parties involved in Canadian aid and simultaneously removes focus from the issue by precluding the necessity to have gender-specific programming at the core of Canada's support for GE (Swiss 2009).

Overall, the diminished place of gender within the Canadian aid program is reflective of periods of earlier resistance and debate over the place of gender in the politics of Canadian aid.[7] There have been suggestions that gender equality is being marginalized because of the politics of a Conservative government trying to please domestic constituencies with anti-GE affinities (Plewes and Kerr 2010). The statistical evidence bears this out, with a more than 10 per cent decline in GE-focused aid in a five-year period (see Table 3). This marginalization does not necessarily link causally to the securitization of aid, but the co-occurrence of these trends cannot be divorced from the broader pattern of Canadian aid being increasingly employed to attain national interests at the expense of poverty reduction or other altruistic aims. At the same time as special pools of funding are being created at DFAIT to address security and conflict issues, CIDA is pulling back from supporting more gender-specific programming and moving instead toward an approach dominated by mainstreaming and diminishing shares of ODA dedicated to GE.

Altruism and National Interest: Gender Equality in the Context of Securitization

The competing motivations for aid encapsulated in the securitization of aid and the concurrent decrease of support for gender equality in Canada's aid highlight the tensions between altruistic concerns associated with GE and the foreign policy or defence concerns associated with securitization. Interview data collected from CIDA officials underline this tension and the ongoing debate about the motivations behind securitization. For instance:

> We don't have any problems with security-system reform. But we're not going to do security-system reform for the sake of security-system reform. We are going to do it because it has an impact on poverty. We're going to do it because it's related to poverty-reduction goals. It's going to make the state better able to use scarce resources ... It's going to make sure that they don't do things with impunity, gender equality, all of those kinds of

things are going to be the values that inform what development
actors do when they undertake these kinds of things ... We're
hearing echoes of the fact that if you're going to do this, it's got
to be in a positive way for positive peace, for positive reasons,
not for negative ones, and certainly not negative ones tied to
"Canadian interests at the core," but more to Canadian values ...
[Interview, 6 February 2007]

This respondent highlights the fact that ssr – only one manifesta-
tion of the securitization of Canadian aid – is something that must
reflect development concerns for poverty reduction and Canadian
values like gender equality and not be tied only to foreign policy
interests deemed "Canadian interests at the core." This illustrates
how, even within CIDA, officials are actively trying to strike a balance between national interest and humanitarianism.

It is difficult, however, to discern how this balancing act between
the dual motivations of altruistic aims and self-interest tied to foreign policy and security is reflected in securitization. Arguably, the
decision to situate the most significant pool for security-related aid
– the GPSF – within DFAIT can be seen as the chief motivation behind
the increased focus on security in Canada's aid. One interview
respondent noted the need for CIDA's Peacebuilding Unit to better
define its mandate in the presence of the new DFAIT mechanism:

Before we didn't really have to define ourselves very well,
because we didn't have a competitor. Now we had the creation
of a $100-million fund per year and with the mandate that
was as open as our mandate was ... So, you have within the
Canadian government an evolving situation around programming and a confusion over roles and responsibilities ... This creation of a GPSF ... was supposed to come to CIDA and then it
got flipped over to Foreign Affairs for a whole bunch of reasons
that are quite fascinating from a political side. [Interview,
23 October 2006]

The CIDA-DFAIT dynamic is clearly one of competing interests
and corresponding competing motivations and mandates. The government's decision, announced in April 2005 as a part of the
International Policy Statement released by the Liberal government
of Paul Martin, to place the GPSF at DFAIT was clearly a political

one, with the specific aim to link a new aid distribution mechanism more closely to Canada's diplomatic and security concerns. The creation of a new dedicated fund to address these concerns through DFAIT-controlled aid is a telling indication of the priority accorded securitization in the political dynamics of aid in Canada. Indeed, a brochure created by DFAIT to promote START and the GPSF in late 2006 highlighted that new mechanisms were necessary for Canada to have a whole-of-government approach to responding to "complex conflicts with important implications for stability and international security" (DFAIT 2006, 1).

In contrast, rather than having a dedicated pool of aid money to draw upon for gender equality – a traditionally strong sector of Canadian aid intervention – one respondent emphasized that as early as 2006 the effect of mainstreaming gender at CIDA displayed a

lack of attention to specific gender-equality programming – in the sense that, if we are mainstreaming, we no longer do targeted interventions, which is a misconception that we're trying to address by stressing our two-pronged approach which allows for both integration of gender-equality issues and results in whatever sectoral work we're doing, but also targeted programming ... So this is a kind of, has been a trap. The use of the terminology "crosscutting" has been problematic because people think of it at the project level, where it does sort of mean integration, and so then think, "Oh, we don't do stand-alone gender equality initiatives anymore!" So we're working to change some of this. I think in a new policy we would have to clarify that because there is continued confusion.

When informed that some of the respondent's colleagues had said that their biggest fear for programming in the peace and security area was that it might be labeled crosscutting and meet the same fate as gender, the respondent continued: "Well, it's interesting, because people have argued both ways. Some are saying we want child rights to be mainstreamed and we want HIV/AIDS issues to be mainstreamed and conflict prevention to be mainstreamed and so be careful where you go with that, because mainstreaming can be a two-edged sword. We all know about policy evaporation and we have concrete proof of that. We're mainstreaming. You just can't see it" (Interview, 4 October 2006).

The seeming evaporation of focused efforts on gender equality at
CIDA and in the larger context of Canada's aid program is enabled
by an increased reliance on mainstreaming as a tool for promoting
equality. This echoes other research which suggests that mainstreaming has the capacity to make gender everyone's responsibility and at
the same time nobody's, attaching significant risk to an overreliance
on mainstreaming as a tactic for pushing gender forward (Tiessen
2007). The fact that gender is being increasingly portrayed as "something" that is done by everything in the Canadian aid program, while
security becomes a more specific targeted objective with reserved
pools of funding, is a reflection of the priority – or the lack thereof
– accorded to the two objectives. That recent statistical reports on
Canadian ODA and international assistance do not calculate the
amount of funding dedicated to GE is indicative of mainstreaming
into oblivion. The 2007–08 fiscal year report states: "CIDA does not
track statistics on gender equality as part of its sectoral profile for
bilateral projects. Instead, gender equality cuts across all sectors and
is considered an integrated component of all programming" (CIDA
2009). In fact, CIDA's most recent *Statistical Report on International
Assistance* for fiscal year 2008–09 does not even contain the word
gender, and itemizes only $900,000 of spending on women's organi-
zations by CIDA (2010). This explicit omission directly contradicts
the DAC's data, submitted to the OECD by the Canadian government,
depicting CIDA and Canada as more actively supporting these initiatives. As mentioned earlier, this trend is reflected also in the more
recent non-renewal of funding for NGOs that do significant work on
women's rights, gender, and development in Canada and abroad
(Plewes and Kerr 2010).

The de-prioritization of gender equality in aid contrasts sharply
with Canada's initiative at the 2010 G8 Summit concerning maternal and child health. Indeed, the sudden appearance of such a priority on the Canadian aid agenda sparked considerable confusion
among observers and critics regarding the provenance of such an
objective (Plewes and Kerr 2010). This is an instance of gender being
instrumentally used to further other foreign policy objectives beyond
the clear humanitarian benefits of improved maternal health. Indeed,
the prestige or reputational bump expected by the government of
Canada from focusing on such issues as it hosted the G8 cannot be
underestimated as a motivating factor for this recent policy turn.
The fact that the decision triggered a significant domestic and

international debate about the place of sexual and reproductive health is worth noting, since it underlines the initiative's highly political nature. In the wake of Senator Nancy Ruth's controversial warning to aid groups, the controversy grew beyond groups and opposition political parties pushing for access to abortion, becoming contextualized in the broader debate about Canadian support for women's rights and the ability of the Conservative government to achieve short-term progress on these issues.

CONCLUSION

My analysis tells two stories regarding the motivations behind aid provision and the instrumentalization of aid to support foreign policy and security objectives in a period of diminishing focus on gender equality. First, securitization can be seen as a direct outcome of the closer relationship that Canadian aid now has with foreign policy and security concerns. In this respect, the securitization of aid can be viewed as part of a larger trend of instrumentalization of Canadian aid. It is indicative of a pendulum swing in the motivations for providing aid, a swing toward self-interest and away from humanitarianism.

Second, despite the recent push in the area of maternal health, gender equality is marginalized along with more altruistic/humanitarian motives. Gender objectives are further diminished by renewed efforts to mainstream these issues across the aid program rather than according them prominence as a strength of Canadian aid. This is not to say that securitization of aid is the direct cause of gender's decline in the Canadian aid sector; instead, gender appears now to become a priority for Canada only when it serves some greater purpose or Canadian interest, whether it is "saving" the women of Afghanistan or making a splash at an international summit around the issue of maternal health.

What does this imply for Canadian aid? How should motives be better managed to address the concerns that arise from the instrumental use of aid as a tool for foreign policy and security objectives? Two options present themselves: 1) move away from areas of Canadian strength around humanitarian issues such as gender and toward priorities that closely align with national self-interests like security; or 2) build on humanitarianism in general, and gender in particular, as key pillars of a Canadian aid program. The

Liam Swiss

first scenario is the one currently being followed by the Canadian
government, as evidenced by the aid disbursement patterns and the
increased ODA role for DFAIT explored above. Distinct departures
from areas of traditional strength would seem destined to undermine the effectiveness of Canadian aid by halting long-term incremental progress made in those sectors previously. Yet, if one believes
that Canada must focus on what it has done well in the past to succeed in the future, then it is clear that Canada's traditional strengths
in GE and other areas of altruistic concern should be accorded a
greater degree of importance within the allocation of aid funds. The
creation of a set pool of funds dedicated to gender-specific interventions and building on Canada's past reputation as a leader in the GE
field would be one step in this direction. This would help to more
closely align altruism and self-interest in Canada's aid program. At
the same time, more examination of Canada's security-related aid,
particularly that delivered by the GPSF and DFAIT, is necessary to
understand better whether the securitization of aid in Canada has
become wholly divorced from the poverty-reduction concerns under
which it is supposed to operate.

NOTES

1 See also Table 1.
2 The analysis that follows is based on Canadian and OECD/DAC data on
  Canadian ODA disbursements, recent reports to Parliament on Canadian
  aid activities, and interviews with respondents working within CIDA. The
  DAC databases on bilateral ODA are the most reliable international source
  of data on aid flows.
3 Sector-allocable aid is the DAC classification of that portion of ODA that
  can be attributed to a specific sector code.
4 A possible explanation for why this 2006 figure is so high might be the
  influence in CIDA at that time of an executive vice-president appointed as
  an informal "gender champion" who reputedly pushed for country programs to focus on GE-specific programming in a concerted way. She left the
  agency in 2007, perhaps accounting for the precipitous drop back to nor-
  mal levels. For more on the effects of such "champions," see Swiss (2009).
5 Because gender equality is a crosscutting issue, there is no specific sector
  created to indicate programming on GE, and instead there is a marker
  attached to all sector-allocable aid which can indicate whether the program is either principally or significantly focused on GE. The distinction

between the two markers would mirror CIDA's designation of programming as either GE-specific or GE-integrated.

6 Unfortunately, at the time of writing, figures for 2009 were not yet
available, making it impossible to confirm whether this trend has
continued.

7 For instance, senior management resistance in the 1980s to expanding
CIDA's capacity to deal with women-in-development issues. For more
on this, see Swiss (2009).

REFERENCES

Andersen, Regine. 2000. "How Multilateral Development Assistance Triggered the Conflict in Rwanda." *Third World Quarterly* 21, no. 3: 441–56.

Black, David R., and Rebecca Tiessen. 2007. "The Canadian International
Development Agency: New Policies, Old Problems." *Canadian Journal
of Development Studies* 28, no. 2: 191–212.

Blanchard, Eric M. 2003. "Gender, International Relations, and the
Development of Feminist Security Theory." *Signs: Journal of Women in
Culture and Society* 28, no. 4: 1289–1312.

Brown, Stephen. 2007. "Creating the World's Best Development Agency?
Confusion and Contradictions in CIDA's New Development Policy."
Canadian Journal of Development Studies 28, no. 2: 203–18.

– 2008. "CIDA under the Gun." In Jean Daudelin and Daniel Schwanen,
eds., *Canada among Nations 2007: What Room to Manoeuvre?*
Montreal and Kingston, ON: McGill-Queen's University Press. 91–107.

Brzoska, Michael. 2003. *Development Donors and the Concept of
Security Sector Reform*. Geneva: Geneva Centre for the Democratic
Control of Armed Forces.

Canadian International Development Agency. 1999. "CIDA's Policy on
Gender Equality." http://www.acdi-cida.gc.ca/INET/IMAGES.NSF/
vLUImages/Policy/$file/GENDER-E.pdf. Accessed 14 December 2011.

– 2006. "Statistical Report on Official Development Assistance, Fiscal Year
2004–2005." Gatineau, QC: Canadian International Development Agency.

– 2007. "Statistical Report on Official Development Assistance, Fiscal Year
2005–2006." Gatineau, QC: Canadian International Development Agency.

– 2008. "Statistical Report on Official Development Assistance, Fiscal Year
2006–2007." Gatineau, QC: Canadian International Development Agency.

– 2009a. "Canada Moves on Another Element of Its Aid Effectiveness
Agenda." http://www.acdi-cida.gc.ca/acdi-cida/ACDI-CIDA.nsf/eng/
NAT-223132931-PPH. Accessed 25 August 2010.

– 2009b. "Statistical Report on International Assistance, Fiscal Year 2007–2008." Gatineau, QC: Canadian International Development Agency.

– 2010. "Statistical Report on International Assistance, Fiscal Year 2008–2009." Gatineau, QC: Canadian International Development Agency.

Cohn, Carol, and Cynthia Enloe. 2003. "A Conversation with Cynthia Enloe: Feminists Look at Masculinity and the Men Who Wage War." *Signs* 28, no. 4: 1187–1207.

Delacourt, Susan. 2010. "Aid Groups Advised to 'Shut the F— Up' on Abortion." *Toronto Star*, 3 May.

Department of Foreign Affairs and International Trade. 2006. "Stabilization and Reconstruction Task Force (START): Mobilizing Canada's Capacity for International Crisis Response." http://www.international.gc.ca/cip-pic/assets/pdfs/library/START_brochure_EN.pdf. Accessed 27 August 2010.

– 2010. "The Global Peace and Security Fund (GPSF)." 14 May. http://www.international.gc.ca/START-GTSR/gpsf-fpsm.aspx. Accessed 17 May 2010.

Ebo, Adedeji. 2007. "The Role of Security Sector Reform in Sustainable Development: Donor Policy Trends and Challenges." *Conflict, Security and Development* 7: 27–60.

Lalonde, Jennifer. 2009. "Harmony and Discord: International Aid Harmonization and Donor State Domestic Influence. The Case of Canada and the Canadian International Development Agency." PhD thesis. Baltimore: Johns Hopkins University.

Lumsdaine, David H. 1993. *Moral Vision in International Politics: The Foreign Aid Regime, 1949–1989*. Princeton, NJ: Princeton University Press.

Macdonald, Ryan, and John Hoddinott. 2004. "Determinants of Canadian Bilateral Aid Allocations: Humanitarian, Commercial or Political?" *Canadian Journal of Economics* 37, no. 2: 294–312.

Maloney, Sean M. 2005. "From Kabul to Konduz: Lessons for Canadian Reconstruction of Afghanistan." *Policy Options* (May): 57–62.

Morgenthau, Hans. 1962. "A Political Theory of Foreign Aid." *American Political Science Review* 56, no. 2: 301–9.

Morrison, David R. 1994. "The Choice of Bilateral Aid Recipients." In Cranford Pratt, ed., *Canadian International Development Assistance Policies: An Appraisal*. Montreal and Kingston, ON: McGill-Queen's University Press. 123–55.

– 1998. *Aid and Ebb Tide: A History of CIDA and Canadian Development Assistance*. Waterloo, ON: Wilfrid Laurier University Press.

Moser, Caroline. 2005. "Has Gender Mainstreaming Failed?" *International Feminist Journal of Politics* 7, no. 4: 576–90.

Moser, Caroline, and Annalise Moser. 2005. "Gender Mainstreaming since Beijing: A Review of Success and Limitations in International Institutions." *Gender and Development* 13, no. 2: 11–22.

Noël, Alain, Jean-Philippe Thérien, and Sébastien Dallaire. 2004. "Divided over Internationalism: The Canadian Public and Development Assistance." *Canadian Public Policy/Analyse de Politiques* 30, no. 1: 29–46.

Organisation for Economic Co-operation and Development. 2005. "Security Sector Reform and Governance." *DAC Guidelines and Reference Series*. Paris: Organisation for Economic Co-operation and Development.

– 2007a. "Aid in Support of Gender Equality and Women's Empowerment." Paris: Organisation for Economic Co-operation and Development.

– 2007b. "Canada: Development Assistance Committee Peer Review." Paris: Organisation for Economic Co-operation and Development.

– 2008. "Aid in Support of Gender Equality and Women's Empowerment." Paris: Organisation for Economic Co-operation and Development.

– 2009. "Development Co-operation Report 2010." Paris: Organisation for Economic Co-operation and Development.

– 2010a. "Aid in Support of Gender Equality and Women's Empowerment." Paris: Organisation for Economic Co-operation and Development.

– 2010b. "QWIDS: Query Wizard for International Development Statistics." http://www.stats.oecd.org/qwids/. Accesssed 21 May 2010.

Otter, Miranda. 2003. "Domestic Public Support for Foreign Aid: Does It Matter?" *Third World Quarterly* 24, no. 1: 115–25.

Plewes, Betty, and Joanna Kerr. 2010. "Politicizing, Undermining Gender Equality." *Embassy*. 5 May.

Pratt, Cranford. 1994a. "Canadian Development Assistance: A Profile." In Cranford Pratt, ed., *Canadian International Development Assistance Policies: An Appraisal*. Montreal and Kingston, ON: McGill-Queen's University Press. 3–24.

– 1994b. *Canadian International Development Assistance Policies: An Appraisal*. Montreal and Kingston, ON: McGill-Queen's University Press.

– 1994c. "Humane Internationalism and Canadian Development Assistance Policies." In Cranford Pratt, ed., *Canadian International Development Assistance Policies: An Appraisal*. Montreal and Kingston, ON: McGill-Queen's University Press. 334–70.

Rathgeber, Eva. 1990. "WID, WAD, GAD: Trends in Research and Practice." *Journal of Developing Areas* 24: 489–502.

– 1995. "Gender and Development in Action." In Marianne H. Marchand and Jane L. Parpart, eds., *Feminism/Postmodernism/Development*. London: Routledge. 204–20.

Rawkins, Phillip. 1994. "An Institutional Analysis of CIDA." In Cranford Pratt, ed., *Canadian International Development Assistance Policies: An Appraisal*. Montreal and Kingston, ON: McGill-Queen's University Press. 156–85.

Swiss, Liam. 2009. "Developing Consensus: The Globalisation of Development Assistance Policies." PhD thesis. Montreal: McGill University.

– 2012. "The Adoption of Women and Gender as Development Assistance Priorities: An Event History Analysis of World Polity Effects." *International Sociology* 27, no. 1: 96–119.

Tiessen, Rebecca. 2007. *Everywhere/Nowhere: Gender Mainstreaming in Development Agencies*, Bloomfield, CT: Kumarian Press.

Uvin, Peter. 1999. "Development Aid and Structural Violence: The Case of Rwanda." *Development* 42, no. 3: 49–56.

Woods, Ngaire. 2005. "The Shifting Politics of Foreign Aid." *International Affairs* 81, no. 2: 393–409.

6

CIDA'S Land and Food-Security Policies:
A Critical Review

DENIS CÔTÉ AND DOMINIQUE CAOUETTE

The 2008–09 global food crisis was a harsh reminder of the central-ity of food security in the international development agenda. Despite some progress made between the 1960s and the late 1990s, the num-ber of undernourished people in the world has been increasing rather than decreasing since 2000 (FAO 2009c). As the number of people living with hunger climbed to over one billion in 2009 as a result of the food and financial crises, halving the proportion of people who suffer from hunger between 1990 and 2015 – a target set for the first Millennium Development Goal (MDG) of eradicating poverty and hunger (UN 2005) – seems increasingly out of reach.

Responding to this crisis, Canada has stepped up its efforts to address the problem of food insecurity through official development assistance (ODA). In May 2009 the Canadian International Develop-ment Agency (CIDA) identified food security as one of its three the-matic priorities. A few months later, at the G8 Summit in L'Aquila, Italy, in July 2009, the Canadian government announced that it would double its investments in support of sustainable agricultural development by committing an additional $600 million over three years, bringing the total to $1.18 billion over the three-year period (CIDA 2009). In April 2010 CIDA launched its Food Security Strat-egy and also became one of the main contributors to the Global Agricultural and Food Security Program – a World Bank funding mechanism.

While there is no doubt that Canada has recently taken initiatives to fight food insecurity overseas, it is still too early to evaluate fully their impact. Nonetheless, these initiatives are grounded in policies that guide specific programs and projects and those policies merit closer examination.

This chapter analyzes CIDA's past and current policies on agrarian issues and food security in order to assess its contribution to the realization of the right to food in developing countries. Such an examination is both timely and important since Canada, under international human-rights law, has obligations as a donor to contribute toward the realization of human rights, not only within its national boundaries but also through its international assistance. We examine Canada's policies toward developing countries to highlight the broader motivations and principles that have guided its interventions in rural areas. Our conclusion is that, though CIDA's policies have improved in many ways, CIDA has usually been influenced by the broader geopolitical context and an implicit commitment to political and economic liberalism, marked by a reluctance to engage in structural changes that would undermine ruling elites, notably access to land. CIDA's policies on land, agrarian issues, and food security also show a specific concern for Canadian commercial interests. While CIDA's emphasis on production and productivity can contribute to improving the right to food of rural populations in developing countries by increasing the amount of food available to them, its deliberate avoidance of social-justice issues such as land reform reflects a clear political choice in favour of a commercial food system based on liberalized market policies. In doing so, the agency sidesteps the key issue of access to land and supports unequal power structures that perpetuate poverty and injustice. As a result, it ends up undermining the right to food that its policies otherwise promote.

To support this argument, we first present a brief historical overview of the evolution of CIDA's land policies from Canada's first foray into international assistance through the Colombo Plan in 1950 until the year 2000, when the adoption of the Millennium Development Goals led to the formulation of CIDA's current land and food-security policies. We subsequently present the key elements of two documents at the core of CIDA's current land policies, *Promoting Sustainable Rural Development through Agriculture: Canada Making a Difference in the World* (2003) and *Increasing Food Security: CIDA's Food Security Strategy* (2010). Finally, we assess CIDA's land policies in relation to the five dimensions of the right to food, as well as the policies' potential contribution to poverty reduction.

CANADIAN AID, FOOD, AND LAND POLICIES: A HISTORICAL REVIEW

After the Second World War, the United States launched economic reconstruction in Western Europe through the European Recovery Plan, better known as the Marshall Plan (1948–51). The plan provided a $12-billion package for the reconstruction of sixteen countries with the explicit aim of preventing and containing communist governments in Europe. Soon, the fear of seeing economically vulnerable states fall into the Soviet Union's sphere of influence extended beyond Europe. In this context, as a member of the Commonwealth and an ally of the United States, Canada began to invest in international assistance as a means to counter communism and rural insurgencies.

Food Aid

Canada first became an international donor in 1950 through its participation in the Colombo Plan. While the stated objective of this plan was "the economic and social advancement of the peoples of South and Southeast Asia" (Colombo Plan secretariat 2010), the underlying motive was to prevent the spread of communism to the region. Canada's contribution to the Colombo Plan was not inspired by land policies as such; instead, there was a strong emphasis on food aid. Canada in fact was motivated more by geopolitical and economic interests than by a charitable desire to improve the lives of the poor. Canadian food aid to South Asia aimed to keep the newly independent states of India, Pakistan, and Ceylon within the Western sphere of influence. Bilateral aid to the region also facilitated the penetration of Canadian businesses into new markets (Dupuis 1984, 104).

For the next twenty-five years (1950–75), Canada did not have specific land policies. In 1960, under pressure from the United States and old colonial powers to take on a larger share of the development-assistance effort, Canada joined the Development Assistance Group of the Organisation for European Economic Co-operation

(OEEC) – superseded in 1961 by the Organisation for Economic Co-operation and Development (OECD) – and its assistance programs began to extend worldwide (Morrison 1998, 6).[1] In the 1960s, Canada expanded its bilateral programming first to the newly independent Commonwealth countries of Africa and the Caribbean, then to francophone African countries, Latin America, and Asian countries beyond the Colombo Plan.

Yet this geographic diversification was not accompanied by clear policies on land and rural development. Food aid was still the major mechanism through which Canada contributed to feeding the poor. However, in developing countries, food aid often depressed agricultural prices while reducing incentives for both domestic food production and agrarian reform (Morrison 1998, 83). In certain instances, Canada's food aid became an impediment to food production. Canadian economic interests translated into rural-development projects, particularly the establishment of agribusinesses in developing countries.

In the mid-1960s, the Canadian government became more enthusiastic about foreign aid. David Morrison describes this period as one of idealism, optimism, and prosperity that fuelled an interest in international development and captured the imagination of Canadians (Morrison 1998, 1). In 1968 CIDA was created and, while food aid remained a major component of Canadian ODA, as a proportion of the total Canadian ODA it fell from 50 per cent to 30 per cent between 1966 and 1970 (Morrison 1998, 83).

Integrated Rural Development

By the 1970s, CIDA had reoriented its agrarian program in the wake of Robert McNamara's famous Nairobi speech in which he announced a shift in World Bank's programming away from the "growth with trickle-down" model to a model of "growth with equity," which prioritizes meeting the basic needs of populations (Morrison 1998, 108). This new basic-needs approach was progressively adopted by most Western aid agencies and included a strong emphasis on integrated rural development, which sought to "extend basic employment, education and health services to the countryside, thus making it an 'integrated' approach" (Carty and Smith 1981, 132). Critics argue that it also sought to "transform subsistence peasant agriculture into commercial, capitalist agriculture by locking the small producer into the agribusiness food system as a consumer of agricultural inputs (seed, fertilizers, chemicals, machinery, technology, etc.) and as a producer of crops suitable for further processing and marketing both nationally and internationally" (Carty and Smith 1981, 132).

Pressed by the 1973 international food crisis that devastated Sub-Saharan Africa, and guided by the new basic-needs approach developed by the World Bank, in 1975 CIDA outlined its first substantial guidelines on land issues in a major policy document entitled *Strategy for International Development Cooperation 1975–1980* (CIDA 1975). In this document, CIDA identified agriculture as a development priority for the very first time and signalled its intention to refocus its assistance on food production and agricultural development to meet the basic needs of the least privileged sections of the populations in the poorest countries of the developing world (Morrison 1998, 117). To achieve these objectives, the strategy relied on integrated rural-development projects.[2] The agency also pledged to allocate at least 33 per cent of its total bilateral aid budget to agricultural and rural development from 1977 to 1982 (Carty and Smith 1981, 130). However, CIDA fell short of its commitment: while the proportion of aid directed to rural development did increase to 29.5 per cent in 1976, Morrison argues that most of that increase should be attributed to "creative relabeling" (Morrison 1988, 126) – it fell again to 17.9 per cent in 1979 (Morrison 1998, 166–7).

Robert Carty and Virginia Smith argued that the 1975 policy generally supported middle-class farmers, excluded the rural poor and landless, and circumvented land reforms in developing countries (Carty and Smith 1981, 130). While CIDA prized "integrated rural development as an important innovation ... no amount of technique or exhortation about the importance of the agricultural sector, even if it helps some small farmers produce more, will be of significant benefit to the world's rural poor without radical changes in land tenure systems" (Carty and Smith 1981, 139–40).

The following examples illustrate some of the contradictions that these projects generated.

Colombia as a Prototype

In 1976, one year after Canada had published its first land policy and shifted its aid focus toward meeting the basic needs of the

poorest populations in developing countries, CIDA "broke ground in
the field of 'new aid' by its involvement in a prototype basic needs
projects" in Colombia (Carty and Smith 1981, 134). While its
$14-million investment made it a minority participant alongside the
Inter-American Development Bank ($64 million) and the World
Bank ($52 million), CIDA still had a strong leadership role in the
project (Carty and Smith 1981, 134).

The objective of the project was to increase food production by
small peasant farmers in Sucre and Cordoba. At that time, one million rural families owned no land at all and 75 per cent of small
owners occupied only 7.2 per cent of land suitable for cultivation in
the country. Conversely, rural elites counted for only 5 per cent of
landowners but monopolized two-thirds of the cropland producing
export crops and products such as coffee and sugar (Carty and Smith
1981, 134–5).

After the Second World War, inequalities in the countryside
increased with the modernization of agriculture, as the government
promoted and subsidized modern estates producing agro-exports.
Most international aid worsened the situation by helping large
estates pay for mechanization, irrigation, and other agricultural
inputs, which led to the development of capitalist agribusinesses and
the expulsion of small peasant farmers from their land (Carty and
Smith 1981, 135). Increasing inequalities also led to the creation of
a strong peasant movement in the 1970s, to which the government
responded by "imprisoning 35,000 federation members and assas-
sinating over 200 militants" (Carty and Smith 1981, 136). CIDA's
main objectives for this project were to raise production and productivity, as well as accelerate the modernization and commercialization of agriculture. These objectives were consistent with the
Canadian government's trade interests, which CIDA promoted by
tying aid to the procurement of Canadian goods and opening new
markets for Canadian goods in Latin America. In fact, half of CIDA's
$14-million commitment was tied to the procurement of Canadian
goods, such as fertilizers, pesticides, electric transmission lines, jeep-
type vehicles, and motorcycles.

Results of this project were less than positive. While the endeavour assisted about 7,500 rural families who already owned between
one and twenty hectares of land, it bypassed 25,000 peasant families
who owned less than one hectare. Thus, the project strengthened
the middle class within the peasantry, leaving the poorest on the

sidelines. Worse, the project circumvented – rather than supported – a twelve-year-old land-reform program that had redistributed only 1.6 per cent of the large estates thus far. As Carty and Smith noted, integrated rural development "avoids land reform and its planners expected that the rural population somehow would be satisfied if just a few among them improved their productivity" (Carty and Smith 1981, 136).

Ghana: Learning the Hard Way

In 1978 Ghana barely qualified for the World Bank's category of a middle-income developing country. At the time, Ghana was dependent on cocoa for 75 per cent of its foreign earnings and poverty was especially acute in the arid north of the country, bordering the Sahara desert. Drought and famine plagued the area and only about half of children survived until the age of five (Carty and Smith 1981, 16).

In the mid-1970s, agricultural assistance and efforts to improve the quality of life in rural areas rose to the top of CIDA's agenda. CIDA described its massive well-installation project in northern Ghana as an outstanding example of its new initiatives. It reported the construction of nearly 900 wells by the end of the 1975–76 fiscal year, "supplying the area with safe drinking water for the first time" (Carty and Smith 1981, 16).

The water project in Ghana had two major flaws. First, the choice of the pump highlights the priority given to Canadian commercial self-interest over value for development. A crew from the CBC's *Fifth Estate* visited the well-digging area in 1978 and discovered that, while CIDA had indeed rapidly completed the first phase of its work, the pumps it purchased from General Steel Wares in Ontario wore out in months, sometimes even in weeks. CIDA kept repairing the malfunctioning pumps and eventually decided to buy new ones from another Canadian company – Monarch Industry in Winnipeg – despite acknowledging that the best pump for the area was one made in India. This is an example of Canadian interests taking precedence over the developing country's rural poor interests (Carty and Smith 1981, 17). Second, CIDA sent staff to Ghana who had little understanding of local culture and failed to inform people of the health benefits of clean water. People were not aware that clean water was better for their health than dirty water and continued to drink dirty water or mix clean water with clay to give it "colour and taste." CIDA subsequently decided to invest in a health-education program and training in pump repairs (Carty and Smith 1981, 127).

The Shift from Development Issues to Managerial Effectiveness

There was much intellectual ferment at CIDA in the early 1970s but, with the appointment of Michel Dupuy as CIDA president in 1977, focus shifted from development issues to an emphasis on managerial effectiveness and integration within the foreign policy apparatus (Morrison 1998, 144). In 1980 Marcel Massé took over the CIDA presidency and tried to bring development back to centre stage. From 1980 to 1983, CIDA refocused its mission and worked to develop coherent principles for Canadian aid (Morrison 1998, 177). In 1981 CIDA adopted three priority sectors: agriculture, energy, and human-resource development.

A few years later, a report on Canada's ODA prepared by the House of Commons Standing Committee on External Affairs and International Trade, *For Whose Benefit*, pointed out that while agriculture often ranked first in ODA commitments, this included "food aid and investments in rural transportation." In its report, the committee cautioned against regarding food aid as a substitute for planned agricultural development projects (SCEAIT 1987, 62). The committee also stressed that "in some countries where there is desperate need, basic human rights have not been observed and the opposite of development is taking place. An all too common example is the lack of respect for the rights of peasant farmers, whether because of the failure to implement land reform or the forced collectivization of agriculture" (SCEAIT 1987, 23).

During the following decade, Canada relied on its 1975 land-policy document to guide its agricultural programming in its ODA. While attention continued to be on integrated rural development, CIDA's priorities started to shift toward specific components of agriculture and food production, such as food self-sufficiency, transportation, storage, small farming marketing, and women's empowerment in rural areas (Morrison 1998). From 1989 to 2003, CIDA supported a host of land-policy initiatives, with a regional focus on the Americas. It emphasized "technical cooperation," channelling aid to aerial photography, Radarsat technology, and land mapping (Caouette 2007). According to critics, during the 1990s CIDA reduced its investment in agricultural development and reframed existing projects around the notion of business development. The result of this two-decade-long downward slide was a lack of sustained and coherent political leadership, and a crisis of funding.

CIDA'S CONTEMPORARY LAND AND FOOD-SECURITY POLICIES

In this section, we assess the two main documents that have defined CIDA's land and food-security policies: *Promoting Sustainable Rural Development through Agriculture: Canada Making a Difference in the World* (2003) and *Increasing Food Security: CIDA's Food Security Strategy* (2010).

The major incentives that led the agency to update and systematize its position on land and food security were the adoption of the Millennium Development Goals (2000) and the World Food Summit: Five Years Later (2002). The adoption of the MDGs prompted Canada to reinvest in food-security and land-policy objectives and to put them in a broader perspective, linking them to other areas of development, such as environmental sustainability and gender equality, the two main crosscutting themes of CIDA's programming. The 2002 World Food Summit served to highlight the international community's disappointingly slow progress in reducing hunger and increasing food security in the context of the MDGs, and to stress the crucial importance of reversing the overall decline in investments in agriculture and rural development. CIDA Minister Susan Whelan responded by launching several consultations with civil society organizations and commissioned a number of studies and discussion papers on land policies in 2002 and 2003. This led to the first substantial revision of CIDA's land and agricultural policies since 1975, presented in a document titled *Promoting Sustainable Rural Development through Agriculture: Canada Making a Difference in the World*.

Promoting Sustainable Rural Development through Agriculture

CIDA sought to update its land and agricultural policies in *Promoting Sustainable Rural Development through Agriculture*. This new policy document revealed a market-led approach to rural development and argued that the causes of rural poverty in developing countries were related to issues of production and market access, rather than insufficient access to land. The policies also emphasized the importance of scientific research as a means to solve problems of rural development, particularly in farming technology and biotechnology. CIDA argued that investing in agriculture could be conducive to the MDGs while contributing to the eradication of poverty and hunger and the promotion of gender equality, as well as ensuring environmental sustainability, human health, and education.

The document's rationale was that, in a market economy, the best land is exploited by the biggest producers while the poor are confined to less productive land. The rural poor's situation can be improved by focusing on increasing productivity by intensifying and diversifying production, as well as increasing market access by investing in infrastructure. Unfortunately, instead of addressing the root cause of rural poverty by promoting greater access to land for the poor, CIDA supported an acceleration from subsistence to commercial farming (CIDA 2003, 13).

While CIDA's 2003 policy document may have demonstrated a renewed interest in agriculture as part of Canadian ODA, it did nothing to promote consistent development-aid policies and strategies. Between 2000 and 2010, the uncertainties engendered by four federal elections and the nomination of five different CIDA ministers affected the agency's planning, which was characterized by a lack of focus and shifting priorities (see Brown, chapter 3, this volume). In the midst of these changes, agriculture and rural development were somewhat sidelined.

A Changing Context and the New Food-Security Strategy

The 2008 international food crisis brought food security and rural development back to the top of the Canadian aid agenda. In 2009 CIDA Minister Bev Oda announced another change in the agency's priorities. Aside from identifying twenty countries of focus, CIDA settled on three thematic priorities for its development aid: food security, children and youth, and sustainable economic growth. It released a new food-security strategy in April 2010, whose main objective was to contribute to poverty reduction. It also aimed to contribute to sustainable development in accordance with the principles of aid effectiveness. In the strategy, Canada's ODA in food security was said to be focused on increasing the availability of food; improving access to food; increasing availability and access to quality nutritious food; increasing the stability of food security; and supporting improved governance of the global food system. Accordingly, agricultural development and land policies were framed as means to support the overarching goal of food security. To increase food security in developing countries, CIDA identified three paths: sustainable agricultural development, food aid and nutrition, and research and development (CIDA 2010a, 3–4).

The choice of sustainable agricultural development as a means to increase food security was rooted in the assumption that developing the agricultural sector in poorer countries is key to achieving sustainable and complex economies. CIDA's objective was to help farmers increase agricultural production and productivity in a sustainable manner that also benefits women. Its programs were expected to produce increased agricultural production and productivity among small-scale rural farmers, especially women, strengthened policies, more accountable institutions, and improved management processes with partner governments.

CIDA considered food aid and nutrition as necessary to address the immediate needs of vulnerable and high-risk populations. Emergency food aid was required to deal with situations of acute food insecurity, while nutrition interventions would reduce the number of child deaths related to malnutrition in developing countries. CIDA's priorities under this path include: supporting the World Food Programme, nutrition interventions, and the use of social-safety nets, including the improvement of the Food Aid Convention; increasing micro-nutrition programming; and strengthening national and regional food reserves and food-crisis alert and prevention systems. The expected results were an increase in the number of lives saved and better overall health, as well as improved quality and effectiveness of food-aid programming.

The third path of action to increase food security was research and development. CIDA linked the decline in agricultural productivity and increased fragility of global food security over the past thirty years to a decline in investment in agricultural research and development. As a result, investment in research was presented as essential to meet current and future food demands.

As a whole, the 2010 food-security strategy redefined the agency's framework on land policies by subordinating them to the overarching priority of food security. While the document presented a general framework for action to achieve food security, it did not address specific land policies. This approach, and the thinking behind it, is found in, and often inferred from, the 2003 document. Together, the

2003 and 2010 documents reiterate CIDA's support for economic liberalism and its emphasis on production, productivity, and market access rather than increased participation and access to land.

CIDA'S LAND POLICIES AND THE RIGHT TO FOOD

The right to food was enshrined in the Universal Declaration of Human Rights in 1948, but it was the shift toward a human-rights-based approach to food security following the World Food Summit in 1996 that led to the elaboration of a more specific definition of the right to food in 1999 (FAO 1999) and guidelines for its realization in 2004. The content of the right to food includes the four pillars of food security (availability, access, adequacy, and sustainability) and the right for people to participate in the design and implementation of policies defining their own food and agriculture systems. Since the vast majority of the people suffering from hunger today live in rural areas, land and food-security policies must support access to land and productive resources to contribute significantly to the realization of the right to food for the most vulnerable communities.

This section examines CIDA's policies through a human-rights lens, based on international donors' obligation to respect, protect, and fulfill human rights through their development assistance, as well as the 2008 Canadian ODA Accountability Act. It also assesses CIDA's land policies in terms of their contribution to realizing the right to food in developing countries by weighing the potential impact of these policies on the five dimensions of the right to food named above.

Origins of the Right to Food

In 1996 the Rome Declaration of the World Food Summit triggered a change in food-security paradigms within international donor agencies by proposing the adoption of a rights-based approach to fight hunger and malnutrition. Although the right to food had been enshrined in Article 25 of the Universal Declaration of Human Rights since 1948,[3] there was still some degree of uncertainty regarding the specific content of that right. For example, Mary Robinson, former UN high commissioner for human rights, argued that a "fundamental misunderstanding in the implementation of the right to food has been the notion that the principal obligation is for the state to feed the citizens under its jurisdiction" (FAO 1998, vii).

The UN Committee on Economic, Social and Cultural Rights provided a more elaborate definition in 1999, arguing that the right to adequate food is realized "when every man, woman, and child, alone or in community with others, has the physical and economic access at all times to adequate food or means for its procurement" (FAO 2007). For the Canadian Council for International Co-operation (CCIC), this was a landmark declaration because it defined three levels of *state obligation* toward the right to food (to respect, protect, and fulfill) and the three *elements* of that right (accessibility, adequacy, and stability of supply) (CCIC 2010, 99).

As the definition of the right to food became clearer, the Food and Agriculture Organization of the United Nations (FAO) adopted in 2004 the Voluntary Guidelines to Support the Progressive Realization of the Right to Adequate Food in the Context of National Food Security. These guidelines were an important step toward the implementation of the right to food because they "represented the first time the international community agreed on the full meaning of the right" (FAO 2007). Although they are not legally binding, the Voluntary Guidelines draw upon international law and provide guidance on the implementation of existing obligations. Since the adoption of these guidelines, the two successive United Nations special rapporteurs on the right to food have further developed the concept and have published several reports highlighting the impacts of agribusinesses, large-scale land acquisitions, trade liberalization, and the food crises, among others, on the right to food.

Canada's Obligation to Implement
the Right to Food through Its ODA

Under international human-rights law, states must *respect, protect,* and *fulfill* all human rights. The obligation to *respect* human rights means to refrain from interfering with the enjoyment of the right. The obligation to *protect* refers to the enactment of laws that create mechanisms to prevent violation of the right by state authorities or non-state actors. The obligation to *fulfill* means to take active steps to put in place institutions and procedures, including the allocation of resources, to enable people to enjoy this right (UNFPA 2008). The state has primary responsibility to contribute to the realization of human rights *within* its own national boundaries. However, as noted by Amnesty International, "states also have obligations when they act beyond their borders to respect, protect, and fulfill economic, social and cultural rights" (Amnesty International 2010). As CCIC observes, the main legal basis for the consideration of the human-rights obligations of states in development assistance can be found in Article 2 of the International Covenant on Economic, Social and Cultural Rights (CCIC 2010, 55).[4]

In 2008 Canada adopted legislation that makes meeting human-rights standards in international assistance a legal requirement. The Official Development Assistance Accountability Act sets three criteria for assessing Canada's foreign aid priorities: in the opinion of the minister responsible for CIDA, ODA must contribute to poverty reduction, take into account the perspectives of the poor, and be consistent with international human-rights standards (see, in this volume, McGill; Brown, chapter 3; and Blackwood and Stewart). As noted by Alex Neve of Amnesty International Canada, the act has helped to secure the recognition of the principle that "human rights obligations do extend beyond our borders" (CCIC 2010, 60).

In relation to the right to food, the ODA Accountability Act represents an opportunity for Canada to implement a human-rights approach to food security. The act can help ensure that the voices of the people living with hunger are heard, that their knowledge is valued, and that Canadian foreign aid spending contributes to a world without hunger (CCIC 2010, 103). However, former CCIC president Gerry Barr argues that, while CIDA has adopted a human-rights-driven approach to its programming, it has been minimalist so far in applying this approach on the ground: "A review of CIDA's internal discussions about the application of human rights standards to its programming practices and choices suggests that CIDA has adopted a minimalist do-no-harm approach to the application of human rights standards ... The Act can be an important tool for CIDA and all concerned with Canada's aid program to chart a more effective and steady future for foreign aid. Sadly, the potential of this landmark legislation will be unfulfilled if government programming and reporting under the act continues to be lacklustre" (Barr 2010).

Availability

The FAO argues that, to ensure food security, a sustainable supply of adequate food must be available (FAO 2008, 5–8). Availability thus relates to the production of food in sufficient amounts, supplied either through domestic production or imports, including food aid, to meet people's needs. While availability of food remains an important pillar of food security, the FAO acknowledges that "after considerable progress in agricultural production, food availability is no longer the main cause of food insecurity" (FAO 2009a, 59). Current food production worldwide is sufficient to feed twelve billion people, nearly twice the world population (UN Human Rights Council 2008, 2). Most occurrences of food insecurity are therefore not caused by a lack of food availability, but rather by the "people's lack of entitlements to gain access to available food" (FAO 2009b, 14). Consequently, land and food policies focusing on production and productivity may succeed in increasing the amount of available food but do not address the main problem of food security, which is one of access.

The main objective of CIDA's land policies is to increase production and productivity of small farms. Because the world's population is constantly growing, CIDA argues, "global food production must increase by 2050 to keep pace with increasing demand" (CIDA 2003, 5). To increase the production and productivity of marginal lands to which small farmers are often confined, CIDA proposes two different approaches: diversification and intensification. The diversification strategies include integrating crop and livestock production, introducing agro-forestry technologies, and matching production with natural-resource endowments. In terms of intensification, CIDA proposes to invest in "appropriate technologies and sustainable production techniques" and in agricultural innovation and research, notably in the field of genomics and biotechnology (CIDA 2003, 9).

On the one hand, CIDA's policy to increase agricultural production and productivity is conducive to the realization of the right to food because it seeks to increase the amount of food available to small farmers. While there is more than enough food available at the global level to feed the entire world population (UN Human Rights Council 2008, 2), the distribution of that food is highly unequal and small farmers on marginal lands can surely benefit from increased levels of production and productivity. Whether that food is consumed directly by the small producers or sold in the market, this should result in increased access to food.

On the other hand, CIDA's land policies do not address the root causes of the lack of food availability and distribution: the fact that small farmers are frequently pushed onto small, marginal lands in the first place. The highly unequal distribution of land in numerous developing countries has led to situations where large corporations and landowners acquire (legally or illegally) the best lands, forcing subsistence farmers to become landless farm workers or cultivate unproductive marginal lands. CIDA's focus on production and productivity for small farmers on marginal land thus implicitly legitimizes the highly unequal distribution of land and landlessness, which are the deeper structural causes of food insecurity in rural areas.

CIDA's active support for biotechnologies as a means to increase productivity is another contentious issue. The special rapporteur on the right to food argues, for example, that research and investments in genetically modified seeds have contributed to a "vertical integration between seed, pesticides, and production to increase corporate benefits" (UN Human Rights Council 2008, 17). Transnational corporations that have increased their control over the food chain and biotechnologies have been the beneficiaries, not small farmers. Thus, CIDA's active promotion of investments in biotechnologies does more to increase the profits of (Canadian) transnational corporations than to help the poor realize their right to food.

Accessibility

Accessibility refers to individuals' physical and economic access to adequate resources for acquiring appropriate foods for a nutritious diet. In other words, people must have access either to natural resources to produce their own food or to economic resources to buy food. However, since about 80 per cent of the people living with hunger (smallholders or agricultural workers, herders, artisanal fisherfolk, and members of indigenous communities) live in rural areas (UNDP 2005), access to land is essential to ensure the enjoyment of the right to food (UN General Assembly 2010, 3). Supporting the realization of the right to food for the most vulnerable communities requires policies that ensure direct access to productive resources to grow food, such as agrarian reform. In the context of an international trade regime that favours developed countries and creates disadvantages for developing states, particularly in the agriculture sector (UN Human Rights Council 2010, 6), land and food-security policies that support the realization of the right to food should also support "agrarian reform that benefits small-scale land holders and promotes security of tenure and access to land" (UN Human Rights Council 2010, 22).

The main aim of CIDA's land policies when it comes to the issue of access is to promote increased income for the poor to buy food (economic access), rather than a direct access to productive resources to grow their own food (land access). CIDA argues that reducing hunger and poverty in rural areas requires mainly that the "income of the rural poor must increase rapidly" (CIDA 2003, 4–5). It assumes that raising agricultural productivity will allow farm labour to find new off-farm employment, notably in agro-based processing (CIDA 2003, 9). CIDA also proposes more active participation in the local and international markets for those who remain in farming, which in the case of the poor would require diversifying their products and increasing their quality. The agency's strategies to help farmers at the local level are the provision of greater access to credit, support for agro-based processing, and the promotion of rural entrepreneurship. At the national level, CIDA supports the removal of "obstacles to international trade currently faced by the poorer developing countries – subsidies, and tariff and non-tariff barriers" so that "agricultural producers have a greater chance to participate in such trade" (CIDA 2003, 15). In general, CIDA also advocates the move "away from a subsistence orientation and government dominance to commercialization," as well as "opportunities to accelerate this process" (CIDA 2003, 13).

The 2003 policy indicates that "improving access, management, and administration of land" is one of CIDA's programming priorities to enhance food security, agricultural productivity, and income (CIDA 2003, 13). In regard to land access, however, CIDA addresses the issue only through a gender-equality lens, stating that its programming "will address the central role of women in agriculture and inequality in women's access to productive resources such as land" (CIDA 2003, 11). This focus on gender equality is certainly important and welcome since women are the main food producers in developing countries and account for a disproportionate 70 per cent of the hungry in the world (UN Human Rights Council 2008, 14). However, the issue of access to land is not only a gender issue. Avoiding a discussion on the larger issue of social justice in rural areas of developing countries, including land distribution or redistribution strategies, is not a mere omission: it reflects a clear political choice in favour of a commercial food system based on liberalized market policies.

While CIDA's policies may somewhat increase employment and income in the countryside, they impede rather than contribute to the realization of the right to food in developing countries because they support a food system that perpetuates and deepens inequalities. Helping marginalized communities in rural areas to make substantial progress toward the realization of the right to food requires policies that support direct access to productive resources to grow food, such as agrarian reform. CIDA, however, argues that the problem of access to land should be addressed through intensification and diversification of production systems rather than through the (re)distribution of land (CIDA 2003,13). Moreover, the commercial food system promoted by CIDA, with its focus on market integration and free trade, undermines the ability of developing countries to design and implement genuine agrarian-reform programs and creates more obstacles for the rural poor to access land. In a system where land is exclusively bought and sold on the market, securing access to land requires financial resources that the rural poor do not have. Research has shown that, even in cases where land distribution is attempted, it does not benefit the poor when the mechanisms of this distribution are market-based (Borras and Franco 2010). On the contrary, "these schemes have provided landlords better and broader means by which they can quickly consummate their evasion from redistributive land reform" (Borras 2005, 125). The special rapporteur on the right to food also notes that market-led agrarian reform shifts the logic of agrarian reform away from a concept of the right to land and redistribution toward a view that access to land is possible only through purchase of the land at market prices, despite a context of historically produced inequities (UN Human Rights Council 2008, 12).

Adequacy

The adequacy of the food that is available and accessible to people also matters to achieve food security. The FAO argues that, to be adequate, food must meet three criteria: it must be nutritional and meet the dietary needs of people; it must be safe for human consumption; and it must be culturally acceptable. Meeting dietary needs requires that "the diet as a whole contains a mix of sufficient nutrients for physical and mental growth, development and maintenance of the body, and physical activity that are in compliance with human physiological needs at all stages throughout the life cycle and according to gender and occupation" (UN ECOSOC 1999, 3). To be safe, food must be free of adverse substances, that is, from "contamination of foodstuffs through adulteration, poor environmental hygiene, and/or inappropriate handling at different stages of the food chain" (UN ECOSOC 1999, 3). Cultural acceptability refers to the need to take into account "perceived non nutrient-based values attached to food and food consumption" (UN ECOSOC 1999, 3).

The right to food can be realized only when people have access to adequate food, meaning that it is safe, nutritious, and culturally appropriate. CIDA recognizes that malnutrition – and not just under-nourishment – has a devastating impact on people's health. To increase not only the quantity but also the quality of the food available to the poor, CIDA stresses the importance of nutrition interventions such as the provision of micronutrients, the diversification of diets, the fortification of staple foods, and school feeding programs (CIDA 2010a, 5). Two of its main areas of focus have been the provision of micronutrients and the fortification of staple foods.

For CIDA, increasing the nutritional value of crops is a priority. The 2003 policy included a priority on "increasing the food and feed value of staple crops of the poor" (CIDA 2003, 13). This was reasserted in the 2010 strategy in which CIDA indicated its intention to "work with the CGIAR [Consultative Group on International Agricultural Research] toward increasing the nutritional value of crops" and helping identify "more nutritional crops" (CIDA 2010a, 7). This is to be achieved through "new science in the areas of genomics and biotechnology" that "can potentially improve crop and livestock adaptation to environmental stress" as well as improve yields (CIDA 2003, 12).

CIDA's commitment to increasing the availability of and access to nutritional food that meets the dietary need of people contributes to the realization of the right to food by fulfilling one of the three criteria of adequacy. However, the means through which CIDA seeks to improve the nutritional value of crops is cause for concern. The agency is a strong supporter of biotechnology and genomic research and relies on this science to improve yields and make crops more nutritional. The potential impact of genetically modified food on health is still unclear and promoting its use could go against another criterion of food adequacy: that food has to be safe for humans to eat. Moreover, the use of genetically modified seeds is already having a strong negative impact on biodiversity and on the ability of farmers to control their production. Strategies promoting the use of biotechnology in agriculture thus have a negative impact on the realization of the right to food because they do not meet all the criteria for food adequacy. They also undermine the sustainability and participation dimensions of the right to food.

Sustainability

The sustainability dimension underpins the previous three and is achieved when the systems through which food is produced are *environmentally* and *economically* sustainable. An environmentally sustainable food system rests on an agricultural model that promotes biodiversity and a sustainable use of water resources, reduces water and soil pollution, and maintains its ability to satisfy the needs of future populations. Agriculture has a key role to mitigate the impact of climate change and to provide adaptation strategies. The economic sustainability of the food system refers to long-term reduction of poverty. It requires increasing the incomes of small farmers by stimulating local demand. Studies have shown that the multiplier effect is far greater when demand is stimulated locally rather than internationally. Land and food policies that promote sustainability encourage ecological agriculture and investments that benefit smallholders directly.

In relation to environmental sustainability, CIDA's 2010 strategy argues that "increased agricultural production and productivity cannot come at the expense of the environment" and that the current agricultural paradigm based on the increased use of fertilizers and fresh water as well as land expansion is not sustainable (CIDA 2010a, 4). Thus, CIDA advocates a move toward "the adoption of sustainable agricultural development wherein agroecological approaches – such as resource conservation, environmental impact mitigation, and climate change mitigation and adaptation – are integral to programming aimed at increasing agricultural production and productivity" (CIDA 2010a, 4). Agroecology can boost farmers' resilience to climate change while minimizing greenhouse gas emissions, combating desertification, and preserving and promoting biological diversity (CIDA 2010a, 4). While concrete results on the ground must now be documented systematically and compared against those linked to traditional chemical-enriched commercial agriculture, this positioning is very encouraging and is likely to have a positive impact on the realization of the right to food.

Participation

The four dimensions examined previously have been characterized by the FAO as the four pillars of food security. The right to food encompasses these pillars, but it also goes beyond them to consider the *means* through which food security is achieved. The realization of the right to food thus also rests on the people's participation in the design and implementation of the policies that define their food system. As Jean Ziegler notes, "the right to food is not about charity, but about ensuring that all people have the capacity to feed themselves in dignity" (Ziegler 2011). Farmers around the world have significant expertise in agricultural techniques that offer high productivity while being ecologically sound. Land and food policies promoting the right to food need to be informed by farmers rather than imposed on them.

For the right to food to be realized fully, food-insecure groups in developing countries, which include most food producers, must be able to participate in the design and implementation of policies that define their food system. CIDA's contribution to the participation dimension of the right to food is mixed. On the one hand, the 2003 policy acknowledges the need for agricultural innovations to be "designed, tested, and transferred using participatory approaches" in order to be effective (CIDA 2003, 13). In its 2010 strategy, CIDA also created a food-security research fund to support research partnerships with developing countries, and identified as expected results the development of specialized expertise for farmers and better access to locally adapted technologies (CIDA 2010a, 7). These elements of CIDA's policies support the participation of farmers in the development of policies and technologies that affect them.

On the other hand, despite some acknowledgment of the importance of farmers' participation in the development of agricultural innovations, CIDA's approach to the governance of the food system is essentially top-down, and weakens farmers' control over their food system. Its promotion of a commercial food system, small farmers' integration into international markets, and new science and biotechnology may actually increase the dependence of the rural poor on transnational corporations.

CONCLUSION

The purpose of this chapter was to examine CIDA's past and current policies on agrarian issues and food security in order to assess its contribution to the realization of the right to food in developing countries. An overview of past policies and an assessment of the role of current CIDA policies on the realization of the five dimensions of the right to food in developing countries shows that, while current policies address all five dimensions of the right to food, which is a considerable improvement over past policies, they include worrying elements that appear to increase social inequalities and they fall short of addressing the key issue of access to land.

Prior to the creation of CIDA in 1968, Canada did not have specific land and food-security policies to govern its international assistance, and it mainly relied on the delivery of food aid to increase the *availability* of food in developing countries. CIDA's 1975 land policy focused mainly on increasing the *availability* of food and *economic access* to food for rural populations of developing countries. It promoted an integrated rural-development approach and refocused assistance away from food aid exclusively toward food production in developing countries. This was a positive development in terms of CIDA's contribution to the realization right to food, since it promoted an increase in the *availability* of food from within developing countries and increased *economic access* to food for some small farmers through a shift toward commercial agriculture.

The case studies of Colombia and Ghana, however, illustrate the shortcomings of the policy in terms of its contribution to two key dimensions of the right to food: *access to land* and *participation*. The CIDA-supported project in Colombia did increase food *availability* and *economic access* to food for the rural middle class. However, it also locked these farmers into a commercial farming system tied to the procurement of Canadian goods (such as fertilizers and pesticides) and circumvented a land-reform program designed to provide *access to land* to the poorest rural families. The Ghana case study provided another example in which Canadian commercial interests took precedence over the interests of the rural poor and showed how the lack of *participation* of the local population in the design and implementation of a rural-development project can negatively affect its outcome.

While maintaining its emphasis on production, productivity, and market access to increase the *availability* of food and the *economic access* to food for rural populations, CIDA also broadened its policies over the years to address the *adequacy, sustainability*, and *participation* dimensions of the right to food. These policies, however, also include elements that have a negative impact on the realization of the right to food. Though CIDA's support for agroecology will likely have a positive impact on environmental *sustainability*, some elements of the agency's policies in relation to adequacy and participation are more contentious. For instance, CIDA recognizes the importance of nutrition interventions, notably through the fortification of staple food, to improve the quality of food. However, at a time when the long-term safety of genetically modified food is still an important concern, CIDA's strong support for biotechnology and genomic research to improve the nutritional quality of crops may compromise the *adequacy* of the food produced. Also, while CIDA's support for the inclusion of farmers in research partnerships to develop locally adapted technologies will increase their *participation*, its promotion of a commercial food system and small farmers' integration in international markets may weaken their control over their own production and increase their dependence on transnational corporations.

In the end, despite some welcome progress, CIDA's current policies continue to fail to address the heart of the food-insecurity problem: the issue of access to land. The fact that half of the world's hungry are smallholder farmers at a time when food production should be sufficient to feed twice the world's population is a clear indication that food insecurity is more a result of an extreme inequality in terms of access to land than of a lack of production and productivity. Thus, while CIDA aims to increase the production and productivity of small farmers on marginal lands, it fails to deal with the reasons why these farmers were pushed onto these marginal lands in the first place. In fact, CIDA's promotion of a commercial farming system further strengthens a structure that leads to the consolidation of large landholdings in the hands of a few and the eviction of subsistence farmers from fertile lands. The agency's land and food-security policies over time may have increasingly contributed to the five dimensions of the right to food, but always in a manner consistent with Canada's own commercial interests and/or commitment to economic and political liberalism, deliberately avoiding the dimensions that required structural changes. What is needed to reduce significantly food insecurity and contribute to the realization of right to food in rural areas of developing countries is genuine land redistribution that will benefit the landless and small farmers. Thus far, CIDA has talked the pro-poor talk, but it has failed to walk the redistribution walk.

NOTES

1 The Development Assistance Group became in 1961 the Development Assistance Committee (DAC). See OECD (2006).
2 Developed and popularized in the 1970s by many OECD donors, integrated rural-development projects (IRDP) sought to address issues and challenges of rural poverty through a systematized and standardized approach that comprised "activities in agriculture, water supply, health, rural infrastructure, and small-scale off-farm enterprises" (Blench et al. 2002, xi.). However, as noted more recently in the context of a new rural-development approach, the IRDP faced many shortfalls, "particularly ... problems with ownership and maintenance of the infrastructure projects (roads, wells etc.), the apparent lack of impact from many years of capacity building within government, and the growing aid/project dependence of government" (Blench et al. 2002, 136; see also Hedlund 1993).
3 Universal Declaration of Human Rights (1948), Article 25. "Everyone has the right to a standard of living adequate for the health and well-being of himself and of his family, including food, clothing, housing and medical care and necessary social services, and the right to security in the event of unemployment, sickness, disability, widowhood, old age, or other lack of livelihood in circumstances beyond his control."
4 Article 2 of the International Covenant on Economic, Social and Cultural Rights (ICESCR). "Each State Party to the present Covenant undertakes to take steps, individually and through international assistance and cooperation, especially economic and technical, to the maximum of its available resources, with a view to achieving progressively the full realization of the rights recognized in the present Covenant by all appropriate means, including particularly the adoption of legislative measures."

REFERENCES

Amnesty International. 2010. *What Are Economic, Social and Cultural Rights?* http://www.amnesty.org/en/economic-and-social-cultural-rights/what-are-escr. Accessed 12 July 2010.
Barr, Gerry. 2010. "What Is Guiding Canada's Aid Spending?" *Embassy*. 26 May.
Blench, Roger, et al. 2002. "Area Development Projects, Poverty Reduction, and the New Architecture of Aid: Volume II – Case Studies." A Sida Evaluation Report, 14 February 2001. Sida Evaluation Series, Stockholm: Swedish International Development Cooperation Agency.

http://www.oecd.org/dataoecd/55/28/35200611.pdf. Accessed
9 December 2011.

Borras Jr, Saturnino M. 2005. "Can Redistributive Reform Be Achieved
via Market-Based Voluntary Land Transfer Schemes? Evidence and
Lessons from the Philippines." *Journal of Development Studies* 41,
no. 1: 90–134.

Borras Jr, Saturnino M., and Jennifer C. Franco. 2010. "Contemporary
Discourses and Contestations around Pro-Poor Land Policies and Land
Governance." *Journal of Agrarian Change* 10: 1–32.

Canadian Council for International Co-operation. 2010. *A Time to Act.
Implementing the ODA Accountability Act: A Canadian CSO Agenda for
Aid Reform.* Ottawa: Canadian Council for International Co-operation.

Canadian International Development Agency. 1975. *Strategy for
International Development Cooperation 1975–1980.* Gatineau, QC:
Canadian International Development Agency.

– 2003. *Promoting Sustainable Rural Development through Agriculture:
Canada Making a Difference in the World.* Gatineau, QC: Canadian
International Development Agency.

– 2009. *Canada's G-8 2009 L'Aquila Commitment for Sustainable
Agricultural Development.* http://www.acdi-cida.gc.ca/acdi-cida/ACDI-
CIDA.nsf/eng/NAD-426114720-LJ5. Accessed 7 September 2010.

– 2010a. *Increasing Food Security: CIDA's Food Security Strategy.*
Gatineau, QC: Canadian International Development Agency.

– 2010b. *Project Profile for Improving Productivity and Market Success
(IPMS)* http://www.acdi-cida.gc.ca/cidaweb/cpo.nsf/vLUWebProjEn/204
3EB543B94745185257019003 1857F?OpenDocument. Accessed
8 October 2010.

– 2010c. *Project Profile for Land Management and Administration –
Canada.* http://www.acdi-cida.gc.ca/CIDAWEB/cpo.nsf/vWebCSAZEn/2
B96C9225B68A36885257140005 8DB9E. Accessed 8 October 2010.

Caouette, Dominique. 2007. "Land Policies and the Rural Poor in the
Official Agendas of International Development Institutions: Some
Critical Reflections." Paper presented at the Annual Conference of the
Canadian Association for the Study of International Development,
University of Saskatoon, 1 June.

Carty, Robert, Virginia Smith, and Latin American Working Group
(LAWG). 1981. *Perpetuating Poverty: The Political Economy of
Canadian Foreign Aid.* Toronto: Between the Lines.

Colombo Plan Secretariat. *The Colombo Plan: History.* http://www.
colombo-plan.org/history.php. Accessed 12 July 2010.

Dupuis, Monique. 1984. *Crise mondiale et aide internationale: Stratégie canadienne et développement du Tiers-Monde*. Montreal: Nouvelle Optique.

Food and Agriculture Organization. 1998. *The Right to Food in Theory and Practice*. Rome: Food and Agriculture Organization.

– 1999. *World Food Summit: 13–17 November 1996, Rome, Italy*. http://www.fao.org/docrep/x2051e/x2051e00.HTM#P83_5958. Accessed 1 July 2010.

– 2002. *World Food Summit: Five Years Later: Resources Mobilization to Ensure the Right to Food*. http://www.fao.org/WorldFoodSummit/sideevents/papers/y6667e.htm. Accessed 5 July 2010.

– 2004. *Voluntary Guidelines to Support the Progressive Realization of the Right to Adequate Food in the Context of National Food Security*. Rome: Food and Agriculture Organization.

– 2007. *The Right to Food. Achieving the Right to Food: The Human Rights Challenge of the Twenty-First Century*. Rome: World Food Day and Special Initiatives Branch, Food and Agriculture Organization.

– 2008. *Methods to Monitor the Human Right to Adequate Food. Volume I: Making the Case for Rights-Focused and Rights-Based Monitoring*. Rome: Economic and Social Development Department, Food and Agriculture Organization.

– 2009a. *The Right to Food. Book 3: Guide to Conducting a Right to Food Assessment*. Rome: Food and Agriculture Organization.

– 2009b. *The Right to Food and Access to Natural Resources Using Human Rights Arguments and Mechanisms to Improve Resource Access for the Rural Poor*. Rome: Food and Agriculture Organization.

– 2009c. *The State of Food Insecurity in the World – Economic Crisis: Impacts and Lessons Learned*. Rome: Economic and Social Development Department, Food and Agriculture Organization.

Hedlund, Hans. 1993. *To End an Aid Programme: The Phasing out Process of the Integrated Rural Development Programme, Eastern Province, Zambia*. Stockholm: Sida.

Morrison, David. 1998. *Aid and Ebb Tide: A History of CIDA and Canadian Development Assistance*. Waterloo, ON: Wilfrid Laurier University Press.

Organisation for Economic Co-operation and Development. 2006. *DAC in Dates: The History of OECD's Development Assistance Committee*. Paris: Organisation for Economic Co-operation and Development.

Standing Committee on External Affairs and International Trade (SCEAIT). 1987. *For Whose Benefit?: Report of the Standing Committee on*

External Affairs and International Trade on Canada's Official Development Assistance Policies and Programs. Ottawa: Queen's Printer for Canada.

United Nations Economic and Social Council (ECOSOC). 1999. 20th Session, General Comment 12. *Substantive Issues Arising in the Implementation of the International Covenant on Economic, Social and Cultural Rights: General Comment 12. The Right to Adequate Food (art. 11)*. E/C.12/1999/5.

United Nations General Assembly. 1966. *International Covenant on Economic, Social and Cultural Rights*, Resolution 2200A (XXI). 16 December.

– 2010. *Promotion and Protection of Human Rights: Human Rights Questions including Alternative Approaches for Improving the Effective Enjoyment of Human Rights and Fundamental Freedoms. The Right to Food. Report of the Special Rapporteur on the Right to Food, Olivier De Schutter*. A/65/281.

United Nations Human Rights Council. 2008. *Promotion and Protection of All Human Rights, Civil, Political, Economic, Social and Cultural Rights, including the Right to Development. Report of the Special Rapporteur on the Right to Food, Jean Ziegler*. A/HRC/7/5.

– 2010. *Preliminary Study of the Human Rights Council. Advisory Committee on Discrimination in the Context of the Right to Food*. A/HRC/13/32.

United Nations Millennium Project Task Force on Hunger. 2005. *Halving Hunger, It Can Be Done*. New York: United Nations Development Programme.

United Nations Population Fund. 2008. *Human Rights: The Human-Rights-Based Approach*. http://www.unfpa.org/rights/approaches.htm. Accessed 5 April 2011.

Ziegler, Jean. 2011. *What Is the Right to Food?* http://www.righttofood. org/new/html/WhatRighttofood.html. Accessed 20 May 2011.

7

Untangling Canadian Aid Policy: International Agreements, CIDA'S Policies, and Micro-Policy Negotiations in Tanzania

MOLLY DEN HEYER

Historical accounts of Canadian aid policy and the structure of Canada's international development assistance reveal a cycle of parliamentary reviews, Senate recommendations, and internal reform programs that continually fail to take root (Morrison 1998). As the main instrument of national aid policy, the Canadian International Development Agency (CIDA) often comes under fire for being a policy-less organization. Despite widespread belief to the contrary, the agency does have a policy framework, albeit a fragmented one with an overabundance of smaller, often contradictory priorities and procedures. In order to understand the causes behind CIDA's inability to articulate a clear set of policies, this chapter addresses the following questions: Who makes aid policy? What is its role? What is the relationship between aid policy and practice?

The chapter explores these questions through a case study of Canadian aid policy and Canada's assistance to Tanzania. I follow the route of policy making and implementation from official government documents "down the rabbit hole" into CIDA's operations in Tanzania. Throughout, I draw from extensive research on aid effectiveness and Canadian aid policy, for which I conducted thirty-six interviews, a policy review, qualitative observation of key donor meetings, and a focus group, in Ottawa/Gatineau and Dar es Salaam between August 2008 and January 2009. The respondents represented CIDA, other bilateral and multilateral aid agencies, the "dialogue process" in Tanzania,[1] the Tanzanian government, and Canadian and Tanzanian civil society organizations (csos). I selected Canadian-Tanzanian development cooperation as my case study because of the two countries' long aid relationship, as well as Tanzania's reputation as an early adopter of aid effectiveness policies.

In the following discussion I use an expanded concept of policy that includes policy influences, official documents, and the nuances of practice. It argues that a holistic understanding of policy reveals the external and internal influences on CIDA that create a contradictory mixture of goals and objectives. Competing agendas make Canadian aid policy documents difficult to draft and maintain over time. Moreover, CIDA's lack of overarching policy and its frequently changing priorities undermine the effectiveness of its practitioners in the field, since practitioners rely on official policies for representation and legitimacy for micro-policy negotiations. Within CIDA, the pressure to show results – and the absence of clear directives – leads to a bureaucratic slowdown as CIDA becomes more risk-averse and centralized. This discussion of Canadian aid policy's inner workings begins with a policy definition, followed by the mapping of CIDA's policy contexts, its official policy framework, and the agency's micro-policy negotiations regarding its assistance programs in Tanzania.

EXPANDING POLICY ANALYSIS

David Black and Heather Smith (1993) argue that analysis of Canadian aid policy must move beyond mere descriptions of policy documents to understanding why and how policy operates. This requires expanding the concept of policy analysis in four new directions. First, the policy analysis employed in this chapter incorporates the concept of discourse to understand how language is used to shape the policy discussions, problems, and proposed solutions. It treats the standard analysis of ministerial statements, strategies, and priorities as a product of a wider negotiation process within which different perspectives and types of knowledge collide to form new ways of understanding issues (Hajer and Wagenaar 2003).

Second, understanding how discourse shapes policy is also critical to grasping the different roles of policy. These roles include the instrumental function of policy documents to provide organizational direction to and coordination of activities, as well as the politically symbolic function of policy to create the perception of consensus, motivate actors, and legitimize practices (van Gastel and Nuijten

2005). Third, the analysis incorporates the micro-policy negotiations embedded in CIDA's day-to-day operations that support the official language of policy documents. These processes involve constant negotiation and the perpetual reinterpretation of key concepts. A diffuse network of smaller negotiations helps inform, frame, interpret, and apply policy. Referring to CIDA, Phillip Rawkins describes how "patterns of activity emerge from an ongoing series of small decisions around projects and programs made by project officers and country directors within their respective areas of discretion. These become codified as routine response and hence part of the 'stuff' of organizational knowledge. Policy is then made incrementally from the pull of individual decisions towards a norm" (Rawkins 1994, 167). As the case study of Canadian aid to Tanzania will demonstrate, practice not only implements policy, it also contributes to its formation, modification, and interpretation.

Finally, analysis must also extend to the wider external influences that shape official policy statements and informal practices. CIDA does not act alone; it is one system embedded in a web of overlapping systems. This web consists of a diverse set of actors and institutions that creates and recreates a complex ecosystem through the accumulation of actions in a negotiated collective process. This web of interactions influences policy formation in a number of ways, ranging from the adoption of new terms and concepts to policy transfers. Thus, analysis must also consider the wider aid ecosystem.

MAPPING CANADIAN AID

In keeping with an expanded definition of policy analysis, I begin the case study by situating aid policy within the context of the Canadian policy landscape. Figure 1 provides a rudimentary cross-section of the ecosystem surrounding CIDA and its Tanzanian field office. Starting at the top of the figure, a set of international organizations generates international discourse around standard policies and practices. Below, CIDA is part of a larger Canadian development-policy sphere in which there is extensive interaction with other departments and agencies. Adding to the complexity, CIDA field offices are embedded in local processes with other donors and recipients at the country level. In the Tanzanian case, these include coordinating with donors in the dialogue process through joint coordination groups, as well as cluster and sector working groups.

Figure 1
The Aid Ecosystem

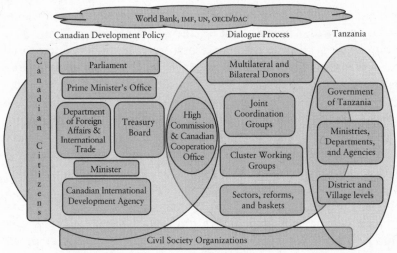

In turn, these groups work with the Tanzanian government, its ministries, departments, and agencies, as well as with local governments. Finally, international and local CSOs span the different spheres. These overlapping systems shape formal and informal understandings of Canadian aid policy.

While Figure 1 is helpful in identifying the primary actors, it is only a static and partial snapshot of a complex system. The categorizations are not based on discrete values, but rather on loose groupings of people who are highly interactive. A more accurate visual representation of the Canadian aid ecosystem would be a beehive of activity, wherein development practitioners circulate through different locations via joint programming, knowledge networks, field postings, and secondments. Development practitioners form epistemic communities that assemble around the globe. They create norms around shared experiences, research, and peer pressure, which in turn facilitate policy transfers among organizations.

Liam Swiss (2010) argues that development practitioners internalize new policy ideas and seek to promote them within their respective organizations. This internalization occurs through several processes. First, organizations such as the Organisation for Economic Co-operation and Development (OECD) set standards and create peer pressure for practitioners to conform. Second, policy makers

often appeal to outside authorities in an effort to convince government officials and development practitioners of their policies' validity. As Swiss's case study of gender policy shows, it is often easier to
justify particular policies and practices if other large donors have
adopted them already. Third, development practitioners often mimic
leaders in their particular field of expertise. The setting of standards,
establishment of authority, and imitation of superiors operate concurrently to create legitimacy around certain policy norms (Swiss
2010). This type of policy influence is a double-edged sword, for,
while sharing research, setting professional standards and ethics,
and identifying lessons learned can improve development practice, it
can also lead to herding behaviour, the uncritical adoption of policy
trends, and frequent policy changes.

The Canadian aid ecosystem contains a wide array of external
influences that help shape policy formation at CIDA. Chris Brown
and Edward Jackson (2009) note that the international development
community has a great deal of influence regarding the types of
Canadian aid delivered and how, but the amount of aid and where it
is directed are determined by the domestic political process. The
Canadian government also sets the regulatory environment within
which aid is disbursed. This combination of influences, from the
international development community and domestic politics, define
the parameters of Canadian aid policy. The following section further
explores the various types of actors present in the Canadian aid ecosystem and how they influence aid policy.

The International Development Community

The international development community intersects with Canadian
aid policy on the topic of technical expertise and aid modalities, or
the "how" of development (Brown and Jackson 2009). International
influence operates at two key points of intersection. The first cross-
roads is present where Canada participates in international organizations (including international financial institutions, the UN and the
OECD) and associations (the Commonwealth, the Francophonie,
G8, G20). International cooperation results in guidelines, agreements, treaties, conventions, and declarations that generate awareness of issues and tether the government to a minimal level of
commitment. The second point of intersection occurs in recipient
countries among development practitioners. In major cities, such as
Dar es Salaam, donors form a community, exchanging information

and coordinating their activities. A number of development practitioners interviewed noted that they felt a high degree of peer pressure to adopt the latest policy trend – in this case, aid effectiveness.

The influence of the international development community is further complicated by the fact that interpretations of aid effectiveness policies vary according to where the actors are situated within the aid ecosystem. Internationally, the OECD's Development Assistance Committee (DAC) sets the standards for aid effectiveness through a series of global studies, reports, High-Level Forums, and peer reviews. Canada, as an OECD/DAC member, fully supports aid effectiveness policies and has generally committed to the key principles enshrined in the Paris Declaration.[2] However, interpretations of these policies shift when they are applied in a Canadian context. Two of the five aid effectiveness principles resonate with Canada's existing domestic focus on accountability. The Canadian version of aid effectiveness emphasizes managing for results and mutual accountability, while minimizing attention to harmonization, alignment, and ownership (Lalonde 2009; and Brown, chapter 3, this volume).

The configuration of aid effectiveness policies changes once again in recipient countries, such as Tanzania. CIDA staff members working in the field must negotiate their interpretations of aid effectiveness policies with the government of Tanzania and its other donor partners in the dialogue process. The government of Tanzania tends to emphasize country ownership and general budget support (GBS), while the donor partners stress coordination and program-based approaches.[3] Such divergent interpretations of aid effectiveness illustrate how different practitioners translate policy as it moves through a sequence of actors and levels within the development industry. In this way, the international community influences wider trends in Canadian development policies. However, this influence diminishes as policies are implemented at the national level. External influence increases again as Canadian policies are implemented within the recipient countries. These varying levels of influence contribute to the variations and occasional contradictions that arise in how policy is interpreted at the international, national, and recipient-country levels.

The Canadian Government

Whereas the international development community influences how development is delivered, the Canadian government determines why, where, and to what extent Canada contributes to international development assistance (Brown and Jackson 2009). Regarding the purposes of Canadian aid, the academic literature reveals deep fissures throughout the federal bureaucracy. Canada struggles to reconcile a humane internationalist approach, based on an ethical obligation to help alleviate global poverty, with a realist approach that seeks to deliver aid while supporting domestic economic and political interests (Pratt 1994). Competing interests involving trade, security, diplomacy, and public opinion further complicate the tension between altruism and self-interest. This ambiguity surrounding aid's purpose weakens CIDA's overall ability to define and defend its policy framework.

Although CIDA is a semi-autonomous agency, it does not have a legislated mandate,[4] and it exists largely under the purview of the Department of Foreign Affairs and International Trade (DFAIT). Except for a brief period in 1979–80, CIDA was not granted a cabinet seat until the junior post of minister of international cooperation was created in 1996 (Morrison 1998, xvii). Even with the junior post, CIDA's lack of political sway is made evident by the fact that, in the fourteen-year period that followed, the position of minister for international cooperation was filled by a succession of eight low-profile politicians.[5]

Like all government departments and agencies, CIDA must jockey for resources in the federal system. CIDA, however, is particularly vulnerable to the political influence of other bodies, such as Foreign Affairs, National Defence, or the Prime Minister's Office. Its broad mandate of development provides an umbrella under which other departments may seek to further their own mandates through strategic "partnerships." Stephen Brown (2008) describes CIDA as being trapped in a policy paradox: increases to CIDA's annual budget and its political profile correlate with a reduction in CIDA's capacity to promote aid policy focused on poverty reduction. This tendency has been amplified with the government's adoption of a whole-of-government approach that promotes policy coherence among departments without resolving the fundamental question of who is setting the standard for policy around which others will cohere.

The relative strength of CIDA's policy framework is of particular importance in terms of how its policies are entangled with the objectives of other departments. As seen in Table 1, CIDA managed only 74 per cent of Canadian official development assistance (ODA)

Table 1
ODA Disbursements by Government Department

Department	2008–09 ODA Disbursement (in $ millions)
Canadian International Development Agency (CIDA)	3,575.19
Finance Canada	676.31
Foreign Affairs and International Trade (DFAIT)	277.70
International Development Research Centre (DRC)	175.75
Citizenship and Immigration Canada	92.05
Royal Canadian Mounted Police	19.61
National Defence	18.79
Health Canada	11.97
Environment Canada	4.04
Labour Canada	1.40
Industry Canada	0.97
Parks Canada	0.47
TOTAL	4,854.28

Source: CIDA 2009a.

in 2008–09 (CIDA 2009a). The remaining funds were divided among several government departments and agencies, including the Department of Finance, which is responsible for contributions to the International Monetary Fund (IMF) and World Bank. While these divisions build on the expertise of different departments, they also hinder CIDA's capacity as the principal provider of development assistance and impede its attempts to build a coherent policy framework for Canadian aid.

The Canadian government's regulatory system also places constraints on CIDA and the ways in which it delivers aid. These restrictions have been compounded with the election of a Conservative government and Parliament's subsequent adoption of the Federal Accountability Act in 2006. While the increased regulation of government finances is generally well received,[6] the act has had a number of unintended effects. As explained below, it has undermined nuanced understandings of accountability by focusing on quantitative indicators and checklists, rather than pursuing a genuine dialogue regarding aid effectiveness. The act also accentuates CIDA's natural tendency toward risk-aversion, to be discussed in the following sections.

This study's research participants expressed concerns over the Federal Accountability Act, as well as CIDA's reliance on approvals from the Treasury Board Secretariat (TBS). The TBS has a particularly difficult relationship with CIDA. Often acting as a gatekeeper, the TBS sets the terms and conditions for international assistance, which include drafting macro-management frameworks, delegating authority, and approving exemptions (Lalonde 2009). The aid officials who were interviewed complained that TBS terms and conditions are often ill-suited to overseas work and place a heavy burden on CIDA staff. In many cases, submissions to the TBS consume a large amount of CIDA staff time, cause lengthy administrative delays, and unnecessarily influence policy decisions. One frustrated CIDA employee noted in 2008 that "the Treasury Board is so unpredictable for us because the Treasury Board is not CIDA. They are at the whim of what is happening politically in the country. But right now we are in a situation where the Treasury Board may not sit, Parliament may get dissolved ... and we are trying to get an approval. It is completely at the mercy of the Treasury Board ... and the Treasury Board has all sorts of other higher priorities."

The lack of a clear legislative mandate, junior minister status, and regulatory frameworks, combined with the political influence of other departments, have left CIDA in a tenuous position from which to negotiate development policy. David Morrison's (1998) detailed review of CIDA's policies illustrates a series of concessions made to Canadian commercial and diplomatic agendas. Accordingly, instead of arguing a position, CIDA "sought to safeguard its autonomy by anticipating what other departments were likely to want of it" (Pratt 1994, 334). While this strategy allows the agency to muddle along in the short term, it has hindered the formation of a long-term aid policy framework for Canada. These policy inconsistencies are evident in CIDA's partnerships with non-governmental organizations (NGOs).

Non-Governmental Organizations

The NGO community interacts with Canadian development policy on issues of aid contributions, recipient countries, and aid modalities. These junctions stem from three activities. First, NGOs generate public awareness of specific issues or events. They are often instrumental in mobilizing the public around easily identified issues such as humanitarian disasters (e.g., the 1980s Ethiopian famine, the 2004 Asian tsunami, the 2010 Haitian earthquake). Second, a number of NGOs also lobby the Canadian government. For example, the Canadian Council for International Co-operation (CCIC) was instrumental in the passing of the ODA Accountability Act in 2008 (see, in this volume, McGill; Brown, chapter 3; and Blackwood and Stewart). Finally, on a smaller scale, NGOs can integrate into the day-to-day functioning of CIDA by creating knowledge networks or managing CIDA projects. For instance, one respondent working for a Canadian NGO described a situation wherein s/he drafted a brief on the latest advancements in her/his field for a CIDA counterpart. The information in the brief was later used at CIDA as the basis for a policy paper on food security. This illustrates how a number of NGOs exert subtle influence within CIDA's policy processes.

In the past, the partnership between CIDA and the NGO community was generally positive with only sporadic periods of contention. Some common complaints from NGOs during this time included bureaucratic delays, excessive paperwork, budget cuts, and inconsistent policies. However, in 2010 sweeping funding cuts to well-respected advocacy organizations, such as KAIROS,[7] Alternatives, MATCH International, and CCIC, sparked fear within the NGO community. The government has remained characteristically circumspect on the issue, suggesting that these programs no longer fit within CIDA's policy framework or priorities. The NGO community, however, claims that these cuts send a clear signal that those who speak out against government policies risk losing their funding (see Smillie, this volume). Furthermore, there may be a long-term policy shift in favour of organizations that provide services, and a concurrent marginalization of advocacy groups (Berthiaume 2010a). Speculation notwithstanding, it is still too soon to tell whether these kinds of funding cuts will weaken the NGO community or prompt it to lobby the government more vigorously.

The Canadian Public

While the Canadian public has some ability to influence the size and direction of aid flows, as demonstrated after the Ethiopian famine and Asian tsunami, the public's lack of awareness of aid's complexity and long-term nature has bred apathy among government officials. A study by Alain Noël, Jean-Philippe Thérien, and Sébastien Dallaire notes, "On average, Canadians think that 10.5 per cent of the national budget is devoted to aid; only twenty per cent know that, in fact, it amounts to less than two per cent" (2004, 34). In actuality, Canada allocated 0.27 per cent of its gross national income (GNI) to aid in 2004, slowly increasing to 0.34 per cent of GNI in 2008 (OECD 2010). This compares poorly to the OECD average of 0.48 per cent in 2009 and the UN target of 0.7 per cent (DAC 2010). The public's shallow commitment to aid was further revealed when the participants in Noël et al.'s study were asked to prioritize budget spending. International development assistance consistently placed last in lists of funding priorities. The government's general lack of commitment to foreign aid was amply demonstrated from the late 1980s to mid-1990s, when a decade of steady cutbacks resulted in an overall 5 per cent decline in government spending. CIDA was subjected to especially drastic cuts, losing 33 per cent of its annual budget during this time (Brown and Jackson 2009, 16).

Several observations may help explain the gap between public perception and reality. First, development differs from other public-policy areas in that the targets or beneficiaries reside outside Canada and do not vote in Canadian elections. This extraterritorial constituency must rely on Canadian CSOs and independent citizens for advocacy and public support. Second, international development has less tangible results than most other government departments. Development results are difficult to measure because of poor data quality, ambiguities of attribution, and the lack of infrastructure and stability in recipient countries. This is further complicated by significant changes in the nature of development work. The development field, and bilateral organizations in particular, currently emphasize scaling-up and increasing donor coordination. In general, donors no longer focus on small, signature projects but rather on larger, program-based approaches. This shift has made development work more bureaucratic and abstract, allowing fewer results to be attributed to specific donors.

Third, the media's coverage of development scandals has shaken the public's faith in international development. Starting in the late 1970s, a series of media reports and books placed a negative spotlight on the development industry's "inept bureaucrats," as well as "corrupt governments" and "victimized poor" in recipient countries.[8] This has encouraged public distrust of development organizations. Misconceptions are accentuated by the many NGOs promoting oversimplified problem-solving scenarios for fundraising purposes. International development's negative and simplistic portrayal in the media only serves to widen the gap between the public's understanding of development and field-level realities. Given this, the Canadian public's preoccupation with trendy issues distracts from long-term opportunities to influence CIDA's policies or indeed the government's disposition toward CIDA

As the above section illustrates, pressures from within the aid ecosystem shape Canadian aid policy. While the international development community often provides the latest policy language and methods, it is Canada's domestic politics that informs where, when, and to what extent aid is delivered. Unfortunately, CIDA's lack of stature within the federal government is further confounded by a nervous NGO community and shallow public support. Meanwhile, CIDA's ongoing lack of purpose and direction has given way to an uneven and contradictory aid policy framework.

THE FICKLENESS OF CIDA'S OFFICIAL POLICY

As explained above, the Canadian aid ecosystem contains a number of cross-pressures that influence CIDA's policies. Rather than managing these pressures, CIDA has allowed itself to be shaped by them, resulting in an official policy framework that is sparse, outdated, and inconsistent. Table 2, "CIDA's Policy Suite," contains a list of policies and their publication dates as shown on the agency's website in the fall of 2011. Of the fourteen documents, two are not dated and four were published before 2000. The last document to contain an overarching policy vision was published in 2002.[9]

The only overarching policy document on CIDA's list is *Canada Making a Difference in the World: A Policy Statement on Strengthening Aid Effectiveness* (2002). This policy document features concepts from the nascent aid effectiveness agenda, including program-based approaches (PBA), ownership, donor coordination, and policy coherence. The "new" language of the time is jumbled with a series of recycled recommendations concerning countries of concentration, untying aid, doubling aid to Africa, and results-based management. While these recommendations are helpful, the document as a whole lacks a coherent vision.

198 Molly den Heyer

Table 2
CIDA's Policy Suite

Policies	
CIDA's Policy for Environmental Sustainability	1992
CIDA's Policy for Performance Review	n/a
CIDA's Policy on Gender Equality	2010*
CIDA's Policy on Poverty Reduction	1996
Policy for CIDA on Human Rights, Democratization and Good Governance	1996
Policy Statement on Strengthening Aid Effectiveness	2002
Results-Based Management Policy Statement	2008
Strategies	
Sustainable Development Strategy	2007–09
Securing the Future of Children and Youth: CIDA's Children and Youth Strategy	2009
Increasing Food Security: CIDA's Food Security Strategy	2010
Stimulating Sustainable Economic Growth: CIDA's Sustainable Economic Growth Strategy	2011
Frameworks	
CIDA's Strategic Planning and Reporting Framework	n/a
The Agency Accountability Framework	1998
CIDA's Framework for Assessing Gender Equality Results	2010

* As mentioned in McGill (this volume), the 2010 gender equality policy is a reissue of the 1999 one, with minor modifications, rather than a new policy.

Source: http://www.acdi-cida.gc.ca/acdi-cida/acdi-cida.nsf/eng/JUD-826145832-Q9M (accessed 6 September 2011).

Conspicuously missing from CIDA's official policy suite is the *International Policy Statement: A Role of Pride and Influence in the World* coordinated by the Paul Martin government and released in 2005. This document attempted to gather all of Canada's foreign policy initiatives under one framework. It contains five chapters, on commerce, defence, development, diplomacy, and a general overview, each of which was released as a stand-alone booklet. The development chapter emphasizes a whole-of-government approach, streamlining aid, enhancing partnerships, and doubling aid to Africa. Common critiques of the paper include excessive moralizing and paternalism around the notion of Canadian values, an indulgent focus on promoting Canadian interests, and the unusual process by which it was produced (Black and Tiessen 2007; Brown 2007). The chapter on development found in CIDA's web archive is stamped with the following statement: "Please note that this was never officially adopted by the Canadian International Development Agency (CIDA). It is available for reference only" (DFAIT 2005). The caveat relegates the document's status to a non-policy statement and highlights partisan involvement and competition over ideas and approaches within and among government departments.

In the absence of overarching policy documents, CIDA has released a number of lists indicating its priority issues and countries of concentration. Between 2000 and 2009, CIDA posted five different lists, resulting in an environment in which the adoption of new priorities often outpaced the organization's ability to redirect programming. For instance, in 2005, CIDA announced that its priorities would be governance, health (with a focus on HIV/AIDS), basic education, private-sector development, environmental sustainability, and the crosscutting theme of gender equity (Office of the Auditor General of Canada 2009). Barry Carin and Gordon Smith (2010) argue that these priorities are vague and could easily be broken down into another twenty-two sectors. The Martin government also attempted to concentrate two-thirds of aid in twenty-five countries, fourteen of which are in Africa. While the policy brought some degree of status and increased resources to the countries of concentration, it failed to narrow the list of recipient countries (Stairs 2005).

The election of Stephen Harper's government in 2006 marked a new era in Canadian politics and placed CIDA in a situation of further uncertainty. International development was not a priority for the Conservative government and the two successive ministers of international cooperation, Josée Verner and Beverley Oda, were also unknown factors, lacking any visible experience on the topic. The only clear international objective of the government was supporting the troops in Afghanistan (Black and den Heyer 2010). Shortly after coming to power, Harper announced that Canada would re-engage with the Western hemisphere. This left many wondering how the government intended to offer more programs in Latin America and the Caribbean, maintain commitments to Afghanistan, and double aid to Africa, while simultaneously concentrating aid in fewer countries. Instead of clarifying a new policy direction, the government issued a series of smaller reviews, financial regulations, and management frameworks for CIDA. This "drip-feed" of vision-less instructions only served to create more inconsistency and confusion within the agency (Gulrajani 2010).

The status of the 2005 list of countries of concentration remained unclear until February 2008, when Minister Oda announced that the agency would concentrate 80 per cent of its aid in twenty countries, of which only six were in Africa. Then, in 2009, Oda made a second announcement that narrowed CIDA's aid priorities to food security, sustainable economic growth, and children and youth. Over the next two years (2009–11), CIDA developed a strategy paper for each priority area.

In 2009 CIDA released a short (seven pages) and quite vague policy document titled *Securing the Future of Children and Youth: CIDA's Children and Youth Strategy*. The strategy contains three objectives: improvement of child and maternal health, higher-quality education and more learning opportunities, and protecting the rights of children and youth (CIDA 2009b). This strategy was later supplemented by the announcement of the Muskoka Initiative on Maternal, Newborn and Child Health during the G8 summit in June 2010. The remaining strategy papers were developed in subsequent years, with the eight-page *Increasing Food Security: CIDA's Food Security Strategy* released in 2010, and the seven-page *Stimulating Sustainable Economic Growth: CIDA's Sustainable Economic Growth Strategy* in 2011.

These intermittent and vague strategies suggest that international development is not a priority for the Conservative government and that, when it does focus on aid, it relies on common charity-oriented archetypes. For example, the Children and Youth Strategy and the Muskoka Initiative can be viewed, quite literally, as motherhood statements. The depiction of women and children as victims of circumstances requiring immediate assistance cannot be contested. However, "victims" and their problems are far more complex than was captured in the strategies. Furthermore, many of the objectives stated in the strategies do not distinguish between humanitarian aid and long-term international development programs that address the roots of poverty. For example, one of the objectives prescribes "food aid and nutrition to provide more flexible, predictable, and needs-based funding to meet the emergency and long-term food and nutrients needs of the most vulnerable and high-risk populations" (CIDA 2010a, 3).

All three of CIDA's new strategies abdicate a degree of responsibility for the conceptualization and execution of polices to multilateral organizations. For instance, the Sustainable Economic Growth Strategy outlines neo-liberal economic policies consistent with the World Bank and IMF. In fact, under the Harper government, in 2007, Canadian contributions to the World Bank's International Development Association (IDA) fund jumped from US$329.1 million to US$653.36 million (OECD 2010). This trend is also reflected in the Food Security Strategy, which defines key terms and policies with reference to the World Bank, the Food and Agricultural Organization, the World Food Progamme, the Consultative Group on International Agricultural Research, and the International Development Research Centre.

While the abdication of policy to multilateral organizations could be seen as a way to avoid domestic interference and promote harmonization between bilateral and multilateral organizations, this is unlikely given CIDA's policy track record. There are no indications from CIDA that the use of multilateral organizations for policy was undertaken with reflection and purpose. It is more likely an administrative shortcut. Further, the mixture of organizations and policies simply replicates contradictions in the international development bureaucracy. As a case in point, the Sustainable Economic Growth Strategy specifically refers to industrialized farming and open markets while the Food Security Strategy continually emphasizes the value of small sustainable farms as a key method of ensuring regular access to food (CIDA 2011; 2010b).

While the government seemed short on policy, NGOs were advocating for change. Most notably, in 2008, the Canadian Council for International Co-operation strongly campaigned for the passage of Bill C-293, the ODA Accountability Act. The act was intended to strengthen Canadian aid policy and assistance by providing clear direction and criteria. It states that the purpose of Canadian aid is to reduce poverty, incorporate the perspectives of the poor, and uphold human rights. However, despite good intentions, the act has gone relatively unacknowledged in government corridors. Two years after the legislation's passage, CCIC reports that the government "technically meets the reporting requirements of the Act, but it fails to fulfill the Act's spirit and intention" (Tomlinson 2010, 1). The ODA Accountability Act could have provided CIDA with the opportunity to rejuvenate Canadian aid policy; instead, CIDA argued that it already meets the act's requirements.

Overall, Canadian aid policy is missing an overarching visionary document that would represent the government's approach to international development assistance. If such a policy document existed, it would outline Canada's contribution to international poverty reduction. The document would provide parameters that could assist CIDA and its partners in building tangible relationships of mutual support and coordination. The lack of such a document, however, has left CIDA rudderless and vulnerable to political intrusions and short-lived development trends. In 2008 one CIDA respondent explained: "CIDA's priorities are a mess. They have shifted so many times that most people are still following the Liberal agenda because they are confused about the messages." This has had a major impact on CIDA's day-to-day operations. Several of CIDA's field staff noted that the lack of official policy makes it difficult to engage in long-term collaboration with other departments, international organizations, and recipient countries. For example, the increase in program-based approaches, such as general budget support and pooled funds, requires CIDA staff to increase their coordination with other donors and recipient countries.[10] Consequently, it is very difficult for CIDA's representatives to participate in international development in the absence of a clear policy to guide their decisions. This type of policy confusion has increased the pressure placed on the smaller negotiations that occur in development practice, as discussed in the next section.

MICRO-POLICY NEGOTIATIONS

A closer look at the Tanzanian case illustrates how problems associated with CIDA's policies extend into the field. At the time of field research in 2008, CIDA was still using a Country Development Program Framework (CDPF) for Tanzania that was issued in 1997 and due to expire in 2002. When this last CDPF was drafted, Canadian aid to Tanzania was in decline, with discussions underway concerning a full withdrawal. The 1997 CDPF focused on smaller projects in primary education, health, and small-enterprise development. Despite the lack of current policy documents, budgets and priorities shifted significantly over the last decade. CIDA re-designated Tanzania as a country of concentration in 2003 and provided the country's aid program with an expanded budget and decentralized administration. Since then, the Canadian aid program has become actively involved in governance, education, health, and private-sector development. [11] Thus, while formal policy development was stalled, informal decisions regarding CIDA's direction and programming in Tanzania were still being made on an ad hoc basis within the agency.

A number of CIDA employees expressed concern over the absence of a CDPF in Tanzania and cited several failed attempts to draft new versions. Efforts to develop a new CDPF were constantly postponed because the decision makers were waiting for evaluation results, the designation of areas of concentration, or elections and ministerial appointments. At one point, the country office did draft a new CDPF, but it was not approved because CIDA's senior management shifted the overall policy direction in the time between the CDPF's submission and its approval. One CIDA respondent noted: "In 2002 is when our CDPF expired. So we went back to the minister and we said there is an evaluation coming up so we wouldn't do the CDPF. We will hold off on it until we have the evaluation done. So she said 'fine.' And we said health and governance is the important priority. And she said, 'Fine, do that.'" Another CIDA respondent expressed annoyance, stating: "Well, we don't have CDPF now. We are operating on the extension of the old CDPF." Despite the lack of official documents, policy decisions are still being made by practitioners on an ad hoc basis in order for their work to continue.

Eventually, CIDA staff supplemented the ad hoc decisions with internal strategies. Staff members in CIDA's Tanzanian country program are designated sector leads on issues such as governance, education, and health. Each sector lead developed a two-page strategy paper to be circulated and reviewed within the country office. Once vetted, the sector strategies were compiled into a ten-page engagement strategy for submission to headquarters. These interim, internal strategies essentially acted as unofficial policies in the absence of more formal directives. While some staff members freely provided me with copies of their two-page strategies, others did not feel comfortable sharing unapproved documents. One of the more cautious staff members described the situation thus: "We are in a bit of an awkward position because they had this country engagement strategy that we were asked to prepare in June [2008]. Version nineteen, I think. It is two pages and one page of projects that come to approval for the next year, and there was a ten-page program document that gave the detailed rationale for the programs. But it is still uncertain as to the status of that document. We were told to operate as if it is approved, but it hasn't been approved ... It is sort of an unwritten understanding that we have backing."

It is important to note that Tanzania's sector strategies were not pulled out of thin air but were patched together from older CIDA policies, speeches, studies, other donor documents, and CIDA's procedures, and customized for the Tanzanian context. In a risk-averse environment, staff members make efforts to accumulate supporting evidence to justify their programming direction. As one CIDA official explained: "It is much easier to make that case if you can just say, we have already done this, this type of policy is exactly what we should be doing, this policy has been approved by so-and-so. It is much cleaner. So when you have to rationalize something when you don't have a clean policy that supposedly tells you what you should be doing – you need to rationalize it."

In the process of cobbling policy together, staff members often face the challenge of accommodating contradictory policy statements. For instance, CIDA's commitment to the Paris Declaration on Aid Effectiveness conflicts with procedures required under the Federal Accountability Act. One CIDA respondent, referring to these two policies, noted: "There is no sort of clear policy over our two policies; these two interpretations can clash without being able to be resolved. Because there is nothing to draw on and say that this approach, this policy trumps, you rely on individuals – individuals are very risk-averse because they have no policy to stand behind to make these calls."

Consequently, differing policies have created a stumbling block for CIDA as it determines whether it should or should not provide GBS to Tanzania. In terms of aid policy, CIDA is committed to the Paris Declaration on Aid Effectiveness, to the G8 initiative to double aid to Africa, and to Tanzania being designated as a country of concentration since 2003. This has resulted in a sharp increase in funding to Tanzania, from CDN$17.49 million in 1998–99 (CIDA 2000) to $36.61 million in 2003–04 (CIDA 2005), reaching $99.43 million in 2008–09 (CIDA 2010b). Under this framework, GBS can promote country ownership and donor coordination, as well as allow CIDA to disburse large sums of money with minimal administrative costs. However, it is difficult for CIDA to disburse GBS under the Federal Accountability Act and the terms and conditions set by the Treasury Board Secretariat. The conflict between aid policy and financial controls has not been resolved, and, as a result, Canada has no clear policy on GBS disbursements. In many cases, the decision to disburse GBS depends on personnel changes in CIDA's senior management and the Treasury Board.

CIDA's administration also contains hidden or invisible structures that influence policy. As proposals move through the system they are vetted by a series of experts working, for instance, in gender, environment, and results-based management, before they are finally approved. One CIDA respondent noted that s/he eventually learned, by word of mouth and personal experience, the types of proposals that would or would not gain approval, thereby illustrating how organizational unwritten norms influence the approval processes. In the case of GBS, several respondents mentioned that CIDA senior management communicated to staff that "it was not the right time" for a GBS submission to the Treasury Board in the months leading up to the 2007–08 financial year. These statements were early warnings that a GBS submission to the Treasury Board would not be approved that year.

These kinds of ongoing micro-policy negotiations are further complicated by varying interpretations of key terms and concepts. A CIDA respondent from the Tanzanian office noted, "Our individuals interpret policy differently than headquarters ... The same words mean different things to somebody who is a financial management advisor than to a program officer sitting in the field." In many cases, conflicts are avoided rather than resolved. Often, practitioners strategically navigate bureaucracy when there is no clear policy or they face obstacles. Skilled practitioners adapt to or bypass administrative roadblocks altogether by using alternative procedures. For example, when CIDA staff in Tanzania realized that they would not likely receive approval for a GBS contribution to the Tanzanian government for 2007–08, they found another way through the policy confusion: CIDA disbursed funds to the World Bank as an executing agency; the World Bank added CIDA's contributions to its Poverty Reduction Budget Support Credit (PRBS) program, which in turn disbursed funds to the Tanzanian government. A CIDA staff member described the situation as follows: "The Treasury Board said, 'We are not going to touch any more submissions until you [CIDA] sort out your countries of concentration.' CIDA hadn't sorted that out yet. So then we couldn't do a GBS submission. And then some senior management didn't seem to be comfortable with budget support. We had very mixed, unclear signals about whether we could proceed with things. So, we had to bundle the Canadian package of budget support with the World Bank's contributions."

While administrative gymnastics are common in all bureaucracies, they still have unintended long-term effects. In the example above, the total contribution to Tanzania was CDN$20 million, minus the World Bank's administrative fees. Frustration among CIDA staff was evident in interviews: "We are the only donor going through Bank right now and we are going to pay five per cent in fees. We just got approval for $20 million and we are going to have to give a million of that to the World Bank and not the people of Tanzania." The scenario also damaged CIDA's reputation with other donors and caused confusion and delays with the Tanzania Ministry of Finance and Economic Affairs. In this case, the unresolved policy conflict between CIDA's aid and accountability frameworks turned into a costly administrative quandary.

THE PROS AND CONS OF MICRO-POLICY NEGOTIATIONS

As this case study shows, a holistic understanding of policy is based on a mixture of official policy documents and micro-policy negotiations in practice. The primary function of a policy framework is to mobilize and maintain political support for international development initiatives, creating a legitimate framework for the day-to-day negotiations that occur in the field (Mosse 2004). Vague policy language may contribute to agreement among partners, but it is also constructed and deconstructed by a series of brokers employing strategic translations. The brokers (consultants, bureaucrats, fieldworkers, and diplomats) interpret and adapt policy as it filters through the development industry (Mosse and Lewis 2006). In CIDA's case, the sparse policy framework correlated with the unstructured nature of micro-policy negotiations in the field. In the Tanzanian field office, policy existed in an unapproved state; was cobbled together, interpreted, and manipulated by administrative procedures; and/or grew out of organizational norms. While most development practitioners interviewed for this study were critical of this policy situation, a few chose to view the situation positively.

For example, some field practitioners saw the lack of official policy as an opportunity to customize policies to the specific needs of the country or program. One respondent noted that policy confusion creates "wiggle room" and went on to explain: "There is always a distinction between the policies and what actually happens on the ground. Sometimes the chaos on the ground provides staff the opportunity to do good work." This was confirmed by a number of Tanzanian officials who noted that one of CIDA's strengths is that its staff listens to the needs of the country and then tries to design programs that meet both the recipient's and CIDA's mandates.

Conversely, a number of CIDA respondents expressed concern over the lack of an overall policy framework, noting: "It affects working in the field in the sense that a strong, coherent and agreed-to framework, that is agreed to by senior management, would help us avoid the flavours of the month." Another respondent noted that a clear policy framework would provide CIDA with a better negotiating position with other donors. S/he stated, "We've been less engaged just because our policy void has put us in a difficult position to engage and be forceful in our interventions." Such staff concerns clearly demonstrate that a lack of official policy correlates with a lack of legitimacy in the field.

Because CIDA has not created a strong official policy framework, it has placed the burden of policy creation on micro-policy negotiations occurring in the field. Moreover, CIDA's fragmented policy framework has failed to generate support for international development assistance or to establish a legitimate base for practitioners. While this may give some practitioners a sense of freedom, it comes with risks. In most cases, the absence of a framework generated insecurity and caution among CIDA staff.

CIDA: APPROACHING PARALYSIS?

As mentioned above, the problems associated with CIDA's fragmented policy framework are seeping through the organization and accentuating the agency's tendency toward risk-aversion and centralization. If the situation worsens, CIDA's bureaucracy may slow to a crawl.

An Element of Risk

The Canadian government's focus on accountability and its lack of an overarching aid policy have created a culture of silence and risk-aversion within CIDA. This was a common theme that emerged from respondents employed inside and outside the agency. One respondent from a Canadian NGO noted that CIDA "has become much more risk-averse ... following the Liberal government, the scandals, and the Conservatives ... now the accountability mechanisms are accentuated, and people are interpreting them very literally. So it gives us very little flexibility." A CIDA respondent noted that these same factors "sent a chill throughout the whole government in Canada about how we conduct business; the processes got even heavier especially in regards to financial management."

While accountability is important, when taken to the extreme it can have negative effects. Development practitioners may seek to protect themselves by adhering to exact procedural accountability, requiring approval, and referring decision making up the chain of command. This overcompensation slows down – and potentially cripples – bureaucratic processes. One CIDA respondent noted that the agency "is allergic to risk ... It is scary the number of risk assessments and analyses and documents and papers that need to come out of the machine before something is approved. We need to go through so many people before it reaches the approval level, and it takes forever."

Beyond overburdening the bureaucracy, the focus on fiduciary accountability can diminish development results. International assistance is difficult, risky, and long term. CIDA and its staff must be able to tolerate a certain level of risk in order to achieve results. This was highlighted in an internal audit in which the auditors noted that CIDA's focus on fiduciary risk blinds it to the necessary risks involved in achieving development results, as well as the risks to its reputation for being ensnared in red tape (Office of the Chief Audit Executive 2008). CIDA's fixation on fiduciary accountability and its risk-averse culture support a highly centralized and bureaucratic administration.

Centralized Administration

The most recent OECD/DAC peer review of Canadian international assistance found that "one of the greatest impediments to Canada's full implementation of the aid effectiveness agenda is CIDA's centralized decision-making structure" (DAC 2007, 57). The centralized administration is reflected in CIDA's low spending authority and lengthy decision-making processes. Several respondents noted the difficulty this creates when carrying out tasks in the field. Spending ceilings for country directors are CDN$500,000 and anything over $5 million must receive ministerial approval. Programs of more than $20 million must be submitted to the TBS for approval (Office of the Auditor General of Canada 2009, 6).[12] These approval levels are low when compared with other donors. For instance, the British Department for International Development's field office in Tanzania can approve up to US$15 million on new commitments, and there are no ceilings for renewed items (Gulrajani 2010, 13). While the low spending ceilings at CIDA are set by the TBS to ensure financial control, they also increase the time and effort required to initiate and implement programs.

Lengthy decision-making processes also bog down CIDA's bureaucracy. A recent review by the auditor general of Canada revealed that the average project approval process involves twenty-eight documents and takes about three and a half years (Office of the Auditor General of Canada 2009, 27). This is especially significant given that donor coordination requires field staff to work with other donors and governments in administering pooled funds. CIDA's delays become its partners' delays and frustrations. One CIDA respondent noted that it was "embarrassing." Another noted, "I sit in a team of people where my colleagues from other donors are making decisions about the way forward, about the financing of the basket. I am being told by my colleagues in headquarters, 'You can't make those decisions.' What am I supposed to tell my colleagues [from other donor agencies]?"

Respondents from Tanzania, including other donors and CSOs, also complained of CIDA's bureaucratic delays. One respondent from the government of Tanzania observed that "the Canadians are always waiting for approvals from head office." Similarly, a respondent from a Tanzanian CSO remarked: "I have been looking at Canadian organizations coming here, working with the local civil society, and they will start developing a proposal and it may take three or four years before the project is proceeding. So if it was something that needed to start within that year then they will miss the boat and that will lead to frustration."

Decentralization has been recommended to CIDA on several occasions. In fact, the agency began a process of decentralization in the early 1990s, before it was halted by budget cuts. Decentralization would have meant higher administrative expenses associated with maintaining offices overseas, but the main benefits would have been the placement of more staff in the field and greater field-level discretion over programming. In 2003 another attempt by CIDA to decentralize was cautiously piloted in six countries, including Tanzania. While some respondents in Tanzania noted that having the director and policy analyst in the field is helpful, they did not think that the decentralization initiative went far enough. A focus group of CIDA staff suggested that the decentralization process was missing three essential elements: delegation of responsibility, control of funds, and authority to make decisions. One CIDA respondent commented that "other donors make decisions here, have the authority to spend in the field, do the due diligence and risk analysis, etc. Everything that we do down here is vetted a hundred times up at headquarters, which, of course, makes us inefficient. It kind of makes us wonder why we have a decentralized program if it is just going to get vetted all over again."

CIDA's policy confusion and micro-management have caused numerous delays in the disbursement of funds. For example, in November 2008 the government of Tanzania prepared and distributed a chart rating the performance of fourteen GBS donors. Each country was given a score between one and five (one being the best) for three categories: timing, predictability, and front-end loading. CIDA scored the worst possible total score of fifteen in the 2004–05 and 2005–06 fiscal years. In 2006–07 disbursements seemed to improve, when CIDA received a score of eight. However, there was no rating for the 2007–08 fiscal year because CIDA was unable to disburse its funds directly to the Tanzanian government and instead rerouted GBS funds through the World Bank. Overall, CIDA received an average score of 12.7 for the three years that it disbursed directly to the government of Tanzania, while the average total score among all fourteen GBS donor partners over the four-year period (including CIDA's poor scores) is 4.5 (Ministry of Finance and Economic Affairs 2008). CIDA's inability to disburse aid in a regular and timely manner, as compared to other donor partners, is a prime indicator that the agency suffers serious organizational maladies.

CONCLUSION

The questions posed at the beginning of this chapter asked who makes aid policy, what its role is, and what the relationship is between policy and practice. Ideally, Canadian aid policy should form a loose but cohesive web that extends to international agreements, government policies, priorities, and strategies, as well as the smaller micro-policy negotiations that occur in practice. By bringing such diverse actors together, the primary function of policy is to generate support, establish legitimacy, and provide a general sense of direction. Unfortunately, this chapter clearly indicates that Canada lacks such an aid policy framework.

Canadian aid policy is situated in a larger aid ecosystem within which a number of influences or cross-pressures interact with policy formation at the international, national, and recipient-country levels. Instead of managing these cross-pressures, the Canadian government has allowed them – and especially its internal politics – to shape its aid policy process. This has left Canada with a fragmented aid policy framework and has exposed CIDA to outside influences, competing agendas, development trends, and political shifts. Internally, in order to compensate for the lack of official policy frameworks, micro-policy negotiations in the field often establish de facto policy. Policies set in the field frequently exist in an unapproved state, are patched together or grow out of organizational norms, and carry various and sometimes conflicting interpretations. CIDA employees also develop ad hoc policies and procedures to navigate through policy confusion. Without official policy frameworks to support their decisions in the field, practitioners often refer decisions up the chain of command in order to avoid risk. As the Tanzanian case study shows, CIDA is becoming increasingly weighed down by an inordinate number of administrative procedures and lengthy delays.

While the Tanzania case study clearly illustrates the need for a renewal of Canadian aid policy, a word of caution is required. In the past, CIDA has attempted to fix its problems by grafting policies onto the existing system and tightening administrative controls. Following this approach again, however, would only accentuate the problems described above. Instead, the renewal process should include a robust policy debate leading up to the creation of an aid policy framework, in addition to the streamlining of priorities and procedures within CIDA. The goal would be to balance the larger policy framework with the micro-policy negotiations that occur in practice. This would provide development practitioners with coherent and legitimate guidance, while still allowing some flexibility for adapting aid programs to local and sometimes changing conditions.

NOTES

1 Aid effectiveness efforts at the country level have resulted in an inter-organizational bureaucracy often referred to as the dialogue process. This fluid structure provides a forum for coordination and policy dialogue between the recipient government and the in-country representatives of donor organizations.

2 The Paris Declaration on Aid Effectiveness (2005) outlines a plan for improving aid effectiveness based on five principles. The first is *ownership*, or the recipient country's ability to effectively plan, coordinate, and manage its own development. The second principle is the *alignment* of donor and recipient countries' development strategies, policies, and procedures. It comes with the caveat that they must strengthen the capacity of government financial-management systems and institute common standards. The third principle is *harmonization*, and it calls for donor coordination involving information sharing, transparency, common agreements, collective action, and the division of labour. The fourth principle, *managing for results*, focuses on building capacity and commitment toward results-based management techniques. Finally, the principle of *mutual accountability* highlights the shared responsibility for strengthening capacity, implementing the national development strategy, and monitoring and achieving results (OECD 2005).

3 According to the OECD/DAC, general budget support "is aid to governments that is not earmarked to specific projects or expenditures items. The recipient government can use it to support its expenditures program as a whole. The aid is mixed with the government's own revenues and disbursed through the government's own financial management system" (OECD 2007, 1).

CIDA defines program-based approaches (PBA) as "a way of engaging in development cooperation based on the principles of coordinated support for a locally-owned program of development such as a development strategy, a sector program, a thematic program, or a program of a specific organization" (CIDA 2008, 1). This includes the aid modalities of GBS and pooled or basket funding.

4 While the ODA Accountability Act (Bill C-293) is legislation, it does not provide CIDA with a clear mandate. Instead, the act outlines three very broad criteria (reduce poverty, incorporate the perspectives of the poor, and uphold human rights) for ODA spending for all federal departments.

5 The ministers for international cooperation from 1996 to 2011 were Pierre Pettigrew, Don Boudria, Diane Marleau, Maria Minna, Susan Whelan, Aileen Carroll, Josée Verner, and Bev Oda.

6 In 2004 the auditor general of Canada, Sheila Fraser, exposed fraud within the Canadian government and the Liberal Party of Canada. It was quickly dubbed the Sponsorship Scandal and resulted in a lengthy public inquiry that highlighted the misuse of public funds and further shook the public's confidence in government spending. In response, the Conservative government drafted the Accountability Act, which, it argued, would address issues of transparency and accountability within the federal government.

7 CIDA rejected KAIROS's funding application in 2009, a move that was the subject of much debate in a parliamentary committee in the fall of 2010. The committee concluded that the paperwork for the funding had been approved, until someone pencilled in the word "not" on the signature page (Berthiaume 2010b).

8 For early critiques of the development industry, see Carty and Smith (1981), Fromm and Hull (1981), Swift and Clarke (1982), Swift and Tomlinson (1991), Hancock (1989), and Ferguson (1993).

9 While the ODA Accountability Act was in place at the time of the research, it was not included in CIDA's policy suite. This is probably due to the fact that it is an act of Parliament, rather than a CIDA policy document.

10 Pooled or basket funding is a type of aid that occurs when a group of donors work together to provide collective funding and administration for a development program.

11 It is interesting to note that, according to CIDA's project browser, the types of activities approved for Tanzania have not changed despite the new 2009 priority areas focusing on children and youth, food security, and sustainable economic growth. This reflects interview data where respondents reported that policy changes take time to implement, and this has led to policy confusion and delays in the organization.

12 While the above figures are official spending ceilings, a number of CIDA staff have indicated that unofficially the ministerial approval levels are much lower. One respondent provided an off-the-record example of programs as small as $100,000 being reviewed by the minister.

REFERENCES

Berthiaume, Lee. 2010a. "Cutting out the Development NGO 'Heart.'" *Embassy.* 9 June.
– 2010b. "Oda: I Don't Know Who Altered KAIROS Memo." *Embassy.* 15 December.
Black, David, and Heather Smith. 1993. "Notable Exceptions? New and Arrested Directions in Canadian Foreign Policy Literature." *Canadian Journal of Political Science* 26, no. 4: 745–74.

Black, David, and Molly den Heyer. 2010. "Canadian Aid Adrift: A Crisis of Conscience?" *The Broker*, 23 (December): 20–3. http://www. thebrokeronline.eu/en/Articles/A-crisis-of-conscience. Accessed 7 March 2012.

Black, David, and Rebecca Tiessen. 2007. "The Canadian International Development Agency: New Policies, Old Problems." *Canadian Journal of Development Studies* 28, no. 2: 191–212.

Brown, Chris, and Edward Jackson. 2009. "Could the Senate Be Right? Should CIDA Be Abolished?" In Allan M. Maslove, ed., *How Ottawa Spends, 2009–10*. Montreal and Kingston, ON: McGill-Queen's University Press. 151–74.

Brown, Stephen. 2007. "'Creating the World's Best Development Agency'? Confusion and Contradictions in CIDA's New Policy Blueprint." *Canadian Journal of Development Studies* 28, no. 2: 213–28.

– 2008. "CIDA under the Gun." In Jean Daudelin and Daniel Schwanen, eds., *Canada among Nations 2007: What Room for Manoeuvre?* Montreal and Kingston, ON: McGill-Queen's University Press. 91–107.

Canadian International Development Agency. 1997. *Official Canadian Development Assistance in Tanzania*. Ottawa: Government of Canada.

– 1997b. *Tanzania, Tufanye Kazi Pamoja: Let Us Work Together*. Ottawa: Government of Canada.

– 2000. *Statistical Report on International Assistance: Fiscal Year 1998–1999*. Ottawa: Government of Canada.

– 2002. *Canada Making a Difference in the World: A Policy Statement on Strengthening Aid Effectiveness*. Ottawa: Government of Canada.

– 2005. *Statistical Report on International Assistance: Fiscal Year 2003–2004*. Ottawa: Government of Canada.

– 2008. *Departmental Performance Report 2007–2008*. Ottawa: Government of Canada.

– 2009a. *Report to Parliament on the Government of Canada's Official Development Assistance*. Ottawa: Government of Canada.

– 2009b. *Securing the Future of Children and Youth*. Ottawa: Government of Canada.

– 2010a. *Increasing Food Security: CIDA's Food Security Strategy*. Ottawa: Government of Canada.

– 2010b. *Statistical Report on International Assistance: Fiscal Year 2008–2009*. Ottawa: Government of Canada.

– 2011. *Stimulating Sustainable Economic Growth: CIDA's Sustainable Economic Growth Strategy*. Ottawa: Government of Canada.

Carin, Barry, and Gordon Smith. 2010. *Reinventing CIDA*. Calgary, AB: Canadian Defence and Foreign Affairs Institute.

Carty, Robert, and Virginia Smith. 1981. *Perpetuating Poverty: The Political Economy of Canadian Foreign Aid*. Toronto: Between the Lines Press.

Department of Foreign Affairs and International Trade. 2005. *Canada's International Policy Statement: A Place of Pride and Influence in the World*. Ottawa: Government of Canada.

Development Assistance Committee. 2007. "Canada: Peer Review." Paris: Organisation for Economic Co-operation and Development.

Ferguson, James. 1993. *The Anti-Politics Machine*, 1st ed. Minneapolis: University of Minnesota Press.

Fromm, Paul, and James Hull. 1981. *Down the Drain? A Critical Re-Examination of Canadian Foreign Aid*. Toronto: Griffin House.

Gulrajani, Nilima. 2010. *Re-Imaging Canadian Development Cooperation: A Comparative Examination of Norway and the UK*. Toronto: Walter and Duncan Gordon Foundation.

Hajer, Maartin, and Hendrik Wagenaar. 2003. "Introduction." In Maartin Hajer and Hendrik Wagenaar, eds., *Deliberative Policy Analysis: Understanding Governance in the Network Society*. Cambridge: Cambridge University Press. 1–30.

Hancock, Graham. 1989. *Lords of Poverty*. New York: Atlantic Monthly Press.

Lalonde, Jennifer. 2009. *Harmony and Discord: International Aid Harmonization and Donor State Domestic Influence. The Case of Canada and the Canadian International Development Agency*. PhD thesis. Baltimore: Johns Hopkins University.

Ministry of Finance and Economic Affairs. 2008. *Medium Term Expenditure Framework and Cross Cluster Strategy*. Dar es Salaam: United Republic of Tanzania.

Morrison, David. 1998. *Aid and Ebb Tide: A History of CIDA and Canadian Development Assistance*. Waterloo, ON: Wilfrid Laurier University Press.

Mosse, David. 2004. "Is Good Policy Unimplementable? Reflections on the Ethnography of Aid Policy and Practice." *Development and Change* 35, no. 4: 639–71.

Mosse, David, and David Lewis. 2006. "Theoretical Approaches to Brokerage and Translation in Development." In David Lewis and David Mosse, eds., *Development Brokers and Translators: The Ethnography of Aid and Agencies*. Sterling, VA: Kumarian Press. 1–26.

Noël, Alain, Jean-Philippe Thérien, and Sébastien Dallaire. 2004. "Divided over Internationalism: The Canadian Public and Development Assistance." *Canadian Public Policy* 30, no. 1: 29–46.

Office of the Auditor General of Canada. 2009. *Report of the Auditor General of Canada to the House of Commons*. Ottawa: Government of Canada.

Office of the Chief Audit Executive. 2008. *Internal Audit Report: CIDA's Management Practices for Program-Based Approach*. Ottawa: Canadian International Development Agency.

Organisation for Economic Co-operation and Development. 2005. *Paris Declaration on Aid Effectiveness*, Meeting Documents. Paris: Organisation for Economic Co-operation and Development.

– 2007. *General Budget Support: General Questions and Answers*. Paris: Organisation for Economic Co-operation and Development.

– 2010. *Statistical Portal*. Paris: Organisation for Economic Co-operation and Development.

Pratt, Cranford. 1994. "Humane Internationalism and Canadian Development Assistance Policies." In Cranford Pratt, ed., *Canadian International Development Assistance Policies: An Appraisal*. Montreal and Kingston, ON: McGill-Queen's University Press. 334–70.

Rawkins, Phillip. 1994. "An Institutional Analysis of CIDA." In Cranford Pratt, ed., *Canadian International Development Assistance Policies: An Appraisal*. Montreal and Kingston, ON: McGill-Queen's University Press. 156–85.

Stairs, Denis. 2005. *Confusing the Innocent with Numbers and Categories: The International Policy Statement and the Concentration of Development Assistance*. Calgary, AB: Canadian Defense and Foreign Affairs Institute.

Swift, Jamie, and Brian Tomlinson. 1991. *Conflicts of Interest: Canada and the Third World*. Toronto: Between the Lines Press.

Swift, Richard, and Robert Clarke, eds. 1982. *Ties That Bind: Canada and the Third World*. Toronto: Between the Lines Press.

Swiss, Liam. 2010. "Promoting Gender Equality as Development Assistance Priority: The Influence of the World Polity and Bureaucrat Agency." Paper presented at the American Sociological Association Meetings. Atlanta, GA. 14 August.

Tomlinson, Brian. 2010. *A CCIC Briefing Note: A Review of the Second Report to Parliament on the Government of Canada's Official Development Assistance 2009-2010*. Ottawa: Canadian Council for International Co-operation.

van Gastel, Jilles, and Monique Nuijten. 2005. "The Genealogy of the 'Good Governance' and 'Ownership' Agenda at the Dutch Ministry of Development Cooperation." In David Mosse and David Lewis, eds., *The Aid Effect: Giving and Governing in International Development*. London: Pluto Press. 85–105.

8

CIDA and the Mining Sector: Extractive Industries as an Overseas Development Strategy

ELIZABETH BLACKWOOD AND VERONIKA STEWART

The overseas operations of Canadian extractive companies have been the subject of increased scrutiny, and frequently mounting criticism, over the past decade, and particularly so since 2008–09. The controversial investment of Talisman Energy in Sudan during the height of the North-South civil war in 1998 served to bring this issue to public attention (CBC 2000). It also set in motion a concerted corporate social responsibility (CSR) movement in Canada, much of it aimed at effecting increased government regulation of overseas extractive operations. The main reasons for this are: 1) Canada is the largest state actor in the global mining industry; 2) Canada currently has virtually no legally binding framework for regulating the activities of its mining companies abroad; and 3) many of these companies are increasingly being accused of various kinds of unethical behaviour, including human-rights abuses, ecological degradation, fuelling community conflict, and engaging in corruption (PDAC 2009). Part of the increased scrutiny concerns the controversial role of Canadian official development assistance (ODA) in facilitating extractive industries in developing countries.

This chapter examines the role of the Canadian government in supporting Canadian mining capital overseas as part of its ODA, in light of the Official Development Assistance Accountability Act (ODAAA) adopted in 2008. The government argues that its support via the Canadian International Development Agency (CIDA) for extractive industries abroad is an excellent example of the "whole-of-government" (WOG) approach, which integrates policy across government departments. However, while there is policy consistency in terms of this support, it conflicts with other stated foreign policy objectives with particular significance for CIDA, as well as ODA objectives as defined by the ODAAA. The government's refusal to regulate Canadian direct investment in extractive industries raises contradictions concerning broader government policy. At the same time, the facilitation of this kind of investment in the global South as carried out by CIDA and other government departments raises a number of issues specific to development policy, especially pertaining to poverty reduction, as well as social and economic development. By examining support for extractive-industry-led development, this chapter analyzes both aid effectiveness and contradictory outcomes in development assistance. Using the ODAAA as framework, it examines ways in which promotion of the extractive sector can be both ineffective and incompatible with Canada's foreign aid objectives.

Key to ensuring that foreign aid complies with the ODAAA are three broad principles outlined in the act: that aid "contributes to poverty reduction; takes into account the perspectives of the poor; and is consistent with international human rights standards" (CIDA 2009b). Growing accusations against mining companies for making inadequate economic contributions to host states, failing to engage meaningfully with affected communities, abusing the local environment, and committing or facilitating acts of violence against protesting host populations suggest that ODA support for extractive industries may fail to comply with one or more of the act's principles.

This chapter begins by situating Canada in the broader context of support for extractive industries and neo-liberal development policy. It then discusses key issues that arise from the pursuit of mining investment as a development strategy. Next, it explains the Canadian government's role in the facilitation of extractive industries abroad. Finally, it utilizes the conditions set out by the ODAAA to evaluate the legality of this support.

MINING AND THE GLOBAL POLITICAL ECONOMY

We must situate the contradictions inherent in providing support to mining capital as a means of achieving poverty reduction and sustainable development within the broader context of mining interests in the global South, as well as international economic trends in facilitating this sector more generally. Concern with the issue of foreign resource extraction and CSR has tended to frame the issue as one pertaining to problems of governance, either at the level of the state or the firm, or a combination of both. In other words, attendant problems are portrayed as the result of corrupt or inept actions taken by individual companies, officials, or governments, or the inability of host governments to reign in the actions of corrupt local actors. Problems are thus construed as local, particular, and individual, rather than as part of a global system mediated by internal and external actors.

Prior to intervention from the international financial institutions (IFIs) throughout the 1980s and 1990s, the mining sector in much of the global South was characterized by high levels of state control, and foreign investment was circumscribed (Bush 2004; Hilson 2001, 27; Hilson and Haselip 2004; Morgan 2002; North et al. 2006; World Bank 1996). Following the debt crisis of the 1980s, the introduction of conditional lending, particularly in the form of structural adjustment programs by IFIs and bilateral agencies, dramatically changed this context by forcing large-scale privatization and the introduction of liberal investment measures. In many cases, the IFIs specifically targeted the mining sector, which they regard as a panacea for economic underdevelopment (Hilson and Haselip 2004, 27). In addition to privatization, countries in the South created liberal mining codes, either at the behest of multi- and bilateral aid agencies, and often with their technical "support," or as a consequence of the competitive pressure to attract foreign direct investment (Morgan 2002). The terms of many of these codes are so favourable to foreign capital that critics argue that little or no benefit accrues to the host state.

In many cases, states receive assistance from countries with significant levels of investment in the host state's mining sector. This has been particularly true of Canada (DFAIT 2009, 3). Canada's ODA therefore presents a strong case for examination, because of both the prominent role Canadian companies play in the global extractive sector and the Canadian state's support to Canadian mining companies abroad. This support occurs directly, via assistance for technical redrafts of mining legislation, financial aid provided to mining companies in various forms, the subsidization of their CSR efforts, lobbying, and embassy support; and indirectly, through building infrastructure in host states and support for broad liberalization measures.

THE UNREALIZED GOALS OF MODERN
MINING-SECTOR DEVELOPMENT

Because Canadian ODA significantly contributes both directly and indirectly to mining operations overseas, it is important to examine the efficacy of using mining as a tool for development. The following discussion demonstrates that, overwhelmingly, extractive industries do in fact fail to meet the economic goals of growth, development, and meaningful job creation in host countries, and may simultaneously cause considerable harm to affected societies and the environments that support them.

Mainstream economic policy has long claimed that increased foreign direct investment (FDI) is a crucial feature of development in Africa and Latin America. Mineral-sector development in particular is widely promoted as a powerful mechanism for economic and, hence, social benefit. There are, however, a number of reasons why many of the supposed benefits of FDI do not materialize in relation to investment in extractive sectors. Orthodox economic accounts place the blame for poor performance on domestic factors such as corruption, poor governance, "Dutch Disease,"[1] a lack of institutional capacity, particularly with respect to the provision of the legal protection of property rights, and the incomplete implementation of structural adjustment and liberalization measures (Auty 2001; Humphreys et al. 2007; Leite and Weidmann 1999; Ross 1999, 2003; Sachs and Warner 2001; World Bank 2003). Accordingly, these accounts call for further domestic reforms with the added objective of creating institutional capacity to support private investment (World Bank 2003, 13).

Conversely, other critics argue that the liberalization measures themselves are not conducive to achieving sustained economic development. The investment protections created through liberalization, such as reductions or exemptions of corporate taxation and the prohibition of industrial policies such as local sourcing requirements, have, they argue, limited the ability of mining to contribute to economic development (Akabzaa 2009; Campbell 2004a; 2006a, 2009; North et al. 2006). Provisions may include generous tax write-offs that allow for "accelerated depreciation," elimination of import duties on capital equipment, 100 per cent foreign ownership of mines, guarantees against expropriation, unrestricted repatriation of profit, and mining royalties of only 1 to 3 per cent (Hilson and Haselip 2004).

There are six major reasons that mining has not created the economic development that its supporters claim: negligible income for host governments based on liberal policies of lowering royalty rates and rates of taxation; mining's inability to provide substantial, stable, and permanent employment, since it is a largely capital-, not labour-, intensive endeavour (Akabzaa 2009; Bush 2009; Campbell 2006a; Ferguson 2006, 196–205; Hilson et al. 2007); the concomitant decline of local farming and fishing industries, where livelihoods are threatened if and when residents are either denied access to resources or their supportive environments are damaged (Pegg 2006, 378); the feeble economic spillover effects and value-added production, particularly since refining and processing frequently take place outside the country of extraction (Bush 2004; Campbell, Belem and Coulibaly 2007; Campbell 2006a; Pradhan 2006; Nunnenkamp 2004; Wise and Mendoza 2005, 80); and the limited usefulness of mining infrastructure to non-mining activities (see Pegg 2006, 381).

In addition, mining is accompanied by changes in the social structure of affected communities, along with associated health risks; conflict between transitory and resident populations; displacement; and environmental destruction. The environmental impacts have potential both to damage the health of surrounding populations and to degrade the land to such an extent that it is rendered useless for future generations (Walde 1992). These impacts occur during all stages of mining: exploration, drilling, actual mining, and post-production waste disposal. The main detrimental effects are deforestation, the contamination of surrounding environments, waste generation, and the pollution and depletion of water sources, with additional degradation to environmentally sensitive areas.

CIDA'S MANDATE AND THE ODAAA

The stated goal of CIDA is to "lead Canada's international effort to help people living in poverty" (CIDA 2010). However, there is an evident contradiction between that objective and the support CIDA provides for extractive industries in developing countries, where a host of social and environmental harms are occurring. Much of the blame for irresponsible mining-sector activities falls on the multinational corporations that engage in the behaviour, or on the host governments that either are complicit with the corporations' behaviour or do not effectively limit it. However, host governments have little option other than to comply with the demands of industry, on account of institutional legal arrangements such as trade and investment agreements or structural adjustment policies mandated by donor agencies and IFIS. Meanwhile, the role of foreign countries in facilitating these processes through FDI creates the conditions in which corporations may act with impunity.

ODA contributes to contradictions concerning the current policy of promoting extractive sector activity in two ways. The first entails the general inefficacy of extractive-sector activity as a vehicle for economic and social development. The record to date in this area is poor, and there is no evidence to suggest it will improve in the near future. The second is more specific to Canadian policy and concerns the trajectory outlined below: the unwillingness of an investor government to regulate effectively the overseas behaviour of its corporate nationals and its willingness to assist companies with questionable records in the areas of human rights or the environment. These actions stand in stark contradiction with the ODAAA.

Prior to the act's adoption in 2008, there was "no legislation clearly defining the mandate and purpose of the Canadian International Development Agency (CIDA) or the parameters of Canada's international development assistance" (Government of Canada 2008). This changed with the new legislation, for the 2008 act lays out three conditions that must be satisfied for all Canadian ODA. As noted earlier, these conditions are that, in the opinion of the minister of international cooperation, assistance contributes to poverty reduction; takes into account the perspectives of the poor; and is consistent with international human-rights standards (CIDA 2009). Initial resistance to the bill from Conservative MPS appears to have signalled the government's firm commitment to pursuing Canadian economic self-interest through CIDA's activities. The bill's main purpose was to entrench poverty reduction as the guiding principle for Canadian ODA. Consequently, it may have been perceived as a threat to the Conservatives' choice of "countries of focus," as well as the application of the whole-of-government approach. Since the early 2000s, the Canadian government has engaged in a new "aid effectiveness" agenda, characterized by a narrowing of target countries and, most recently, a shift in focus away from poorer countries in Africa toward wealthier ones in Latin America (Brown, chapter 3, this volume). This also encompasses the adoption of the WOG approach, an attempt to harmonize policy objectives across government sectors. Commentators have noted that, although policy consistency may be a laudable goal generally, in the case of foreign aid it has often served to subordinate altruistic and humanitarian concerns to those of other government policy aims, such as security, trade, and investment (Brown, chapter 3, this volume; Brown 2008; Smillie 2004, 15).

Though not supported by the then minority Conservative government, the bill did receive unanimous support from opposition members. It subsequently faced resistance from Conservative senators who appeared to be concerned that that the focus on "poverty reduction" would constrain the ability of ODA to put "the tools on the table for economic improvement" (Segal 2007). "Tools" for economic improvement are currently articulated through CIDA's "sustainable economic growth priority," which provides a number of avenues for advancing Canadian commercial interests, the loss of which may also have been a reason for anxiety over the bill. In fact, a CIDA spokesperson's comments to the media at the time reflected precisely this concern: "Bill C-293 would take away the ability of the government to determine how best aid can advance Canada's interests" (Nicole Lascelle, cited in Bailey 2007). Given the recommendations of an earlier Senate report that the Canadian government should concentrate "all bilateral development aid [to Africa] on countries in Sub-Saharan Africa that are aggressively undertaking economic and political reforms ... to develop their private sectors and create a favourable investment climate" and "should enhance Canada's commercial profile in Africa" (SSCFAIT 2007, 63, 109), it is perhaps of little surprise that legislative measures that might conflict with this priority would face considerable resistance. Nonetheless, after numerous amendments, the bill was passed.

In the broader context of mounting criticism over neo-liberal development policy, and concerns that CIDA might be becoming less transparent and subject to a distinct ideological trajectory under the Conservative government, a new wave of scrutiny appears to be focusing on the agency (e.g., Gordon 2010; Burron 2010; Engler 2009; Keenan 2010). However, neither increasing attention to the current expression of Canadian interest in ODA nor the act itself appears to have altered policy in this respect. The government remains committed to voluntary CSR as a means of policing industry overseas. The recent $26.7-million investment of CIDA in "supporting Canada's

Corporate Social Responsibility (CSR) Strategy for the Canadian International Extractive Sector" (launched in March 2009), as well as the implementation of the $20-million "Andean Regional Initiative for Promoting Effective Corporate Social Responsibility" in Colombia, Peru, and Bolivia (CIDA 2011), reflect this position. CIDA's facilitation of Canadian mining capital abroad provides a particularly illustrative account of how development assistance does not conform to the ODAAA, at least the spirit if not the letter of the law.

THE CANADIAN CONNECTION

This section discusses the significance of the Canadian mining sector worldwide, Canadian companies' varied detrimental impacts on the countries in which they operate, and the Canadian state's lax regulatory framework for overseas extractive industries. The discussion then turns to Canadian government involvement in the facilitation of these industries, with specific reference to the linkages between Canadian development and trade institutions consistent with the WOG approach. Finally, it evaluates the government's support for the extractive sector in relation to the stipulations of the ODAAA mentioned above.

The Canadian Role in the International Mining Sector

Canadian companies represent over 75 per cent of mining and exploration companies worldwide (DFAIT 2009, 3), and 57 per cent of the world's mining companies are listed on the Toronto Stock Exchange (TSX) and TSX Venture Exchange (NRC 2010, s. 1.5). Latin America represents the largest destination for overseas Canadian direct investment in mining, and Canadian companies constitute the largest proportion of exploration investment in Latin America, the Caribbean, and Africa (MAC 2010, 35; see also Gordon 2010, 184).

As discussed previously, a host of negative economic, social, and environmental impacts are associated with global mining operations, and, as the world's extractive-industry leaders, Canadian companies' activities have not been an exception. The following section discusses some of the more recent and severe impacts associated with Canadian mining companies' foreign operations, but by no means does it provide an exhaustive list of transgressions.

Arguably, the worst outcomes pertaining to mining are those that involve increases in violence and conflict. In Peru, a CIDA country of focus and recipient of aid supporting extractive-industry development via CIDA's Hydrocarbon Assistance Project, status as the fastest growing economy in Latin America is accompanied by a dramatic increase in "socio-environmental" conflicts. The number of these conflicts has jumped from 8 to 200 in five years, and violent conflict in the country is said to be at its highest since the quashing of the Shining Path rebellion in the 1990s (Pegg 2006, 376–87). Canadian companies Barrick Gold and Manhattan Minerals have been accused of being complicit in the violence, specifically that related to the quelling of protests at mining sites or the assassination of leaders of the anti-mining movement (Engler 2009, 82–3).

In Colombia, where CIDA has aided in creating a favourable investment climate for mining, resource-rich regions are the source of 87 per cent of the forced population displacements, 82 per cent of the violations of human rights and international humanitarian law, and 83 per cent of the murders of union leaders (Erauw 2009, 171). Mining and oil operations also often take place "in areas subject to armed conflict and forced displacement, on lands 'abandoned' due to violent pressure on the communities, or whose title has changed hands over the last decade due to paramilitary pressure" (MiningWatch 2009, 2). After the CIDA-sponsored restructuring of Colombian mining regulations, independent and often poor miners were required to sign a government contract within three years of the regulations coming into effect or lose their mines. As many miners had been forced off their lands or were living under paramilitary threat at the time, they were unable to sign the necessary contracts and therefore forfeited their property (Gordon 2010, 168).

Violent conditions have likewise been reported in Tanzania at the Bulyanulu mine project (previously owned by Canadian company Sutton Resources before its takeover by Canada's Barrick Gold), where, in the lead-up to the project, fifty artisanal miners are reported to have been buried alive by a concert of company officials and local authorities who backfilled the occupied mineshaft (Gordon 2010, 215).

On issues of the environment, Canadian companies have been similarly implicated. In one example, the Peruvian government, which has received considerable CIDA support for technical reform to its mining sector, halved the size of a planned national park along the Amazonian border between Peru and Ecuador created to protect indigenous territories and key headwaters, with local indigenous people blaming the favourable treatment given to the Canadian mining company Dorato Resources (Moore 2011, 10). In Guyana, contamination as a result of waste by-products has occurred and "representatives of indigenous communities filed a suit in a Canadian court after a tailings dam failure caused massive environmental contamination at a Canadian mine in their country" (Keenan 2010, 30).

Mining may also have further environmental impacts in ecologically sensitive areas. For instance, the Pascua Lama mine along the border between Argentina and Chile is among the most controversial projects of Barrick Gold. Barrick plans to "move" twenty-five acres of glaciers that block access to ore deposits at the site, as well as divert a river for cyanide-solution production, causing concern and unrest among local residents, who claim that Barrick's exploration processes have already accelerated the recession of local glaciers (Gordon 2010, 210). Another notable environmental impact is that of Canada's Goldcorp Marlin mine in Guatemala, which, according to the company's own reports, uses 250,000 litres of water per hour. Environmental organizations have calculated that "the amount [of water] used at the mine in a single hour amounts to what an average local family uses in twenty-two years" (Van de Sandt 2009, 34). This industrial usage of water has the potential to restrict the amount of water available to local people now and in the future.

The Failure to Regulate

As mentioned above, CIDA does not have a mandatory CSR framework regulating the corporations to which they provide financial assistance. Nor does it require that companies conduct social-impact assessments before investing abroad. Nonetheless, many companies do claim that CSR is a central component of their operations.

A private member's bill aimed at regulating extractive industries, Bill C-300, defeated in 2010, would have regulated the relationship between several key Canadian government agencies, namely Export Development Canada (EDC), the Department of Foreign Affairs and International Trade Canada (DFAIT), and the Canadian Pension Plan (CPP); established a set of binding standards for companies seeking support from these agencies; and created a complaints mechanism to investigate corporate compliance (Keenan 2010, 34).

Instead, government policy has shifted the focus of accountability from Canadian regulators to the countries where Canadian companies invest (Keenan 2010, 33). Perpetuating a regulatory vacuum, CIDA focuses on the promotion of voluntary CSR, which it claims is a central component of its operations, and "good governance" aimed at improving public-sector capacity in developing states. The Canadian government's only discussion of legal regulation pertains to the issue of bribery of foreign officials. Here, the Canadian government may in certain instances be obligated, in compliance with international conventions, to apply the principle of extraterritoriality with respect to its jurisdictional reach (DFAIT 2009, 14). Yet the same principle is rejected when it comes to other areas of corporate regulation.

CIDA Support for Extractive Industries Abroad

Along with the failure to regulate adequately its overseas extractive industries, the Canadian government makes a concerted effort to facilitate their penetration into these markets. In recent years, as part of the WOG approach, the government has increasingly emphasized the .policy integration of the various departments involved in the international arena. Support for mining occurs across various departments and takes a number of forms. These range from direct financial support from CIDA for CSR projects and technical support to revise mining codes, to EDC financing, CPP investment in the mining sector, lobbying initiatives on behalf of Canadian commercial interests, infrastructure support, and the promotion of liberalization more generally through involvement in IFIs and trade and investment agreements.

A broad examination of CIDA's development strategy, with reference to its "country of focus" program, reveals a telling trend in Canadian development priorities. Nine of the twenty CIDA countries of focus have among the top twelve largest reserves of the six most important metals in world mining, which represent 63 per cent of global production (see list in WIR 2007, 85). Peru, a recipient of considerable FDI and ODA from Canada, holds the second-highest level of reserves and is the second-largest producer of copper, the world's second most important mined metal. Many minerals that do not constitute significant proportions of global mining production but are nonetheless vital for industrial purposes, or highly valued as in the case of gemstones, are not reflected in these totals. Uranium, diamonds (gem and industrial quality), columbite-tantalite (coltan), phosphate, nitrogen, and titanium are but a very few of such minerals. If one considers just these minerals, another seven countries of focus are added to the above list of major sources of minerals (see USGS 2011), bringing the total to sixteen of the twenty countries of focus. Moreover, many of them are dependent on mining. A 2002 World Bank report found that mining is dominant (50 per cent or more of exports) in Jamaica; crucial (15 to 50 per cent of exports) in seven (Peru, Ukraine, Mali, Bolivia, Guyana, Ghana, Tanzania); and relevant (5 to 15 per cent of exports) in Senegal and Indonesia (World Bank 2002, 17).[2]

In January 2011 Bev Oda, the minister of international cooperation, stated that CIDA had already disbursed $5,024,344 on projects related to the extractive sector for the current fiscal year, all of which were in the Americas, and that 70 per cent of this funding was to be directed toward "strengthening the resource governance and municipal government capacity to plan, manage, and deliver community development initiatives to achieve long-term sustainable development results" (MiningWatch 2011a, 1). "Strengthening resource governance" has often meant the creation of investment conditions highly favourable to foreign mining capital. CIDA has been involved in the restructuring of investment legislation, in the continuation of the wider trend of lowering of royalty rates for extractive industries, and in mineral exploration and development, with noteworthy impact in Bolivia, Peru, Colombia, and, on the African continent, Guinea, Mali, Zimbabwe, Botswana, Namibia, and Tanzania (Campbell 2004b; Campbell et al. 2007; CCIC 2006,17). Such a technical approach masks interests and outcomes that are inherently political, as evidenced by assessments of the socio-economic and environmental impacts of mining (Campbell 2006b).

CIDA support for mining is not confined to providing technical assistance for broad objectives such as redefining regulatory frameworks and creating liberal investment environments. It has also facilitated extractive activities in highly specific forms throughout the various stages of sector development, such as exploration, CSR programming, mine closure, and reclamation. As Bonnie Campbell (1998) explains, CIDA played an active role in the development of

Zimbabwe's mining sector, supporting exploration activities such as the provision of aeromagnetic surveys, "training of local mining experts, [and] upgrading the quality and availability of information for investors, the benefits [of which] are now being enjoyed by junior Canadian mining companies" (Smith quoted in Campbell 1998, 30). Subsequently, Canadian companies were able to secure a large number of the exploration licences granted by the Zimbabwean state (Campbell 1998, 30; Akabzaa 2009, 31). Similarly, in Tunisia, CIDA devoted over $2.3 million to a project related to collection of the country's digital geographical data (Northern Miner 2002).

CIDA also has recently devoted considerable financial resources to aiding Canadian extractive companies in meeting their CSR "obligations." Financial support often manifests in programs that support corporate responsibility or environmental improvements, such as Barrick Gold's reforestation project in Peru, which received $499,445 from CIDA. Barrick Gold is contributing $150,000 to this project. It is the world's largest gold company, posting yearly earnings of $3.3 billion in 2010 (Barrick Gold 2010, 3), thus raising questions surrounding the need for some of the world's largest and most profitable mining companies to receive assistance for such projects (Coumans 2011). Mining watchdogs have also raised concerns as to whether this particular project is an independent development project or constitutes reforestation of Barrick's mine site, which they argue should be the responsibility of the company, not the Canadian taxpayer (Ling 2011).

The promotion of voluntary CSR has been posited as a way of ensuring ethical standards for Canadian overseas operations of the extractive industry. The previously mentioned support is part of the broader Canadian strategy of supporting CSR in its extractive industry, where "DFAIT has created a $170,000 CSR Fund to assist Canadian offices abroad and in Canada to engage in CSR-related activities" (DFAIT 2009). Likewise, the recently signed free-trade agreements with Colombia and Peru "include CSR provisions that are directed at the Parties, encouraging them to promote voluntary principles of responsible business conduct with their business communities" (DFAIT 2009). This support can be situated in the context of the promotion of Canadian industry and a seeming unwillingness to impede the companies' profits or operations. For instance, the current CSR program, aptly called *Building the Canadian Advantage: A Corporate Social Responsibility Strategy for the Canadian*

International Extractive Sector, notes that extractive industries make a "major contribution to Canadian prosperity" and that Canadian investment in the extractive sector abroad can "result in a win-win outcome both for the economy of Canada and those of resource-rich developing countries" (DFAIT 2009). Portraying developing countries as winners in these relationships is, however, debatable. What is clear is that the WOG approach results in significant support for extractive industries provided through ODA, CIDA in particular.

Recent examples of this include the September 2011 announcement of four new "natural resource projects" in Africa and South America as part of both CIDA's "Sustainable Economic Growth Strategy" and DFAIT's CSR strategy mentioned above. The largest of these, the Andean Regional Initiative, will see $20 million directed to Colombia, Peru, and Bolivia to "strengthen the capacity of local governments and communities to implement sustainable development projects for the well-being of people living near extractive operations and will improve dialogue between communities and the private sector" (CIDA 2011). CIDA provides no explanation as to why ODA is being targeted to people living in mining areas, as opposed to those living in any other region. Certainly, a number of benefits for mining companies could feasibly accrue from such assistance. Most notably, an improvement in the living conditions of those living in mining regions could stem the widespread conflict that surrounds many mining operations, particularly in Latin America. Indeed, the second objective, improving dialogue between residents and mining companies, suggests that this is a concern. In fact, in November 2011, the Canadian government announced $4.9 million for "Conflict Management and Prevention in the Extractive Sector" in Peru, admitting that social conflicts, "a large majority of which are linked with extractive industries," have increased in the past four years as the extractive sector has expanded (Office of the Prime Minister 2011).

Mining and energy investment is the third-largest component of Canadian FDI (stocks) abroad, and the Canadian government claims that this investment generates "significant additional exports from Canada" (DFAIT 2009). The economic importance of the Canadian mining industry explains in part the government's active role in supporting the sector. However, the mining sector is not unique in benefiting from Canadian foreign policy and trade and investment strategies, nor is Canada anomalous in facilitating the overseas expansion of capital. Rather, analysis of this support must be situated in the broader context of the global political economy, characterized by unequal relations of exchange between the global North and South which are produced and maintained by neo-liberal institutional arrangements. These institutional arrangements include the international financial architecture, notably the World Bank, the International Monetary Fund (IMF), and the Bank of International Settlements, investment and trade regimes such as the World Trade Organization, and myriad investment treaties and foreign debt regimes. It is also comprised of donor agencies and a rapidly growing body of private and public agencies proffering expertise, monitoring, and technical assistance. Ardent state promotion of FDI, and the unwillingness of states to adequately mitigate pernicious corporate behaviour, thus reflect not merely the behaviour of "bad" states, a discrete aberration of duty to serve the "public interest," diminished influence vis-à-vis the power of capital, or the coalescence of corporate and political elite rule. Rather, they are the political and legal expression of capitalism.

Other Governmental Support

Coordination between CIDA and Export Development Canada, a state-owned "crown corporation" that provides financing and insurance to facilitate Canadian exports and overseas investments, is often difficult to pinpoint directly. This is especially true given that the EDC is exempt from the Access to Information Act (Gordon 2010, 167). However, considerable EDC support of extractive industries in Colombia notably occurred alongside CIDA's rewriting of mining codes (reducing royalty rates and social and environmental protection). During the same period, the EDC was involved in the promotion of the commercial extractive industry, including the provision of a US$160-million line of credit to Colombia to enable that country to purchase Canadian equipment for the Cerrejón Zona Norte coal mine, from which Canada imports coal. Of notable concern here is the fact that this mine has caused the mass displacement of the Wayuu indigenous people (CCIC 2006, 17). The EDC's sizeable support to extractive companies via "loans to facilitate the export of mining equipment" and "the use of Canadian consultants – cartographers, geological surveys, etc." (Campbell 1998, 29) is illustrative of Canadian government focus on mining, and is similar to trends reflected in CIDA's "countries of focus" program. In fact, extractive companies (mining, oil, gas) are the single greatest recipients of backing from the EDC. As Karyn Keenan notes: "In 2008, EDC facilitated Canadian business in the Latin American extractive sector worth more than $4 billion and is poised to expand its support for the Canadian mining industry in the region. With new offices in Santiago and Lima, EDC now has a permanent presence in Brazil, Chile, Mexico, and Peru, countries that, together with Argentina, were the top five destinations for Canadian mining capital in Latin America from 2002 to 2008" (Keenan 2010, 31).

Another notable Canadian contribution to Canadian extractive industries overseas is through the Canadian Pension Plan, a publicly administered fund to which most working Canadians are legally required to contribute – holding equity worth $2.5 billion in publicly traded Canadian mining companies with operations in developing countries (Keenan 2010, 31). Though not governed by the ODAAA, CPP has contributed loans and investments to a number of Canadian companies whose human-rights records have been recently challenged by activists and residents of mining communities, and by those non-governmental organizations (NGOs) and media outlets that tell their stories. One such company is Anvil Mining, operating in the Democratic Republic of Congo, where the company, by its own admission, was complicit in offering logistical support to the military's suppression of an unarmed uprising in a town neighbouring Anvil's Dikulushi mine in Katanga province (Gordon 2010, 221).

THE THREE TESTS: HOW CIDA MEASURES UP AGAINST THE LEGAL REQUIREMENTS OF THE ODAAA

This section seeks to evaluate CIDA's compliance with the ODAAA, particularly its stipulation that that foreign aid contribute to poverty reduction, take into account the perspectives of the poor, and be consistent with international standards of human rights (CIDA 2009b). Here, the discussion turns from a general overview of the problems associated with viewing mining as a vehicle for development to the more specific conditions governing the provision of Canadian foreign aid in the context of the tenets of the ODAAA.

Poverty Reduction

Broadly, the promotion of extractive-sector development in mineral-rich states does not meet the stated goals of sustainable economic development and poverty reduction. Where economic growth due to the mining sector does occur, there is considerable evidence that this growth does not translate into poverty alleviation and may offer disparate benefits to different social groups (Ross 1999, 2003, 2004). As the significant decline of FDI to countries of the global South between 2000 and 2003 demonstrates, FDI remains a relatively volatile means of capital formation in many parts of the world, especially those heavily dependent on commodity export (Nunnenkamp 2004; Esanov and Heller 2010; UNCTAD 2009). This is especially the case in extractive sectors, where mineral prices are subject to high levels of instability (UNCTAD 2007; Pegg 2006, 378). In the past century, and increasingly since 1970, primary commodity prices have increased in volatility when compared to prices for manufactured goods (Pegg 2006, 378). For instance, in Guinea – where, as previously noted, CIDA helped liberalize mining legislation – the mining sector contributed 92 per cent of exports in 2004. However, the corresponding income acquired through these export receipts has decreased dramatically in recent years: from 74 per cent in 1986 to 26 per cent in 1996 and 18 per cent in 2004 (Campbell 2009, 67; see also IMF 2006, 48, 55; Integrated Framework 2003, 3).

In Colombia, where, by 2004, Canadian companies "held the dominant share of the larger companies' exploration market" (Gordon 2010, 209), CIDA provided over $10 million in technical and financial support to redraft Colombian mining legislation. The redraft took place without the consultation of potentially affected indigenous communities, weakened pre-existing environmental and social safeguards, and created investment conditions very favourable to foreign companies – including a reduction of royalties to 0.4 per cent, down from the previous 10 to 15 per cent (CCIC 2006, 17). In January-June 2002, the mining sector represented 1.14 per cent of jobs, which fell to 0.92 per cent of jobs after the mining legislation was implemented, despite an increase in investment (Gedicks 2011, 17). Of perhaps greater concern to many observers was the fact that the Canadian organization receiving CIDA funds for this project hired lawyers who represented "half of the mining companies registered in Colombia's national mining registry" (Ramírez 2005). Similarly, in Peru in 2002, CIDA contributed $9.6 million – aiming, purportedly, to provide technical assistance and support to Peru's Ministry of Energy and Mines, but in reality enhancing the rights of private investors (Gordon 2010, 168). In Guinea, too, CIDA contributed to liberalizing the mining code, which "practically dropped any reference to environmental protection" (Campbell 1998, 31).

Where technical assistance for mining-code revisions has resulted in reductions in royalties, as in Colombia and Tanzania, these activities do not appear to meet the ODAAA condition that ODA must contribute to poverty reduction. CIDA support in this regard is ineffective, because of the prior-mentioned failures of mining to contribute positively to economic development. It may also be perceived as facilitating harm when mining contributes to conflict, job loss, or environmental degradation.

Perspectives of the Poor

In many instances, Canadian government policy appears to have explicitly violated the ODAAA provisions that require development strategies to take into account the perspectives of the poor. This occurs through support to companies that do not adequately consult affected communities, through the provision of technical assistance without consulting local populations, and through public-relations activities.

An enduring and pervasive complaint made by mine-affected communities across the globe is the failure of mining companies to adequately consult indigenous populations. This was the case in Colombia, where CIDA contributed $10 million for redrafting mining legislation. In many cases, such consultation is a legal requirement, either through domestic legislation or, for those states that have ratified International Labour Organization (ILO) Convention No. 169, through international law. The non-compliance with this legal obligation can be seen as both a failure to take into consideration the perspectives of the poor and a breach of human rights. Two prominent cases involve Canadian mining giant Goldcorp's operations in Guatemala and Honduras, where accusations that Goldcorp failed to respect communities' rights to consultation and consent, as well as their health, water, property, and right to life, have been verified by a number of third parties – including an in-house human-rights assessment conducted by Goldcorp in Guatemala (MiningWatch 2011a; MiningWatch 2011b).

Support for companies that have come under criticism from local indigenous groups also extends into the diplomatic realm. In Guatemala, the Canadian ambassador published an opinion piece in a local newspaper praising the Marlin mine project, countering the claims of the project's indigenous opponents (Keenan 2010, 31). Likewise, according to an insider representative of the Canadian company Corriente Resources, whose operations in Ecuador have been associated with violent conflict and allegations of human-rights abuses, "the Canadian Embassy in Ecuador has worked tirelessly to effect change in the mining policy – including facilitating high-level meetings between Canadian mining companies and President Rafael Correa" (Keenan 2010, 31). Similarly, Corriente participated in a meeting at which "the Canadian ambassador expressed the government of Canada's concerns regarding changes to Ecuador's regulatory framework" (Keenan 2010, 31). In Peru, in 2005, the Canadian Embassy threatened Canadian Lutheran World Relief with cuts to its government funding if it chose to support Peruvian NGOs that opposed mining development or those that did legal-defence work for affected populations (MiningWatch 2011b). In Honduras, the 2009 military coup was hailed as an "investment opportunity" for Canadian mining company Aura Minerals and others that accompanied Canadian Ambassador Neil Reeder on an official government visit in February 2010 (MiningWatch 2010). Though not specifically related to CIDA development assistance, these instances exemplify the Canadian government's support for its overseas commercial interests, even when such support is in violation of other policies and, in many cases, international human-rights law.

Human Rights

Supporting an industry that is largely believed to be endemically associated with violence (see Collier and Hoeffler 2000; Collier 2004; Ross 1999, 2003, 2004) may contravene the ODAAA stipulations that development assistance comply with international human-rights standards. As previously mentioned, CIDA has greatly facilitated the mining sector in Colombia, where mining activities have been widely associated with violence and displacement: "Local trade unionists say that eighty-seven per cent of the nearly four million people displaced by Colombia's armed conflict over the last two decades were fleeing municipalities in mining regions. Eighty-nine per cent of the trade unionists who have been murdered were active in those same municipalities" (Arsenault 2007).

The Canadian government has supported companies that have been accused of human-rights violations in other countries as well. In the Philippines, CIDA has provided support to TVI Pacific, a mining company with a less-than-stellar human-rights record. In its Filipino operations, TVI did not adequately comply with a local law requiring free, prior, and informed consent of indigenous peoples (MiningWatch 2005). Meanwhile, despite being slated for "community development projects," CIDA funding funnelled through the company appears to violate the ODAAA. This violation occurs through CIDA's failure to address adequately the needs of the local population by first conducting a peace and conflict impact assessment – a practice common with CIDA projects throughout the region, but not in this case – and through its sponsorship of a company with a disreputable human-rights record (MiningWatch 2005).

As noted earlier, CIDA has also funded a reforestation project by Barrick Gold. Problematically, the company is the subject of recent controversy over allegations of "gang rapes and other human rights abuses" by security guards at its Porgera Joint Venture mine in Papua New Guinea. In response to this issue, Peter Munk, Barrick's CEO said, "It would be impossible to police the behaviour of 5,550 employees, particularly in countries where gang rape is a cultural habit" (quoted in Posner 2011). CIDA's support for Barrick, a company that apparently not only avoids its responsibility to protect the communities in which it operates but also – in light of the above statement – bears considerable contempt for the people affected by its activities, therefore seems hostile to the ODAAA mandate on human rights.

Given CIDA's direct support for companies charged with violating human-rights standards, it would appear that the ODAAA is being contravened in several serious ways through the agency's actions. The increased violence associated with mining operations in Peru, Colombia, Tanzania, and elsewhere suggests that CIDA's activities in facilitating mining interests in those countries are in direct violation of the third provision of the ODAAA, which states that ODA must abide by international human-rights standards.

CONCLUSION

As the largest state actor in the international extractive sector, the Canadian government's regulatory framework for Canadian mining companies operating overseas has important implications for the human-rights, social, and environmental context of FDI in the global South. This is especially true given Canadian commercial trespasses of environmental sustainability, ILO Convention No. 169 protecting the rights of indigenous peoples, and human rights – with special relevance to several CIDA countries of focus. The government's steadfast refusal to implement stronger regulatory mechanisms for Canadian mining companies abroad conflicts with its simultaneous promotion of good governance as development policy.

This apparent contradiction appears to extend even further when one analyzes the role of CIDA in *facilitating* Canadian extractive-sector development in the South. While a business case might be made for forgoing regulation with respect to government facilitation of extractive industries in many policy arenas (e.g., EDC, DFAIT, CPP, etc.) – that is, it could be argued that it is the mandate of the Canadian government to foster Canada's economic well-being – it is difficult to apply this logic to an organization whose primary objective is, purportedly, not to enhance Canadian economic interests but rather to execute Canada's "international effort to help people living in poverty" (CIDA 2009a). Although the rhetoric of new governance models attempts to address the lack of "state-capacity and efficient bureaucracy," the emphasis placed by these models on lowering taxation and royalties in order to attract investment raises important questions about the efficacy of FDI in generating state revenue. As discussed, there are also many real and potential social and environmental harms associated with mining operations, especially in the absence of a strong regulatory framework (in both host states and corporate home states) to safeguard local interests. CIDA's role as a "development" agency that uses technical assistance to reduce or limit potential regulatory frameworks in host countries is a contradiction in terms.

In light of the corporate malfeasance of some Canadian extractive industries operating abroad, it is our conclusion that compliance and accountability for CSR must be enforceable and legally binding. We also believe that a comprehensive social and environmental CSR framework should be instituted not just in terms of ODA or CIDA support but as a comprehensive regulatory architecture to standardize the activities of Canadian multinational corporations abroad. A robust consultation process with affected communities should also be mandatory, with final decisions on project launches complying with international law in this area.

Greater transparency and accountability of CIDA also needs be guaranteed. CIDA does not currently provide information on programming projects that are under consideration. Further, even once these projects are approved, access to information regarding them may still be limited. Support for extractive activities can be rolled out in a number of forms that are not readily identifiable in CIDA's project-disclosure information. For example, the reforestation project in Peru involving Barrick Gold falls under the "Public Policy and Public Sector Reform Fund." Rather than be explicitly identified as related to mineral development, extractive-sector support may be channelled through technical assistance, capacity building, public-sector reform, natural-resource management, advanced technical and managerial training, energy generation and supply, and trade and investment. In the absence of Access to Information requests, it is difficult to determine if and how these projects contribute to extractive activities. Even with such requests, information may not be forthcoming if the requests are unsuccessful (Gordon 2010, 375; OICC 2010).

Despite the fact that the ODAAA came into effect only in June 2008, and many of the examples listed above happened prior to that, International Cooperation Minister Bev Oda suggested in 2011 that the funding of development projects in mining-affected areas and in conjunction with mining companies and participating NGOs may form an increasingly common component of ODA (MiningWatch 2011c). Barring the implementation of mandatory regulations and oversight of companies receiving CIDA funding, ODA that supports Canadian mining interests overseas appears likely to continue to violate the principle tenets of the ODAAA.

By adopting the ODAAA, the government created a legal mandate concerning ODA, albeit one that is significantly less robust than the framework called for by proponents of mandatory regulation. The question now arises as to whether official complaints and lawsuits may now be lodged against the government under the act, thereby possibly encouraging a more strict enforcement of its principles. The latter could also be interpreted more broadly – where ODA activities have both direct and indirect consequences. Though access to the Canadian legal system is expensive, and therefore somewhat prohibitive for complainants from poorer regions, the ODAAA nevertheless represents a potential avenue for holding CIDA to account for supporting activities which may involve the contravention of human rights or inflict serious environmental or social harm.

NOTES

1 Refers to a phenomenon said to occur wherein a country's manufacturing and agricultural sectors become less competitive as a result of increased or significant production and export of natural resources.
2 These figures do not include petroleum and natural gas, which are also important extractive industries in several "countries of focus."

REFERENCES

Akabzaa, Thomas. 2009. "Mining in Ghana: Implications for National Economic Development and Poverty Reduction." In Bonnie Campbell, ed., *Mining in Africa: Regulation and Development*. London and New York: Pluto Press. 25–65.

Arsenault, Chris. 2007. "Foreign Firms Cash in on Generous Mining Code." *IPS News Agency*. http://www.ipsnews.net/news. asp?idnews=39755. Accessed 14 June 2011.

Auty, Richard. 2001. "The Political Economy of Resource-Driven Growth." *European Economic Review* 45: 839–46.

Bailey, Sue. 2007. "Canada 'an Appalling Laggard' as Tories Shun Foreign Aid Bill: NDP." *Canadian News Press*. 27 March.

Barrick Gold. 2010. *Annual Report 2010*. Toronto: Barrick Gold Corporation.

Brown, Stephen. 2008. "CIDA under the Gun." In Jean Daudelin and Daniel Schwanen, eds., *Canada among Nations 2007: What Room for Manoeuvre?* Montreal and Kingston, ON: McGill-Queen's University Press. 91–107.

Burron, Neil. 2010. "No Smoking Gun – Yet: Canadian Democracy Assistance in Bolivia." *NACLA Report on the Americas*, May/June: 35–42.

Bush, Ray. 2004. "Undermining Africa." *Historical Materialism* 12, no. 4: 173–201.

– 2009. "Soon There Will Be No-One Left to Take the Corpses to the Morgue: Accumulation and Abjection in Ghana's Mining Communities." *Resources Policy* 34: 57–63.

Campbell, Bonnie. 1998. "Liberalization, Deregulation, State Promoted Investment – Canadian Mining Interests in Africa." *Minerals and Energy – Raw Materials Report* 13, no. 4: 14–34.

– 2004a. "Peace and Security in Africa and the Role of Canadian Mining Interests: New Challenges for Canadian Foreign Policy." *Labour, Capital and Society* 37: 98–129.

– ed. 2004b. *Regulating Mining in Africa: For Whose Benefit?* Uppsala, Sweden: Nordiska Afrikainsitutet.

– 2006a. "Better Resource Governance in Africa: On What Development Agenda?" *Minerals and Energy – Raw Materials Report* 21, no. 3: 3–18.

– 2006b. "Good Governance, Security and Mining in Africa." *Minerals and Energy – Raw Materials Report* 21, no. 1: 31–44.

– ed. 2009. *Mining in Africa: Regulation and Development.* London and New York: Pluto Press.

Campbell, Bonnie, Gisele Belem, and Vincent Nabe Coulibaly. 2007. "Poverty Reduction in Africa: On Whose Development Agenda?" Oxfam No. 2007–01.

Canada. 2008. "Notes on Bill C-293: An Act respecting the Provision of Official Development Assistance Abroad (Official Development Assistance Accountability Act)." http://www.parl.gc.ca/Content/LOP/ ResearchPublications/prb0631-e.htm. Accessed 18 April 2011.

Canadian Broadcasting Corporation. 2000. "Talisman Oil Operations Prolong Sudan Civil War." 11 November. http://www.cbc.ca/news/ canada/story/2000/02/14/talismanooo214.html. Accessed 18 June 2011.

Canadian International Development Agency. 2003. "Expanding Opportunities through Private Sector Development." July. http://www.dsp-psd.pwgsc.gc.ca/Collection/CD4-9-2003E.pdf. Accessed 23 February 2011.

– 2009a. "Mission and Mandate." http://www.acdi-cida.gc.ca/acdi-cida/ ACDI-CIDA.nsf/eng/NIC-5493749-HZK. Accessed 12 May 2011.

– 2009b. "The Official Development Assistance Accountability Act." http://www.acdi-cida.gc.ca/acdi-cida/ACDI-CIDA.nsf/eng/FRA-121185349-JB8. Accessed 13 June 2011.

– 2010. "CIDA's Business Process Roadmap, Version 4.3." http://www. acdi-cida.gc.ca/INET/IMAGES.NSF/vLUImages/RoadMapper cent 202010/$file/V2-2010_RoadMap_Update_Program_English.pdf. Accessed 11 June 2011.

– 2011. "Minister Oda Announces Initiatives to Increase the Benefits of Natural Resource Management for People in Africa and South America." Press Release, 29 September. http://www.acdi-cida.gc.ca/acdi-cida/ACDI-CIDA.nsf/eng/CAR-929105317-KGD. Accessed 17 November 2011.

Clark, Timothy David, and Liisa North. 2006. "Mining and Oil in Latin America: Lessons from the Past, Issues for the Future." In Liisa North, Timothy David Clark, and Viviana Patroni, eds., *Community Rights and Corporate Responsibility: Canadian Mining and Oil Companies in Latin America*. Toronto: Between the Lines: 1–16.

Collier, Paul, and Anke Hoeffler. 1998. "On Economic Causes of Civil War." *Oxford Economic Papers*, 50: 563–73.

Coumans, Catherine. 2011. "CIDA Subsidizes Mining's Social Responsibility Projects." *MiningWatch Canada*. 22 February. http://www.miningwatch.ca/en/cida-subsidizes-mining-s-social-responsibility-projects. Accessed 23 May 2011.

Department of Foreign Affairs and International Trade. 2009. "Building the Canadian Advantage: A Corporate Social Responsibility (CSR) Strategy for the Canadian International Extractive Sector." Ottawa: Department of Foreign Affairs and International Trade.

Engler, Yves. 2009. *The Black Book of Canadian Foreign Policy*. Winnipeg and Black Point, NS: Fernwood Publishing.

Erauw, Gregg. 2009. "Trading away Women's Rights: A Critique of the Canada-Colombia Free Trade Agreement." In *The Canadian Yearbook of International Law, 2009*. Vancouver: University of British Columbia Press.

Esanov, Akram, and Patrick Heller. 2010. "Broken Boom: The Impact of the Economic Downturn on Resource-Dependent Countries." Revenue Watch's *Boom, Bust and Better Policy* Series.

Ferguson, James. 2006. *Global Shadows: Africa in the Neoliberal World Order*. Durham, NC: Duke University Press.

Gedicks, Al. 2011. "Mining in Colombia: Engine of Growth or Resource Curse." http://www.colombiasupport.net/2011/Mining-in-Colombia.pdf. Accessed 20 May 2011.

Gordon, Todd. 2010. *Imperialist Canada*. Winnipeg: Arbeiter Ring.

Hilson, Gavin. 2001. "Mining and Sustainable Development: The African Case." *Minerals and Energy* 16, no. 2: 27–36.

Hilson, Gavin, and James Haselip. 2004. "The Environmental and Socioeconomic Performance of Multinational Mining Companies in the

Developing World Economy." *Minerals and Energy – Raw Materials Report* 19, no. 3: 25–47.

Hilson, Gavin, Natalia Yakovleva, and Sadia Mohammed Banchirigah. 2007. "'To Move or Not to Move': Reflections on the Resettlement of Artisanal Miners in the Western Region of Ghana." *African Affairs* 106, no. 424: 413–36.

Humphreys, Macartan, Jeffrey Sachs, and Joseph Stiglitz, eds. 2007. *Escaping the Resource Curse.* New York: Columbia University Press.

Integrated Framework. 2003. *Guinea: Diagnostic Trade Integration Study.* http://www.integratedframework.org/files/guinea_dtis-vol1_25nov03. pdf. Accessed 12 April 2011.

International Monetary Fund. 2006. *Guinea: Selected Issues and Statistical Appendix.* IMF Country Report No. 06/25, Washington, DC: International Monetary Fund.

Keenan, Karyn. 2010. "Canadian Mining, Still Unaccountable." NACLA Report. https://www.nacla.org/node/6555. Accessed 12 April 2011.

Leite, Carlos, and Jens Weidmann. 1999. "Does Mother Nature Corrupt? Natural Resources, Corruption, and Economic Growth." Working Paper. Washington, DC: International Monetary Fund.

Ling, Justin. 2011. "Canada Gets Cuddly with Mining Companies." *The Dominion* 75. 7 February. http://www.dominionpaper.ca/articles/3814. Accessed 25 May 2011.

Mining Association of Canada. 2010. "A Report on the State of the Canadian Mining Industry: Facts + Figures 2010." Ottawa: Mining Association of Canada.

MiningWatch. 2005. "38th Parliament, 1st Session: Subcommittee on Human Rights and International Development of the Standing Committee on Foreign Affairs and International Trade." http://www.mining-watch.ca/en/38th-parliament-1st-session-subcommittee-human-rights-and-international-development-standing-committ. Accessed 16 June 2011.

– 2007. "Honduras: Demonstrators Push for a New Mining Law." http://www.miningwatch.ca/en/honduras-demonstrators-push-new-mining-law. Accessed 12 May 2011.

– 2009. "Dangerous levels of Arsenic Found near Tanzania Mine." http://www.miningwatch.ca/en/dangerous-levels-arsenic-found-near-tanzania-mine. Accessed 15 June 2011.

– 2011a. "Affected Communities from the Americas Demand That Canadian Mining Industry Respect Their Rights." http://www.mining-watch.ca/en/affected-communities-americas-demand-canadian-mining-industry-respect-their-rights-0. Accessed 14 May 2011.

– 2011b. "Canadian Government Abdicates Responsibility to Ensure Respect for Human Rights." http://www.miningwatch.ca/en/canadian-government-abdicates-responsibility-ensure-respect-human-rights. Accessed 19 June 2011.

– 2011c. Correspondence between Catherine Coumans, director of MiningWatch Canada, and Bev Oda, Canadian minister of international cooperation. http://www.miningwatch.ca/sites/miningwatch.ca/files/1877_001.pdf. Accessed 18 June 2011.

MiningWatch Canada and CENSAT-Agua Viva. 2009. "Land and Conflict, Resource Extraction, Human Rights, and Corporate Responsibility: Canadian Companies in Colombia." Ottawa: Inter Pares.

Moore, Jen. 2011. "Canadian Mining Policy in Practice." Presentation to the Community Movements Conference at Trent University, 12 February. http://www.miningwatch.ca/en/canadian-mining-policy-practice. Accessed 28 May 2011.

Morgan, P.G. 2002. "Mineral Title Management: The Key to Attracting Foreign Mining Investment in Developing Countries?" *Transactions of the Institution of Mining and Metallurgy* 111: B165–B170.

Natural Resources Canada. 2010. *Overview of Trends in Canadian Mineral Exploration 2009*. Ottawa: Natural Resources Canada.

North, Liisa, Timothy David, and Viviana Patroni, eds. 2006. *Community Rights and Corporate Responsibility: Canadian Mining and Oil Companies in Latin America*. Toronto: Between the Lines Press.

Northern Miner. 2002. "Canada Helps Tunisia Develop Mineral Wealth." *Northern Miner* 88, no. 16: 5.

Nunnenkamp, Peter. 2004. "To What Extent Can Foreign Direct Investment Help Achieve International Development Goals?" *World Economy* 27, no. 5: 657–77.

Office of the Information Commissioner of Canada. 2010. "CIDA Report Card 2008–2009." http://www.oic-ci.gc.ca/eng/rp-pr_spe-rep_rap-spe_rep-car_fic-ren_2008-2009_24.aspx. Accessed 14 December 2011.

Office of the Prime Minister. 2011. "Press Release: Conflict Management and Prevention in the Extractive Sector." 12 November. http://www.pm.gc.ca/eng/media.asp?id=4480. Accessed 14 December 2011.

PDAC. 2009. "World Exploration Trends: A Special Report from Metals Economic Group for the PDAC International Convention 2009." Metals Economic Group.

Pegg, Scott. 2006. "Mining and Poverty Reduction: Transforming Rhetoric into Reality." *Journal of Cleaner Production* 14, nos. 3–4: 376–87.

Posner, Michael. 2011. "Special Report: Barrick Owner's Story: From
    Rugs to Riches." *Globe and Mail.* 20 March.
Pradhan, Jaya Prakash. 2006. "Quality of Foreign Direct Investment,
    Knowledge Spillovers and Host Country Productivity: A Framework of
    Analysis." Working Paper. Institute for Studies in Industrial Development.
Ramírez, Francisco. 2005. *The Profits of Extermination: How US
    Corporate Power is Destroying Colombia.* Munroe, MI: Common
    Courage Press.
Ross, Michael L. 1999. "The Political Economy of the Resource Curse."
    World Politics 51, no. 2: 297–332.
– 2003. "Oil, Drugs and Diamonds: The Varying Role of Natural
    Resources in Civil War." In Karen Ballentine and Jake Sherman, eds.,
    *The Political Economy of Armed Conflict: Beyond Greed and
    Grievance.* Boulder, CO: Lynne Reiner Publishers. 47–70.
– 2004. "How Do Natural Resources Influence Civil War? Evidence from
    Thirteen Cases." *International Organization* 58 (winter): 35–67.
Sachs, Jeffrey D., and Andrew M. Warner. 2001. "The Curse of Natural
    Resources." *European Economic Review* 45: 827–38.
Segal, Hugh. 2007. "Comments of Senator Hugh Segal." *Hansard*, May 2007.
Smillie, Ian. 2004. "ODA: Options and Challenges for Canada." Ottawa:
    Canadian Council for International Co-operation.
Standing Committee on Foreign Affairs and International Trade. 2005.
    *Mining in Developing Countries – Corporate Social Responsibility:
    The Government's Response to the Report of the Standing Committee on
    Foreign Affairs and International Trade.* Ottawa: Government of Canada.
Standing Senate Committee on Foreign Affairs and International Trade.
    2007. "Overcoming 40 Years of Failure: A New Road Map for Sub-
    Saharan Africa." Ottawa: Government of Canada.
United Nations. 2002. "International Conference on Financing for
    Development: Facilitator's Working Paper." New York: United Nations.
United Nations Conference on Trade and Development. 2007. *World
    Investment Report 2007: Transnational Corporations, Extractive
    Industries and Development.* New York and Geneva: United Nations
    Conference on Trade and Development.
– 2009. *The Least Developed Countries Report 2009: The State and
    Development Governance.* New York and Geneva: United Nations
    Conference on Trade and Development.
United Nations Education, Scientific and Cultural Organization. 2009. *UN
    World Water Development Report 3.* New York and Geneva: World
    Water Assessment Programme.

United States Geological Survey. 2011. "Mineral Commodity Summaries 2011." Washington, DC: Department of the Interior.

Van de Sandt, Joris. 2009. "Mining Conflicts and Indigenous Peoples in Guatemala." The Hague: Cordaid.

Walde, Thomas. 1992. "Third World Mining: No Limits to Pollution." *Raw Material Report* 8, no. 3: 4–6.

Wise, Raul Delgado, and Ruben del Pozo Mendoza. 2005. "Mexicanization, Privatization, and Large Mining Capital in Mexico." *Latin American Perspectives* 32, no. 4: 65–86.

World Bank. 1996. "A Mining Strategy for Latin America and the Caribbean." Washington, DC: World Bank.

– 2002. *Treasure or Trouble? Mining in Developing Countries.* Washington, DC: International Finance Corporation.

– 2003. *Extractive Industries Review: Striking a Better Balance.* Washington, DC: World Bank.

WorldWatch Institute. 2003. *State of the World Report.* New York: Norton and Company.

9

Between Indifference and Idiosyncrasy: The Conservatives and Canadian Aid to Africa

DAVID BLACK

Since the Conservative Party won the 2006 federal election, many commentators have accused the Canadian government of "walking away from Africa" (Ignatieff 2010). When it comes to foreign aid, this is not, strictly speaking, accurate. According to the 2009–10 Annual Report to Parliament of the Canadian International Development Agency (CIDA), 48 per cent of CIDA's planned aid disbursements were to be spent in Africa (CIDA 2010, 7). The government made much of Canada being the first G8 government to fulfill its pledge to double aid to Africa, as it did – in part by recalculating the base from which it began – between 2003–04 and 2008–09. Total Canadian aid to Africa reached record highs in 2008 and 2009: about $1.3 billion (OECD/DAC online statistics). Additionally, the Harper government championed its Muskoka Initiative on Maternal, Newborn and Child Health at the G8 Summit in June 2010, committing $1.1 billion over five years toward an international initiative that has the potential to be more beneficial to African women and children than to those of any other continent (CIDA 2011c, n.p.).[1]

Even so, it is also clear that the government's disposition toward Africa has changed, and diminished, from that of virtually every other Canadian government in the post-decolonization era, in ways that have had a significant effect on Canadian aid. In this chapter, I will argue that this changed disposition can be captured by the twin themes of indifference and idiosyncrasy. By idiosyncrasy I am not referring here to the role of key individuals – although, as in most other policy domains under the current Conservative government, it is clear that Prime Minister Stephen Harper casts a long shadow over the direction and character of aid policy, albeit more indirectly than directly. Rather, I am referring to what Jennifer Lalonde has characterized as the emergence of "a distinctly Canadian aid effectiveness agenda" (Lalonde 2009, 170; see also, in this volume, Brown, chapter 3; and den Heyer).

In short, while CIDA now talks the talk of "aid effectiveness," echoing the language of the broader aid effectiveness agenda that has come to dominate the international aid regime since the early 2000s, it has deviated from these principles by stressing the more Canada-centric elements of accountability to Canadians – managing for results and restructuring of CIDA – over those that would require multilateral collaboration (harmonization) and responsiveness to recipients' priorities or "ownership" (alignment). One can argue that the latter form the true core of the international aid effectiveness agenda, and therefore that CIDA under the Conservatives has been relatively unconcerned with the efforts of the wider donor community to forge shared priorities and modalities, at least at the level of political leadership and overriding policy direction.[2] Whatever one thinks of the Paris Declaration principles and the aid effectiveness agenda, the recent prevalence of Canada-centric policy reforms represents a distinct break from the long-term, if incompletely achieved, trend toward greater coordination/conformity with harmonized multilateral aid practices (see Black et al. 1996; Black 2006).

Underpinning and preceding this idiosyncratic turn in Canadian aid policy, however, is a bedrock of indifference toward aid generally, and aid to Africa specifically. In short, one searches in vain for influential members of the cabinet and caucus who have more than a passing knowledge of, interest in, or commitment to things African. Similarly, there is no discernible constituency for CIDA and development aid, understood in the traditional "humane internationalist" terms of a particular acceptance of obligations relating to global poverty as an extension of the long-term interests of rich countries (see Pratt 1989, 14), among the current crop of Conservative politicians. This is not to suggest that there is no support for compassion toward the less fortunate, as witnessed particularly in humanitarian responses such as that in post-earthquake Haiti (see also Conservative Party of Canada 2006, 45). However, there is no real conviction that aid can or should be a means toward the long-term objectives of

reducing systemic poverty and inequality, but rather a strong disposition to deploy Canadian aid in ways that reflect more narrowly
understood political, security, and economic self-interest.

In order to develop these themes, it is first necessary to sketch the
backdrop to present Conservative aid policies in Africa by briefly
reviewing the trajectory of aid to Africa under previous Liberal governments. I will then discuss the "reframing" of aid policy under the
Harper Conservatives, and the protracted period of drift that marked
their first three years in office. Finally, I will analyze the recent emergence of a new, more focused, and ostensibly "effective" set of aid
priorities, and what they reveal about current dominant attitudes
and approaches to aid and development.

BORN-AGAIN AFRICANISTS?
THE CHRÉTIEN AND MARTIN LIBERALS

There is a historic irony in former Liberal leader Michael Ignatieff's
criticism of the Conservative government for "walking away from
Africa," since his Liberal predecessors in the Chrétien government
(with Paul Martin as finance minister) presided over the deepest
cuts in the history of the Canadian aid program. Official development assistance (ODA) is estimated to have decreased by 33 per cent
in real terms between 1988–89 and 1997–98, compared with a
22 per cent decline in defence spending and cuts of 5 per cent to all
other programs in the same period (Morrison 1998, 413). The aid-
to-gross national product (GNP) ratio declined from 0.49 per cent in
1991–2 to 0.25 per cent in 2000, dropping Canada well down the
donor "league table" (sixteenth of twenty-two states in 2000) of the
Organisation for Economic Co-operation and Development (OECD).
Aid to Africa was hit hardest of all, with declines in bilateral aid
between 1990 and 2000 of 7.2 per cent for Africa, 3.5 per cent for
the Americas, and 5.3 per cent for Asia (NSI 2003, 78). The disarray
caused by these cuts to Canadian aid programming throughout the
continent was considerable, as was the demoralization they caused
within CIDA. Indeed, one could plausibly argue that the Liberals'
approach to aid to Africa in this period and the Conservatives'
approach since 2006 are near mirror images of each other. The
Liberals actually *cut* aid substantially, all the while maintaining a
rhetorical veneer of interest in Africa partly through the high profile
of Lloyd Axworthy's "Human Security Agenda" and associated

priorities, such as the Ottawa Treaty to Ban Landmines, civilian protection, and the promotion of the "Responsibility to Protect,"[3] each of which found particular resonance in Africa. The Conservatives, on the other hand, have more or less *maintained* existing aid spending commitments, while rhetorically signalling a retreat through their emphasis on Latin America and the Caribbean along with other real and perceived slights of long-standing African partners (discussed in greater detail below). This has proven needlessly counter-productive for the government, not least in terms of Canada's thwarted attempt to secure a seat on the UN Security Council in 2010, and raises the question of *why* the Conservatives would be so unconcerned with potential diplomatic ramifications.

By the early part of the new millennium, however, the Liberals – having presided over a fiscal turnaround – re-engaged African issues with considerable vigour and a high political profile. Prime Minister Jean Chrétien, in the legacy-minded twilight of his political career, embraced the opportunity presented by a select group of African leaders' proposal for what became the New Partnership for Africa's Development (NEPAD), making a G8 concentration on Africa, through the Africa Action Plan (AAP), a principal focus of the 2002 Kananaskis Summit. Although one could argue, in light of the cuts of the 1990s, that this political embrace of Africa was akin to a deathbed conversion, it was nevertheless focused, strategic, and sustained. Chrétien "double-hatted" one of the country's ablest diplomats, Robert Fowler, as his G8 Summit sherpa and his personal representative for Africa, helping to ensure the centrality of Africa on the G8 agenda and the successful negotiation of the AAP. Chrétien himself travelled extensively on the continent to build support for his initiative in anticipation of the Summit, and the government buttressed its diplomatic effort with the $500-million, five-year "Canada Fund for Africa," billed as "a showcase for Canadian leadership in pursuit of effective development through a series of large-scale, flagship initiatives in support of NEPAD and the G8 Africa Action Plan" (CIDA 2002, 26; see CIDA 2003 for details). This was accompanied by a sustained reinvestment in CIDA at a rate of an additional 8 per cent per year, with particular emphasis on Africa. The increase in the aid budget nevertheless managed only to maintain CIDA's relative mediocrity in the OECD context, given increased aid budgets elsewhere.[4]

Chris Brown and Edward Jackson (2009, 19) argue that, "if anything, Chrétien's successor, Paul Martin, was even more committed to Africa." It is true that in various ways the Martin government sustained and extended the government's renewed interest in Africa, within CIDA and beyond it. At the 2005 Gleneagles G8 Summit, Canada confirmed it would at least double its ODA between 2001 and 2010, and committed to doubling aid to Africa even more quickly, between 2003–04 and 2008–09, on what was then projected to be a base figure of $2.8 billion. When the Martin government's foreign policy "blueprint," the 2005 International Policy Statement (IPS), finally emerged, it asserted that "Canada has played an important role in bringing African issues onto the global agenda, within the G8 and other forums. We will continue to press forward, in close collaboration with other partners in Africa and other donors, to support regional initiatives such as NEPAD" (CIDA 2005, 23).

Controlling for the inevitable hyperbole of such documents, two features of this statement should be emphasized. The first is the degree to which the Martin government was showcasing, in this and other places, its ongoing engagement with the politics of African development. In short, through the first half decade of the 2000s, "Africa" was made a hallmark issue by two successive Liberal governments. This was an accentuation of, but not a fundamental departure from, the interest in African issues and countries demonstrated by previous Canadian governments, both Liberal and Conservative, extending back to the early 1960s. The second is the degree to which this engagement was premised on ongoing collaborative structures and processes. These extended beyond the G8 to, for example, the Africa Partnership Forum – an inclusive forum of African leaders and the continent's major multilateral and bilateral donors launched at the Evian G8 Summit in 2003 (see Cargill 2010, 8–10) – and, even more broadly, the 2005 Paris Declaration on Aid Effectiveness. Indeed, the IPS also reiterated the commitment made in CIDA's 2002 statement, *Canada Making a Difference in the World: A Policy Statement on Strengthening Aid Effectiveness*, that "the principles of aid effectiveness – local ownership, greater partnership, donor harmonization, policy coherence and a focus on results – [would be placed] at the core of Canada's development cooperation program" (CIDA 2005, 6).

Given the notoriously wide dispersal of CIDA's bilateral recipients, the IPS went on to announce the concentration of two-thirds of bilateral aid in twenty-five "development partner countries," with bilateral assistance "increasingly concentrated in sub-Saharan Africa"

(CIDA 2005, 23). The government subsequently placed fourteen African countries on the twenty-five-country list, with a fifteenth, Sudan, being prioritized under a separate "Failed and Fragile State" window.[5] While Denis Stairs (2005) has convincingly demonstrated that this exercise in concentration was largely illusory, at least in terms of significantly reducing the dispersal of Canadian ODA, it did matter in at least one significant way. Countries designated as core development partners became the focus of medium- to long-term program planning, with increased numbers of CIDA personnel assigned to them both at headquarters and in the field along with somewhat increased budgets. This in turn enabled CIDA officers attached to these country programs to participate more fully and actively in the collaborative program-based approaches and intra-donor and donor-recipient governance structures that were increasingly institutionalized in recipient countries in the context of the international aid effectiveness agenda (see, for example, den Heyer 2012).

In sum, when the Harper minority government took office in January 2006, there was every indication that the die had been cast: Canada – and CIDA – was committed to steadily increasing aid budgets, a somewhat more focused aid program (in terms of both bilateral recipients and priority themes[6]), and a growing emphasis on Africa.

THE POLITICS OF INDIFFERENCE:
THE CONSERVATIVES AND AID TO AFRICA

Even before the new Conservative government took office in January 2006, however, an insightful analysis of public attitudes toward development assistance had demonstrated that Canadians on the partisan political right, including (at the time) both Progressive Conservative (PC) and Reform Party supporters, were far less inclined to support development aid than those in the centre or especially on the left. Alain Noël, Jean-Philippe Thérien, and Sébastien Dallaire (2004) note that polls conducted in 2000 for the Canadian Election Survey showed that only 10 per cent of those who considered themselves PC or Reform supporters favoured increased aid spending, compared with 40 per cent of those who supported the New Democratic Party (NDP) and 20 per cent who self-identified as Liberals. The overall picture, they argue, was that support for "humane internationalism" as manifested in foreign aid was much more fragile and divided than had traditionally been thought.

Unsurprisingly therefore, the Harper Conservatives took office with little on the record concerning aid, and nothing that would suggest a strong commitment to global poverty reduction. Their election platform, for example, said only that a Conservative government would:

- Articulate Canada's core values of freedom, democracy, the rule of law, human rights, free markets, and free trade – and compassion for the less fortunate – on the international stage;
- Advance Canada's interests through foreign aid, while at the same time holding those agencies involved in this area accountable for its distribution and results; and
- Increase spending on ODA beyond the current projected level and move towards the OECD average level. [Conservative Party 2006, 45.]

These vague and somewhat contradictory intentions contrasted with the precise and ambitious targets for enhancing the capacity and prestige of the Canadian Forces in the next plank of the platform. The combined emphasis on "compassion for the less fortunate," with its redolence of Christian charity, and on an interest-based calculus for the deployment of aid suggested a relatively limited and instrumental approach. Similarly, emphasis on accountability for its distribution and results reflected the deep skepticism of the Conservative base concerning the value of aid, and the ability of those agencies responsible for its distribution (notably CIDA) to do this work effectively. At the same time, the third point reflected a concern with international burden sharing and respectability among Canada's Western peers – even as the government abandoned the target of 0.7 per cent ODA/gross national income (GNI).

In sharp contrast to previous Progressive Conservative governments (see Clark 2007, 2), the Conservative caucus and cabinet contained no members with a clearly established interest in Africa. Their collective disposition was, and has remained, largely indifferent to this part of the world.[7] This broad disposition also applied to more inclusive manifestations of multilateralism, including the UN, the Commonwealth, and large-scale conference diplomacy such as the processes by which the Paris Principles and Accra Agenda for Action on international "development cooperation" were negotiated; and to much of the traditional non-governmental "development community" in Canada, with whom Conservative party relations were at best distant. A full discussion of *why* this disposition prevailed is beyond the scope of this chapter. However, it is clear that foreign policy thinking within the new government was strongly influenced by American conservative think-tanks and intellectuals; that the government's conception of "internationalism" was largely focused on strengthened relationships with traditional friends and allies, starting with the United States; that its leadership favoured a more "hard-headed," rational-utility-maximizing approach to international relations *beyond* traditional Western allies and alliances; and that this broad world view saw little to no advantage in becoming enmeshed in Africa's challenges. Fairly early in the life of the new government, this disposition was firmly reinforced by a report of the Standing Senate Committee on Foreign Affairs and International Trade, entitled *Overcoming 40 Years of Failure: A New Road Map for Sub-Saharan Africa* (2007). While purporting to advocate a new approach to relations with Africa, the report's key messages included the premise that African governments and leaders were the principal architects of their own misfortune, owing to an "unacceptable and pernicious" governance record; and that CIDA – an "ineffective, costly, and overly bureaucratic" agency – had "failed to make a foreign aid difference" and needed a radical overhaul, up to and including consideration of its abolition (Senate of Canada 2007, VII, IX, and XI). These conclusions were firmly in line with the predisposition of much of the Conservative caucus and its electoral base. The implications of the government's broad orientations will be further explored in the next section of this chapter.

In the absence of a constituency of any consequence for aid or for Africa, but with a government that had, as Joe Clark has put it, "a prudent regard for keeping Canada's word in the G-8" (Clark 2007, 3), the result for the first several years of the "Harper era" was a policy (if it can be so described) of drift. This was overlaid with periodic portends of more far-reaching changes which, taken together, effectively tied the hands of the makers and practitioners of Canadian aid and limited their ability to participate fully in, or commit to, medium- and long-term aid policy programming either bilaterally or multilaterally.

Among the changes that did emerge, it was clear from the outset that the government would prioritize Canada's military engagement in Afghanistan. This had profound implications for CIDA and

Canadian aid. Although not among the twenty-five priority countries for bilateral aid on the IPS list, Afghanistan rapidly became the
largest bilateral-aid program in Canadian history, reaching $280 mil-
lion by 2008–09 (CIDA 2011a, n.p.). It was supported by a large
Afghanistan Task Force which absorbed a disproportionate share of
CIDA's human resources, including the unprecedented assignment of
a CIDA vice-president. Yet the agency's performance in the unfamil-
iar and inhospitable political and security terrain of Afghanistan has
been widely criticized and deepened its reputation for ineffectiveness
(see Brown 2008, 95–8).

Rhetorically, the prime minister signalled a shift in priorities
toward greater emphasis on the Americas – ironically while attending the Heiligendamm G8 Summit in June 2007 that, like most summits since 2001, had a strong focus on Africa. This was widely
interpreted to reflect not only a comparative lack of interest in Africa
but a partisan desire to distance Canada's new Conservative government from the "Liberal brand," which the government took to
include an (over)emphasis on Africa. However, neither the ostensible
new tilt toward Latin America and the Caribbean, nor a prospective
move away from Africa, were tangibly reinforced by substantive aid
policy decisions for nearly two more years, reflecting the bedrock
lack of political interest in the "aid file" from the prime minister and
his government.

Indeed, aside from an ill-conceived (and now superseded) Office
for Democratic Governance announced in October 2006, and a more
admirable September 2008 announcement that aid was to be fully
untied by 2012/13, there were *no* substantive policy announcements
beyond the Afghanistan file for more than three years. Everyone who
was concerned with aid to Africa knew that changes were in the
works, but few were consulted, inside or outside the agency, and
those who may have been consulted by the tight circle around the
minister certainly were not at liberty to discuss publicly the directions
that might be taking shape. For major bilateral programs, ostensibly
guided by multi-year Country Development Program Frameworks
(CDPFs), it was clear that their existing frameworks were either obso-
lescent or indeed lapsed (see den Heyer, this volume).

The results of this apparent policy drift or vacuum were, as noted
above, debilitating for CIDA officers and their governmental and
non-governmental partners. In the absence of any clarity concerning
future directions, they could not fully commit to, let alone lead

within, the intra-donor planning processes that the aid effectiveness agenda prioritized. Similarly, project-planning processes with various implementing agencies became mired in multiple layers of approval and indecision, behind which lay an absence of clarity of purpose. For example, the auditor general of Canada (2009) reported that the average length of time for CIDA project approval was three and a half years. While a variety of explanations can be suggested for this absence of clarity regarding aid policy priorities, the end result can only be interpreted as reflecting a profound lack of concern with, or seriousness about, Canada's development programming and its consequences in Africa.

AN IDIOSYNCRATIC APPROACH TO AID EFFECTIVENESS

In an essay published in 2006, soon after the Conservatives took office, I concluded that, taken together, the thematic foci, selection criteria for core development partners, and new aid modalities that had come to the fore in Canadian aid policy over the first half-decade of the 2000s reflected a trend toward convergence with the dominant ideas and practices of the aid effectiveness agenda, and thus the international aid regime. This, in turn, continued a halting but nevertheless persistent tendency toward convergence that had been apparent for considerably longer (see Black 2006; Black et al. 1996). It was clear even then, however, that the Conservatives were likely to be less interested in both aid to Africa and the consensus principles of the international aid regime than their predecessors. Indeed, when the Conservatives' policy direction for Canadian aid to Africa finally began to come into focus, with key announcements in the first part of 2009, their conception of aid effectiveness was largely a "made in Ottawa" one, with little discernible reference to or influence from the broader international trends to which CIDA was still formally committed.

The fullest statement of the government's "New Effective Approach to Canadian Aid" came in International Cooperation Minister Bev Oda's May 2009 speech at the University of Toronto (Oda 2009b). In it, she asserted: "We pledge to make Canada's international assistance program more efficient, more focused, and more accountable. In short, more effective." The speech reiterated the steps already taken toward untying aid and reducing the number of bilateral countries of focus, while introducing three priority themes of "increasing food security, stimulating sustainable economic growth, and securing the future of children and youth." In addition, she outlined two "complementary [foreign policy] themes" to which aid resources would also be allocated – democracy promotion and ensuring security and stability. The implications of these themes will be addressed shortly. What is germane at this stage is that, in the entire speech, there was not a single mention of the principles and practices of harmonization or alignment (whether using these or comparable terms), which are cornerstones of the Paris Declaration. In short, there was no mention of the multilateral (as opposed to Canadian) aid effectiveness agenda.

This point needs to be carefully qualified. It is clear that, for good or ill, there is still support for, and commitment to, the broader multilateral aid effectiveness agenda within CIDA itself, as reflected in "CIDA's Aid Effectiveness Action Plan (2009–12)" issued later in the same year.[8] That plan, unlike Minister Oda's speech, is explicitly anchored in Canadian multilateral commitments to the Millennium Development Goals (2000), the Monterrey Consensus (2002), the Paris Declaration (2005), and the Accra Agenda for Action (2008). It contains quantifiable commitments to conduct country missions jointly with other donors (33 per cent), and analytic work jointly with other donors (50 per cent) by 2012–13. Similarly, it commits to channelling "at least fifty per cent of funding to the government sector through country systems, or state to the host government the rationale for using any separate systems" by 2012–13 (CIDA 2009, 5). All of this seems to indicate continued commitment to the collaborative modalities of the aid regime – though what precisely these commitments mean in practice remains unclear and a matter for careful scrutiny.

Even so, at the political level of key policy decisions regarding priority countries and themes, both the minister and government seem to have shown a cavalier disregard for the implications of their decisions on the ability of CIDA programs to participate in (let alone lead) shared multilateral processes. This underscores the degree to which the minister on the one hand, and much of her agency on the other, seem not only to have different approaches to aid policy implementation, but to exist in a relationship of mutual suspicion (see Brown 2009; also Smillie 2010). The government's apparent lack of concern with the implications of its policy decisions for multilateral dynamics and interests can be illustrated in a number of ways.

The first, and most prominent, was the government's abrupt decision, in February 2009, to reorient its bilateral aid to twenty "countries of focus," down from the previous government's list of twenty-five. In the process, it dropped eight of the fourteen African countries that had been included as priority partners in the Martin government's list of twenty-five, including a number of very long-standing bilateral recipients from both Commonwealth and francophone Africa.[9] The new list provided the most tangible evidence to date of the government's announced intention to refocus on the Americas, with the addition of new priority partnerships with Colombia, Haiti, Peru, and the Caribbean region. Almost as striking, however, was the ham-fisted way in which the announcement was handled, with no prior consultation with affected countries or indeed other long-standing development "partners" among the donor and non-governmental organization (NGO) communities. The political impact was, to say the least, unhelpful given the government's forthcoming "moment in the sun" as host of the twin G8 and G20 Summits in June 2010, as well as its failed campaign for a seat on the UN Security Council, since successful Canadian campaigns in the past had rested heavily on African support. The announcement was belatedly followed by several fence-mending and damage-control representations to African diplomats in Canada (for example, Oda 2009a), but the pertinent point for this analysis is that the government was neither attuned to, nor concerned with, the multilateral ramifications of this decision. It was, in short, focused on its own idiosyncratic conception of aid effectiveness, defined in terms of accountability to Canadians and concentrated focus.

Similarly, the new thematic foci of children and youth, food security, and sustainable economic growth, along with the vague foreign policy priorities of democracy promotion and ensuring stability and security, reflected the government's *own* priority setting, with little regard for broader collaborative efforts. Just how these thematic priorities were arrived at remains unclear to those outside the minister's inner circle. There is nothing inherently undesirable about the government's particular priorities, or inconsistent with those pursued in the broader international aid regime. The key problem was that the *process* by which they were arrived at and operationalized militated against consultation with key partners, and the ability of those implementing CIDA policy to do so in a timely, transparent, or consistent manner. Moreover, the pre-determination of Canadian strategic priorities took no apparent account of recipient-country priorities, in contravention of Paris Declaration principles of ownership and alignment. Once again, the priorities were announced, in May 2009, without discernible consultation inside or outside CIDA.[10] The agency organized consultative roundtables some three months *after* the new priorities were announced on how they should be implemented. After many more months of delay, CIDA released sparse (six- to eight-page) strategy documents for each theme. The Food Security Strategy, for example, was released in early 2010; the Sustainable Economic Growth Strategy, which had become the default category for CIDA's previous and relatively long-standing emphasis on governance, was not released until late October 2010.

There is much that could be said about this extraordinarily protracted process of thematic priority setting. The point here, however, is the impact it had on those trying to plan, approve, and oversee projects and programs on the ground in African (and presumably other recipient) countries – even those with relatively large, high-priority programs. In short, both the length and opacity of the approval process, and the fetishizing of focus ("focus within focus," as a Canadian aid official in Ethiopia put it), made it extremely difficult for CIDA personnel to engage in longer-term, multi-donor, collaborative commitments – a hallmark of the aid effectiveness agenda – and to be both responsive and reliable in their commitments to "partners" in developing countries. The logic of *Canada's* aid effectiveness agenda was, from the perspective of at least some CIDA program officers, a step backward toward an emphasis on "outputs" instead of "outcomes" – a preoccupation with the tracking of specific results from Canadian aid dollars regardless of (and potentially at the expense of) a broader concern with systemic outcomes to which Canada was one of several contributors. In the meantime, Canadian policy makers were often forced to delay, prevaricate, and in some cases renege on major commitments, while awaiting clarification on what the agency's new priorities would be, and how they would be interpreted and implemented. Any planning efforts were beset by uncertainties, delays, and multiple layers of approval. For example, by February 2010, the new Ethiopian country strategy (to replace the one for the five-year period ending in 2008–09) had already been through thirty-two versions (interview with Canadian aid official, Addis Ababa, February 2010). These processes, which the government highlighted as reflections of its commitment to "more effective" aid, therefore unfolded at the expense of CIDA's ability to participate in and support the international aid effectiveness agenda.

The disconnect between the government's approach to aid policy making and the elements of the broader aid effectiveness agenda to which CIDA was still committed through its 2002 policy statement, *Canada Making a Difference in the World*, was reflected in the results of the auditor general's fall 2009 analysis of the agency. The report was critical of CIDA's lack of progress on its 2002 commitments to align with recipient priorities, harmonize its efforts with other donors, and make more extensive and predictable use of program-based approaches. It concluded: "Many of the weaknesses we identified can be traced back to a lack of corporate management processes to guide and monitor the implementation of CIDA's aid effectiveness commitments ... it has yet to develop a comprehensive strategy for implementing its commitments" (Auditor General 2009, 3). Without discounting CIDA's own well-known management travails, however, the agency's failure to make good on its aid effectiveness commitments must also be attributed in large measure to a lack of political leadership from successive ministers and governments. This lack of leadership reflects, in part, the very slow and opaque process of decision making concerning new priority countries and themes – along with the low priority given to aid – and more recently an obsession with focus and domestic accountability that is very difficult to square with the fundamental imperatives of decentralized responsiveness and collaboration that are at the core of the transnational aid effectiveness agenda.

CONCLUSION: A SHALLOW RE-ENGAGEMENT

The history of Canadian aid to Africa, particularly over the past twenty years, has been marked by substantial reversals of political and material fortune. This can be seen as part of a longer pattern of consistent inconsistency in Canadian attention toward Africa (see Black 2010). What are the prospects for renewed commitment under a more internationally engaged Conservative government?

Through much of 2010, there was some evidence of an effort to increase Canada's visibility and refurbish the country's image on the continent. It is clear that much of this was tied to the tardy, and ultimately embarrassingly unsuccessful, bid for a non-permanent seat on the UN Security Council for 2011–12. Whereas, as noted by Joe Clark (2007), there was a striking paucity of ministerial visits to Africa for the first several years of the Harper era, the first four months of 2010 saw three visits in rapid succession – by Foreign Minister Lawrence Cannon to the opening Summit of the African Union in Addis Ababa in January; by International Trade Minister Peter Van Loan to Kenya and South Africa in March; and by Governor General Michaëlle Jean to Senegal, the Democratic Republic of Congo, Rwanda, and Cape Verde in April. These followed the fence-mending representations to African missions in Canada noted previously (Oda 2009a).

The material basis for the claim that "Canada's history and friendship with Africa is strong and long-standing," and that "we will make responsible, meaningful commitments and keep them" (Oda 2009a), rested heavily on two foundations. The first was the argument, noted above, that Canada was the first G8 government to meet its commitment to double aid to Africa, a year ahead of the target date of 2009–10.[11] The fact that this resulted in a relatively modest total commitment of $2.1 billion was not dwelt upon (see Johnston 2010). However, the flagship initiative of the Harper government's image makeover, as well as a centerpiece of the G8 Summit in June 2010, was the Muskoka Initiative mentioned earlier. First articulated in Harper's speech to the World Economic Forum (WEF) in January 2010, the initiative was anchored by the $1.1-billion commitment of new money by the Canadian government announced during the Muskoka Summit. Also at the Summit, the G8 committed to provide a total of $5 billion in "catalytic" funding over the 2010–15 period, with the aim of generating in excess of $10 billion in new funding from all donors for this collective effort to accelerate progress on Millennium Development Goals 4 and 5.[12] By September 2010, the initiative was said to have generated $7.3 billion in new funding for maternal and child health (Toycen 2010). By November, it was announced that 80 per cent of Canada's $1.1-billion contribution would go to seven countries in sub-Saharan Africa, as Canada's own implementation plans were finally articulated (O'Neill 2010).[13]

At the time of writing, this initiative is still in a formative stage and so cannot be adequately analyzed here. Broadly speaking, it seems uncharitable to criticize an effort to address these self-evidently praiseworthy objectives. Indeed, the cynic might note that the initiative was cleverly targeted to disarm potential critics: Who, after all, could oppose its objectives? Nevertheless, setting this effort in fuller context suggests that it masks as many uncertainties and weaknesses as it addresses. First, and most important, the commitment was formulated at the same time as the March 2010 budget made this announcement:

> With the achievement of the $5-billion aid target,[14] future IAE [International Assistance Envelope] spending levels will be capped at 2010–11 levels and will be assessed alongside all other government priorities on a year-by-year basis in the budget. Relative to the planning track in the September 2009 Update of Economic and Fiscal Projections, which assumed automatic ongoing growth for international assistance spending of eight per cent per annum, this results in savings of $438 million in 2011–12, rising to $1.8 billion in 2014–15. [Department of Finance 2010, n.p.]

In other words, the Canadian government was, at best, "flatlining" aid, resulting in an anticipated decline in ODA as a percentage of GNI from 0.32 per cent in 2009/10 to 0.26 per cent over the next few years. The problem here is not simply the decision, in the context of an austerity budget, to target aid once more for a disproportionate share of cuts, and glibly accept further erosion of Canada's already desultory performance. It is that, when the overall budget is no longer growing, the "targeted" and "focused" effort to make progress on maternal and child health comes effectively *at the expense of* a broader commitment toward poverty reduction, and thus the systemic underpinnings from which both maternal and child-health failures arise and on which sustainable progress needs to be built. The prime minister's words in introducing this initiative at the WEF in Davos are telling: "Let us close with something where progress is possible, if we are willing. It concerns the link between poverty and the appalling mortality among mothers and small children in the Third World. Did you know that every year over half a million women die in pregnancy and nearly nine million children die before their fifth birthday?" (G8 Information Centre 2010b, n.p.). In this statement, the prime minister effectively articulates a choice to address the *effects of* poverty on maternal and child health, rather than the underlying conditions of poverty to which it is explicitly linked. It is to be hoped, of course, that this initiative will save many lives, notably in Africa. Yet the choice to overlook and, implicitly, accept the underlying condition raises doubts about sustainability, and where the effects of poverty will be deflected *to* if they are successfully tackled in the area of maternal and child health.

The second point to note is the relatively late and apparently improvised character of this initiative. Here, it is instructive to compare the Muskoka Initiative with the Chrétien government's efforts to animate the Africa Action Plan prior to the Kananaskis G8 Summit in 2002 (Fowler 2003). First, the scope and ambition of the Chrétien government's approach was far broader – coming as it did in response to African leaders' NEPAD initiative – while the diplomatic focus and effort behind it was far more protracted and sustained. In brief, it was launched directly from the Genoa Summit in 2001, and was led diplomatically at the highest level by the Prime Minister's Summit sherpa and personal representative for Africa, Robert Fowler. Canada committed through the March 2002 Monterrey Consensus to sustained increases in aid spending with particular emphasis on Africa, and well before this it announced a special $500-million Canada Fund for Africa to amplify its diplomatic effort in the federal budget of December 2001. The prime minister's personal prioritization of this focus was underscored by travel to six African countries to discuss the initiative, along with consultations at the UN, Commonwealth, and Francophonie (see Chrétien 2007, 558).

By contrast, Prime Minister Harper's initiative on maternal and child health was not mooted prior to his Davos speech, less than six months before the G8/G20 summits, and does not seem to have been anticipated within CIDA, where staff were left scrambling to give life to the project, with minimal information or guidance (interviews with CIDA officials, February 2010; Pearson 2010). The lack of planning and reflection was soon exposed by controversial mixed messages over whether the government would or would not support contraception and abortion within this initiative.[15] Further, the decision on how much money the government would allocate to the initiative was announced just as the G8 Summit was beginning, attenuating any prospect of leading by example. The announced commitment of $1.1 billion in new funding over five years was, on the one hand, substantially more than the Chrétien government's $500-million Canada Fund for Africa, but, on the other, roughly the same as the Harper government's outlay for the three days of the combined G8 and G20 summits in Huntsville and Toronto, putting the relative level of the government's commitment into relief. Plans for how the money would be spent were announced several months later (see CIDA 2011d).

The point of this comparison is not to cast the Harper government in an unflattering light by highlighting the virtues of the Liberal initiative. After all, as noted previously, the Liberal initiative on the Africa Action Plan was characteristically long on ambition and modest on concrete resource commitments, while coming in the wake of the draconian cuts to aid spending in the 1990s under the same leadership. The comparison does underscore, however, some of the distinctive characteristics of Canadian aid policy making under the Harper Conservatives: a lack of sustained attention and consultation, leading to tardy or improvised initiatives; and an emphasis on tightly focused, readily "branded" initiatives consistent with the Conservatives' distinctive interpretation of "results" and "accountability." In short, indifference and idiosyncrasy. In the meantime, the ability of Canadian aid policy makers to participate actively in the larger debates and dynamics of the international aid regime, particularly in Africa, continues to decline.

NOTES

1 Since Africa has a greater need in this area than other regions, it is likely that it will receive a large share of the assistance.
2 It is fair to say that, in the field and within the agency, CIDA personnel are still highly sensitive to the ongoing effort to work more collaboratively with their peers, and are therefore frustrated by the apparent lack of concern with this effort on the part of their political leadership.
3 Articulated and popularized by the Canadian-sponsored International Commission on Intervention and State Sovereignty. See http://www.idrc.ca/EN/Resources/Publications/Pages/IDRCBookDetails.aspx?Publication ID= 240. Accessed 3 March 2012.
4 By 2007, Canada's ODA was ninth in terms of total volume and fifteenth as a percentage of GNI in the twenty-two-member Development Assistance Committee (DAC) of the OECD (See Brown and Jackson 2009, 5). For more on this "moment" in Canadian policy toward Africa, see Black (2004) and Fowler (2003).

5 Core development partners in Africa were to be: Benin, Burkina Faso, Cameroon, Ethiopia, Ghana, Kenya, Malawi, Mali, Mozambique, Niger, Rwanda, Senegal, Tanzania, and Zambia. It is noteworthy, in terms of Canada's historic multilateral commitments to the Commonwealth and the Francophonie, that seven of these countries were Commonwealth member states and seven were Francophonie members. One – Cameroon – was a member of both, and one – Ethiopia – was a member of neither.

6 Outlined in the IPS as: good governance, health (with a focus on HIV/ AIDS), basic education, private-sector development, and environmental sustainability, with gender equality as a crosscutting theme.

7 Some close to the government would argue that indifference is too weak a characterization and that the attitude of at least some Conservative parliamentarians may be closer to disparagement or disdain. For an analysis of this disposition, see Black (2009).

8 See CIDA (2011b); also Brown and Jackson (2009).

9 Specifically, Benin, Burkina Faso, Cameroon, Kenya, Malawi, Niger, Rwanda, and Zambia. For an insightful account of the impact in one of these – Malawi – see York (2009).

10 This relatively isolated approach to policy making, and the absence of consultation especially with long-established development NGOs and NGO coalitions in Canada – most notably the Canadian Council for International Co-operation (CCIC) – reflected a pattern of growing estrangement between the government and many Canadian civil society organizations (CSOs) concerned with development. This pattern was highlighted by CIDA's abrupt and controversial decisions not to approve new funding for the Canadian church coalition, KAIROS, ending a thirty-five-year funding relationship, and later CCIC, in November 2009 and July 2010 respectively (see Smillie, this volume). These decisions have not been explained beyond the dubious rationale that the work of the two organizations did not fit with CIDA's new thematic priorities. They do, however, reflect a trend toward the instrumentalization of aid funding relationships with CSOs, based on the government's interpretation of its priorities. In this regard, it is consistent with the idiosyncratic character of Conservative aid policies and policy making.

11 This, as many commentators have noted (but many seem now to have forgotten), overlooks the controversy surrounding the government's 2007 "recalculation" of the magnitude of this commitment, effectively reducing it by some $700 million by using a different baseline for the 2003–04 starting point. For one discussion, see Black (2009).

12 Reducing under-five mortality by two-thirds; and reducing maternal mortality by three-quarters and achieving universal access to reproductive health by 2015. For the text of the Muskoka Initiative, see G8 Information Centre (2010a).

13 These countries were Mozambique, Mali, Malawi, Nigeria, South Sudan, Ethiopia, and Tanzania. Other country foci for the initiative were Afghanistan, Haiti, and Bangladesh.

14 The result of the commitment made at the Gleneagles G8 Summit in 2005 to double total aid spending between 2001 and 2009–10.

15 The final decision was yes to contraception but no to abortion. See Gavai (2010).

REFERENCES

Auditor General of Canada. 2009. "Report to the House of Commons, Chapter 8: Strengthening Aid Effectiveness – Canadian International Development Agency." Ottawa: Office of the Auditor General of Canada.

Black, David. 2004. "Canada and Africa: Activist Aspirations in Straitened Circumstances." In Ian Taylor and Paul Williams, eds., *Africa in International Politics*. London: Routledge. 136–54.

– 2006. "Canadian Aid to Africa: Assessing 'Reform.'" In Andrew Cooper and Dane Rowlands, eds., *Canada among Nations 2006: Minorities and Priorities*. Montreal and Kingston, ON: McGill-Queen's University Press. 319–38.

– 2009. "Out of Africa? The Harper Government's New 'Tilt' in the Developing World." *Canadian Foreign Policy* 15, no. 2: 41–56.

– 2010. "'Africa' as Serial Morality Tale in Canadian Foreign Policy." Paper presented to the annual meeting of the Canadian Association of African Studies, Carleton University, Ottawa, May.

Black, David, and Jean-Philippe Thérien, with Andrew Clark. 1996. "Moving with the Crowd: Canadian Aid to Africa." *International Journal* 51, no. 2: 259–86.

Brown, Chris, and Edward Jackson. 2009. "Could the Senate be Right? Should CIDA Be Abolished?" In Allan M. Maslove, ed., *How Ottawa Spends, 2009–10*. Montreal and Kingston, ON: McGill-Queen's University Press. 151–74.

Brown, Stephen. 2008. "CIDA under the Gun." In Jean Daudelin and Daniel Schwanen, eds., *Canada among Nations 2007: What Room for*

Manoeuvre? Montreal and Kingston, ON: McGill-Queen's University Press. 91–107.

– 2009. "CIDA under Attack (from Its Own Minister)." *The Mark.* 24 June.

Canadian International Development Agency. 2002. "Canada Making a Difference in the World: A Policy Statement on Strengthening Aid Effectiveness." Gatineau, QC: Canadian International Development Agency.

– 2003. "New Vision, New Partnership: Canada Fund for Africa." Gatineau, QC: Canadian International Development Agency.

– 2005. *A Role of Pride and Influence in the World: Development.* International Policy Statement. Ottawa: Government of Canada.

– 2009. "CIDA's Aid Effectiveness Action Plan (2009–12)." http://www. acdi-cida.gc.ca/acdi-cida/ACDI-CIDA.nsf/eng/FRA-825105226-KFT. Accessed 7 December 2009.

– 2010. "Report to Parliament on the Government of Canada's Official Development Assistance 2009–2010." Gatineau, QC: Canadian International Development Agency.

– 2011a. "Afghanistan – Funding." 3 August. http://www.acdi-cida.gc.ca/ acdi-cida/ACDI-CIDA.nsf/eng/JUD-12514411-QD6. Accessed 2 December 2011.

– 2011b. "Aid Effectiveness Agenda." 29 November. http://www.acdi-cida. gc.ca/acdi-cida/ACDI-CIDA.nsf/eng/FRA-825105226-KFT. Accessed 2 December 2011.

– 2011c. "Maternal, Newborn and Child Health." 25 November. http:// www.acdi-cida.gc.ca/acdi-cida/ACDI-CIDA.nsf/eng/FRA-127113657-MH7. Accessed 2 December 2011.

– 2011d. "Minister Oda Announces Global Health, Nutrition and Disease Prevention Initiatives." 28 November. http://www.acdi-cida.gc.ca/acdi-cida/ACDI-CIDA.nsf/eng/FRA-103117396-TE2. Accessed 2 December 2011.

Cargill, Tom. 2010. "Our Common Strategic Interests: Africa's Role in the Post-G8 World." London: Chatham House.

Chrétien, Jean. 2007. *My Years as Prime Minister.* Toronto: Alfred A. Knopf.

Clark, Joe. 2007. "Is Africa Falling off Canada's Map?" Remarks to the National Capital Branch of the Canadian Institute of International Affairs, Ottawa. 6 November.

Conservative Party of Canada. 2006. *Stand up for Canada: Federal Election Platform.* 13 January.

den Heyer, Molly. 2012. "The Reshaping of Aid Effectiveness Policies in the International, Canadian, and Tanzanian Contexts." PhD thesis. Halifax: Dalhousie University.

Department of Finance. 2010. *Budget 2010: Leading the Way on Jobs and Growth.* 4 March. http://www.budget.gc.ca/2010/plan/chap3e-eng.html. Accessed 14 December 2011.

Fowler, Robert. 2003. "Canadian Leadership and the Kananaskis G8 Summit: Towards a Less Self-Centred Canadian Foreign Policy." In David Carment et al., eds., *Canada among Nations 2003: Coping with the American Colossus.* Don Mills, ON: Oxford University Press. 219–41.

G8 Information Centre. 2010a. "Muskoka Declaration: Recovery and New Beginnings." http://www.g8.utoronto.ca/summit/2010muskoka/communique.html. Accessed 2 December 2011.

– 2010b. "Statement by the Prime Minister of Canada at the 2010 World Economic Forum." http://www.g8.utoronto.ca/summit/2010muskoka/harper-davos.html. Accessed 2 December 2011.

Gavai, Avinash. 2010. "How the Rest of the G8 Stacks up on Contraceptives, Abortion." *Embassy*, 31 March. http://www.embassymag.ca/page/view/contraceptives-03-31-2010. Accessed 4 March 2012.

Ignatieff, Michael. 2010. "Rebuilding Canada's Leadership on the World Stage." Speech to the Montreal Council on Foreign Relations, Montreal. 2 November.

Johnston, Patrick. 2010. "Canadian Generosity Tumbles." *Globe and Mail*, 23 September.

Lalonde, Jennifer. 2009. "Harmony and Discord: International Aid Harmonization and Donor State Domestic Influence: The Case of Canada and the Canadian International Development Agency." PhD thesis. Baltimore: Johns Hopkins University.

Morrison, David. 1998. *Aid and Ebb Tide: A History of CIDA and Canadian Development Assistance.* Waterloo, ON: Wilfrid Laurier University Press.

Noël, Alain, Jean-Philippe Thérien, and Sébastien Dallaire. 2004. "Divided over Internationalism: The Canadian Public andn Development Assistance." *Canadian Public Policy* 30, no. 1: 29–46.

North-South Institute. 2003. *Canadian Development Report 2003.* Ottawa: North-South Institute.

Oda, Bev. 2009a. "Speaking Notes for the Honourable Beverley J. Oda Minister of International Cooperation for a meeting with African Ambassadors to Canada." Ottawa. 26 October.

– 2009b. "Speaking Notes for the Honourable Beverley J. Oda Minister of International Cooperation at the Munk Centre for International Studies." Toronto. 20 May.

O'Neill, Juliet. 2010. "Funds Earmarked for Maternal and Child Health in 10 Impoverished Countries." *Ottawa Citizen*. 1 November.

Pearson, Glen. 2010. "Maternal Health Pledge Sows Confusion." *Embassy*. 3 February. http://www.embassymag.ca/page/view/pearson-02-03-2010. Accessed 4 March 2012.

Pratt, Cranford. 1989. "Canada: An Eroding and Limited Internationalism." In Cranford Pratt, ed., *Internationalism under Strain: The North-South Policies of Canada, the Netherlands, Norway, and Sweden.* Toronto: University of Toronto Press. 26–69.

Senate of Canada. 2007. *Overcoming 40 Years of Failure: A New Road Map for Sub-Saharan Africa*. Ottawa: Standing Committee on Foreign Affairs and International Trade.

Smillie, Ian. 2010. "High Time for a Minister Who Understands the Role of Aid." *Globe and Mail*. 7 January.

Stairs, Denis. 2005. "Confusing the Innocent with Numbers and Categories: The International Policy Statement and the Concentration of Development Assistance." Calgary, AB: Canadian Defence and Foreign Affairs Institute. http://www.cdfai.org/currentpublications.htm. Accessed 14 December 2011.

Toycen, Dave. 2010. "Maternal, Child Health Go beyond Politics." *Embassy*. 22 September. http://www.embassymag.ca/page/view/toycen-09-22-2010. Accessed 4 March 2012.

York, Geoffrey. 2009. "Banned Aid." *Globe and Mail*. 30 May.

10

Tying up the Cow:
CIDA, Advocacy, and Public Engagement

IAN SMILLIE

Usai den tie cow na dae e dae eat grass. (A cow grazes where it is tied.)
– Old Sierra Leonean proverb

ADVOCACY AND CIVIL SOCIETY: THE CONCEPT

In 1993 Harvard University professor Robert Putnam published a book about Italy that would have important ramifications for wider understanding about the role of civil society and development. Putnam explored the reasons for the vast difference in economic development and the quality of governance between northern and southern Italy. He found that many of the apparent and intuitive explanations were faulty. It was not about climate or geology or natural resources. In some of these respects, the south was better endowed than the north. A major difference was the growth in the north – and the absence in the south – of what Putnam called "horizontal collaboration." In the south, vertical hierarchies prevailed, civil society was stunted, and development was slow. In the north, however, voluntary associations, communes, and guilds had become well established as far back as the twelfth century, creating social contracts that required political leaders to share power with others. A rich network of associational life led to the professionalization of public administration with "remarkably advanced systems of public finance ... land reclamation, commercial law, accounting, zoning, public hygiene, economic development, public education, policing and government by committee" (Putnam 1993, 126).

Making Democracy Work: Civic Traditions in Modern Italy was important because it refreshed – with new evidence from a new setting – what others, including John Locke, G.W.F. Hegel, and Tom Paine, had written about the importance of civil society in contributing to democracy, and to the environment required for sustainable economic development. Alexis de Tocqueville wrote expansively in the 1840s on the subject of community, voluntarism, and the creation of associations in his influential *Democracy in America*. Many of these ideas were resuscitated and given new life by Putnam's study.

The Putnam work came at a critical moment. The Cold War had just ended, and instruments of the state in the former Soviet bloc had atrophied with unforeseen speed. There had been no need for civil society organizations (CSOs) as service providers before the collapse of the Berlin Wall, because, in the ultimate welfare state, government took care of everything. Moreover, there was no desire on the part of government for civil society as a vehicle for "horizontal collaboration" and associational life because that might have fostered dissent.

With the advent of capitalism, or free markets, or whatever passed for these concepts in the post-Gorbachev era, CSOs were needed for just about everything: for health care, for educational services, for the provision of welfare to children, the disabled, the elderly, and anyone else the state had lost its ability to serve. CSOs were also seen – as they had been by de Tocqueville and now Putnam – as harbingers of democracy: organizations that could serve as advocates on behalf of their constituents; watchdogs in volatile political economies; teachers who could educate people about their rights as well as their responsibilities. In some ways, "civil society" became an alternative expression for democracy in countries where the term "democracy" had been comprehensively devalued by the communist state.

Western aid agencies with experience in Latin America, Asia, and Africa flocked to the former Soviet bloc, and "capacity building" for newly formed CSOs became the order of the day. This in turn led to new ways of looking at civil society in the developing countries of the South. There, the end of the Cold War gave long-overdue impetus among donors to the notion of "good governance." There too, CSOs were now seen as carriers of the democracy gene, acting as advocates, watchdogs, and expressions of popular opinion. For example, it became *de rigueur*, even essential, for governments to consult with local CSOs in the creation of all Poverty Reduction

Strategy Papers, the gateway to International Monetary Fund and World Bank funding.

While all of this may have been new to donor governments in the 1990s, and perhaps unwelcome to some recipient governments, it was hardly new to mature CSOs. Advocacy has been around for a very long time. Historically, all manner of CSOs have been formed *solely* for the purpose of public education and political advocacy, while others have seen advocacy as an important adjunct to their service function. In the late eighteenth and early nineteenth centuries, some anti-slavery societies, most notably in Canada and the United States, had as a partial purpose the provision of assistance to escaped slaves. However, they and their British counterparts had as their main objective a distinct political purpose: the ending of slavery.

History is rich with similar examples: the liberation of the Congo from Belgium's King Leopold in the first years of the last century; the campaign for the British social reforms of 1906–11; women's suffrage movements in the first half of the twentieth century; the creation of the Geneva Conventions on the treatment of the victims of war. The concept is mirrored in small and large ways in all manner of domestic Canadian CSOs today. Bodies organized to assist those with impairments, for example – physical, sensory, cognitive, or developmental – provide a wide variety of services to their clientele, often supported by government. However, they are also concerned about the rights of those they work with. Like their service provision, the promotion of these rights is often supported by government. The same is true of organizations working to protect the environment. It is not enough to simply plant trees; existing plant life must be protected. For that to happen, environmental organizations must educate the public and decision makers, and they may very well have to lobby politicians.

Arriving at the idea of "lobbying politicians," we edge into murky water, especially where government funding is concerned, so let us set that aside for a moment and examine the role of international development organizations in the field of advocacy. First, however, a broad description of advocacy: advocacy in the field of international development is variously known as policy dialogue, public engagement, development education, public participation, social action, and sometimes campaigning. It may take on high-profile, openly political characteristics, or it may be a discrete, low-profile activity.

It may be aimed directly at governmental decision makers in Canada or abroad, or it may use proxies such as the cultivation of public opinion and other vehicles.

Advocacy is likely to have one of two broad goals. The first is to build and maintain a constituency for development assistance – however this may be understood – as support for an organization's service function. The second has to do with change: changes in understanding, behaviour, policies, and relationships that improve the objective indicators of development in poor countries. This chapter will show that, while a great deal of emphasis has been placed on the former goal, often in ways designed to enhance organizational income, much less has been invested in the latter one – not least because it can result in income *reduction*.

BUILDING THE CONSTITUENCY

Arguably, "building the constituency" is where the greatest effort has been placed on public engagement and advocacy work by international development non-governmental organizations (NGOs). It is almost exclusively where the effort has been placed by the Canadian International Development Agency (CIDA): outreach to Canadians on development challenges in poor countries, with descriptions of successful aid projects "showcasing best practices in international development," as CIDA put it in a 2010 press release (CIDA 2010a, n.p.). Today's NGO websites are replete with good-news stories about what is being accomplished and what more can be done through development assistance. The development *problématique* in such cases is situated almost exclusively in the developing world, and the solution is more of what we know works.

A Google search using the words CIDA + public + engagement turns up numerous effusive NGO testimonials to this approach. World Hope International (WHI), a small Ottawa-based NGO founded in 2001, explains its public engagement and its relationship with CIDA as follows:

There is a clear alignment between CIDA and WHI Canada objectives. CIDA's priorities are poverty reduction, democratic governance, private sector development, health, basic education, equality between women and men, and environmental sustainability. Through its broad mission to bring hope and healing to a hurting world, WHI Canada focuses on poverty reduction, health and basic education. To date, WHI Canada has received CIDA funding to implement two public engagement projects, and two international development projects. The public engagement projects are consistent with CIDA's focus on engaging Canadians as global citizens. [World Hope 2010, n.p.]

Another NGO, the Canadian Association for Community Living (CACL), puts it this way: "CACL, with the support of the Canadian International Development Agency (CIDA), is raising awareness and engaging with Canadians and Canadian-based development NGOs on the need to combat global poverty and exclusion of people with intellectual disabilities, and to ensure that international development efforts – including poverty reduction strategies and the Millennium Development Goals – are inclusive of people with intellectual disabilities" (CACL 2010, n.p.).

CIDA's Mass Media Initiative is one vehicle of support for this kind of enterprise. In recent years it has funded dozens of projects that have resulted in festivals, exhibits, articles, radio, film, and television programs.[1] Many, if not most, deal with specific issues, projects, or organizations, and many become useful fundraising tools for the organization in question.

The dividing line between public engagement and fundraising is blurry. CIDA will not actively finance an NGO's direct fundraising efforts, but it is hard to imagine that the production of a film, for example, about the work of Plan International, co-financed and managed by Plan Canada, would not contribute to the image and – directly or indirectly – Plan's fundraising effort. CIDA contributed $90,000 to Plan Canada in 2008–09 for a half-hour film that would in effect do precisely that. According to CIDA's website:

"Because I Am a Girl" is a half-hour documentary profiling the lives of three girls (from Haiti, Sudan, and Colombia) whose stories are reported through the eyes of young Canadian journalists (MTV Canada female hosts). Examining a variety of development issues through the role of Canadian organizations, the documentary focuses on the impact of these issues on juvenile girls ... The full thirty-minute documentary [was] launched on MTV Canada and [had] a second-window opportunity on CTV, airing between September 2008 and September 2009. [CIDA 2010b, n.p.]

More often than not, the messages contained in programs like this present poverty as a technical problem, the product of hostile forces of nature or blind social forces, or a vicious circle that can (and must) be broken by outside intervention in the form of education or health care or food or microfinance. However, almost everyone working in the field of international development, including the authors of the most emotive NGO fundraising appeals, knows that the problems of poverty – and the solutions – are more complicated than that.

CHANGING THE DEVELOPMENT DYNAMIC

Deep-seated poverty in developing countries has to do with history, with trade and investment, with governance, and with power imbalances that leaned one way during the bipolar Cold War period and in other ways since. Technical solutions can be important, but alone they are rarely the answer, and many of the issues needing attention may lie well beyond the borders of the country in question.

Broader understanding of the development dynamic has manifested itself in different kinds of messaging. One type has to do with who is at fault: for example, "the rich" or a nuanced version of same. Messages here treat the problem as a sin of omission, one that can be explained or solved in a variety of ways:

- By the provision of more development assistance. This might, for example, manifest itself in campaigns for donor governments to reach the 0.7 per cent of gross national income/official development assistance (GNI/ODA) target.
- By changing behaviour in the North: high standards of living in the North (or rates of consumption, environmental degradation, etc.) cannot continue without simultaneously impoverishing others. The imbalance must be redressed.
- By resolving outstanding trade disparities: the removal of subsidies from Northern agricultural products; the removal of Northern trade barriers to Southern goods.

In the 1960s and 1970s debates such as these were conditioned and sharpened by a bitter and polarizing fight against apartheid in South Africa, a struggle with which many Northern development organizations identified; by liberation wars in Angola, Mozambique,

Rhodesia (as Zimbabwe was then known), and Guinea-Bissau; and by the war in Vietnam. Additionally, some NGOs were caught up in campaigns against abuses in developing countries by multinational corporations. The long-running campaign against Nestlé for its unscrupulous promotion of baby formula in Africa during the 1970s was emblematic of this approach. Others joined more generic campaigns such as an effort by the United Nations Conference on Trade and Development (UNCTAD) during the 1970s and 1980s to create a "New International Economic Order," one that would improve terms of trade and create a better deal for countries whose economies were dependent on one or two primary products, such as jute, sisal, coffee, cotton, tea, or bananas.

Among Canadian NGOs, Oxfam Canada was one of the first to stake its claim in this area. In 1972 it stated:

> We can no longer appear to be solely preoccupied in the intricate and demanding business of raising and dispersing funds while we know that fundamental social, economic and political injustices exist which all the aid in the world will never remove. We are at a point in our history when we run the risk of being seen as lacking in conviction and honesty if we do not show that we understand the underlying causes of poverty and underdevelopment, that we are unwilling to tolerate them and that we wish to help remove them insofar as we can. [Lissner 1977, 195, citing Oxfam Canada's booklet "Education," 1972]

During the 1970s, the Canadian University Service Overseas (CUSO) – then one of the largest NGOs in Canada – adopted what at the time looked to some like strident positions on such issues. Its advocacy on behalf of Southern African liberation movements was seen as giving comfort to terrorists, and its support – moral as much as anything else – for South Africa's African National Congress was regarded as giving comfort to communism.[2] As late as 1983, a group calling itself Canadians for Foreign Aid Reform (C-FAR) published a booklet entitled CUSO and Radicalism, which stated that "a closer investigation of CUSO's activities brings to light a very strong political bias supporting left-wing and socialist, even openly communist countries and groups" (Lapajne 1983, 1).

It is easy to forget that, while the Cold War ended with a whimper less than a decade later, it was as alive and as virulent during the

1980s – the Reagan years – as it had ever been. Canada's ambivalent attitude during the 1960s and 1970s toward South African apartheid and the Southern African liberation struggles has been airbrushed from collective memory, helped along by the latter-day efforts of Brian Mulroney to persuade Margaret Thatcher that apartheid could not survive.[3] So it is easy to forget that organizations that spoke about such issues, about the shortcomings of Canadian government policy or the role of multinational corporations in Southern Africa, were regarded by many with suspicion and by some as "left-wing and socialist, even openly communist."

There are parallels today: it is commonplace for campaigning environmentalists, human-rights workers, and the like to be written off as deluded romantics, or anti-business, or "just in it for the money." It is much less controversial to "feed the children" or to "save the children" or to "adopt" the children than to deal with the difficult and complex realities that make it impossible for the parents of these children to look after them properly themselves. When faced with a choice between the difficult and the less difficult, between insults and praise, between something that may damage an organization's income and a money spinner, great fortitude is required to take the road less travelled – even occasionally.

LEGAL LIMITATIONS

There is confusion, not least in the minds of some NGO managers and their boards, about what levels of advocacy are permissible under Canada's regulations for non-profit organizations and charities. In fact, charity regulations are frequently cited for the diffident advocacy undertaken by so many international development organizations. This is almost certainly a case of wilful suspension of belief and selective attention, of hearing what one wants to hear rather than the facts.

Non-profit organizations can engage in as much advocacy as they want. Regulatory constraints deal only with the income and expenditure boundaries that they must, as not-for-profit organizations, adhere to. *Charitable status*, if it is sought from and granted by the Canada Revenue Agency (CRA), confers additional rights and responsibilities on non-profit organizations. The principal right is the ability to issue receipts that can be used by donors as tax deductions. A $100 donation to a Canadian charity, for example, will cost the giver about $75, depending on his or her rate of income tax. The difference – money foregone by the government of Canada – represents indirect support by the government to the charitable sector. As a result, the government, quite correctly, wants to ensure that this money is used for genuinely charitable purposes, and so the rules and responsibilities for charities are more rigorous than they are for non-profits without charitable status.

Under the Income Tax Act, a registered charity can be involved in non-partisan *political* activities as long as it devotes "substantially all" of its resources to charitable activities. Any political activities have to help accomplish the charity's purposes and they must remain incidental in scope. Acceptable political activities are described in detail by the CRA, but they fall generally under the concept of urging – either directly or through the public – elected representatives or public officials, Canadian or otherwise, to adopt or change laws, policies, or decisions. The general financial limitation on such activities is 10 per cent of an organization's total resources, although the proportion may rise to as much as 20 per cent for smaller organizations.

Public-awareness campaigns are different, and are not treated as political activities. According to the CRA:

> A charity's public awareness campaigns aim to give useful knowledge to the public to enable them to make decisions about the work a charity does or an issue related to that work. When a registered charity seeks to foster public awareness about its work or an issue related to that work, it is presumed to be taking part in a charitable activity as long as the activity is connected and subordinate to the charity's purpose. In addition, the activity should be based on a position that is well-reasoned, rather than information the charity knows or ought to know is false, inaccurate, or misleading. [CRA 2010, n.p.]

In all of this, a great deal of interpretation is required, but a great deal of latitude is allowed. Conservative think-tanks like the C.D. Howe and Fraser institutes, whose primary purpose is to influence public policy, are registered charitable organizations. The Conference of Defence Associations Institute "promotes public debate on national security and defence issues" and receives government funding to do so (CDAI 2010, n.p.). It is a charitable organization. So are the North-South Institute (NSI) and Amnesty International.

The limitations on public engagement are guided by common sense and, obviously, by an organization's purpose and its concerns about the sensitivities of its funders. For organizations highly dependent on government funding, and those for whom income maximization and service provision are key, the boundary walls around public engagement may be more constraining than for others, but they are almost entirely self-constructed.

In other words, there are no limitations placed by the Canadian Revenue Agency on charitable organizations that might want to engage the public on issues related to trade or tariffs, human rights, or the size and quality of Canadian development assistance, because this would be, as the CRA puts it, "connected and subordinate to the charity's purpose." The issue is not whether CSOs *can* engage in this kind of work. It is not even whether they should. It is whether they see this kind of activity as an essential part of their mandate, or simply an adjunct, an ancillary activity that can be used to raise an organization's profile and funds. It is, of course, one thing to consciously decide that such activities are not germane to an organization's mandate. It is another to avoid them out of fear that private donors will not understand, or worse, that institutional donors will react to unpalatable messages by shooting the messenger.

The following sections of this chapter will examine what happens when CSOs are caught in CIDA's crosshairs. There is a growing concern that the warning shots of years past have been transformed into a shoot-to-kill policy. The chapter will conclude with a more fundamental concern: a worry that the idea of civil society as an "essential ingredient of democracy, [one that] helps citizens find a voice to be more effective participants in political life,"[4] has been transformed by the Harper government into a concept that perceives NGOs as little more than junior service providers, operating at the pleasure – and the behest – of government.

BITING THE HAND THAT FEEDS

The federal government has always been of two minds about how, and even whether, to support the public-engagement activities of Canadian CSOs working in the field of international development. This is not new. What is now called "public engagement" was in the 1970s and 1980s called "public participation" and more frequently "development education," a term with a vaguely condescending

Orwellian ring to it, a bit like "attitude adjustment" or "behaviour modification." While governments – both Liberal and Progressive Conservative – were in those days supportive of constituency-building development education – of the type done today by organizations like Plan Canada and World Hope International – they did not appreciate being hectored about their political stance on Southern Africa, much less on the volume and quality of their aid program. Nor did they like being asked by the media and by opposition members of Parliament why the government was providing support to voices that came across as shrill, radical, and sometimes abusive.

Measured criticism was acceptable, but only up to a point. For example, during the early 1980s the North-South Institute, which received the bulk of its income from CIDA, published a series of detailed studies on Canadian aid to Bangladesh, Haiti, Senegal, and Tanzania. Describing an ill-advised automated bakery project, the institute's report on Tanzania stated that "poor judgment by CIDA can result in aid of dubious benefit, aid whose negative consequences are extended well beyond the original initiative" (Young 1983, 106). The bakery project was by then more than "dubious"; it was an acknowledged and a well-publicized disaster.[5] The NSI report was even more cautious about Canada's other major investment, in the Tanzanian railway sector. The report spoke of its "potential to be highly positive" but added a non-judgmental yet vaguely suggestive nuance: "It is too early to judge how effective and well-balanced Canadian aid to the railway sector has been" (Young 1983, 105).

CIDA and the government at large could support and even tolerate a certain level of criticism of this type, perhaps viewing it as useful "policy dialogue." However, sometimes the criticism went too far. In 1991 the Canadian Council for International Co-operation (CCIC) issued a "report card" that was much more critical of Canada's aid program than anything the North-South Institute had ever published, comparing CIDA's performance unfavourably against a major 1987 CIDA policy paper, *Sharing Our Future*. Soon after the appearance of the report card, CIDA President Marcel Massé called in CCIC's executive director and gave him a dressing down on the grounds that this kind of publication would demoralize the Canadian public and strengthen CIDA's critics in Parliament. Many of the larger CCIC members, NGOs that contributed the bulk of the organization's membership income, were also unhappy about the report card, fearing, perhaps, that some of the government's displeasure might rub off on their own CIDA funding (Brodhead and Pratt 1994, 104).

Watchdogs, of course, are not supposed to bite the hand that feeds, and hand-biting analogies have never been far from the fore in CIDA's thinking about its support for development education or policy engagement. Organizations like CUSO that failed to understand the sometimes unspoken boundaries found their applications for development education funding refused. Finally, after years of ongoing debate and controversy, in 1995 the Liberal government scrapped CIDA's public-participation program entirely. NGOs that received multi-year program funding from CIDA were permitted to spend up to 15 per cent of their CIDA contributions on public engagement, but it would take another four years before a wider program of CIDA support would be reintroduced.

During 2009 and 2010, something more dramatic occurred. Stephen Harper's Conservative government began defunding Canadian organizations whose "messages" it did not like. This was not a defunding of their advocacy work, it was a 100 per cent cancellation of all CIDA funding, often without explanation or warning. In 2009 KAIROS, an ecumenical organization sponsored by Canada's mainstream churches, had all of its CIDA funding cancelled – despite a positive CIDA evaluation – because CIDA Minister Bev Oda said that it did not "fit" with CIDA priorities (Woods 2009). Immigration Minister Jason Kenney said that the cut reflected the government's "zero tolerance policy" towards anti-Semitism (Whittington 2009), apparently mixing up the Canadian KAIROS with one in Palestine that had called for boycotts against Israel. Despite the mix-up, the decision stood, perhaps because the Canadian KAIROS did have critical things to say about Israeli occupation of Palestinian territory, things the Canadian government did not like to hear.

Alternatives, a Montreal-based organization, was also severely cut, apparently for similar reasons. The government also went through the Montreal-based Rights and Democracy with a scythe because of its tiny amounts of support for three "unacceptable" organizations in the Middle East. Women's groups and organizations working in reproductive health were axed in conjunction with the government's announcement that it would no longer fund abortion services overseas. In addition, in 2010, the Canadian Council for International Co-operation saw a forty-year partnership with CIDA dry up overnight, without a rational explanation,[6] although undoubtedly the group was penalized because it had gone to bat for member organizations that had previously been chopped. This was a totally new phenomenon: cuts not just to a questionable advocacy project, but complete cancellation of all support to entire organizations.

Some of the organizations in question will survive the slash-and-burn approach of the Harper government and may be stronger for it. Their voice, now free of funding chill, will be more independent and may express more clearly what they think. However, if they are membership organizations like CCIC, the present situation may do the opposite. It may provide an excuse for member organizations to cut back on their own advocacy, focusing even more attention on service delivery and eschewing even the half-hearted advocacy of previous years.

When the cuts came to CCIC, a CIDA official told its CEO, Gerry Barr, that something good had come out of it, in the sense that CCIC members and others had rallied around with funding, and with the independence that would accompany it. However, as Barr puts it, "something good was wrecked as well."[7] In fact, several things were wrecked, including the jobs of three-quarters of CCIC staff and any remaining idea that CIDA, under the Harper administration, could be a reliable "partner" for Canadian CSOs. Something else that was damaged was a sense of common purpose among Canada's NGO community: some went out of their way to praise a CIDA G8 "initiative" on maternal and child health (MCH), while also criticizing others for concerns about a concomitant CIDA decision to exclude abortion services from any reproductive-health projects. If NGO praise for CIDA's MCH initiative aimed to liberate substantive new funding for an important Millennium Development Goal, it probably failed. If it aimed to give embattled CIDA Minister Bev Oda a positive photo-op in front of the Parliament Buildings, it succeeded admirably. If it aimed to divide the Canadian NGO community, it may have succeeded there too.

Something else was happening as CIDA took the axe to advocacy. A new, and at the same time very old-fashioned, idea of civil society was emerging from the CIDA bunker. NGOs should be seen and not heard. They should revert to the role of service providers, working on service delivery, largely in sectors and countries of CIDA's choosing, regardless of the fact that these have changed a dozen times in as many years. As part of CIDA's new "development effectiveness principles," it looked as though NGOs would now revert to project-by-project funding under a dizzying array of new rules and procedures, and a requirement that each proposal include "exit strategies that ensure results achieved are sustainable" (Tomlinson 2010, 4).

In a powerful article on the dangers of over-controlling development assistance, former United States Agency for International Development (USAID) administrator Andrew Natsios writes about what he calls the two tensions in development programming: accountability and control versus good development practice. He says that the balance "has now been skewed to such a degree in the U.S. aid system (and in the World Bank as well) that the imbalance threatens program integrity" (Natsios 2010, 3). He could be describing CIDA, and not least its increasing heavy-handedness with CSOs. Natsios goes on to say that the control element "ignores a central principle of development theory – that those development programs that are most precisely and easily measured are the least transformational, and those programs that are most transformational are the least measurable" (Natsios 2010, 4). This is not to say that NGO programs are more transformational than others (although they probably are). It is to say that CIDA's efforts to control Canadian CSOs have never been greater, adding to the chill on almost any kind of serious developmental advocacy.

Something else is being lost in all this as well, something inherent in the Putnam idea of civil society. According to Putnam and others who have written about civil society, its strength comes not just from speaking out – advocacy – but from the willingness of government and others to listen. When government listens to civil society, it takes advantage of a powerful tool for good governance. Listening does not mean that a government must act on what it is hearing, but listening to a range of views can help leaven and improve the policy process. When voices are silenced, governments become deaf and lose the ability to discern. There is no more enduring image of a collapsing autocracy than the ubiquitous mob tearing down the outsized statue of a leader who, until the day before his downfall, knew he was feared, but who probably also believed himself to be wise, respected, and admired.

There is not a little irony in the fact that, while CCIC was awaiting – in vain – an explanation from CIDA as to why its funding was being cut, Foreign Minister Lawrence Cannon was attending a high-level ministerial meeting of the Community of Democracies in Poland in July 2010. Here, at least in theory, the importance of civil society was understood and articulated in terms that went far beyond basic service delivery. In remarks that Canadian NGOs would undoubtedly find ironic, if not hypocritical had they been made public, Cannon said:

> It is no secret to those of us in the room that a vibrant, established and pluralistic civil society is an essential ingredient of democracy. Civil society helps citizens find a voice to be more effective participants in political life. But beyond its role as a check and monitor, civil society is an important bridge to help governments connect to the people they serve and build positive relationships. Civil society is also a means through which citizens can contribute to thriving social, cultural, and economic sectors that are characteristic of healthy democracies.[8]

CONCLUSION: VOICELESS SERVICE PROVISION?

There is no obligation on the part of government to fund the advocacy work of CSOs, but in doing so a government can promote two things. The first is a wider constituency of citizen voices, including some who may find the public square crowded by those with outsized resources. Second, it can promote a quality of voice that might not find its way into the public square if it had to rely solely on private resources. Civil society can, in fact, do everything that Cannon described, but not if CSOs operate in fear that something they say might antagonize the government and bring them to the edge of financial ruin.

Nor is there an obligation for a charitable organization to engage in public-education and advocacy work – with or without government funding. However, the development problems of the poorest countries cannot be solved by aid alone, much less by NGO projects. Moreover, by dealing exclusively in development as feel-good opportunities for Canadians who want to "adopt" a child or dig a well, some of Canada's most prominent CSOs miss the bigger picture and present a misleading image to Canadians. It is not only, or even mostly, about "showcasing best practices in international development." It is about fixing what's broken all around the showcase. It is not about building a more efficient underground railway with "exit strategies" and "sustainable results"; it is about ending slavery.

The trade-off for cso s, and for governments that weigh the value in supporting them, has pitted voice against service provision instead of making them complementary. It has also created a situation in which many of Canada's largest international organizations have succumbed to the politics of income maximization, holding their collective tongue on issues that are fundamental to the mandate they have set for themselves.

NOTES

1 For a current list, see http://www.acdi-cida.gc.ca/cidaweb/cpo.nsf/vWebCC En?OpenView&RestrictToCategory=2217. Accessed 27 February 2012.
2 The author was executive director of cuso between 1979 and 1983.
3 Canadian government ambivalence toward the struggle against apartheid is described at length in Freeman (1997).
4 The irony of this brief quotation, from remarks made by Foreign Minister Lawrence Cannon in July 2010, will become apparent when it is repeated toward the end of the chapter.
5 Writing in the *Toronto Sun* three decades later, Peter Worthington (2010) raked over the coals of the ill-fated bakery project and all of the media attention it received.
6 cida Minister Bev Oda told ccic that it could reapply for funding if and when it had some overseas-development projects to peddle (author's discussion with ccic Executive Director Gerry Barr Ottawa, 20 July 2010).
7 Author's discussion with Gerry Barr, Ottawa, 20 July 2010.
8 Unlike most other speeches made by the minister, since defeated in the 2011 federal election, this one was not made available on his website or that of the conference. The excerpt quoted here was supplied by a government source who wants to remain anonymous. This fear of being identified as the source of a minister's speech says as much about the Harper government's attitude toward "a vibrant, established and pluralistic civil society" as anything else.

REFERENCES

Brodhead, Tim, and Cranford Pratt. 1994. "Paying the Piper: cida and Canadian ngos." In Cranford Pratt, ed., *Canadian International Development Assistance Policies: An Appraisal*. Montreal and Kingston, on: McGill-Queen's University Press. 87–119.

Canada Revenue Agency. 2010. "Policy Statement." http://www.cra-arc.
  gc.ca/chrts-gvng/chrts/plcy/cps/cps-022-eng.html#P107_9478. Accessed
  21 July 2010.
Canadian Association for Community Living. 2010. http://www.CACL.ca/
  english/projects/CIDA.asp. Accessed 13 July 2010.
Canadian International Development Agency. 2010a. "Minister Oda
  Announces Next Step to CIDA's Aid Effectiveness." 22 July. http://www.
  acdi-cida.gc.ca/acdi-cida/ACDI-CIDA.nsf/eng/CEC-722111726-KXG.
  Accessed 23 July 2010.
– 2010b. "Project Browser: Project Profile for 'Because I Am a Girl.'"
  http://www.acdi-cida.gc.ca/CIDAWEB/cpo.nsf/vWebCCEn/4FBAB6381
  3A89F41852574280037237F. Accessed 13 July 2010.
Conference of Defence Associations Institute. 2010. "About CDA Institute."
  http://www.cda-cdai.ca/cdai/about-cdai. Accessed 21 July 2010.
Freeman, Linda. 1997. *The Ambiguous Champion: Canada and South
  Africa in the Trudeau and Mulroney Years.* Toronto: University of
  Toronto Press.
Lapajne, Branka. 1983. *CUSO and Radicalism.* Toronto: Centre for
  Applied Research.
Lissner, Jørgen. 1977. *The Politics of Altruism.* Geneva: Lutheran World
  Federation.
Natsios, Andrew. 2010. "The Clash of the Counter-Bureaucracy and
  Development." Washington, DC: Center for Global Development. http://
  www.cgdev.org/content/publications/detail/1424271. Accessed 17
  August 2010.
Putnam, Robert. 1993. *Making Democracy Work: Civic Traditions in
  Modern Italy.* Princeton, NJ: Princeton University Press.
Tomlinson, Brian. 2010. "Partnerships with Canadians: A Renewal of the
  Mandate of Canadian Partnership Branch: A Review by the Canadian
  Council for International Co-operation." Ottawa: Canadian Council for
  International Co-operation. July 2010. http://www.ccic.ca/_files/en/
  media/CCIC_Analysis_of_Partnership_with_Canadians_en.pdf.
  Accessed 17 August 2010.
Whittington, Les. 2009. "Anti-Semitic Charge Angers Aid Group." *Toronto
  Star.* 18 December. http://www.thestar.com/news/canada/article/740510-
  --anti-semitic-charge-angers-aid-group. Accessed 27 February 2012.
Woods, Allan. 2009. "Ottawa Starves Climate Critics of Cash on Eve of
  Eco-Summit." *Toronto Star.* 3 December. http://www.thestar.com/news/
  canada/article/733939--ottawa-starves-climate-critics-of-cash-on-eve-of-
  eco-summit. Accessed 6 September 2010.

World Hope International. 2010. "World Hope Canada and CIDA." http://
www.worldhope.ca/index.php?option=com_content&view=article&id=
17&Itemid=58. Accessed 13 July 2010.

Worthington, Peter. 2010. "A Hurting Hand: It's Better to Spend Money
Probing Worthiness of CIDA than Wasting It on Foreign Aid." *Toronto
Sun*. 29 March. http://www.torontosun.com/news/columnists/peter_
worthington/2010/03/26/13372541.html. Accessed 6 September 2010.

Young, Roger. 1983. *Canadian Development Assistance to Tanzania*.
Ottawa: North-South Institute.

11

CIDA'S New Partnership with Canadian NGOs: Modernizing for Greater Effectiveness?[1]

STEPHEN BROWN

In the 1980s the Canadian International Development Agency (CIDA) was a world leader in the recognition of the importance of non-governmental organizations (NGOs) as development actors in their own right. Through its Partnership Branch, CIDA provided Canadian NGOs with support to broad programs (as opposed to short-term projects) and even in some cases with core funding over a number of years, that is to say, financing that was not designated for a specific project or country but rather for the NGOs themselves to spend as they saw fit. Most of CIDA's funding to NGOs supported work in countries and sectors identified by the NGOs themselves, based on their long-term involvement with actors from the global South. The NGO financing mechanism was based on trust, nurtured by close relationships that often spanned decades. Canada's innovative approach for supporting Canadian NGOs served as an inspiration to other bilateral aid agencies (Morrison 1998, 21).

The terms of the relations between CIDA and NGOs became more difficult in the 1990s, as the government sought to assert control over the content and destination of the funding delivered by the NGOs. Tensions grew further in 2009, when CIDA abruptly ended funding to a number of prominent NGOs, sending a chill through the development NGO sector. In July 2010 the minister of international cooperation, Bev Oda, announced a new "Partnership with Canadians," including important changes to CIDA's relationship with Canadian NGOs, as part of the government's efforts to "modernize our foreign aid and improve its effectiveness" (CIDA 2010b).

This chapter analyzes this new partnership within the context of broader trends in Canada's official development assistance (ODA) since 2000. It seeks to determine to what extent the new funding mechanisms will modernize CIDA's partnership with Canadian NGOs for increased effectiveness.

I find that the changes in the funding mechanisms are in line with two important recent trends: 1) CIDA and the broader Canadian government's increased centralization and control of foreign aid; and 2) the government's increasing instrumentalization of development assistance and CIDA. Though the government continuously invokes modernization and especially effectiveness to describe the changes, the new partnership modalities actually constitute, in important ways, a clear step backward. They undermine the contributions of NGOs as development actors and decrease aid effectiveness from a development perspective, even if they may help the government reach other objectives. Rather than enhance the CIDA/NGO partnership, these new measures are further eroding CIDA's already fraught relationship with Canadian NGOs.

THE PARTNERSHIP BETWEEN DONORS AND NORTHERN NGOS

NGOs based in Canada and other countries of the global North have a privileged relationship with Southern NGOs, while CIDA and other bilateral aid agencies normally have much closer ties with Southern governments. Canadian NGOs can thus play a very important role in representing the perspectives of the poor and advocating for their priorities. The signatories of the Accra Agenda for Action, including the Canadian government, have recognized this independent role: "We will deepen our engagement with CSOs [civil society organizations] as independent development actors in their own right whose efforts complement those of governments and the private sector. We share an interest in ensuring that CSO contributions to development reach their full potential ... We will work with CSOs to provide an enabling environment that maximises their contributions to development" (Accra Agenda for Action 2008, 4). CIDA also recognizes that NGOs can do things CIDA itself cannot, particularly in very poor countries: "Civil society organizations which possess well-developed capacity and strong links with the most vulnerable people are key partners for CIDA" (Canada 2002, 10).

The use of "partnership" to describe donor-NGO relations is rather euphemistic, given that the donor generally "pays the piper" and therefore gets to call the tune.[2] Sally Reith, in her analysis of this relationship, argues that the term partnership actually "disguis[es] the reality of the complex relationships in imbalances of power and inequality, often expressed through the control of one 'partner' over the other" (Reith 2010, 447). In most donor countries, this imbalance has increased over time, especially since the 1980s, when a growing number of donors increasingly found NGOs to be useful for their own purposes, notably by circumventing the state in recipient countries in an era of donor-imposed structural adjustment and government downsizing. The subsequent expansion of donor funding – and of NGOs – has left NGOs more dependent than ever on donors and therefore "increasingly vulnerable to donor demands" (Reith 2010, 448; see also Edwards and Hulme 1996). Reith notes: "Because donors control the funding it is often their goals that are pursued. Donors' funding requirements often imply that they have an agenda, and it is up to the NGOs to demonstrate how they can fit in with it, where failure to do so results in rejecting of funding applications" (Reith 2010, 450). Consequently, NGOs have become much more hesitant to challenge donor policies, as well as more likely to "manipulate information to their own advantage, reinforcing the notion of mutual distrust" (Reith 2010, 452). The "New Aid Agenda" also erodes NGOs' legitimacy by turning them into the voice of donors in the South, rather than the voice of the South in the land of the donors, and reduces NGOs' downward accountability, that is, to beneficiaries (Edwards and Hulme 1996, 966–8).

In Canada, the CIDA/NGO relationship was not always as antagonistic as it became in the 2000s. Starting in the late 1960s, CIDA received proposals from Canadian NGOs and funded successful ones on a 3:1 ratio, sometimes even better. As Tim Brodhead and Cranford Pratt (1996) recognize, NGOs may have designed proposals based on what CIDA was likely to finance and CIDA did earmark certain funds for specific purposes, but CIDA was essentially responsive to the priorities determined by Canadian NGOs, normally set jointly with Southern NGOs. CIDA recognized that Canadian NGOs could work with many actors in the global South better than a large government agency based in Canada. Several NGOs could criticize Canadian aid policies and practices without fear of their applications being denied in retaliation. Its responsiveness to NGO-led initiatives placed CIDA at the forefront of its donor peers by the mid-1980s. Further, CIDA adopted as its own several issues advocated by the NGOs, including recognizing the role of women in development and the importance of human rights. CIDA took two additional steps forward: first, by allocating multi-year funding to Canadian NGOs' broader programs, and not just specific projects; second, starting in the early 1990s, by providing core funding to some larger NGOs with a proven track record (Brodhead and Pratt 1996, 91–8).

Countervailing forces were also at play, within CIDA and the Canadian government as a whole. For assistance to some recipient countries, CIDA no longer valued Canadian NGOs for their insight into grassroots needs. Instead, the Canadian government itself identified priority needs and gave Canadian NGOs contracts to implement projects to address those needs, which often aligned with Canada's own interests (Brodhead and Pratt 1996, 101). By the mid-1990s, while aid budgets were shrinking, CIDA was seeking even greater control (Brodhead and Pratt 1996, 114). Canada's (1995) new foreign policy statement, *Canada in the World*, further compelled the realignment of Canadian ODA with Canada's own foreign policy interests, including measures such as funding NGOs only in government-identified priority sectors, for aid in general or for the relevant recipient country, albeit still in a responsive manner (Rudner 1996, 207–8). By then, CIDA's relationship with NGOs resembled far more closely the model analyzed by Reith, presented above. As funding levels dropped, NGOs had to devise more creative and competitive ways of raising resources, including private donations from individual Canadians, and not always with the same success. The NGOs most successful in fundraising in the late 1990s and early 2000s were those related to children (often via child sponsorship), linked with churches, or the local branches of international NGOs, such as Oxfam Canada, CARE Canada, and Save the Children Canada (Caouette 2008, 119–23).

CIDA'S NEW PARTNERSHIP WITH CANADIAN NGOS

It is in this context of a deteriorated relationship that CIDA restructured in 2010 its framework for working with NGOs. The changes eliminated some initiatives and reorganized CIDA's Partnership with

Canadians Branch. The latter now manages two programs. The first, the Global Citizens Program, seeks to raise Canadian public awareness of development issues, encourage and disseminate knowledge about development, and foster the participation of youth (CIDA 2010b). The second program, known as Partners for Development, redefines CIDA's relationship with various types of Canadian organizations, including large and small NGOs. This chapter addresses only the latter program, because the former finances what is essentially development education rather than development activities.

Under the new funding mechanisms, CIDA will award, over a five-year period, $110 million to large NGO projects (defined as those with budgets above $2 million) and $30 million to smaller ones (budgets under $2 million). Canadian NGOs will respond to periodic "calls for proposals" from CIDA, some of which will be narrowly defined in accordance with the government's geographic and thematic priorities, such as Haiti (deadline for submissions November 2010) and maternal and child health (deadline January 2011). Selection criteria were:

- Sound governance
- Support of Canadians
- Relevance to CIDA's mandate and coherence with Canadian Government policy
- Results
- Development effectiveness. [CIDA 2010b, 2011b]

As part of this new process, the Partners for Development Program will allocate half its funds to proposals for projects in CIDA's twenty "countries of focus" and 80 per cent of funds will support projects that "align" with its three "priority themes" (CIDA 2010b).[3] This chapter now turns to the analysis of those mechanisms.

NEW DIRECTIONS AND TRENDS IN CANADIAN FOREIGN AID

The redefinition of CIDA's partnership with Canadian NGOs follows two key trends in foreign aid since the early 2000s at CIDA and, more broadly, within the Canadian government at large. This section analyzes in turn the changes in the partnership in light of these two trends.

Centralized Control

For decades, critics have faulted CIDA for being excessively bureaucratic and for its cumbersome administrative procedures. Compared
to other countries' bilateral aid agencies, power is very centralized at
CIDA headquarters. CIDA managers in the field and in Gatineau,
Quebec, have low levels of authority to approve projects and exten-
sions. They often must obtain approval from their superiors in a
process that requires a lot of time (see den Heyer, this volume).
According to a report by the Office of the Auditor General (2009,
27–8), "most of the projects required the Minister of International
Cooperation or the Treasury Board to approve them" and the processes took an average of more than three and a half years.

   CIDA is not the only government agency affected by such high levels
of control. After the election of the Conservatives in 2006, the Prime
Minister's Office required advance approval of any civil servant's public remarks, which had the effect of gagging the bureaucracy. The
desire to control communications extended to organizations that
receive CIDA funding. In 2009 CIDA sought to amend its contribution
agreements with partners to prevent them from making any public
pronouncement on their project without obtaining CIDA approval at
least sixty days in advance. (As with many of these changes, it is not
clear if CIDA initiated this or if it was at another actor's behest.)

   Instead of decentralizing power, CIDA is often seeking to increase
its control. The new "partnership" between CIDA and Canadian
NGOs will also, in several ways, further increase CIDA's control over
the content of the NGOs' activities, especially concerning the specific
programs that it finances. The reconfigured relationship will limit
the diversity of approaches and ensure that the NGOs' activities follow more closely the government's geographical and sectoral priorities. As noted above, 80 per cent of funding will go to activities
relating to the three themes that the government identified and
50 per cent will go to the twenty countries of focus.

   NGOs, of which many are already very dependent on CIDA funding, will become even less independent, despite the fact that a hallmark of civil society is its autonomy from the state. Canadian NGOs
are increasingly turning into CIDA executing agencies, especially
when they compete against each other in response to "calls for
proposals" to provide services in target countries or to address
themes chosen by the government. CIDA will thus decreasingly take

advantage of the value-added that Canadian NGOs derive from the privileged relationship with their partners in developing countries. If they want to receive public funding, NGOs that specialize in countries and sectors that are not CIDA priorities will either have to redirect their programs and partnerships with southern organizations toward Canada's priority themes or develop new partnerships in countries of focus where they have little or no experience. Otherwise, they will have to compete for the 50 per cent of funds available for lower-priority countries and the mere 20 per cent that will go to non-priority themes. The alternative is to obtain other sources of financing or reduce the size of the organization.[4]

These stipulations create partnerships and programs based on supply (CIDA's priorities) rather than demand (needs in the South). This contradicts international norms of aid effectiveness, which emphasize the local ownership of development strategies and the alignment of donors' programs with them. Those principles were spelled out very clearly in the Paris Declaration on Aid Effectiveness (2005), which Canada signed. To be fair, CIDA could counter that its priorities are based on real needs, which is true; however, CIDA's "partnership" modalities force the NGOs to operate in specific areas and constrain them from using their aid in an agile, adaptive way, in conjunction with Southern partners, which is a key component of NGOs' value-added.

Among the criteria listed above, one in particular explicitly expresses the government's desire to control NGOs: "Relevance to CIDA mandate and coherence with Canadian Government policy." In and of itself, CIDA's mandate should not pose any problems. According to the website that announces the new partnership framework, CIDA's mandate is "poverty reduction" (CIDA 2010b), which is clear, easy to understand, and already applicable to most NGOs' activities. However, the longer version, in the *About CIDA* section of CIDA's website, defines the agency's mandate as: "Manage Canada's support and resources effectively and accountably to achieve meaningful, sustainable results and engage in policy development in Canada and internationally, enabling Canada's effort to realize its development objectives" (CIDA 2009b).[5] Since Canada's "development objectives" are nowhere defined, they are open to self-interested interpretation by the Canadian government.

The second part of this criterion, "coherence with Canadian Government policy," provides further cause for concern. The "backgrounder" on the website stipulates that "proposals for funding support ... must be consistent with Canadian government policy" (CIDA 2010b). The obligation is repeated in the application guide-lines, phrased as the necessity to avoid "contraven[ing] Canadian government and foreign policy" (CIDA 2010a, 8). The examples given include anti-terrorism legislation and UN conventions. However, they all relate to existing government legislation and legal obligations, whereas the language of the guidelines is far more broadly encompassing, stating that NGOs' activities must be coherent with government *policy*, which is far more arbitrary and subject to change (Canadian policy can be whatever the government *du jour* says it is). Not only is Canadian policy is a vague term, subject to multiple interpretations, but the requirement of being consistent with it could have an important censoring effect on Canadian NGOs. Any NGO that criticizes Canadian policies would ipso facto not be consistent with Canadian policy. How could a Canadian NGO work, for example, with Palestinian human-rights organizations without criticizing Israel? Such activities would contradict Canadian policy.[6]

The problem is even more fundamental than that. NGOs are val-ued specifically because their perspectives are different from states' – whence the recognition of their complementarity and the need to support them, as discussed above. Indeed, their "development man-date includes monitoring and fair critical comment on government policy directions" (Tomlinson 2010, 5), a crucial democratic right. However, when they relinquish advocacy work, let alone criticism, NGOs increasingly resemble executing agencies and service providers (see Smillie, this volume). These new funding mechanisms risk replacing sustained relations of solidarity with the South with sim-ple, short-term apolitical charity. It will be interesting to see which NGOs receive CIDA funding in the future, where they work, and what their approach to development is.

Instrumentalization

Conflicting motives have always underpinned ODA, including Canada's, with altruism rubbing shoulders with diplomatic, com-mercial, and security interests (SCEAIT 1987, 7; Morrison 2000, 15). The relative importance of each, however, may vary. Scholars have noted that Canada's self-interest became increasingly prominent over the course of the 1990s (Pratt 2000; Rudner 1996). This trend accelerated, especially in its security dimension, after the attacks of

11 September 2001 and the subsequent invasions and wars (Brown 2007, 2008). After 2007, one can also trace the rise of commercial self-interest, notably in Canada's relations with other countries in the Americas, including in CIDA's new list of countries of focus, announced in 2009 (see, in this volume, Blackwood and Stewart's discussion on support to the Canadian mining sector).

New initiatives in Canadian foreign aid thus increasingly reflect the Canadian government's objectives, rather than those of developing countries or the needs of the poor themselves. In other words, the Canadian government is, more and more, instrumentalizing CIDA and ODA for goals other than international development. Nowhere is this policy shift more apparent than in Afghanistan, which almost overnight became Canada's top aid recipient. In 2007–08, for instance, the Canadian government disbursed 6.2 per cent of its foreign aid to Afghanistan (OECD 2010, 244), a large part of which went to Kandahar province, where Canadian Forces were deployed.

Even though many suspected this had always been the case, CIDA included for the first time in 2009 among its official criteria the recipient country's "alignment with Canadian foreign policy priorities" when selecting its twenty "countries of focus" (CIDA 2009a), although it has nothing to do with the needs or capacities of recipients. Even the ODA Accountability Act, passed in 2008, cites the need for Canadian development assistance to be consistent with "Canadian foreign policy," as well as "the principles of the Paris Declaration on Aid Effectiveness" (Canada 2008, para. 2[1]), two concepts that can actually be contradictory.

As mentioned above, the Paris Declaration focuses on the need for donors to align their activities with the priorities of the recipient country and to coordinate among themselves. Nominally, CIDA's new partnership guidelines recognize the importance of local ownership, so that projects "respond ... to needs, priorities and approaches identified by the local partner(s)" (CIDA 2010a, 19). This closely corresponds to the principles of the Paris Declaration. In practice, however, the Canadian government's decision to concentrate its activities in specific countries and themes is based to a large extent on self-interested criteria and not the Paris principles (see Blackwood and Stewart, this volume).[7] The new criteria for assessing Canadian NGOS' proposals also insert Canadian self-interest into the NGOS' work, and additionally, as discussed above, the requirement that NGOs' programs be coherent with Canadian government priorities strongly encourages – practically obliges – them to align their work with Canadian government goals, not the priority needs of the global South, and to refrain from criticizing the Canadian government. Here again, the government is instrumentalizing NGOs for political reasons.

From this perspective, it is hard to justify the use of public funds such as ODA to contribute to the criticism of government policies. Even though public debate is a hallmark of democracy, Conservative politicians do not seem to understand the value of pluralism when it comes to ideas and opinions, nor the importance of defending the rights of those most in need. The government's decision to deny funding in 2009–10 to several NGOs deemed too critical, including the Canadian Council for International Co-operation (CCIC) and KAIROS (see Smillie, this volume), is reminiscent of the justification given by John Baird, at the time president of the Treasury Board, for the abolition of the Court Challenges Program of Canada: "I just don't think it made sense for the government to subsidize lawyers to challenge the government's own laws in court" (Sossin 2006).

In the past, CIDA and the NGOs collaborated closely and made common cause on various fronts. Brodhead and Pratt (1996, 98) describe a relationship based on trust between CIDA's NGO Division and Canadian NGOs. CIDA found the Canadian Council for International Co-operation, the well-respected umbrella organization for development NGOs, a useful interlocutor on aid issues. In the early 1990s, when CIDA was threatened with budget cuts, CCIC led campaigns to rally support for the agency (Brodhead and Pratt 1996, 93, 111). This relationship of trust has since been severely eroded – in both directions. Instead, mutual distrust now characterizes the relationship between CIDA and Canadian NGOs – or worse, for those whose funding was not renewed for seemingly arbitrary reasons. NGO officials recognize that in many cases, notably the rejection of KAIROS's funding application, decisions are made at the political level (in the minister's office or perhaps the Prime Minister's Office) rather than by CIDA staff. Nonetheless, as long as the government instrumentalizes foreign aid for political reasons, NGOs will regard CIDA policies and decisions with greater suspicion. This will not prevent most of them from applying for funding anyway, even when the parameters of the calls for proposals are likewise politicized, but it has sabotaged the working relationship between the two sides, to the detriment of the quality of Canadian foreign aid.

MODERNIZATION FOR GREATER EFFECTIVENESS?

As mentioned above, the new partnership framework is presented as a contribution to modernizing Canada's foreign aid in order to improve its effectiveness. This section seeks to determine if there are good reasons to believe it will have that effect.

Let us begin with the concept of modernization. Broadly speaking, any change may be called a modernization, whether it has a positive or negative effect. CIDA, of course, is trying to portray the changes in a positive light: the old system is no longer working well and needs to be updated. Under the new framework, CIDA will once again only finance Canadian NGOs' individual projects and programs in response to specific calls for proposals, thus dropping its most innovative aspects: the responsive approach and core funding. Though technically one could call the new modalities a modernized partnership, it is actually a significant step backward.

Next, what about the impact on aid effectiveness? Any analysis is immediately faced with the problem of the definition of effectiveness. Does it refer merely to the capacity to create economic growth, as the World Bank (1998) defined it? Or does it follow the usage of the Organisation for Economic Co-operation and Development (OECD), epitomized by the Paris Declaration (2005), according to which effectiveness is based on the principles of local ownership, harmonization among donors, alignment with recipient-country systems and objectives, results, and mutual accountability?

Since 2002, the Canadian government has used the goal of aid effectiveness to justify almost all changes to foreign aid policy and practices, even where there is no a priori reason to expect them to have any positive impact on effectiveness by either definition (Canada 2002). An examination of important Canadian aid trends demonstrates that, with the exception of the decision to untie aid, there is no reason to believe that the changes will lead to greater effectiveness. Some measures, in fact, have a negative effect, such as the emphasis on obtaining short-term, visible results (see Brown, chapter 3, this volume).

It is not yet clear what the effects will be of the concentration of resources in a subset of countries and sectors. There are nonetheless

reasons to question the benefits of such restrictions from a development perspective. The very act of changing geographic and thematic
priorities, which occurs with every new government or even CIDA
minister, *decreases* the effectiveness of aid, since it contributes to aid
volatility and unpredictability and undermines partnerships that are
important for development to take place (see Brown, chapter 3, this
volume). It is also unclear how Canadian NGOs will become more
effective if they are pressured "to artificially change the countries
where they program and to alter programmatic areas of work in
which they and their partners have particular expertise and impact"
(Tomlinson 2010, 3). Finally, granting project-specific, short-term
funding will harm Canadian NGOs' capacity to work with Southern
actors on the basis of a sustained, strong partnership, thereby reducing long-term impact.

Since "aid effectiveness" does not have a fixed meaning, the
Canadian government, especially under the Conservatives, uses the
term as a blanket justification for its own political preferences,
including in its partnerships with Canadian civil society organizations. NGOs, such as KAIROS, can be denied CIDA funding potentially because they criticized government policy, but are unhelpfully
told by the CIDA's minister's office that it is because their proposal
did not "closely align with our aid effectiveness strategy" (Mackrael
2010, A4). CIDA can also invoke an applicant's mismatch with its
thematic priorities, even when the proposal from KAIROS – to use
the same example – focused on governance, which is on CIDA's list
of crosscutting themes.

Another way to justify the rejection of an application for funding
of an NGO that focuses on research and advocacy (which will always
involve some criticism of government policies) is to contend that
such activities do not contribute to visible outputs on the ground.
When, for instance, CIDA did not renew its grant to CCIC in 2010,
Minister of International Cooperation Bev Oda, on being asked in
the House of Commons why the government had taken this decision,
stated: "We have many NGO organizations [sic] and partners [unlike
the CCIC, presumably] that are actually feeding children who are
starving, that are actually improving the health of mothers and children in sub-Saharan Africa and protecting the rights of women and
children in the Congo" (Berthiaume 2010). Oda's parliamentary secretary, Jim Abbott, explained more explicitly that the government
does not want to fund such organizations as CCIC because they

allegedly do not contribute to effective aid: "The government is working to make our aid more effective. The opposition wants to see our international aid go to Ottawa lobbyists. Our government wants to see our international aid actually help the world's poor" (Parliament of Canada 2010). Nonetheless, at least in theory, "CIDA values the contributions of knowledge partners" such as CCIC. CIDA's Partners for Development Program web page argues: "Though they may not deliver aid directly, they do play a vital role in identifying transformative and innovative development practices that can help improve the effectiveness of development and/or undertake evidence-based research and policy development" (CIDA 2011b). In fact, CIDA continued to fund the CCIC's provincial counterparts.

Not all Canadian NGOS are worthy of support and none has any automatic entitlement to CIDA funding. Poorly conceived proposals should be rejected – though working together on the development of the project (as actual partners, if that is possible) could help avoid low-quality submissions. There is a logical case to be made for holding a competitive process – competition can raise the quality of proposals and, through more narrowly defined "calls," facilitate the ranking of proposals – but, as explained above, the top-down determination of priorities by the government ignores other expertise and is far more likely to be self-interested. An extensive review of the literature, conducted in the mid-1990s, concluded that Western donors should abandon "contract culture" in favour of "funding arrangements which provide predictability and stability in the long term" (Edwards and Hulme 1996, 969). Similarly, a 2002 study found that the "marketized" competition among NGOS has deleterious effects, including dysfunctional outcomes facilitated by induced opportunistic behaviour. Its conclusion regarding the preferability of "longer-term, general-use funds for reputable INGOS [international NGOS] that would then be free to make better choices" (Cooley and Ron 2002, 38) sounds remarkably like CIDA's erstwhile provision of core grants. The abandonment of the latter, along with the demise of the responsive approach, strips the CIDA/NGO relationship of its most innovative features.

CONCLUSION

The modalities of CIDA's new partnership with Canadian NGOS fit snugly within the two trends in Canadian foreign aid examined above: CIDA's increasingly centralized control and the government's growing instrumentalization of CIDA and ODA more broadly. Under the new partnership framework, CIDA regulates more closely the activities of the NGOs it funds and ensures that the majority align with the agency's geographical and thematic priorities. The government, however, did not choose those priorities because of their greater effectiveness in promoting development, but rather, to a great extent, according to its self-interest, notably in the choice of countries of focus.

The Canadian government is progressively extending the reach of its control over ODA. It has reoriented its bilateral aid according to security considerations (Afghanistan) and commercial interests (the Americas). It has also begun to reassess its multilateral aid to better reflect Canadian foreign policy (United Nations Relief and Works Agency for Palestine Refugees). The closer control of Canadian NGOs' activities and their thematic and geographic reorientation to align more closely with CIDA's priorities and Canadian foreign policy allows the government to complete the picture.

The new partnership with Canadian NGOs further reduces their autonomy and their capacity to respond to the needs of the Southern partners. If they want to continue to enjoy CIDA funding, they have to submit to its conditions. Rather than a modernization, as CIDA presents it, the new relationship is a step backward. It also – and this is surely one of the government's intents – muzzles NGOs by strongly discouraging them from criticizing government policies.

Despite CIDA's references to the international principles of aid effectiveness, as expressed in the Paris Declaration and the Accra Agenda for Action, the new partnership with Canadian NGOs contradicts those norms in significant ways. If such CIDA initiatives lead to an increased effectiveness of ODA, there is little reason to believe that it will be in the interest of countries in the global South, and even less so if each new minister or government redefines CIDA's priorities. Instead, these modalities could well be more effective in supporting more self-interested foreign policy: that is, gag the organizations that disagree with Canadian development-related policies, subordinate NGO activities to the Canadian government's interests, discourage them from advocacy work, and reduce their functions to the execution of projects, preferably in countries and sectors chosen by the Canadian government. These measures will further harm CIDA's reputation, at home and abroad, as well as Canada's standing as an important global actor, both already suffering greatly.

NOTES

1 For discussions that enriched this chapter's analysis, I am grateful to the participants in a workshop organized by the Association québécoise des organismes de coopération internationale, held in Montreal on 22 October 2010. I also thank Maxime Michel, Rosalind Raddatz, Ian Smillie, and a CIDA employee who needs to remain anonymous for their helpful suggestions and comments.

2 The title of Brodhead and Pratt's (1996) book chapter, "Paying the Piper: CIDA and Canadian NGOs," alludes precisely to that metaphoric relationship.

3 Since 2009, the twenty "countries" of focus are: Afghanistan, Bangladesh, Bolivia, Caribbean Regional Program, Colombia, Ethiopia, Ghana, Haiti, Honduras, Indonesia, Mali, Mozambique, Pakistan, Peru, Senegal, Sudan, Tanzania, Vietnam, Ukraine, and West Bank and Gaza (CIDA 2009a). CIDA also announced in 2009 the following priority themes: 1) increasing food security; 2) securing the future of children and youth; and 3) stimulating sustainable economic growth (CIDA 2011d).

4 One must nonetheless recognize that one or two themes are open to creative interpretation, especially sustainable economic growth. Moreover, CIDA has identified three crosscutting themes: environmental sustainability, equality between men and women, and governance. It is unclear whether some specific activities are to be included or not. NGOs can take advantage of this ambiguity by using priority or crosscutting themes to frame their activities. The government, however, can also use the ambiguity and, in its case, interpret the parameters more restrictively in order to justify turning down requests for funding.

5 It is worth noting that this mandate is defined in technocratic language that refers to management, results, and policy making, but never to fighting poverty or inequality.

6 These trends are not limited to bilateral aid. In 2010, for instance, the Canadian government reallocated its annual contribution to the UN Relief and Works Agency for Palestine Refugees in the Near East, better known by its acronym UNRWA. Henceforth, the funding would not go to the UN agency's treasury. Instead, it would be paid directly to its food-aid program. The Conservative government can thus support the basic needs of Palestinians without contributing to a critique of the Israeli government, which it supports almost unconditionally.

7 For examples of more selfless aid policies, see the discussion in McGill's and Gulrajani's chapters in this volume, notably the case of the United Kingdom.

REFERENCES

Berthiaume, Lee. 2010. "Cutting out the Development NGO 'Heart.'"
    Embassy. 9 June. http://www.embassymag.ca/page/view/cicc-06-09-
    2010. Accessed 3 March 2012.

Brodhead, Tim, and Cranford Pratt. 1996. "Paying the Piper: CIDA and
    Canadian NGOs." In Cranford Pratt, ed., *Canadian International
    Development Assistance Policies: An Appraisal*, 2nd ed. Montreal-
    Kingston, ON: McGill-Queen's University Press. 87–119.

Brown, Stephen. 2007. "'Creating the World's Best Development Agency'?
    Confusion and Contradictions in CIDA's New Policy Blueprint."
    Canadian Journal of Development Studies 28, no. 2: 213–28.

– 2008. "CIDA under the Gun." In Jean Daudelin and Daniel Schwanen,
    eds., *Canada among Nations 2007: What Room to Manoeuvre?*
    Montreal and Kingston, ON: McGill-Queen's University Press. 91–107.

Canada. 2002. *Canada Making a Difference in the World: A Policy
    Statement on Strengthening Aid Effectiveness*. Hull, QC: Canadian
    International Development Agency.

– 2008. *Official Development Assistance Accountability Act*. Ottawa:
    Department of Justice.

Canadian International Development Agency. 2009a. "Countries of
    Focus." 13 August. http://www.acdi-cida.gc.ca/acdi-cida/ACDI-CIDA.
    nsf/eng/JUD-51895926-JEP. Accessed 25 May 2011.

– 2009b. "Mission and Mandate." 5 August. http://www.acdi-cida.gc.ca/
    acdi-cida/ACDI-CIDA.nsf/eng/NIC-5493749-HZK. Accessed 25 May
    2011.

– 2010a. "Application Guidelines Development Projects ($2M and Over)."
    December. http://www.acdi-cida.gc.ca/INET/IMAGES.NSF/vLUImages/
    Partnership/$file/2mplus-guidelines-eng.pdf. Accessed 26 May 2011.

– 2010b. "Minister Oda Announces Next Step to CIDA's Aid
    Effectiveness." 22 July. http://www.acdi-cida.gc.ca/acdi-cida/ACDI-
    CIDA.nsf/eng/CEC-722111726-KXG. Accessed 25 May 2011.

– 2011a. "Global Citizens Program." 25 March. http://www.acdi-cida.
    gc.ca/acdi-cida/ACDI-CIDA.nsf/eng/FRA-325121615-M48. Accessed
    26 May 2011.

– 2011b. "Partners for Development Program." 25 March. http://www.
    acdi-cida.gc.ca/acdi-cida/ACDI-CIDA.nsf/eng/FRA-325122215-M7Y.
    Accessed 26 May 2011.

– 2011c. "Partnerships with Canadians Programs." 25 March. http://
    www.acdi-cida.gc.ca/acdi-cida/ACDI-CIDA.nsf/eng/JUD-
    11291243-N24. Accessed 26 May 2011.

– 2011d. "Priority Themes." 28 February. http://www.acdi-cida.gc.ca/acdi-cida/ACDI-CIDA.nsf/eng/FRA-1015144121-PWW. Accessed 26 May 2011.

Caouette, Dominique. 2008. "Les organisations non gouvernementales canadiennes: Bilan et perspectives." In François Audet, Marie-Eve Desrosiers, and Stéphane Roussel, eds., *L'aide canadienne au développement*. Montreal: Presses de l'Université de Montréal. 111–39.

Cooley, Alexander, and James Ron. 2002. "The NGO Scramble: Organizational Insecurity and the Political Economy of Transnational Action." *International Security* 27, no. 1: 5–39.

Edwards, Michael, and David Hulme. 1996. "Too Close for Comfort? The Impact of Official Aid on Nongovernmental Organizations." *World Development* 24, no. 6: 961–73.

High Level Forum on Aid Effectiveness. 2005. *Paris Declaration on Aid Effectiveness*. March.

– 2008. *Accra Agenda for Action*. September.

Mackrael, Kim. 2010. "Ottawa Ignored CIDA Green Light When It Halted Aid Group's Funding." *Globe and Mail*. 28 October.

Morrison, David R. 1998. *Aid and Ebb Tide: A History of CIDA and Canadian Development Assistance*. Waterloo, ON: Wilfrid Laurier University Press.

– 2000. "Canadian Aid: A Mixed Record and an Uncertain Future." In Jim Freedman, ed., *Transforming Development: Foreign Aid for a Changing World*. Toronto: University of Toronto Press. 15–36.

Office of the Auditor General of Canada. 2009. "Chapter 8. Strengthening Aid Effectiveness – Canadian International Development Agency." *Report of the Auditor General of Canada to the House of Commons*. Ottawa: Government of Canada.

Organisation for Economic Co-operation and Development. 2010. *Development Co-operation Report 2010*. Paris: Organisation for Economic Co-operation and Development.

Parliament of Canada. 2010. *House of Commons Debates*. 40th Parliament, 3rd Session, Number 083. 22 October.

Pratt, Cranford. 2000. "Alleviating Global Poverty or Enhancing Security: Competing Rationales for Canadian Development Assistance." In Jim Freedman, ed., *Transforming Development: Foreign Aid for a Changing World*. Toronto: University of Toronto Press. 37–59.

Reith, Sally. 2010. "Money, Power, and Donor-NGO Partnerships." *Development in Practice* 20, no. 3: 446–55.

Rudner, Martin. 1996. "Canada in the World: Development Assistance in Canada's New Foreign Policy Framework." *Canadian Journal of Development Studies* 17, no. 2: 193–220.

Sossin, Lorne. 2006. "An Axe That Harms Democracy: Court Challenges
    Program Played Key Role in Settling Equality Rights." *Toronto Star*.
    28 September.
Standing Committee on External Affairs and International Trade. 1987.
    *For Whose Benefit? Report on Canada's Official Development
    Assistance Policies and Programs*. Ottawa: House of Commons.
Tomlinson, Brian. 2010. "Partnerships with Canadians: A Renewal of the
    Mandate of Canadian Partnership Branch. A Review by the Canadian
    Council for International Co-operation." Ottawa: Canadian Council for
    International Co-operation. July.
World Bank. 1998. *Assessing Aid: What Works, What Doesn't and Why*.
    Washington, DC: World Bank.

12

The Politics of Reforming Canada's Foreign Aid Policy

ADAM CHAPNICK

Discussions of foreign aid reform in Canada seem to inspire regret and despair. In early 2011 the University of Ottawa's Pierre Beaudet commented that "there is a bit of a funeral-parlour atmosphere with CIDA's [the Canadian International Development Agency's] public servants and the NGO [non-governmental organization] community ... They are very depressed" (Chapel 2011, 4).[1] Not long before, an opinion editorial by Gerry Barr (2010, 9) – at the time, the president and chief executive officer of the Canadian Council for International Co-operation, an umbrella organization of Canadian development NGOs that has since seen its government funding discontinued – described CIDA as "exhausted, unclear, and unable to focus." The agency has been unwilling to "do the right thing," he claimed, before using the words "sadly" and "lacklustre" in his final paragraph. Similar frustration echoes in articles by other prominent aid advocates. The McLeod Group's Ian Smillie (2010, 8), for example, denounced the governing Conservatives for "killing Canada's efforts in some of the world's poorest countries and damaging our once proud reputation as a thoughtful, generous leader in development assistance."[2] Smillie's chapter in this volume is similarly pessimistic.

That these authors' comments are well intentioned is indisputable; all three have dedicated their professional lives to providing support to the world's less fortunate. Nor are their instincts to bring concerns about the state of the Canadian government's development-assistance policy into the popular realm ill-advised. In the political world that is Ottawa, it is difficult to effect change without a media-savvy public profile. Moreover, as Smillie has suggested, advocacy might indeed be necessary to enable a genuinely transformative global development-assistance strategy. However, the distress evident among the advocates, a feeling that resonates in many chapters of this volume, reflects exaggerated expectations of the importance, or potential importance, of official development assistance (ODA) to Canadian political decision making. Too often, lofty, unrealistic aspirations impede the development of sound, politically informed strategic thinking that might eventually advance the aid agenda in Canada and beyond.

The political climate in Ottawa is critical to any understanding of the prospects for foreign aid reform. Behaviour on Parliament Hill, rarely admirable to begin with, has been in a state of near-constant decline since the onset of a series of minority governments in 2004. And, while the Conservatives' majority victory in 2011 seemed to spawn a degree of improvement in members' attitudes, that change did not last. Among the many smear campaigns waged by the political elite, most notable for analysts of international affairs is the Conservative Party's successful effort to diminish former Liberal leader Michael Ignatieff for having too much experience outside Canada (Ignatieff 2011). Foreign policy more generally has become a tool of partisan politics: the government has denied the federal opposition involvement in the formulation of Canada's international strategy, and the opposition has largely ignored successful government initiatives on the world stage.

In this political environment, when foreign aid policy is viewed as a tactic rather than an inherent responsibility of the state, one cannot expect rapid progress on the ODA file. Advancements are necessarily constrained by what others have called the facts of Canada's "national life" (Bland 2000). For the purposes of clarity and simplification, in the case of development assistance, these constraints span three broad categories: 1) the role of political incentives in managing the federal appetite to effect change; 2) the influence of constituency advocacy, or lack thereof, on efforts to move development assistance to the forefront of the political agenda; and 3) the impact of the contemporary Canadian political environment on the federal government's inherent conservatism.

This chapter expands on these constraints within the context of the arguments made thus far in this collection by examining ODA through the political perspective of Canadian strategic decision makers. It assesses the prospects for progress and outlines a series of recommendations intended to enable development-assistance advocates to better position themselves to effect change within the contemporary Canadian political environment. It is a pragmatic assessment that refuses to put too much faith in the unlikely event that a transformative leader or leadership strategy will all of a sudden raise foreign aid to the top of Ottawa's international agenda. Instead, it emphasizes more realistic expectations, incremental progress, strategic advocacy, and the fostering of a spirit of non-partisanship at the decision-making level.

BRINGING THE POLITICS IN: THE FACTS OF NATIONAL LIFE

Effective management of political change is rarely possible without the prior establishment of legitimate expectations. If one claims too much, the public will necessarily be disappointed with the results. Deliberately underestimating one's capacity for change can similarly alienate the supporters whose advocacy is needed to implement new policy. It is therefore critical that Canadian proponents of foreign aid reform recognize the systemic and cultural governance structures that pervade the policy-making process. Those structures can be organized around three themes: political incentives; constituency advocacy; and the contemporary political environment.

The Role of Political Incentives

Analyses of Canada's international policies regularly emphasize the role of "entrepreneurial leadership" in the policy-making process (Tomlin et al. 2008, 2). Nilima Gulrajani and Hunter McGill's references to Britain's Clare Short in this volume are consistent with such an observation. Policy, such references confirm, is made by individuals. In a democracy, policy makers are typically influenced by the impact of their decisions on the possibility of re-election or promotion within government. Logically, then, ambitious politicians are attracted to popular issues, while matters that fail to capture the voters' attention tend to be managed by a combination of idealists (who are willing to forsake professional advancement to pursue an issue that resonates personally) and (more commonly) also-rans (politicians who, for whatever reason, are unlikely to achieve significant power within government). Of these three groups of individuals, Canadian development-assistance policy has tended to attract the latter two, neither of which has been adept at advancing significant

strategic initiatives. The reasons that ODA has failed to interest policy entrepreneurs stem from three facts of national life that cannot
be ignored by reform advocates, many of whom (such as McGill, in
this volume) express concern over the lack of political will among
the Canadian policy establishment to effect real change.

*No Canadian election has ever been determined by a party's stance
on foreign aid.* Historically, the vast majority of national elections
have focused on domestic issues, be they the state of the Canadian
economy, political accountability, or a combination of the two
(Duffy 2002; Clarke et al. 2009). It follows that there is little incentive for today's party leaders to spend significant time thinking about
– or developing strategy to promote – effective outcomes in international development assistance. When the Conservatives were first
elected in 2006, for example, they had based their campaign on a
forty-six-page platform called *Stand up for Canada*. Foreign aid did
not appear in their literature until page 44, which included the single
statement: "Foreign aid has been used for political purposes, not to
ensure genuine development." The following page included two
additional bullets, ironically pledging to "Advance Canada's interests through foreign aid, while at the same time holding those agencies involved in this area accountable for its distribution and results,"
and to "Increase spending on Overseas Development Assistance
beyond the currently projected level and move towards the OECD
average level" (Conservative Party of Canada 2006, 44, 45). There is
little reason to believe that this thinking has since varied.

*The international development-assistance portfolio has rarely
been taken seriously by any Canadian government, and never for a
sustained period of time.* To highlight the recent situation, between
1996 and 2010, CIDA was led by eight different junior cabinet ministers. Minister Beverley Oda (first appointed in 2007) is the first of
these eight to serve for more than twenty-eight months, and she
came to the position without significant professional experience in
international affairs. When she arrived, her agency had already, in
the words of two analysts, "suffered more reviews than any government endeavour" (Carin and Smith 2010, 4), and more followed,
not to mention significant criticisms of Oda's managerial ability.[3]
The succession of ministers and reviews has created what development-assistance expert Bernard Wood (2007, 230) has described as
a "vacuum of strategic direction," which has prevented innovation
as well as the possibility of long-term policy implementation. To

quote Wood again: "Development cooperation has retained a side-show status in Ottawa. It has been viewed as worthy, but it has been neither powerful enough nor adequately structured to resist all manner of interference and arbitrary change in priorities and direction" (230). Molly den Heyer's chapter in this volume makes a similar case. It is therefore hardly surprising that the aid portfolio is not sought after by ambitious Canadian politicians, nor is it seen by the Prime Minister's Office as a stepping stone to greater political influence. In simple terms, cabinet ministers who can, or who aspire to, make a difference do not gravitate to CIDA. And, since it is rare that a prime minister will strive to effect radical change in an area that does not produce votes, it is understandable that reform efforts to this date have not produced sustained, fully funded shifts in policy.

Canada has fallen so far behind the world leaders in international-development assistance that there are comparatively few policy initiatives that might generate notable, sustainable political credit beyond the national borders. Ever since Lester B. Pearson won the Nobel Peace Prize for his performance during the Suez Crisis, Canadians who concern themselves with international affairs have been preoccupied with the idea of global leadership (Chapnick 2010). Praise from abroad is politically attractive because it provides external, and therefore less partial, validation of government initiatives. Moreover, positive external assessments of Canadian accomplishments abroad tend to have a notable, positive impact on domestic opinion of those same activities. Although experts on ODA, such as this volume's Stephen Brown, have proven that legitimate judgments of aid effectiveness must be based on recipient-determined outcomes, not donor inputs, donor-initiated proposals accompanied by major international investments – such as Canada's 2005 pledge to double its aid to Africa or its decision to spearhead a 2010 G8 (Muskoka) commitment of over $7 billion to maternal and child health (MCH) – remain best positioned to garner the desired accolades from a global audience that has yet to accept fully the implications of recipient-based policies.[4]

Some might respond that Prime Minister Stephen Harper's 2010 MCH initiative – discussed, mostly critically, in several of this volume's chapters – is evidence that development policy has become politically attractive. Indeed, in spite of the controversy over whether donor countries would fund legal access to abortion, Harper's effort was endorsed by a number of international aid experts, suggesting at least the potential for a residual, positive impact at home. As the Conservative government looks back at the value of the initiative to its domestic political position, however, it will have to consider the findings of pollster Nik Nanos. According to Nanos (2010), in spite of the extensive coverage of the MCH initiative in the international press, Canadians believed that the most important issue facing G8 leaders at their summit in Huntsville was global warming. The Conservative signature proposal "didn't even come close" to achieving similar support (22). Between the abortion controversy and such statistics, there is little reason for the Conservatives to look back at their ODA initiative as good politics.

At the strategic-policy level, as both Gulrajani and McGill note in their chapters, Canada's allocation of approximately $5 billion to ODA in 2009 left it ranked in the middle of the Organisation for Economic Co-operation and Development (OECD) pack (by comparison, the United States provided close to $40 billion) and slightly worse in percentage of gross national income (Canada has never come close to Sweden's 1 per cent). A 2010 government announcement that the aid budget would be frozen indefinitely suggests that those rankings will only worsen (Clark 2010). *Sustainable* global leadership in international development assistance, an effort that Stephen Brown's chapter 3 concedes would require a significant national commitment of new money, should therefore not be expected from Ottawa in the short term.

In sum, politics is about choices, and Canadian policy entrepreneurs have traditionally made choices with their political futures in mind. Foreign aid policy in Canada has a history of political unimportance. Its lack of vote-gaining ability has deprived external advocates of the political tacticians needed on the inside to make significant, sustainable policy change easily achievable. Over time, as a number of authors here have demonstrated, the Canadian government's neglect of development assistance has caused the country's relative standing as an international donor to decline significantly. These factors, taken together, do not imply that effecting sustainable change in Canadian ODA policy is impossible. (Indeed, the negative tone of this chapter thus far should not be interpreted as resignation or even despair.) They do suggest, however, that advocates must develop more realistic expectations. There are real, empirical reasons that making a difference, even when the recipe for doing so is clear, can be difficult.

The Impact of Constituency Advocacy

When the political incentives to pursue a given strategic approach are not easily evident, it is up to external advocates to manufacture new ones, or to engage in what is typically known as agenda setting. Effective constituency advocacy can increase the political attractiveness of issues that might otherwise be ignored by governments. Public outcry in 2010 over the Conservative government's musings about changing the lyrics of Canada's national anthem, for example, made front-page headlines and forced an immediate denial of any such plans.[5] In the case of development assistance, constituency advocacy in Canada has typically been unreliable and largely ineffective. Moreover, the problems are not easily overcome. The challenges represent three additional aspects of Canada's national life.

There is no natural domestic, voting constituency to advocate on behalf of CIDA *and foreign aid supporters.* Health care, education, and taxation policy are perennial election issues because they affect all Canadians. Care for the elderly is a regular concern in political circles because older Canadians vote in proportionally high numbers. The Canadian defence industry has a reasonably strong advocacy base because of the number of veterans living across the country and the respect with which members of the Canadian Forces are typically held in public-opinion surveys. In contrast, as Molly den Heyer and David Black note in their chapters, effective international development assistance is recipient-driven, and those recipients are citizens of other countries who cannot vote in Canadian elections. And, while there is no question that an effective development-assistance policy will provide domestic benefits in the long term, such gains are difficult to illustrate, or quantify, during an election campaign. Moreover, Canadians living in conditions reminiscent of those faced in some developing countries – indigenous peoples on particularly substandard reserves, children and single mothers trapped in abject poverty, the ill and infirm who lack reliable access to health care – are less likely than wealthy Canadians to vote. And, if they do cast a ballot, it is difficult to blame them for failing to advocate increases to Canadian social spending abroad while they experience the effects of insufficient funding for similar causes at home. To summarize, the lack of a natural and reliable domestic voting constituency poses a significant challenge to individual and group efforts to raise ODA reform to the forefront of the political agenda.[6]

Popular support for foreign aid in Canada is fickle and shallow.
Canadians see themselves as a compassionate people. Indeed, when
an international crisis strikes, they are among the quickest and most
generous to respond. They are also among the most active in terms of
remittances. This makes Canada an ideal partner in international
disaster-relief efforts, as well as in emergency humanitarian-assistance
projects more generally. However, neither those who open their wal-
lets generously in times of international emergencies nor those who
remit thousands of dollars to relatives still living abroad necessarily
support a sustained, national commitment to long-term, government-
sponsored development aid. Indeed, surveys have demonstrated
repeatedly that Canadians are more than willing to accept reductions
to the ODA budget to further other objectives (Environics 2010).

The public response to the 12 January 2010 earthquake in Haiti is
a case in point. Although Canadians were proud of their government's leadership role initially, six weeks after the crisis began just
28 per cent of those surveyed told the polling firm Harris-Decima
that the government should make a ten-year commitment to help the
country rebuild (Canadian Press 2010b, A16). Less than four months
later, while the three leading parties contesting the British federal
election pledged to shield London's international development-
assistance budget from the most significant spending cuts since the
Second World War, the Canadian government was hardly criticized
for its decision to make development assistance suffer the brunt of
its first effort to reduce the deficit. This combination of initial enthusiasm followed by a lack of sustainable popular commitment to ODA
has developed among reform advocates – who are prone to focus on
the former and neglect the latter – an inflated sense of the extent of
public support for their cause. Their unrealistic view affects the
strategies that they use to shape the political agenda and magnifies
the disappointment that they feel when they are unsuccessful.

*NGO and CIDA advocacy on the foreign aid file has been largely
ineffective.* Non-governmental organizations are the bodies in
Canada with the greatest incentive to lobby the government to
increase support for international development initiatives. They are
not, however, ideal advocates. First, the ever-expanding number of
NGOs prevents them from speaking with a single voice on the political stage. Indeed, as Ian Smillie notes in his discussion of the conflict
within the non-governmental community over the Muskoka
Initiative, the contours of NGO opinion – although certainly more

sophisticated and nuanced – are hardly different from those of the Canadian public: both NGOs and Canadians alike are divided over the rightful purposes of development assistance (Tomlin et al. 2008).[7] It is therefore too easy for governments to reject one advocate's argument in favour of another's.[8]

Second, as lobbyists, NGOs lack strategic focus. As Stephen Brown notes in chapter 3, perennially unsuccessful efforts to increase Canada's support for international development assistance in pure dollar terms, or in terms of gross national income in anything but the best of economic times, for example, are not inherently consistent with calls for the government to make all development assistance recipient-driven. (Recipients' needs have nothing to do with the state of the Canadian economy or with the ability of the Canadian government to invest in them.)

Finally, by relying so heavily on government support, NGOs are limited in the strategies that they can use to pursue their goals effectively. Recent decisions by CIDA to eliminate funding to particular organizations, described in more detail in Smillie's chapter, might well have been unfounded and short-sighted (KAIROS 2010; Brown and Jackson 2009). They are, nonetheless, the logical political outcome when an ideologically motivated (then) minority government seeks to mobilize its base and limit dissent. This is not to suggest that NGOs should therefore refrain from criticizing government policies or end their engagement in what Smillie describes as public-awareness campaigns, but rather to point out that public criticism is a political action that can result in political consequences and that these consequences must be kept in mind when NGOs plan their advocacy strategies.

CIDA itself has been no more successful. Between its lack of consistent leadership, its ever-shifting priorities, its "policy of risk avoidance" (Wood 2007, 242), and its inability to demonstrate significant successes, four challenges discussed throughout this volume, the organization has not made the work of its advocates easy (Brown and Jackson 2009).[9] Calls from the Senate to consider abolishing the organization altogether have further damaged public trust (Segal 2007).

In sum, the aid lobby in Canada is in a poor position to effect change. It lacks a substantial, reliable domestic constituency to make its voice heard; it serves an ambivalent general public whose initial enthusiasm for ODA raises high hopes but whose genuine commitment to the cause is less strong; and its public leadership is neither strategically nor politically united to a sufficient extent. While these limitations do not prevent development assistance from reaching the top of the political agenda, there is no question that they make such a journey exceptionally difficult.

The Role of the Contemporary Political Environment

Although ODA reform advocacy has been difficult in the past, the state of the contemporary Canadian political environment makes the challenges of today far greater. An effective national strategy requires long-term planning, unselfish behaviour, and a non-partisan approach to policy development and implementation. It must be attractive enough to withstand changes in governmental leadership, unexpected international economic and political shocks, and popular and therefore politically appealing fads and trends. Even an effective ODA policy with a durable strategic framework will be vulnerable to the short-term focus of most Canadian political leaders today. The problems are multifold.

Today's Canadian governments operate in an environment that discourages strategic international policies. At one level, the Conservatives' definitive electoral victory in 2011 should be good news for development-assistance advocates (Mazereeuw 2011). With a majority of the seats in the House of Commons, the prime minister can now take bolder risks and implement more strategic (and perhaps less popular) policies that will have at least four years to demonstrate preliminary results. Moreover, the time available to establish new political norms should make it more difficult for successor governments to renege on previous commitments. However, when the governing party has broader political goals – such as making Canada "a conservative country, full of people more inclined to vote Conservative" (Ivison 2009) – it has less incentive to govern cooperatively. Moreover, when the political opposition displays a marked inability to hold the government to account in a politically meaningful manner – be that the consistent failure of the Liberals to do so while serving as the Official Opposition from 2006–10 or the ineffective response of the New Democratic Party (NDP) to the minister of labour's rigid imposition of a settlement during the 2011 postal strike – the governing party has every reason to engage in a game of political brinkmanship, which it has done repeatedly without significant electoral repercussions.

Such tactical and operational successes have led to the infusion of ideology into strategic-level discussions of foreign aid policy. The Harper government's decision to prevent Canadian aid dollars targeted for maternal and child health to be spent on access to (legal) abortions, for example, betrays – in the strategic sense – its previous commitment to untie all Canadian aid. Whereas Ottawa had initially recognized that recipient countries were best placed to determine how to maximize the effectiveness of aid contributions, political exigencies appear to have motivated the Conservatives to impose their own ideological vision on Canada's recipient partners.[10] So long as the Harper team continues to strive to effect a permanent change in Canada's social fabric, such political tactics will continue.

The politicization of Canadian international policy interferes with long-term, strategic planning. Politics is, regrettably, often about immediacy. Indeed, Canadians have been conditioned by recent election campaigns to expect ongoing evidence of what Ottawa has done for them lately. Voters demand quantifiable results that can be felt at the personal level, and evidence of such results is more easily demonstrated in the domestic realm: lowering taxes allows citizens to keep more of their paycheques; investing in infrastructure creates new roads and funds public transit; spending on social programs can lead to better-equipped hospitals and schools.

International policy in Canada is more complicated. For one, as David Black and others have noted in this volume, the relevant constituencies are generally not Canadian. Second, because Canada is not a great power, it is often in its interest to act through coalitions and alliances, bodies in which decision making is shared and policies do not always conform fully to Canadian preferences (Keating 2002). Third, and this is particularly true in the case of ODA, international development-assistance projects are generally long term, preventative in nature, and not conducive to providing immediate, quantifiable evidence of success (Lancaster 2009; den Heyer, this volume). Improving the level of education within a society, for example, takes a generation. Reducing the rate of infant mortality can take just as long. Such initiatives require long-term commitments that almost always exceed the length of time that any political party holds power. Effective foreign aid policy must therefore be predominantly non-partisan, for only an approach that can be sustained through a series of elections has a real chance of success (Chapnick 2008–09). Until the mood in Ottawa becomes more open to cross-party cooperation, the opportunities for significant foreign aid reform will necessarily be limited.

*The current national and international fixations with comprehen-
sive approaches to international policy are not compatible with best
practices in development assistance.* The idea of marshalling all of a
government's resources from across a variety of departments to
manage issues of international security is intuitively appealing
(Mantle 2008). Among their many benefits, intragovernmental linkages promote policy cohesion and reduce redundancy. As it relates to
development assistance, however, as Stephen Baranyi and Anca
Paducel make clear in their chapter's analysis of the Canadian contribution to the mission in Afghanistan, the comprehensive approach
to conflict management risks compromising the recipient-driven
methodology that is so critical to long-term success in development-
assistance projects. Recent Canadian policy reflects the paradox.
During the international policy review of 2005, CIDA identified
twenty-five development partners based, at least in part, on those
countries' ability to use foreign aid effectively. Afghanistan was not
on the list. Nevertheless, thanks to Canada's overwhelming military
and diplomatic commitment to Afghanistan through NATO, that
country became Ottawa's foremost aid recipient. This example is not
meant to diminish the need to aid Afghanistan. Rather, it suggests
that a distinction must be made between wartime reconstruction
(now often known as stability operations) – which is best coordinated by the Department of Foreign Affairs and International Trade
(DFAIT) and can be directed to any given state for any length of time
– and development assistance – ideally coordinated by an institution
devoted exclusively to long-term developmental aims.

There is a strong argument to be made in favour of DFAIT's
Stabilization and Reconstruction Task Force having been given the
lead in providing civilian assistance in Afghanistan; whether CIDA
should have been so heavily involved requires a different debate.
Nonetheless, such a discussion will not occur so long as political
decision makers insist on pursuing their current understanding of
the importance of comprehensiveness to the management of international security issues. Until such views evolve, CIDA will continue to
involve itself in countries that lack the capacity to use Canadian
contributions effectively.

REASONS FOR HOPE

Although this assessment of the implications of Canada's national
life for foreign aid policy has emphasized the negative, it nonetheless

reveals a series of opportunities for progress. Some of these ideas, it is worth noting, are introduced convincingly by Nilima Gulrajani earlier in this volume.

Opportunities at the Political Level

The unattractiveness of the foreign aid portfolio is, ironically, also what could make it irresistibly appealing to the right prospective cabinet minister.[11] Since there has never been aggressive competition for the international-cooperation responsibilities in Canada, a knowledgeable, opportunistic member of Parliament could establish him- or herself as the party's leading expert on the subject fairly easily. As three analysts of international policy making in Canada have suggested, "leadership in the development arena has come from individuals who display remarkable qualities of imagination, insight, personal drive, and ambition, even when the odds are stacked against them" (Tomlin et al. 2008, 176). An individual with such motivation and expertise would command respect in cabinet committees, making it more likely that the views of CIDA would be heard at the highest political levels. A capable minister would also benefit from the low expectations that are typically associated with a file that has a reputation for failure. Small successes in ODA policy would appear relatively larger than they would otherwise. Finally, in an era that has seen endless calls for Canadians to promote their brand abroad (Potter 2009), a successful foreign aid strategy could provide an ideal way ahead.

Moreover, there is reason to believe that such an opportunity could appear shortly. Minster Oda will be seventy when the next federal election takes place in 2015. Should she choose not to run for office again, she will likely be asked to give up her portfolio sufficiently in advance of the next election so as to give her successor an opportunity for significant exposure within the cabinet in advance of the campaign. That exposure could create the window necessary to begin the process of real change.

Opportunities at the Constituency Level

Although there is no natural domestic constituency to advocate a more informed and effective Canadian approach to ODA, Prime Minister Harper's MCH initiative demonstrates that – should a future campaign be executed with greater political tact – development assistance, with its focus on those most in need, could be shaped to have cross-party political appeal. Beyond the controversy, the Muskoka Initiative earned the Conservative government praise from reputable and powerful NGOs and private organizations, such as the Bill and Melinda Gates Foundation. While domestic support for long-term development assistance is shallow, Canadian public opinion remains sympathetic to the basic concept of providing aid to people in need. In the words of two political scientists, "it is Canada's more activist international policies that resonate with citizens' definitions of what it means to be Canadian" (Berdhal and Raney 2010, 1004). The political challenges of introducing a significant development-assistance initiative in Canada might therefore be overcome by a shrewd campaign built around a sense of patriotism.

Finally, the non-governmental community is capable of change. Ironically, the 2010 government decision to end funding for CCIC could become the impetus for non-governmental organizations across Canada to better coordinate and differentiate their efforts to support and promote development assistance as a national priority. NGOs most reliant on government grants might focus more comprehensively on policy implementation, for example, leaving advocacy work to organizations whose survival is less dependent on their relationships with the federal treasury. Such action would take leadership, and compromise, but major policy changes frequently occur in times of crisis, and much of the NGO community has come to see the efforts of the Harper Conservatives as sufficiently problematic to merit radical adjustments.[12]

Opportunities Stemming from the General Political Environment

One of the ironic benefits of Canada's relatively limited support of international development assistance at the official level is that significant improvements to Canadian policy would not be excessively costly. Increasing ODA noticeably, for example, and thereby providing the government with the flexibility necessary to pursue a comprehensive, recipient-based strategy more effectively, would cost far less than the $490 billion that will be required to fulfill the Canada First Defence Strategy (Canada, Department of National Defence 2010). The long period of time often necessary to see significant development results could also be politically beneficial. In the contemporary Canadian political environment, where every government failure has typically been magnified exponentially, a strategy that is not designed to produce immediate results, if presented as such, becomes immune from legitimate criticism. Making development aid a priority, if done with best practices in mind, is therefore both low-cost and low-risk. Finally, given Canadians' disillusionment with all of their political leaders, there is incentive for the major parties to appear conciliatory. A government that reaches out to the opposition to establish a more collaborative and less partisan approach to ODA might therefore improve its reputation among non-aligned voters.

In sum, the bleakness of the prospects for significant foreign aid reform is also advocates' greatest source of hope. A policy entrepreneur with legitimate aspirations to improve Canada's performance in international development assistance would face relatively little competition in acceding to the relevant ministerial portfolio. Having become a minister (admittedly a junior one), that individual would benefit from low expectations and an opportunity to reframe political understandings of ODA around the Canadian brand. Because of the lack of risk associated with it, a well-designed ODA initiative could have political appeal and could obtain support from a coalition of advocates eager to make a difference. Finally, the cost of such an initiative would be manageable, even in challenging economic times.

THE WAY AHEAD IN POLITICAL TERMS

Given the constraints of Canadian national life, how might ODA reform advocates move forward? Here are four suggestions.

Accept Political Realities

The daunting challenges faced by recipients of development assistance, along with the awareness of the complicity of elements of the developing world in failures to alleviate global poverty, too often lead reformers to ignore the systemic barriers facing policy makers in democratic states. In politics, expectation management is critical. In Canada, the chances that a government in Ottawa will invest significant political capital in an ambitious foreign aid strategy are severely limited, and there is no argument, however pragmatic, that will inspire immediate change. Reform advocates must therefore be wary of stressing the negative, lower their expectations to more realistic levels, and aim for achievable objectives. More specifically, while the Millennium Development Goals (MDGs) are legitimate, based on high-quality research, and absolutely necessary, endless criticism of the Canadian government for failing to meet them will serve little purpose. For one, the MDGs cannot be met by Canada alone, so no decision in Ottawa can guarantee critical satisfaction. More important, as the current Canadian government has demonstrated through its dismissive attitude toward Canada's obligations under the Kyoto Protocol, there is little reason to believe that any form of political pressure would compel Prime Minister Harper to compromise his party's stated priorities in order to pursue a set of international standards, particularly if they were established before the Conservatives took power. Advocates should instead aim for smaller victories, like their success in making maternal and child health a G8 agenda item, and build the political momentum necessary for greater advancements later. Focusing on the positive will not only improve public perceptions of foreign aid, it will also make the development-assistance portfolio more politically attractive to current and prospective ministers.

Take Things One Step at a Time

One of the simplest, and most achievable, initiatives that might be pursued by reform advocates is to formally (and legally) differentiate emergency aid from development assistance. Whether it be by promoting legislation that distinguishes between the two efforts more clearly in the federal budget, or by campaigning to remove humanitarian assistance from CIDA's areas of responsibility, there is no question that popular understandings of ODA would improve if such a distinction were clearer. Setting apart responsibilities for development assistance might also support attempts to track CIDA's performance in genuine official *development*-assistance projects.

Reorient NGO Advocacy

Divisions among and within NGOs, while natural, are a tremendous inhibitor of Canadian political efforts to reform both CIDA and foreign aid policy more generally. Disputes over, for example, whether to participate at all in initiatives that involve military forces, over whether political advocacy is consistently necessary, and over the purpose of development assistance – the latter two subjects are discussed in greater detail by Ian Smillie in this volume – prevent aid reform advocates from making their voices heard effectively on the federal stage. NGOs need a single message, supported by both the anglophone and francophone aid communities, if they hope to make a consistent impact in the political sphere.[13] That message should focus on recipient-driven sustainable poverty-reduction strategies, the implementation of which will require all-party cooperation, predictable funding, and a willingness to somehow exempt foreign aid from the irresponsible diatribes that have typically made up the twenty-first century's version of Question Period.

Decrease the Partisanship

Reform advocates, including many contributors to this volume, too often come across – inadvertently or not – as critics of the sitting government, as opposed to critics of Canadian performance. The difference might be subtle, but it is nonetheless crucial. Arguably, no government in Ottawa has ever met reform advocates' complete expectations. While some might have failed more brilliantly than others, there is no evidence to suggest that a simple change in government, or even, as Gulrajani suggests, governing structure will lead to a dramatic improvement in Canada's ODA performance. Vilifying the current government is therefore counter-productive, particularly when Ottawa has yet to dedicate sufficient effort to the ODA file to effect real, long-term strategic change in either a positive or a negative manner. Far better would be more even-handed analysis of the current government's efforts, applauding what good has taken place (the commitment to untie Canadian aid, for example), and noting areas that still require significant improvement (meeting the intention the Official Development Assistance Accountability Act, discussed in detail in the chapters by Denis Côté and Dominique Caouette and by Elizabeth Blackwood and Veronika Stewart, would be one). The easier that advocates make it for the opposition to disparage the government's ODA policies, the less likely it is that discussions of foreign aid will ever become sufficiently non-partisan so as to invite long-term, well-thought-out, sustainable strategies.

CONCLUSION

As this volume aptly demonstrates, there is no paucity of serious research describing the challenges facing CIDA and Canada's ODA program more generally. There is also no doubt that the proposals of many of the authors here would indeed enhance Canada's global impact, and reputation, in the field of sustainable poverty reduction. Nonetheless, in the Canadian liberal-democratic framework, sometimes being able to identify problems and propose reasonable solutions is not enough. Serious analysis and strategic planning is often beholden to fortuitous timing and a little bit of luck. The best reformers can do for now is to stay positive while continuing to develop the understanding, unity, and widespread non-partisan commitment needed to effect change when the policy window finally does open.

NOTES

1 This comment is confirmed empirically by Nilima Gulrajani in her chapter in this volume.
2 See also Schram (2010), McAskie (2010), and Pearson (2011). The Ottawa-based McLeod Group advocates an increased and improved role for Canada on the international stage; see http://www.mcleodgroup.ca.
3 For a commentary on CIDA's repeated exercises in self-examination, see Office of the Auditor General (2009), specifically "Chapter 8. Strengthening Aid Effectiveness: Canadian International Development Agency." On criticism of Oda, see Clark (2011).
4 For an example of how international favour can be politically advantageous, see CTV News (2003).
5 For the intensity of the response, see the more than 2,000 comments to a CBC (2010) website story which recounts the Throne Speech in which the intention to consider changing the lyrics was announced.
6 On the role of the public in the policy-making process, see Gidengil et al. (2004).
7 For a summary of the broader international aid debate, see Gulrajani (2011).
8 Note the differences, for example, between the proposals of Harris and Manning (2007) and the McLeod Group (2010). See also Chapnick (2008), Tomlin et al. (2008), and Pratt (2000).
9 On the history of CIDA, see Morrison (1998).
10 On the politicization of the MCH debate, see Canadian Press (2010a).
11 There is precedent for a major political figure choosing a relatively innocuous cabinet position. In 1895 Britain's Lord Salisbury offered Joseph Chamberlain any portfolio he wanted in the British government (apart from foreign affairs or leader of the House of Commons). To Salisbury's surprise, Chamberlain chose to become colonial secretary, a position that he viewed as ideal to advance Britain's position in the world.

12 On the challenges faced by NGOs because of the Harper government's approach, see Berthiaume (2010).
13 The absence of French-language references in English Canadian research on foreign aid highlights the stark divide between the two communities.

REFERENCES

Barr, Gerry. 2010. "What Is Guiding CIDA's Aid Spending?" *Embassy*. 26 May.

Berdhal, Loleen, and Tracey Raney. 2010. "Being Canadian in the World." *International Journal* 65, no. 4: 995–1010.

Berthiaume, Lee. 2010. "Cutting out the Development NGO Heart." *Embassy*. 9 June.

Bland, Douglas. 2000. "Everything Military Officers Need to Know about Defence Policy-Making in Canada." In David Rudd, Jim Hanson, and Jessica Blitt, eds., *Canadian Strategic Forecast 2000: Advance or Retreat? Canadian Defence in the 21st Century*. Toronto: Canadian Institute of Strategic Studies. 15–29.

Brown, Chris, and Edward T. Jackson. 2009. "Could the Senate Be Right? Should CIDA Be Abolished?" In Allan M. Maslove, ed., *How Ottawa Spends 2009–2010: Economic Upheaval and Political Dysfunction*. Montreal and Kingston, ON: McGill-Queen's University Press. 151–74.

Canadian Press. 2010a. "Anti-Abortion Activists Praise Harper's Maternal-Health Stand." *Globe and Mail*. 13 May. http://www.globeandmail.com. Accessed 2 July 2010.

– 2010b. "Canadians See Bigger Role for Charities." *Toronto Star*. 18 February. A-16.

Canadian Broadcasting Corporation. 2010. "O Canada Lyrics to Be Reviewed." 3 March. http://www.cbc.ca/arts/music/story/2010/03/03/o-canada-anthem.html. Accessed 29 June 2010.

Carin, Barry, and Gordon Smith. 2010. *Reinventing CIDA*. Calgary, AB: Canadian Defence and Foreign Affairs Institute.

Chapnick, Adam. 2008. "Canada's Aid Program: Still Struggling after Sixty Years." *Behind the Headlines* 65, no. 3.

– 2008–9. "The Golden Age: A Canadian Foreign Policy Paradox." *International Journal* 64, no. 1: 205–21.

– 2010. "Victims of Their Own Success? Canadians and Their Foreign Policy at the Onset of the Cold War." *Zeitschrift für Kanada-Studien* 30, no. 1: 9–23.

Chappel, Kate. 2011. "Groups Brace for Tough Times on Aid Spending."
   Embassy. 16 March.

Clark, Campbell. 2010. "Priorities Shift as Tories Put Foreign Aid on Ice."
   Globe and Mail. 5 March. http://www.theglobeandmail.com. Accessed
   5 March 2010.

– 2011. "In Wake of Oda Controversy, Ottawa Must Explain Why
   Decisions Are Made." *Globe and Mail*. 16 February. http://www.
   theglobeandmail.com. Accessed 17 February 2011.

Clarke, Harold D., Allan Kornberg, and Thomas J. Scotto. 2009. *Making
   Political Choices: Canada and the United States*. Toronto: University of
   Toronto Press.

Conservative Party of Canada. 2006. "Stand up for Canada." http://www.
   cbc.ca/canadavotes2006/leadersparties/pdf/conservative_platform
   2060113.pdf. Accessed 15 June 2010.

CTV News. 2003. "Bono Urges Canada to Lead the Fight for Africa."
   15 November. http://www.ctv.ca/servlet/ArticleNews/story/
   CTVNews/1068857137936_19/. Accessed 29 June 2010.

Department of National Defence. 2010. "*Canada First* Defence Strategy."
   http://www.forces.gc.ca/site/pri/first-premier/index-eng.asp. Accessed
   6 July 2010.

Duffy, John. 2002. *Fights of Our Lives: Elections, Leadership, and the
   Making of Canada*. Toronto: HarperCollins.

Environics Institute. 2010. *Focus Canada 2010: Public Opinion Research
   on the Record. Serving the Public Interest*. http://www.environicsinstitute.
   org/research-focuscanada2010.html. Accessed 1 April 2011.

Gidengil, Elisabeth, et al. 2004. *Citizens*. Vancouver: University of British
   Columbia Press.

Gulrajani, Nilima. 2011. "Transcending the Great Foreign Aid Debate:
   Managerialism, Radicalism, and the Search for Effectiveness." *Third
   World Quarterly* 32, no. 2: 199–216.

Harris, Mike, and Preston Manning. 2007. *Vision for a Canada Strong
   and Free*. Vancouver: Fraser Institute.

Ignatieff, Michael. 2011. "My Name Is Michael Ignatieff, and I Am
   Canadian." *Globe and Mail*. 29 June. http://www.theglobeandmail.com.
   Accessed 29 June 2011.

Ivison, John. 2009. "A Tory Guide to a Blue Canada." *National Post*.
   13 November. http://www.nationalpost.com. Accessed 9 February 2010.

KAIROS. 2010. "Urgent Action: Restore Canadian International
   Development Agency (CIDA) funding to KAIROS." htttp://www.
   kairoscanada.org/index.php?id=645. Accessed 6 July 2010.

Keating, Tom. 2002. *Canada and World Order: The Multilateralist Tradition in Canadian Foreign Policy*, 2nd ed. Don Mills, ON: Oxford University Press.

Lancaster, Carol. 2009. "Sixty Years of Foreign Aid: What Have We Learned?" *International Journal* 64, no. 3: 799–810.

Mantle, Craig Leslie. 2008. *How Do We Go about Building Peace While We're Still at War? Canada, Afghanistan and the Whole of Government Concept.* Ottawa: Canadian Forces Leadership Institute.

Mazereeuw, Peter. 2011. "Development Groups Hope Majority Brings Change." *Embassy.* 11 May.

McAskie, Carolyn. 2010. "Canadian Aid – More, Not Less, Is Needed." In Fen Osler Hampson and Paul Heinbecker, eds., *Canada among Nations 2009–2010: As Others See Us.* Montreal and Kingston, ON: McGill-Queen's University Press. 343–50.

McLeod Group. 2010. "Development Assistance." http://www.mcleod group.ca/topics/development/index.html. Accessed 29 June 2010.

Morrison, David R. 1998. *Aid and Ebb Tide: A History of CIDA and Canadian Development Assistance.* Waterloo, ON: Wilfrid Laurier University Press.

Nanos, Nik. 2010. "Global Warming Most Important Issue for Canadians at G8 and G20 Summits." *Policy Options* (June): 22–5.

Office of the Auditor General. 2009. *2009 Fall Report of the Auditor General of Canada.* http://www.oag-bvg.gc.ca/internet/English/parl_oag_200911_08_e_33209.html. Accessed 2 July 2010.

Pearson, Glen. 2011. "Lighting the Tinder around CIDA." *Embassy.* 23 February.

Potter, Evan H. 2009. *Branding Canada: Projecting Canada's Soft Power through Public Diplomacy.* Montreal and Kingston, ON: McGill-Queen's University Press.

Pratt, Cranford. 2000. "Alleviating Global Poverty or Enhancing Security: Competing Rationales for Canadian Development Assistance." In Jim Freedman, ed., *Transforming Development: Foreign Aid for a Changing World.* Toronto: University of Toronto Press. 37–62.

Schram, John. 2010. "Canada and Africa: Where Has Canada Gone?" In Fen Osler Hampson and Paul Heinbecker, eds., *Canada among Nations 2009–2010: As Others See Us.* Montreal and Kingston, ON: McGill-Queen's University Press. 181–7.

Segal, Hugh. 2007. "Overcoming 40 Years of Failure: A New Road Map for Sub-Saharan Africa." Report of the Standing Senate Committee on Foreign Affairs and International Trade, February.

Smillie, Ian. 2010. "CIDA and the Money Doublers." *Embassy*. 19 May.
Tomlin, Brian W., Norman Hillmer, and Fen Osler Hampson. 2008.
    Canada's International Policies: Agendas, Alternatives, and Politics.
    Don Mills, ON: Oxford University Press.
Wood, Bernard. 2007. "Managing Canada's Growing Development
    Cooperation: Out of the Labyrinth." In Jennifer Welsh and Ngaire
    Woods, eds., *Exporting Good Governance*. Waterloo, ON: Wilfrid
    Laurier University Press. 225–51.

CONCLUSION

Taking Stock, Looking Ahead

STEPHEN BROWN AND ROSALIND RADDATZ

This book provides diverse viewpoints from which to understand and assess the performance of Canadian foreign aid and its main provider, CIDA, as well as to consider how to improve it. In this concluding chapter, we seek to identify convergences and divergences among the various chapters and see to what extent we can draw a multidimensional portrait of CIDA and Canadian aid policy. We also try to identify gaps in our collective knowledge and ways in which they might be filled.

ASSESSING CIDA AND CANADIAN FOREIGN AID

While the chapters share no common characterization of CIDA's capacity and effectiveness, they all point to important deficiencies. Whether based on an analysis of CIDA and Canadian foreign aid in isolation or in comparison to other donors, the portrait of CIDA that emerges is one of profound mediocrity (especially in the contributions by Blackwood and Stewart, Brown's chapter 3, Côté and Caouette, den Heyer, Gulrajani, McGill).

This is hardly surprising. We know from donor rankings how Canada compares to its peers in the Organisation for Economic Co-operation and Development's Development Assistance Committee (OECD/DAC), including through the comparison of quantitative data. For instance, in 2009–10, the Canadian government's level of generosity, as measured by the ratio of official development assistance (ODA) to gross national income (GNI), put it in fourteenth place among the twenty-three DAC donor countries – below the DAC average and nowhere near the UN target set in 1970. A World

Bank-sponsored index on the quality of aid ranked Canada even worse: twenty-first out of twenty-eight bilateral donors (Knack et al. 2010).

Numerous authors in this volume attempt to understand more qualitatively why Canada does not rank higher. Some do so through focused comparisons. Both McGill and Gulrajani argue that not only is Canada providing foreign aid that is inferior in quality and quantity to that of Norway, Ireland, and the United Kingdom – countries generally acknowledged as providing competent aid – it is noteworthy for its lacklustre performance in several specific areas. The analysis in this book breaks down various components of Canada's second-rate performance. This is not an exercise in CIDA-bashing. The book tries not to reiterate the decades-old, oft-repeated litany of criticisms, including excessive red tape, over-centralization, a lack of focus, and a score of other complaints. Instead, we focus on new criticisms, for instance, the only partial implementation of the ODA Accountability Act, or new perspectives on old ones, such as the implications of mixed motives for Canadian aid.

The Lack of Policy and Vision

Several contributors highlight the lack of an overarching aid policy framework and up-to-date sectoral policies, under both Liberal and Conservative governments (Brown's chapter 3, Côté and Caouette, den Heyer, Gulrajani, McGill, Swiss). This contrasts unfavourably with the White Papers in Ireland, Norway, and the United Kingdom, which set out a coherent vision of longer-term development assistance. For example, CIDA's flavour-of-the-month approach to sectoral priorities has prevented Canada from intervening effectively in the food and agricultural sector, as it appears, disappears, and reappears on CIDA's list of priorities (Côté and Caouette). Policy is often improvised and not expressed explicitly, leaving CIDA officials and their counterparts to cobble together policy guidance in a piecemeal fashion from different sources (Brown's chapter 3), causing CIDA employees, especially those in the field, to become overly risk-adverse and subsequently approach operational paralysis (den Heyer). A few contributors note how Canada has fallen behind in areas where it once led, including gender, support to civil society organizations, and poverty reduction (Brown's chapter 11, McGill, Swiss). The latter is especially surprising, given that Canada's 2008 legislation specifies that poverty reduction is the overarching focus of Canadian aid. Together, the contributions paint a sobering picture of CIDA's lack of both vision and a coherent policy framework and how that hinders the effectiveness of Canadian foreign aid.

For years, critics often complained that CIDA was a policy *taker*, not a policy *maker*. Starting in 2008, however, Canada has taken a few bold initiatives that break away from the donor consensus. Among the most notable is the announced shift away from Africa toward the Americas – though it is unclear how this will concretely modify the distribution of Canadian aid, given other initiatives that may favour Africa, such as the Muskoka Initiative on maternal and child health (MCH). While many of our contributors call for greater government vision and direction, bold new policy making could well take CIDA in a direction that most critics would disapprove of. At times, an old policy or none at all can actually be better than a "bad" one.

Effectiveness and Accountability

As explained in this book's Introduction and discussed in other chapters (Baranyi and Paducel, Black, both Brown chapters, den Heyer, Gulrajani, Swiss), the Canadian government participates actively in the international "aid effectiveness" agenda, including by its attendance at the prominent meetings in Paris (2005), Accra (2008), and Busan (2011), which places emphasis on principles such as alignment with recipient countries' development planning and harmonization with other donors. On the domestic front, however, it employs the principle of effectiveness very differently. It emphasizes accountability to Canadian taxpayers through visible, usually quantifiable, short-term results, even if these come at the expense of responsiveness to recipients' priorities, accountability to recipients, cooperation among donors, and long-term change (Black, Brown's chapter 3, den Heyer, Gulrajani, McGill, Smillie). This approach clashes with the nature of much development assistance, which is long term, not always causally obvious, frequently preventive, multifaceted, and often channelled through government institutions and combined with contributions from other donors. As a result, CIDA often cannot conveniently point out specific achievements that can be directly traced to its aid, especially for its major programs (as opposed to small-scale, lower-impact, stand-alone projects), which in turn makes it vulnerable to charges of being ineffective. The Canadian government's preoccupation with visible results means that short-term, one-time, "marketable" aid projects are being privileged over the less visible, ongoing, integrated projects that are the benchmark of effective developmental aid.

The promise of greater effectiveness that accompanies new government initiatives makes it harder for critics to oppose such measures, especially since the alternate narrative cannot be easily reduced to sound bites. The fact remains that there is no consensus on the right way of "doing development" and, as a result, more experimentation is needed on what might work and where. Under such circumstances, aid outcomes – insofar as they can be ascertained – may prove disappointing. Rather than being seen as failures and a waste of taxpayer money, such instances could be turned into learning experiences that will inform future aid interventions. Donors undermine their own learning process and thus future effectiveness when they claim that they know what works and will be able to account for every cent spent.

As Canada provides more assistance to countries in active or recent conflict, including so-called fragile states, results are more difficult to achieve and communicate to the Canadian public. Faced with these challenges, Canada and other donor governments have adopted "whole-of-government" approaches to bring together government departments that have something specific to contribute or might otherwise be working at cross-purposes. As some chapters warn, this risks reorienting foreign aid to meet goals other than development, notably security (Brown's chapter 3, Swiss), and furthermore, as argued in the Introduction, prioritizing donor self-interest ahead of poverty reduction in recipient countries flies in the face of the concept of aid effectiveness. At a more fundamental level, it even calls into question the validity of labelling such activities development assistance. However, non-aid government departments can sometimes work with aid agencies on poverty alleviation and other development concerns. While the "securitization" of Canadian aid did take place in Afghanistan, that does not mean that it inevitably follows a whole-of-government approach. Sudan and especially Haiti provide important counter-examples, though they also support concerns about how much aid can achieve in zones of great insecurity or very difficult circumstances (Baranyi and Paducel) – in other words, its effectiveness in such contexts.

The current international consensus underscores the need for donors to focus their aid in a limited number of countries and sectors as a means to increase their effectiveness. The DAC, notably in its peer reviews of donors, strongly reinforces this norm. Accordingly, two of this volume's chapters criticize Canadian aid for being too scattered when compared to other donors (Gulrajani, McGill). Ever since Jean Chrétien's government defined nine core countries for Canadian assistance in 2002, successive Canadian governments have tried to decrease the fragmentation of Canadian aid. Paul Martin's government expanded the list to twenty-five in 2005, with a focus on Africa. Stephen Harper's government reduced it to twenty in 2009, with more of a focus on the Americas. In doing so, it substituted comparatively better-off countries for many poor ones and privileged countries with which Canada had economic ties, notably as partners in free-trade agreements and destinations for Canadian-based mining companies (Blackwood and Stewart, Brown's chapter 3, McGill). Even if greater focus makes for more effectiveness, it is hard to make the case that three different lists of priority countries – as well as three different sets of priority sectors – generated in the same decade can produce the stability and predictability necessary for aid effectiveness.

Further impediments to CIDA's effectiveness are its internal structures and lines of authority. CIDA is a highly centralized organization, which is not necessarily a problem in itself. However, the agency's centralized policies mean that field offices have little authority to commit new financing, which slows down the approval process, in turn hampering Canada's ability to participate in programming jointly with other donors (den Heyer, Gulrajani). The potential for paralysis increases with the lack of explicit and internally coherent policy guidance from CIDA itself.

Living up to Commitments

There has always been ambiguity around the fundamental motivations of Canada's and other donors' aid programs. Humanitarianism and selflessness compete with self-interest, be it commercial, diplomatic, or security-related. The relative sway of any of these varies over time. However, the main overall trend since 1986, if not earlier, according to various contributors, has been a consistent increase in self-interested motives (Black, Blackwood and Stewart, both Brown chapters, Côté and Caouette, Swiss). Part of this could be due to a lack of clear definition of the purpose of Canadian aid, notwithstanding the generally ignored ODA Accountability Act, discussed below. The lack of a shared understanding and commitment to aid, as CIDA tries or is expected to be all things to all people, limits the agency's ability to define and execute a policy. Given these divergent views and interests, defining an overarching mandate would prove very difficult and may be an overambitious goal for the time being (Chapnick). Even a clear definition of purpose might be found wanting by many contributors to this volume, notably if it principally emphasized Canadian interests.

Regardless of Canada's "true" motivations with respect to aid, the Canadian government has set targets and made certain commitments, to which it might be held accountable. The most famous one is the target of 0.7 per cent of GNI to be spent by the government on development assistance. Canada has also subscribed to the Millennium Development Goals (MDGs). These goals and targets, however, are by no means binding. The Canadian government never set a firm date by which it would achieve the 0.7 per cent target – despite decades of unprecedented economic growth – comparing poorly with European Union countries that committed to increase their foreign aid to 0.7 per cent of GNI by 2015. Whereas previous Conservative and Liberal governments all reiterated the 0.7 per cent target, even as they failed to reach it, the Harper government actually dropped the commitment on aid volume. As for the MDGs and economic and social rights, such as the right to food, they do not assign responsibility to any specific actor, making it more difficult to demand accountability for Canada's contributions or lack thereof. The global economic downturn of 2007–09 caused many donors to cut back on aid spending (Canada froze and later cut its aid budgets), even as the crisis increased needs in the global South. As a result, it is increasingly clear that many of the MDGs will remain unattainable, especially in Africa, but no one in particular will be liable for the shortfall.

Likewise, while the Paris Declaration and related documents on aid effectiveness provide guidance to CIDA and other development actors, they contain provisions only for monitoring. They are not framed as obligations and cannot be enforced or compelled in any way. As a member of DAC and a signatory of the Paris Declaration and subsequent aid effectiveness documents, in principle Canada endorses a definition of aid effectiveness based on local ownership of the development process and cooperation among donors in alignment with recipient countries' development plans. But in practice, at least to its domestic audience, the government invokes "effectiveness" to justify an array of policy initiatives, even ones that go against the Paris principles. Consequently, Canada's use of aid effectiveness is one that focuses on quantifiable results and "accountancy" to taxpayers, at the expense of accountability to aid recipients, coordination, and national ownership (Black, Brown's chapter 3, den Heyer, McGill, Smillie). The Canadian electorate, moreover, is relatively uninterested in aid issues, which acts as a disincentive for governments to make greater contributions (Black, Chapnick).

As mentioned above, unlike the other donors mentioned in this volume, Canada lacks a broad, clearly articulated, and integrated aid strategy – a "grand design" for development assistance that would define its goals, motives, and means. The absence of a national policy framework might not simply be a result of government unwillingness to draft such as document. CIDA is part of a complex matrix made up of multiple actors, subject to competing and contradictory internal and external influences, with discordant goals. These make aid policy documents hard to draft (den Heyer). For example, while international community norms (such as those embodied in the Paris Declaration) influence types of aid and how it is distributed, the Canadian government determines how much aid it will deliver and where it will be directed.

The lack of such a framework also renders it more difficult to assess how well CIDA is performing in relation to its obligations. The 2008 ODA Accountability Act was designed to fill that void. With very strong support from civil society, the act was passed in Parliament against the will of the Conservative minority government, but not before it was watered down. While it was intended to focus Canadian aid firmly on fighting poverty, in practice it achieved little besides an additional annual report. Several contributors consider CIDA insufficiently committed to poverty reduction, noting that the preferred government strategy is to ignore the act as much as possible (Blackwood and Stewart, Brown's chapter 3, Côté and Caouette, McGill). Even the auditor general's (2009) report did not use the act as a standard against which CIDA policies and performance could be measured. Instead, the auditor general used a half-forgotten 2002 CIDA policy statement on aid effectiveness, which – as the report noted in detail – did little to guide the agency's actions.

Policy Coherence and the Instrumentalization of Aid

Aid alone is insufficient for development; donors' complementary commercial, economic, social, and environmental policies can also contribute to development and poverty reduction. As explained in the Introduction, a major feature of the international discourse on aid effectiveness and an important one for Canada is *policy coherence*. This term refers to the degree to which various government departments work together for a common goal, which could be either development in the South (policy coherence for development) or one more closely in line with the donor's national interests. The whole-of-government approach is the means by which a country achieves such coherence, which is seen as an important way to improve effectiveness (be it for aid/development or something else).

Sweden is generally considered one of the countries with the best policy coherence for development. In the UK, the Department for International Development was given a clear ministerial lead for all development-related programs, making Britain a model of policy consistency. Canada, by way of contrast, is deemed to lack policy coherence and continuity. Here again, Canada's want of a clear vision for international development assistance is limiting. Without an overarching strategy for aid and engagement with the global South, it is difficult for the Canadian government to consider in a systematic way the consequences of Canadian public policy on developing countries.

That Canadian international policy lacks coherence is not a recent observation. In fact, no Canadian government has ever stated a clear national intent to pursue policy consistency for development. On this subject, there is some disagreement among the book's chapters: McGill stresses the importance of policy coherence for development; Blackwood and Stewart, Brown's chapter 3, and den Heyer warn that policy coherence may hinder rather than help Canadian development efforts; and Baranyi and Paducel argue that the whole-of-government approach can have a positive or negative impact on development, depending on the circumstances.

Just as states have multiple and mixed motives and intents, so too do the agencies and departments within government. Like policy coherence, national self-interest is not per se a negative thing, nor is it necessarily at odds with development. Much depends on how the national interest is framed. Nonetheless, the competing interests that emerge from the simultaneous pursuit of political, commercial, security, and development goals tend to disfavour an orientation based mainly on effective development assistance – especially in conflict-affected countries and "fragile states." The impact of mixed motives on aid/development effectiveness is the elephant in the room that the Canadian government (and its DAC peers) hope observers and critics will ignore. It also complicates the elaboration of an overarching aid policy framework. It is in this context that governments often instrumentalize aid for non-development purposes, potentially via a whole-of-government approach, and invoke "feel-good" development issues or effectiveness concerns to legitimize self-interested measures that do not constitute improvements on previous policies or are unlikely to improve the impact of aid from a development perspective (Blackwood and Stewart, both Brown chapters, den Heyer, Gulrajani, Swiss).

No donor country can claim its aid program to be entirely devoid of self-interest. In this respect, as is true of its peers, Canada's approach to foreign aid reflects both altruistic concerns and national self-interest. However, depending on the domestic political climate of the time and the perspective of those in power, one or the other of these has had greater influence on aid policy. The Canadian government's approach to aid has always oscillated between commercial, trade, and foreign policy concerns and perceptions of aid as an altruistic benefit for the world's poorest countries (Brown's chapter 3, Côté and Caouette, Swiss). Since the mid-2000s, Canada has reasserted national interests in its aid. Despite very different national and international contexts, its aid is influenced by many commercial and diplomatic interests similar to those that prevailed prior to CIDA's establishment, with additional security concerns in a post–9/11 global context (Brown's chapter 3, Swiss).

Charting the vagaries of aid motivations over time illustrates why it would be simplistic to cast any specific party in power as the villain of the story. Canadians forget that, throughout the 1990s, the Chrétien government decimated ODA spending. Ironically, toward the end of his mandate, concerned with developing a lasting legacy, Chrétien became a champion for aid and Africa. The Martin government sought to re-establish Canada's presence on the world stage, during which time major aid programs were folded into the whole-of-government approach, which was then used in Afghanistan as a means to mollify the US for Canada's refusal to participate in the invasion of Iraq. As noted, in the years since it came to power, the Harper government has yet to define with any clarity its approach to foreign aid, with observers trying to determine its intent through occasional vague press releases and ministerial speeches. There is good reason to be suspicious: from its very inception, the Reform Party (precursor to the Conservatives) expressed little interest in foreign policy and development assistance, especially regarding Africa, so it should come as no surprise that the Harper government has revealed itself as rather indifferent to these, favouring instead a rapprochement with the United States, especially during the administration of George W. Bush (Black, Brown's chapter 3).

Against those patterns of relative continuity and small changes in policy, an examination of CIDA's support to Canadian nongovernmental organizations (NGOs) suggests that the Harper government has made a clear break with previous governments. Where the Liberals tinkered with funding modalities, infusing at times more trust toward and at others more control over the NGOs that CIDA funded, under the Conservatives important modifications in practice and regulations in 2009–10 have fundamentally changed the nature of this "partnership." The government limited NGOs' ability to apply for funding for projects that the NGOs identified with their own partner organizations in the global South. Instead, most funding will go to NGOs with projects in CIDA's priority sectors and countries. Consequently, NGOs will be often reduced to being providers of short-term services to alleviate poverty, rather than actual partners in development that have some comparative advantages of their own. This will hinder their efforts to change power structures and eliminate poverty, thereby hampering the effectiveness of NGOs' own development assistance (Brown's chapter 11, Smillie).

The Canadian government and other donors increasingly recognize the benefits of policy coherence and the role that non-aid policies can play in promoting international development. To advance the aid effectiveness agenda in a meaningful way, they would do well to explore further the non-aid components of *development* effectiveness. This would necessarily include placing far greater emphasis on policy coherence *for development* rather than policy coherence *tout court*. Championing such an initiative would be an excellent way for the government to burnish CIDA's and Canada's international image, something from which they could increasingly benefit.

Canada's Declining Reputation

Canadians are prone to believing that their country is held in very high regard among its donor peers and in the global South. It is true that Canada has a strong track record of assistance to a great number of countries (a side effect of the fragmentation of its aid) and that it was once an intellectual leader among DAC donors, most notably on the importance of gender issues and the complementary role that NGOs play with regard to government-to-government aid. The Canadian government also played an important part in 2002–05 in placing Africa at the core of development concerns, particularly at G8 summits. Since 2006, however, the government's position on all three issues has slipped dramatically.

CIDA long demonstrated a clear commitment to gender equality. In fact, throughout the 1980s, many other donors widely considered the agency's gender policies to be pioneering and visionary. However, since the election of the Conservative government in 2006, Canada has not only lost its leadership status in regard to gender equality, the issue itself is no longer treated as a crucial component of development aid. CIDA has shifted its programs from endeavours that support women's rights and empowerment to activities that target service delivery to women (McGill, Swiss). Meanwhile, the UK has assumed the mantle of leadership and innovation in gender equality (McGill). The Muskoka Initiative, launched at the 2010 G8 Summit in Huntsville, Ontario, tried to regain some lost ground by funnelling resources to maternal and child health. However, the government's efforts were compromised by confusion over whether contraception would be included (initially no, but then yes) and access to abortions (which were excluded, creating a different standard of care for Canadian women and their counterparts in the global South) (Black, Brown's chapter 3, Chapnick, Smillie). The government also suggested that more attention would be paid to Africa, since that is where MCH needs are greatest. This further reinforced an impression, shared by many policy observers, that CIDA and the broader Canadian government were simply making up development policy as they went along.

Some other policy decisions have further hurt Canada's international reputation, such as the shrinking place of Africa in CIDA's aid program, including through the delisting of eight African countries of concentration in 2008; the increased control being exerted over CIDA-funded NGOs; and the freezing of aid budgets in 2010 (Black, Brown's chapter 11, Smillie). The effects are cumulative, as countries in the global South, especially Africa, along with Southern organizations that partner with Canadian NGOs and Canada's peers in the DAC, all note Canada's loss of leadership and its fading commitment to foreign aid. Canada's international standing depreciated further with a number of unpopular government positions, such as recalcitrance regarding the reduction of greenhouse gasses, culminating in the government's unilateral withdrawal from the Kyoto Protocol in 2011, and its near unconditional support for Israel. Hard evidence is elusive, but Canada's failure to obtain a seat on the UN Security Council in 2010 could plausibly be a result of its increasingly tarnished reputation.

WHAT IS TO BE DONE?

All contributors to this volume share a normative concern about poverty in the global South and want to see the Canadian government deliver better aid. All of them have criticized how the Canadian government develops foreign aid policy and administers foreign aid, especially since 2000, often in comparison to well-performing donor peers. Many point to the politicization of Canadian foreign aid as a major source of dysfunction in both policy and programming. Authors also show how partisan and political manipulation by successive governments, as well as political actors' over-involvement in what should often be non-partisan or technical decisions made by civil servants, have greatly interfered with the ability of CIDA's aid professionals to use their skills to deliver effective aid. Short-term domestic electoral considerations thus subvert basic development principles such as long-term relationships and a predictable flow of resources.

Few contributors, however, elaborate on what the Canadian government should do to improve its aid performance and fewer still describe how to compel it to take the necessary steps to do so (Chapnick is a notable exception). Therein lies the rub. Clearly, this volume was never meant to be a how-to manual for reforming CIDA and Canadian aid. In fact, six policy papers and other studies, listed in the Introduction, address this very issue. Here we outline the implicit and explicit policy recommendations made by contributors to this volume. They can be divided into four non-mutually exclusive strategies: institutional reform, political leadership, public pressure, and legal action.

Institutional Reform

Many debates on how to reform CIDA focus on its governance structures. Those who mostly support foreign aid as a humanitarian imperative tend to advocate a strong minister leading a full-fledged, independent government department (as opposed to an agency with a junior minister). Those whose primary concern is national self-interest in Canadian foreign policy (rather than the needs of developing countries, though the two are not always incompatible) generally support CIDA's absorption into the Department of Foreign Affairs and International Trade. Agency governance reform, however, would be no panacea (Gulrajani) and no contributor to this volume presents it as a major component of their diagnosis of CIDA's ills.

Political Will

Many contributors identify a lack of political will to be the main impediment to improving Canadian aid policy (Brown's chapter 3, Chapnick, Gulrajani, McGill). In many instances, authors point to measures and new initiatives that are unlikely to improve aid effectiveness and suggest alternative approaches. The problems are not hard to understand, but they are unlikely to be addressed as long as decision makers lack the personal or national interests to do so. The leadership necessary to carry out effective and meaningful changes would need to come from one or a few highly motivated and competent individuals (as argued by Chapnick, Gulrajani, McGill) and would likely require the support of the prime minister and other key members of cabinet (the happy constellation of factors that led the UK to establish a strong ministry dedicated to international development). An aid champion in cabinet would also be necessary to direct the preparation and adoption of an aid-focused White Paper. Canada has had no such figure for a very long time. The conditions were ripe in 2000–06, at the end of Chrétien's tenure as prime minister and during Martin's short-lived government, for such a figure to emerge.

Yet no one did. As a result, many aid policy initiatives during that period were motivated principally by Canadian interests (Black, Brown's chapter 3).

Public Pressure

Several chapters note the consequences of weak public support and the benefits of public pressure (Black, Chapnick, den Heyer). After all, Canadians demonstrated great generosity with the people of Haiti after the 2010 earthquake and the countries affected by the 2004 tsunami in Asia (Black, Brown's chapter 3, Chapnick, den Heyer). This impelled the Canadian government to top up its own contributions quite significantly. These examples, however, pertain to sudden and highly visible natural disasters, not long-term development challenges – and such generosity is not extended equally to all countries in urgent need of assistance (Canadians provided relatively little assistance, for instance, to the millions of Pakistanis directly affected by widespread flooding in 2010). The government is clearly not immune to public opinion, especially on issues of import to its electoral base. An uncoordinated groundswell of opposition to the Harper government's mere mention of the possibility of revising the lyrics to O Canada caused the government to repudiate the idea overnight. Strategic public, non-partisan advocacy can have an important effect on government behaviour, especially when the window of opportunity opens in the form of a potential aid champion in Parliament (Chapnick).

Legal Action

Several contributors mention the disappointing impact thus far of the 2008 ODA Accountability Act (Brown's chapter 3, Côté and Caouette, McGill). However, it may prove more useful in the future than it has to date. Its provisions on human-rights obligations and its focus on poverty and the perspectives of the poor could be used in court to hold the government accountable for infringement of those rights (Blackwood and Stewart). Individual litigants, Canadian NGOs, or even actors from developing countries could initiate lawsuits against the Canadian government. It is hard, however, to predict what the courts might decide, since the phrasing of the act is sometimes ambiguous and therefore remains open to judicial interpretation.

AREAS FOR FURTHER RESEARCH

This book did not set out to provide a coherent assessment of CIDA and Canadian aid policy. Nonetheless, the various chapters, despite their different approaches and perspectives, are remarkably complementary. Amid the convergences, there were very few divergences. One, mentioned above, was on the effect of whole-of-government approaches and policy coherence on development assistance. Some contributors argued in favour, while others warned of risks; these are not incompatible perspectives per se, especially since the risks did materialize in Afghanistan. One chapter actually confirmed that the fears of the securitization of aid were justified, not only in Afghanistan but also in the Darfur region of Sudan. However, in some cases, policy coherence did favour development, as in South Sudan and Haiti (Baranyi and Paducel).

A second issue of divergence is the question of aid fragmentation and its detrimental effects on aid effectiveness. Two authors implicitly accepted it as a given (Gulrajani, McGill), while another raised the possibility that the fragmentation might not be inherently deleterious (Brown, chapter 3). More research is required on Canada's and other countries' aid programs to ascertain its actual effects and confirm or reject (or provide greater nuance to) the general consensus in the DAC that donors should further concentrate their aid programs and adopt "policy-coherent," whole-of-government approaches to support development objectives more effectively.

A few issues are not covered by this volume, some by design, others not. For instance, CIDA's humanitarian assistance is not addressed. It was excluded because humanitarian operations are generally (though decreasingly) oriented toward short-term assistance rather than long-term planning. They are also emergencies that can literally emerge unexpectedly overnight. Policy in this area is quite different from development assistance and cannot be related to the various donor policies and norms discussed throughout this volume, such as aid effectiveness principles. Complex debates are taking place around humanitarian assistance (particularly in the realm of intervention), but they are generally quite separate from the ones in development assistance.

For similar reasons, in the context of a volume that had to be limited in size, no effort was made to include a chapter on the topic of Canada and multilateral institutions. Multilateral aid is a very important topic and, moreover, an understudied one in the Canadian case. However, the decision was made to limit discussions to bilateral aid, including the support to NGOs that also participate in this form of development assistance. Similarly, the book does not address the issue of the global "aid architecture" – the set of diverse institutions that make aid policy and deliver aid assistance though a number of different mechanisms – and Canada's participation in discussions on reforming it. Recent and ongoing changes include the expansion of the DAC, the transition from the G8 to the G20, and the creation of the UN-based Development Cooperation Forum, where not only rich or middle-income countries but also the poorest ones can be heard. One of the implications of the growing prominence of non-DAC donors, such as Brazil, China, and India, is that Canada's share of global development assistance – and its influence – is shrinking.

It would nonetheless have been useful to include a contribution from an expert in Canadian public policy to discuss interdepartmental relations in Ottawa and clarify how, where, and by whom decisions affecting Canada's foreign aid are made. Moreover, because most contributors to this volume centre their analysis on policies and practices from the point of view of the donor country's capital and agency headquarters, with only a few partial exceptions (Blackwood and Stewart, Côté and Caouette, den Heyer), more discussion is warranted on the effects of foreign aid as practised in specific recipient countries. A more comprehensive study would be helpful to further elucidate the results, perceptions, and critiques of Canadian aid in recipient countries. It is there, not in donor capitals, that one can assess the actual impact (or lack thereof) of new aid initiatives, including the drive to focus on fewer countries, policy coherence, and the evolving aid effectiveness agenda, as well as the level of compliance with international and domestic commitments and obligations.

Clearly, much work remains to be done on Canadian foreign aid. This volume by no means seeks to provide all of the answers or even ask all of the important questions. Rather, it should be seen as a well-intentioned contribution to the burgeoning interest in and studies of CIDA and Canadian aid policy mentioned in the Introduction. We hope it will attract the critical attention of a range of people who share similar concerns and that it will elicit further contributions to the collective debate surrounding the ways Canada can best make important contributions around the world.

REFERENCES

Auditor General of Canada. 2009. "Chapter 8. Strengthening Aid Effectiveness – Canadian International Development Agency." *Report of the Auditor General of Canada to the House of Commons.* Ottawa: Office of the Auditor General of Canada.

Knack, Stephen, Halsey Rogers, and Nicholas Eubank. 2010. "Aid Quality and Donor Rankings." World Bank Policy Research Working Paper. Washington, DC: World Bank.

Contributors

STEPHEN BARANYI is associate professor of international development and global studies at the University of Ottawa. His research focuses on the challenges and contradictions of peacebuilding, security-sector reform, and development in fragile states, especially Haiti. His recent work has appeared in the *Journal of Peacebuilding and Development* (2011), the *Canadian Journal of Development Studies* (2011), *Fixing Haiti: MINUSTAH and Beyond* (United Nations University Press 2011), and his edited book titled *The Paradoxes of Peacebuilding Post-9/11* (UBC Press 2008).

DAVID BLACK is director of the Centre for Foreign Policy Studies and professor of political science and international development studies at Dalhousie University. His research has focused on Canada and Sub-Saharan Africa, the foreign policy of post-apartheid South Africa, and sport in international relations and development. His work on Canada and Africa, including development assistance, has been published in the *Canadian Journal of Development Studies*, *Canadian Foreign Policy*, *International Journal*, and numerous edited collections.

ELIZABETH BLACKWOOD is a PhD candidate in political science and a graduate research associate at the Centre for Global Political Economy at Simon Fraser University. Her research is in the area of trade and investment, with a focus on the regulation of extractive industries and investment law. In 2008 she conducted field research in Guatemala, documenting the effects of open-pit mining on rural communities. She has also studied in West Africa, researching the political economy of structural adjustment programs.

STEPHEN BROWN is associate professor of political science at the University of Ottawa. His main research interests are foreign aid, democratization, political violence, peacebuilding, and transitional justice, mainly in relation to Sub-Saharan Africa. His prior work on CIDA and Canadian aid policy has appeared in, among other places, the *Canadian Journal of Development Studies* (June 2008), *Canada among Nations 2007* (McGill-Queen's University Press 2008), *L'aide canadienne au développement* (Presses de l'Université de Montréal 2008), and *Readings in Canadian Foreign Policy: Classic Debates and New Ideas*, 2nd ed. (Oxford University Press 2011). He is currently co-editing a book on the securitization of foreign aid.

DOMINIQUE CAOUETTE is associate professor in the Department of Political Science and director of the East Asian Studies Centre of the Université de Montréal. He has published articles in *Kasarinlan: A Philippine Quarterly of Third World Studies*, *Pacific Focus*, *Geography Compass*, *Canadian Journal of Development Studies*, and *Possibles*, and has contributed chapters to a number of books, including *Neopatrimonialism in Africa and Beyond* (Routledge 2012), *L'État néopatrimonial: Genèse et trajectoires contemporaines* (Presses de l'Université d'Ottawa 2011), *L'altermondialisme: Forums sociaux, résistances et nouvelle culture politique* (Écosociété 2010), *La politique internationale en questions* (Presses de l'Université de Montréal 2009), and *L'aide canadienne au développement* (Presses de l'Université de Montréal 2008). Recently he co-edited *Solidarities beyond Borders: Transnationalizing Women's Movements* (UBC Press 2010) and *Agrarian Angst and Rural Resistance in Contemporary Southeast Asia* (Routledge 2009).

ADAM CHAPNICK is associate professor of defence studies at the Royal Military College of Canada and deputy director, education, at the Canadian Forces College. His recent publications include *Canada's Voice: The Public Life of John Wendell Holmes* (UBC Press 2009) and "Canada's Aid Program: Still Struggling after Sixty Years" (*Behind the Headlines*).

DENIS CÔTÉ is a doctoral candidate in political science at the Université de Montréal. He is the coordinator of the Asia-Pacific Working Group of the Canadian Council for International Co-operation and recently published an article in the *European*

Journal of East Asian Studies entitled "Ripe for a New Asian Multilateralism? ASEAN and Contemporary Regional Dynamics" (2011). His contribution to this volume is made purely in his personal capacity.

MOLLY DEN HEYER recently obtained her PhD from Dalhousie University in Halifax. Her dissertation traces how aid effectiveness principles are transformed as they move through the international development community, starting with global discourse and then filtering through Canadian aid policy to the dialogue process in Tanzania. Her other research interests include interdisciplinary research methods, critical alternative development theory, discourse analysis, participation, development administration, policy, planning, and evaluation.

NILIMA GULRAJANI is research fellow at the Global Economic Governance Programme at Oxford University. She was formerly assistant professor in the Department of Government and the Department of International Development (DESTIN) at the London School of Economics and Political Science. Her research interests lie at the intersection of public management and development studies, and deal primarily with theories of development management, comparative organizational dynamics of donor agencies, and aid effectiveness. Her work has been published in journals such as *Public Administration Review*, *Third World Quarterly*, and *Public Administration and Development*. She is currently the co-convenor of the Development Studies Association Study Group on Development Management.

HUNTER MCGILL is an international development policy consultant and senior fellow at the School of International Development and Global Studies at the University of Ottawa. His consulting practice focuses on good bilateral donor practice, aid effectiveness, and humanitarian assistance. He spent thirty years at CIDA and worked at the OECD for five years as head of peer review and evaluation operations for the Development Assistance Committee (DAC).

ANCA H. PADUCEL is a master's student in international relations/political science at the Graduate Institute of International and Development Studies in Geneva. Her main research interests are in conflict and security, particularly the challenges of peacebuilding, state building, and development in fragile states, as well as regional integration, especially in Sub-Saharan Africa. She recently published a working paper with the North-South Institute titled "Gender Equality and Fragile States Policies and Programming: A Comparative Study of the OECD/DAC and Six OECD Donors" (2011).

ROSALIND RADDATZ is a Trudeau Scholar completing her doctorate at the University of Ottawa. Her dissertation examines the relative influence of power and resource sharing, civil society, international intervention, and mediation in negotiated peace agreements in Sierra Leone and Liberia. Other research interests include mass violence/genocide, peacebuilding, institutional accountability, transitional justice, and post-conflict gender issues, primarily in relation to Sub-Saharan Africa.

IAN SMILLIE has lived and worked in Africa and Asia. He was a founder of the Canadian NGO Inter Pares and was executive director of CUSO. He has worked at Tufts and Tulane universities and widely as a development consultant. He is the author of several books, including *Freedom from Want: The Remarkable Success Story of BRAC* (Kumarian Press 2009) and *Blood on the Stone: Greed, Corruption and War in the Global Diamond Trade* (Anthem Press 2010). Smillie helped develop the fifty-five-government "Kimberley Process," a global certification system to halt the traffic in conflict diamonds. He was the first witness at Charles Taylor's war crimes trial in The Hague and he chairs the Diamond Development Initiative.

VERONIKA STEWART is a master's student in the sociology program at Simon Fraser University. Her research interests are critical political economy, the activities of extractive industries in developing nations, and Third World approaches to international law. She is currently a research intern at the Committee for Workers' Capital in Vancouver.

LIAM SWISS is assistant professor of sociology at Memorial University. His research and teaching interests include international development, foreign aid, gender, security, and globalization. Recently, his research on aid has examined the intersection of globalization with

bilateral foreign aid policy around issues of gender equality and
security from a comparative perspective. His work has been published in journals such as *American Sociological Review*, *International Sociology*, *Qualitative Sociology*, and *International Journal of
Comparative Sociology*. He worked previously for CIDA on Canada's
aid program in Pakistan.

Index

Economic Growth Strategy, 201,
223, 230, 258. *See also* Official
Development Assistance
Accountability Act
Canadian Lutheran World Relief,
235
Canadian Public Service Employee
Survey, 13, 66
Canadian University Service
Overseas (CUSO), 274–6, 280
Canadians for Foreign Aid Reform
(C-FAR), 275
Cannon, Lawrence, 260, 282–3
capacity building: in developing
countries, 44, 122–3, 227–8,
230, 238, 270; in former Soviet
bloc countries, 270. *See also*
Paris Declaration on Aid
Effectiveness
Cape Verde, 260
capitalism, 231, 270
CARE Canada, 290
Caribbean: food aid, 162; mining
industry, 224; priority region for
Harper government, 18, 80, 90,
97, 99, 199, 249, 254, 257
Carin, Barry, 199
Carroll, Aileen, 212n5
Carty, Robert, 163, 165
C.D. Howe Institute, 277
Center for Global Development,
14, 25–6, 34, 40–1, 45, 47, 49n1.
See also rankings of aid donors
Ceylon, 161
charitable status. *See* Canada
Revenue Agency
charity, 179, 200, 252, 294
children and youth: priority theme
for Harper government, 29, 91,
112, 120, 123, 137, 168, 200,

256–7. *See also* maternal and
child health
Chile, 226, 232
China, 3, 89, 100, 127, 138, 342
Chrétien, Jean, 5, 89–90, 93, 97–8,
248, 262, 331, 339; legacy projects, 4, 80, 95, 99, 249, 335. *See
also* Liberal government
civil society organizations: consultations on policies, 28, 167, 270;
contributions to democracy, 270,
278, 282–3, 293–4, 296;
estrangement from Canadian
government, 264n10, 281, 287,
298, 328; importance in development, 7, 18, 32, 43, 67–8, 122,
189, 270–1, 287–8. *See also* non-
governmental organizations
Clark, Joe, 253, 260
Clean Development Mechanism, 39
climate change, 9, 26, 29, 40, 42,
47, 100, 178, 310
Colombia: capitalist agribusiness,
164, 180; free-trade agreement
with Canada, 229, 331; mining
industry, 224–5, 228, 230–1,
233–6; priority country for
Harper government, 35, 257
Colombo Plan, 160–2
commercial interests: agribusiness,
162, 171; influence on aid policy,
4, 7, 94–5, 138, 160–1, 165,
180–1, 192, 194, 222–3, 227–8,
230, 235, 237, 294–5, 300, 331,
335; Latin America, 80, 97, 99,
164, 224; United Kingdom, 36,
70
Commission for Africa, 5
Commission on International
Development (1969), 25

Export Development Canada, 226–
7, 231; coordination with CIDA,
231–2
extractive industries: benefits to
Canadian mining companies, 10,
18, 230; Canadian companies
abroad, 10, 17, 217, 219–24,
237, 331; Canadian government
support for, 218–22, 224, 227–
30, 232–8, 331; changes in social
structure of host states, 217, 221,
225, 234, 237; corruption and
violence in, 217–19, 225, 230,
234–5; effect on indigenous communities, 226, 231, 233–7; environmental degradation, 17,
217–18, 220–2, 224–6, 233–4,
237, 239; exploitation of host
states, 17, 218–19, 221, 224;
government regulation of, 217–
19, 222, 224, 226–7, 231, 237–8;
human-rights abuses, 217, 222,
225, 232, 234–7, 239; liberalization measures, 219–20, 227–8,
231, 233–4; privatization, 219;
structural adjustment programs,
219–20, 222
extraterritoriality, principle of, 227

failed states, 5, 15, 93, 251; Failed
States Index, 109. *See also* fragile
states
Federal Accountability Act (2006),
193–4, 213n6; conflict with
existing aid commitments, 204
Fifth Estate (CBC), 165
food aid, 161–2, 169, 173, 180,
200; impediment to domestic
food production, 162, 166; untying of, 29, 33–4, 84

Food Aid Convention, 169
food insecurity: structural causes,
17, 159–60, 173–4, 181. *See also*
food aid
food security, 100, 118, 167, 175;
biodiversity, 177–8; criteria for
adequacy of food, 176–7; in
Haiti, 117; human-rights-based
approach to, 170, 172; hunger,
41, 159, 167–8, 170, 172, 174–5;
malnutrition, 169–70, 172, 177;
means to achieving, 16, 160,
169–70, 172–81; nutrition, 91,
169, 177, 181, 200; participation
of farmers in reform and innovation, 179, 181; priority theme for
Harper government, 16, 29, 91,
121, 159, 168, 200, 256–7; in
Sudan, 121; sustainable supply
of food, 172–3, 178. *See also*
biotechnology; CIDA, land and
food policies; global food crises;
right to food
foreign aid: academic study of, 3,
10–11, 139–40, 192, 299, 321–2;
budget freeze, 4, 310, 332, 338;
Canada's international standing,
24, 46, 85, 89, 96–7, 99–100,
206–7, 259–61, 300, 305, 310,
322, 336–8, 342; centralization
of control over, 19, 187, 208–9,
282, 287–8, 290, 292, 299–300,
331; changes since 2000, 3–5, 12,
79–80, 84, 89, 95, 98, 136, 196,
288, 292–7, 300, 331, 335, 338;
competing interests, 40, 49n3,
147, 149–50, 187, 192, 211, 218,
221, 294, 328, 333–5; diplomatic
interests, 4, 7, 15, 120, 126, 142,
151, 194, 294, 316, 331, 335;

Minna, Maria, 212n5
Monarch Industry, 165
Monterrey Consensus (2002), 5, 47, 256, 262
Morrison, David, 12, 71, 162, 194
Mozambique, 274
Muggah, Robert, 117
Mulroney, Brian, 276
multi-bilateral finance, 59–61
multilateral spending, 59–61, 64, 110, 121, 247, 300, 341–2
Munk, Peter, 236
Munro, Lauchlan T., 56
Muskoka Initiative on Maternal, Newborn and Child Health (2010), 43, 200, 246, 260, 262, 309–10, 312, 318, 329, 337. *See also* maternal and child health

Namibia, 228
Nanos, Nik, 310
national anthem (Canada), 311, 340
national ownership: alignment of aid with recipient country priorities, 5, 8–9, 56, 64, 82, 92, 191, 247, 256, 293, 297, 329, 333; goal of development, 32–3, 82, 92, 99, 114–15, 119, 122–3, 191, 197, 247, 293, 295, 329, 332–3. *See also* Paris Declaration on Aid Effectiveness
NATO alliance: Canada's contribution to, 95, 99, 123, 316
Natsios, Andrew, 282
natural resource curse. *See* extractive industries
neo-liberal approach: to development, 5, 109–10, 118, 201, 218, 223

neo-liberal market mechanisms, 16, 175, 231
Nestlé, 275
Netherlands, 25
Neve, Alex, 172
New Democratic Party, 251, 314
New Partnership for Africa's Development (NEPAD), 249–50, 262
Noël, Alain, 196, 251
non-aid policies for development: elimination of trade and tariff barriers, 9, 31, 39, 47, 84, 93, 274; environmental protection, 9, 274; immigration, 9; importance of, 24, 26, 38, 40–1, 48, 82, 87, 93, 283, 330, 334, 336; political costs of, 10; reducing subsidies to domestic industries, 9–10, 274; technology transfers, 9. *See also* whole-of-government approach
non-governmental organizations, 3, 98; creation of knowledge networks, 195; importance in development, 18, 67, 100, 110, 117, 124, 270, 287–90, 293, 342; lack of strategic focus, 313, 320; lack of unified voice, 313, 320–1, 332; loss of funding, 18, 278, 280, 287–8, 290, 296, 313, 318, 336; oversimplification of development problems, 197, 272, 274, 276, 283, 290; partnerships with CIDA, 194–5, 272, 281, 287–300, 318, 336–8, 342; role as service providers, 18, 195, 270–1, 278, 281–4, 292, 294, 300, 318, 336. *See also* civil society organizations

North-South Institute, 109, 122,
277, 279
Norway, 12, 14, 34; Ministry of
Foreign Affairs, 14, 55; model of
donor performance, 55–6, 58,
64, 68–9, 73; ODA/GNI target,
25, 59; NORAD, 59, 70; political
vision for aid policy, 70–1; public
support for foreign aid, 67;
White Papers on aid, 71, 328.
See also bilateral spending

Oda, Beverley, 13, 28–9, 35, 46,
96–7, 168, 199–200, 212n5, 228,
238, 256, 280–1, 287, 298, 308,
317; criticism of CIDA, 86, 90,
255
Office for Democratic Governance,
254. *See also* democracy, promotion of
official development assistance. *See*
foreign aid
Official Development Assistance
Accountability Act (2008), 48,
97–8, 170–1, 195, 201, 295;
CIDA's compliance with, 18, 44,
217–18, 221–2, 224, 232, 234–6,
238–9, 321, 328, 332–3; three
criteria for ODA funding, 29–30,
172, 212n4, 218, 222, 232, 340
Organisation for Economic
Co-operation and Development:
DAC Network on Gender, 42;
definition of effective aid, 191,
297; Development Assistance
Committee (DAC), 8, 30, 33–4,
49n1, 54, 82, 87, 89, 97, 108,
341–2; study of Canada's alignment with national priorities, 8.
See also DAC peer reviews

Organisation for European
Economic Co-operation, 161–2
Organization of American States,
90
Organization of the Petroleum
Exporting Countries, 35
Ottawa Treaty to Ban Landmines,
249
Oxfam Canada, 275, 290

Paine, Thomas, 270
Pakistan, 94, 112, 148, 161; flooding (2010), 340
Palestine, 280; human-rights organizations, 294
Pan-American Health
Organization, 116
Papua New Guinea, 236
Paris Declaration on Aid
Effectiveness (2005), 7, 9, 25, 28,
60, 84, 98, 250; Canada's commitment to, 8, 20n3, 84, 92, 108,
115, 121, 123–4, 191, 204, 332;
importance of recipient countries' priorities, 5, 92, 98, 123,
258, 293, 321, 329; principles of,
14, 33, 56, 82, 127n1, 212n2,
247, 252, 256, 258, 293, 295,
297, 300, 333
Patrick, Stewart, 123
peacebuilding, 91, 120, 122, 125,
139
peace dividend, 79
peacekeeping, 39, 42, 120, 125
Pearson, Lester B., 25, 72, 89;
Nobel Peace Prize, 309;
Pearsonian idealism, 98–9
Pergau Dam (Malaysia), 36
Peru, 35, 224–5, 227–8, 230, 232,
234–6, 257; free-trade agreement